WWJD Today?

Daily Time with Jesus

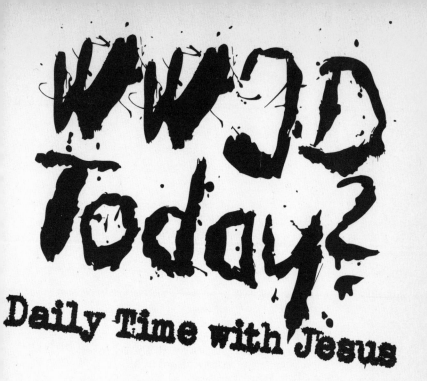

WWJD Today?

Daily Time with Jesus

A Devotional

Brian Shipman

BROADMAN
&HOLMAN
PUBLISHERS

Nashville, Tennessee

0-8054-1688-9

Published by Broadman & Holman Publishers, Nashville, Tennessee
Page Design: Anderson Thomas Design
Editorial Team: Vicki Crumpton, Janis Whipple, Kim Overcash
Page Composition: PerfecType

Dewey Decimal Classification: 242
Subject Heading: TEENAGERS—PRAYER-BOOKS AND DEVOTIONS
Library of Congress Card Catalog Number: 98-19141

Unless otherwise stated all Scripture citation is from the NIV, the Holy Bible, New International
Version, copyright © 1973, 1978, 1984 by International Bible Society.

Library of Congress Cataloging-in-Publication Data
Shipman, Brian K.
    WWJD Today? : daily meditations
        p.   cm.
    Summary: A collection of devotional readings and Bible verses presenting the life of
Jesus as a blueprint for daily choices made by Christians, in such areas as thankful-
ness, popularity, generosity, and obeying God's will.
    ISBN 0-8054-1688-9 (pbk.)
    1. Bible. N.T. Gospels—Meditations. 2. Teenagers—Prayer-books and devotions—
English.
        [1. Prayer books and devotions.]
        I. Title.
        BS2555.4.S55   1998
        242'.63—dc21

                                                                98-19141
                                                                     CIP

3 4 5 02 01 00

Dedication

To my bride, Jennifer,
who believed in me more than I did.

To a true friend, Mike,
who encouraged and inspired me.

To the youth group
of Colonial Hills Baptist Church
in Cedar Hill, Texas,
who constantly amazed me
by doing the things that Jesus would do.

Acknowledgments

This book would not be in print were it not for the selfless giving of a handful of very important people.

My wife, Jennifer, who pulled me out of writer's block time and time again with her creative ideas and who patiently sacrificed her own time so that I could finish this project.

My dear friends, Mike and Vanise Hinesly, who, besides helping proofread, made me laugh, took me away from my troubles, and encouraged me to keep going.

Greg Morris, who showed me the eye in the hurricane, and his wife, Donna, who unselfishly offered herself as editor-in-chief.

Bob Henry, my mentor, who showed me that every obstacle has a doorway through it.

Sheila Ochsner, who led me to Jesus through her living testimony.

My parents, Dale and Kathy, who raised me in a wonderful home and taught me who Jesus was.

Introduction

Though I grew up in church, my place on Sunday morning was the back row. I sat with about ten other teenagers, passing notes and laughing. I never paid much attention to the sermons. Frankly, I thought they were boring. I figured if I listened, then my life would be boring too. I didn't want to live a boring life. I wanted my life to be different—full of excitement and wonder. I never heard anything exciting or wonderful about Jesus, so why did I need Him?

One of those Sundays, however, I remember being jolted from my slumber. A young woman sang a solo right before one of those boring sermons, and for the first time in my life I heard something about Jesus that fascinated me. The song was "Rise Again" by Dallas Holm. It started with Jesus saying, "Go ahead. Drive the nails in my hand. Laugh at me where you stand." I was intrigued. I wondered how Jesus could be so calm in the face of pain and death. I was amazed at how confident Jesus was that He would rise again.

My interest in Jesus faded as I entered high school. I was so busy making friends and having a great time that I forgot all about the song and the sermons and the Sunday school lessons. I didn't care about the Bible. I cared about *now*. I wanted to experience life to the fullest.

One day, however, Jesus interrupted my regularly scheduled program. I noticed that one girl in our youth group was different from everyone else. She didn't pass notes. She *took* notes on those boring sermons. She prayed. She read the Bible. I thought to myself, *How boring!* However, the more I watched her life, the more I liked what I saw. She was kind and patient and caring and confident. Her life seemed full of excitement and wonder. Suddenly, I realized that she had something I didn't. She had Jesus.

I finally stopped struggling and let go. I asked Jesus to come into my heart, forgive me of my sin, and be the Lord of my life. When Jesus took over my life that day, I had an insatiable thirst to know everything about Him. I began reading the Bible like there was no tomorrow. I was captivated by everything He said and everything He did. I wanted to be like Him. I wanted to be like Jesus.

This book is the product of my unending investigation of Jesus' life. My desire for you as you read the pages is that you will be as fascinated with Jesus as I am. This book is divided into weekly segments. Each week contains six devotions followed by a seventh-day review. Take the time each day for six days to read the devotion and the corresponding Bible passages. On the seventh day, flip back through the devotions and remind yourself of what you have learned and how you have put your faith into practice. If you have a question about a particular topic, check the index.

The life of Jesus is a blueprint for building your life. He experienced the same kinds of circumstances and struggles you do. By examining what He did in certain situations, you can follow His example.

Jesus had to deal with parents who didn't understand Him. He had siblings who made fun of Him. He faced some type of rejection almost every day. His schedule was constantly interrupted. Someone Jesus knew very well committed suicide. One of Jesus' closest friends died, and He wept. One of His family members was put in jail and eventually given the death penalty. He was often homeless and poor. Sometimes people made up lies about Jesus and spread rumors about Him. At a time when He needed His friends the most, they all ran out on Him. He had to do things that He didn't want to do. He had many enemies. He experienced indescribable pain. He was humiliated in front of His family and friends. He died like a common criminal.

Thankfully, Jesus was never overcome by His difficulties. He rose again. His life was full of excitement and wonder. He had very close friends. He walked on water. He opened the eyes of the blind. He healed the sick and raised the dead. He prayed constantly. His words amazed everyone who heard Him speak. People were always glad to see Him. He accomplished all of His dreams and goals. He still lives today.

You, too, can have a life that is full of excitement and wonder. How? Walk with Jesus. Spend time reading His Word, learning how He lived. When you face similar situations, ask yourself, "What would Jesus do right now if He were me?" Then answer that question by following Jesus' example.

Is your faith still in the boat? Are you just watching Jesus from the sidelines? Get up. Step out of the boat. Walk with Jesus on the water. Learn from the Master. Walk where He walked.

*I have given you an example so that you can do
the same things I have done for you.*
(John 13:15, author's paraphrase)

Private Eye

Luke 1:1–4

When Colleen chose her science project, she thought it would be fairly simple. All she had to do was go to all the schools in her school district, take a water sample from the different drinking fountains, and label the time and place that she did it. Then she would perform a simple test on each sample to determine the amount of lead in the water. As expected, when she began making bar charts of the results of her tests, they all contained small but harmless amounts of lead—except for one.

The high school choir room had a drinking fountain, and Colleen's tests showed that it had so much lead in the water that it was life-threatening to drink. So Colleen took the results of her testing to the school administration to see what could be done. The administration took Colleen's tests seriously, but to be sure of the results they performed their own tests. Sure enough, the water had dangerous levels of lead in it. So, the school district reworked the pipes, changed out the fountain, and redid the tests. Now, thanks to Colleen, the water is safe to drink.

Colleen started out with a simple school project but ended up making national headlines with her discovery. The school district carefully investigated Colleen's claims and found them to be true. Because they were true, action had to be taken.

The writers of the four Gospels, including Luke, started living simple lives like everyone else but ended up making headlines in the Bible with their discovery that the Son of God had come to earth as a human. Luke, a doctor, carefully investigated all the eyewitness reports about Jesus and decided to make his own science project—which he wrote down and sent to a friend named Theophilus. To this day, people are still investigating the claims of the four Gospels. Some believe; some do not. One fact remains: if the claims are true, *action must be taken*.

You are about to start an incredible journey through the life of Jesus as you read the eyewitness accounts. Make a commitment now to carefully investigate the stories about Jesus by having a devotion (quiet time) with God each day in prayer and Bible study. Then decide what action to take—something specific you can do to become more like Jesus.

Having a daily quiet time with God is important. Do you agree with that statement?

_____

Why? _____

Do you currently have a daily quiet time? _____

If not, do you think you could start one today? _____

Ask God to help you set aside time for Him each day. Pray that He will speak to you as you read the Bible. Become a private investigator of God's Word, just like Dr. Luke did. You'll be amazed each day at what you find and how it will change your life.

I Like Your Style

John 1:1–18

In a popular movie, a CIA agent is convinced that an assassin will attempt to take the President's life soon. No one believes him, but the agent keeps trying to tell everyone that this gun-wielding maniac is coming. While everyone ignores the agent's warnings and labels him a fool, the assassin secretly plans his insidious plot. The dastardly deed will be committed during a banquet with a plastic gun that can evade standard metal detectors.

Finally, at the last possible moment, the secret service agent spots the assassin near the President. He breaks out in a sprint, arriving not a moment too soon. He leaps into the air between the would-be assassin and the President. A shot rings out. The agent goes down, but the President goes away unharmed. Even though no one believed the agent, his story was true all along—the assassin really was coming.

John the Baptist was trying to convince the people around him that God was coming to earth as a human to save everyone from their sins. Most people laughed. A few people got angry. Some really believed what John said was true. John gave his life to a message that most people thought was crazy. After all, the idea of God Almighty shrinking Himself down to our size seems farfetched. However, it turned out to be true. While everyone else went about their own business, God quietly slipped into the world to change it forever.

You can change the world like John the Baptist did. How? Follow John's example. First, make sure you know the message. John knew that Jesus was real and that He could change lives. Because Jesus has changed your life, you can be sure He can change others. Second, share the message in a creative way. John dressed up in strange clothes, ate weird food, and told his message while waist deep in the middle of a river. That's creative.

John's style won't necessarily be yours. You can develop your own style of sharing God's love. You might share Jesus by bringing friends to your youth group where they can hear God's Word. You could have a party at your house where Christian music and a message (by you or a peer) is included. You might even call a non-Christian friend on the phone and share with him or her about how God recently answered one of your prayers.

Do you have friends who are not Christians? ____

Is it important that they hear the good news about Jesus? ____

Write down one creative way that you could share Jesus with one of these people in the next day or so. _____

Pray that God will give you the courage to share Jesus with someone else this week. Be creative. Choose your own style. You can make a difference.

Background Check

Matthew 1:1–17; Luke 3:23–38

> *"So, what does your dad do?"*
>
> *The question caught Colton off guard. He stared into his locker, pretending to hunt for something. "Oh, I can't explain it. He sits in a little room all day. You know how it is."*
>
> *In actuality, Colton's father was in prison, sitting in a little room all day doing time. Colton was so ashamed that he never told anyone. Thinking about his convict father haunted him every day. Colton walked in silence to his next class.*
>
> *Colton's mom was a waitress, working double shifts at a local truck stop. He wasn't proud of that either. His older brother had left home last year, leaving Colton the only man in the house.*
>
> *"Hey," said Colton's friend Steve, "why don't we go to your house after school and play this new video game I got this weekend? I've got it here with me in my backpack."*
>
> *Colton thought about the one-room apartment his mother could barely afford and said, "No, I can't. I've got to . . ." His words trailed off as he searched for an excuse. "I've got to finish some homework. I'm really behind."*

Colton was ashamed of his family—the things they did and the consequences on his life. Many times he blamed them for the problems he faced with friends and at school. Did you realize, though, that Jesus had some questionable characters in His family tree as well?

Read today's passage. Wipe that blank stare off your face—all those names aren't as boring as you might think. Check out Matthew 1:5. Rahab was King David's great-grandmother and an ancestor of Jesus. But did you know she was a prostitute? You can read her story in Joshua 2–6. Did you know that King David was an adulterer and a murderer? Read his story in 2 Samuel 11–12. Some of Jesus' ancestors were famous; some, not so famous. Some were great, and some were downright evil. In spite of His family problems, He still became everything He was intended to be.

Have you ever been ashamed of your family situation? _____

Have you ever been upset with God for giving you the family or home that you have?

_____

Jesus knows how you feel. How do you feel when you think about your family problems?

_____

Take time right now to pray and thank God for who you are, who your family is, and the home that He has given you. That might be difficult, considering your situation, but thank God anyway. Even if you have family problems, God will fulfill His plan for *you,* just like He did for His own Son.

For further reading on this subject, look at 1 Thessalonians 5:18; Jeremiah 29:11–13; Psalm 139:13–16; and Acts 17:26–28.

Speechless

Luke 1:5–25

Ross woke up screaming. His wife, Megan, calmed him down—again. Every night Ross had nightmares about the dead body he found while on an underwater salvage expedition. The dead man had been in his sunken boat for days, and his body had bloated to twice its size. The image still haunted Ross.

Ross answered the phone the next day and his face fell. It was another salvage job with a possible fatality. Ross gathered his gear and headed out the door. "Pray for me," he pleaded with Megan. Megan did pray. She prayed, "Dear Lord, please don't let Bob find a dead person in that sunken boat."

Offshore, Ross went down to the sunken boat several times but could not find anyone. Ross was relieved, but his supervisor suggested one more try. Ross went down and peered around with his flashlight. Out of the corner of his eye, he spotted a human foot. Trembling, Ross grabbed the ankle to pull out the body. The foot jerked back in response! Ross's heart raced. He worked his way through the debris and shot upward to find himself in a small pocket of air, face to face with a terrified stranger. He was alive! The man had survived in that sunken boat for almost two days. Megan's prayer had been answered—just not in the way she expected.

In today's passage, Zechariah's prayer was answered so unexpectedly it frightened him. He couldn't believe his ears when the angel spoke. Zechariah had prayed for so long that perhaps he just didn't believe anymore.

How's your prayer life? Rate your prayer life on a scale from 1–10, with 10 being the best.

_____

What is the biggest thing you prayed for during the past year? _____

Did you get an answer? _____ *If not, do you think you prayed enough?* _____

Our God is an awesome God, and He wants to do great things for you. But if you don't ask, you won't receive. Keep asking, even when the answer seems to be delayed. Here are a few tips on improving your prayer life. Make this **A.C.T.S.** outline your guideline for praying.

1. **A**doration. Praise God first. When you do, you will realize how big He is. Then you will have faith to ask for big answers.
2. **C**onfession. Admit to God where you've failed. Forgive anyone else who may have hurt you. Know that God has forgiven you.
3. **T**hanksgiving. Thank God for what He has already done for you in the past and present.
4. **S**upplication. Tell God about all your needs. Keep asking every day and wait for His answer in His time.

Unexpectedly Pregnant

Luke 1:26–38

Imagine for a moment that your name is Mary and you're fifteen years old. You have a crush on a guy named Joe who lives a few blocks down from you. You and Joe take frequent walks to the edge of town where there is a steep cliff overlooking a beautiful valley. There the two of you sit and talk for hours about your future together. Joe, on the shy side, has asked you to marry him; and you have said yes. The date is not set just yet, and you still wonder if you made the right decision. But for now, the two of you walk back to town, hand in hand, just happy to have each other.

Joe kisses you goodnight on your front porch, and you silently slip inside your home just before dark—as requested by your overprotective mother. You walk past the living room where Mom is sewing and Dad is reading a copy of the Nazareth Times. You head to your room, close the door, and plop down on your bed. You pull a pillow under your chin and daydream, wondering what the future holds. Will you have a big wedding? Is Joe the right guy? What will your children be like?

Today's passage starts right here. Suddenly, a strange visitor interrupted Mary's thoughts with an important message. Mary believed the angel's message that she would become the mother of the Son of God. Can you imagine what it was like the next day when she walked out to the edge of town with Joseph? What was she going to tell him? "Joseph, I'm pregnant. Let me explain."

Mary probably had plans for her life. She wanted to marry Joseph, have kids, raise a family, and have a good life. Then a messenger from another world showed up and offered her a life far beyond her wildest dreams. Mary could have said, "No, thank you. I already have plans." Or, she might have said, "Please don't choose me. Go find someone else." Mary, however, chose to let her life be interrupted by God. She listened and obeyed.

Sometimes God wants to get your attention with a message. He periodically interrupts your regularly-scheduled life with a quiet time, a sermon, a conversation with your parents, or a cloud-speckled sunset. He whispers to you that He has chosen you to do something special.

Do you ever wonder what God's will is for your life? _____

How can you find out? _____

What should you do when you discover His will? _____

God not only has a will for your life, He has a will for your week—and for your day. Ask the Lord to show you His will. When He speaks, listen and obey—just like Mary did.

A Womb with a View

Luke 1:39–56

Amber was pregnant, and she couldn't tell her parents because her father would kill her. She and her boyfriend rounded up the $300 it would cost for an abortion. They planned to skip school next Tuesday and take care of her "problem."

Amber's friend Susan was a Christian who didn't turn her back on Amber during this difficult time. Susan patiently pleaded with Amber to do one thing: "Come and get an ultrasound first so you can see what you're getting rid of. If you're brave enough to dispose of it, then you're brave enough to look at it first."

Amber, resistant at first, finally gave in the day before her abortion. Susan's parents paid for the procedure. The clinic had Amber lie down on a table while they spread something like Vaseline on her stomach. Then, they turned on a little screen and placed an electronic gismo on the jelly. Suddenly, an image appeared on the screen. What Amber saw made her cry—a beating heart, a tiny human-like form with hands and feet, dancing around inside her. Amber decided to keep her baby because she fell in love with what she saw.

In today's passage, Mary was less than one month pregnant with Jesus. She went to see Elizabeth, who was about six months pregnant with John the Baptist. Notice what happened when Mary walked into Elizabeth's house. The six-month-old "fetus" in Elizabeth's womb leaped for joy when the three-week-old "fetus" in Mary's womb came near. John the Baptist sensed the presence of Jesus before either one of them had been born. He did a little dance inside his mother.

Some people say the Bible has nothing to say about abortion. However, today's passage proves differently. It is a simple story about two women and two unborn children. All four were given some part in the story because all four were alive. God had a plan for each one.

The Bible teaches that unborn children are alive. Does that give them equal rights with people who have already been born? _____

What can you do to help protect the life and rights of unborn children?

_____

Maybe you can't change the laws, but you can make a difference. How?

- If you know someone who is pregnant and planning an abortion, don't turn your back on her. Love her because God loves her. Offer to help her through this difficult time. Ask your parents or youth pastor about a local crisis pregnancy center that will help pay her medical expenses and provide clothes, diapers, and food.
- Don't be afraid to state your opinion on abortion. Never state your opinion hatefully, but let others know that you simply believe the unborn child has a life worth living. Tell people what the Bible says about it.
- Ask God to help you rescue at least one unborn child in your lifetime.

Weekly Bible Study and Prayer Review

Bible Study

Look back through some of the Scriptures you read this week. Write down the one verse or passage that God used to speak to you.

_____

_____

_____

_____

*Memorize this verse or passage. You can do it if you spend just
a few minutes saying it to yourself.*

Now, think of at least one situation you will probably face soon in which you could use this Scripture to help you make the right decision. Write down that situation below.

_____

Quote the Scripture when you face this situation, and live by it.

Prayer Time

*Take a few moments to praise God for who He is.
Now take a few moments to thank God for things He has done for you.
Now ask God to make you into the person He wants you to be.
Ask God to use you to help others become closer to God.*

Below is your prayer list for the week. Keep it updated each week. If your prayer isn't answered this week, carry it over to next week's list.

Request	Date of Original Request	Date Answered
_____	__/__/__	__/__/__
_____	__/__/__	__/__/__
_____	__/__/__	__/__/__
_____	__/__/__	__/__/__
_____	__/__/__	__/__/__
_____	__/__/__	__/__/__
_____	__/__/__	__/__/__
_____	__/__/__	__/__/__
_____	__/__/__	__/__/__

*Pray for the things on your list and trust God to provide.
Forgive anyone you have not yet forgiven.
Ask God to forgive you for any unconfessed sin in your life.
Ask God to keep you out of trouble with sin.
Acknowledge that God is in complete control of your life
and will take care of everything.*

Johnny, Be Good

Luke 1:57–80

Alicia was the star of the youth choir. She could sing like no one else. Every time she sang a solo in church, the adults lavished her with praise.

Alicia could quote Bible verses better than anyone else in her Sunday school class. She could recite all of the books of the Bible in order. She was friendly to new people in the youth group. She treated the older members with respect. Alicia was the most popular girl in church.

At school, however, Alicia was different. She had a reputation on the drill team for being an easy target for the guys. She cheated on her tests just like everybody else. She went to parties where she experimented with drugs. Alicia was the most popular girl in school.

Alicia wanted to be popular at church and school, so she set up two different versions of herself. The first version did things that would make people at church admire her. The second version did things that would make people at school like her. She did whatever it took to get noticed.

In today's passage, John the Baptist's birth did not go unnoticed. His dad talked about how great he would be. Everyone at the party expected John to grow up and be great. John was the most popular guy in town. Notice, however, what John actually did with his life. Instead of becoming Mr. Popularity, John moved to the desert, where no one could see him. John didn't care whether he was noticed or not. He put God in charge of his popularity. Later, John did emerge into the public eye. People from all over the world heard about him. He became so great that Jesus said John the Baptist was the greatest man who ever lived.

Sometimes we do what we do to be noticed. We want people to accept us, say good things about us, and give us a pat on the back. Playing the popularity game can get tough, though. If you are a Christian playing the game, it forces you to lead two lives—one at church and the other everywhere else. You try to maintain your image by wearing masks and pretending to be someone you aren't. People may accept you, but are they accepting you or a false image of you?

Have you ever played the popularity game, pretending to be someone you aren't just to be accepted? _____

Name something that you did solely to be noticed by someone else.

_____

How would your life change if you stopped trying to be popular?

_____

Put Jesus in charge of your popularity. Ask God to help you take off the masks you have been wearing. Don't be afraid to be yourself. God accepts you just the way you are.

Bad Reputation

Matthew 1:18–25

Your name is Joe. You're a decent guy and you've always tried to do the right thing. You've prayed all your life that God would give you a godly wife, and you thought that prayer was answered when you met Mary. You fell in love with her and asked her to marry you. She seemed so sweet! you thought. But now, all that is over. She's pregnant. And she's giving you some crazy story about how an angel came to her and told her she would give birth to God's son. "Yeah, right! God's son. That's just too much for me to handle."

So, you think about your options. You could spread rumors about Mary's pregnancy all over town and ruin her reputation—but you really don't want to hurt her like that. You could claim responsibility for the pregnancy, but then both your reputations would be ruined, and you'd be lying. So, you finally decide the right thing to do for both you and Mary is to break off the engagement quietly so that Mary isn't too disgraced. You've made up your mind. You'll do it tomorrow. It's late now, and you need some sleep. So you lie down and . . .

Today's passage tells the rest of Joe's story. Joseph had a big decision to make. Should he have believed the dream? If he did take Mary to be his wife, what would everyone else think? Joseph had just received instructions from God that could possibly have ruined his reputation. Joseph finally decided it was worth risking his own reputation so that Jesus could come into the world.

Suppose God wants you to reach out to one of those people at school who no one likes. Suppose He wants you to share Jesus with the people who have a bad reputation.

What if He wants you to sacrifice your own reputation for the sake of bringing Jesus into someone else's world? Could you do it? _____

Think of a time when you had a chance to bring Jesus into a conversation or activity at school. Did you do it, or were you too embarrassed?

_____

What can you do next time to help bring Jesus into someone else's world?

_____

Pray that God will give you the wisdom and courage to put your reputation on the line for Jesus this week. Don't be afraid to stand up for Him the next time you have a chance.

A Terrible Day

Luke 2:1–7

It was just an ordinary day for Bob at the construction site. He had rigged a pulley at the top of a five-story building. Through the pulley ran a rope attached to a barrel full of bricks sitting on a ledge. Bob had finished his job and now wanted to clean up. He was at the bottom of the building. The barrel of bricks was at the top. He prepared to lower the bricks with the rope and pulley.

Bob pulled on the rope to lower the bricks, but the bricks were too heavy. He hung on to the rope and was pulled up the building as the bricks came down. Halfway up, Bob and the barrel met and crashed. Barely managing to hold on to the rope, he continued up the building until he hit his head and jammed his fingers in the pulley. At the same time, the barrel hit the ground and the bottom broke open. All the bricks fell out. Now Bob was heavier than the barrel, causing him to sail down the building and meet the barrel halfway. Crash! Bob landed on the pile of bricks and accidentally let go of the rope. The barrel then came back down the building and landed on top of Bob.[1]

Bob had one tough day. He could probably ask God, "Why me?" A lot of things happen to us that make us want to ask God, "Why me?"

In today's passage, Joseph and Mary had a problem. They lived in Nazareth, and Caesar had issued a decree demanding everybody to go to the town where their ancestors were born to pay taxes. Great! thought Joseph. We're broke as it is, and the trip to Bethlehem is going to take weeks! When they finally arrived in Bethlehem, there was no place to have a baby in but a smelly cattle stable. Joseph could have said, "God, look. Mary is having Your child. Can't You give us some special treatment?"

Chances are, you are going through something right now and asking God, "Just what do You think You're doing?" You may have problems with acne, parents, friends, or something more serious. You may hate the way God has made you. You may have a problem you just can't imagine getting through. You wonder where God is.

Have you ever asked God, "Why?" _____

If you could ask God "why" about anything right now, what would it be?

_____

There is a reason for everything. For instance, if Joseph and Mary hadn't gone to Bethlehem, Jesus wouldn't have been born there like Micah 5:2 promised. God knew what He was doing. God had everything worked out just right. The same is true for you. Everything you're going through has a purpose.

Ask God to help you see past your bad times. Look for the good in what God is doing in your life. For further study, read Romans 8:28.

Not a Nobody

Luke 2:8–20

Marsha absolutely hated her legs. They were strong, but they were bigger and straighter than the legs of the "pretty" girls, like the cheerleaders. All of her life she hated her legs. She felt like all of the guys went after the girls with legs that had more curve to them.

One day Marsha met a guy named Anthony who really liked her. He never said anything about her legs. He seemed to enjoy her appearance very much. He often told her how beautiful she was. Once Marsha asked Anthony how he could like her ugly legs. He simply said he really liked strong, sturdy legs on a girl.

Marsha still was not satisfied but refused to bring up the subject again. Then one day Anthony took Marsha to meet his mother. Anthony's mom was crippled. Both of her legs were skinny, crooked, and weak. She couldn't stand or walk without help. Tears welled up in Marsha's eyes. She realized that Anthony loved her legs because they were strong—something lacking in his mother.

Anthony really loved Marsha. She probably asked, "Why would you pick me? My legs are so ugly!" Anthony's reason for picking Marsha had a lot to do with the way her legs looked. He liked what she hated.

In today's passage, angels told some shepherds about the birth of Jesus. Of all the people to announce the birth of the King of kings and Lord of lords, why did God pick those shepherds? There were a lot of great religious people and rulers of Jerusalem and all sorts of other important people to tell. Why would God pick smelly shepherds out in the fields to announce the birth of Christ? Apparently God liked something He saw in the shepherds. After all, God's only Son was the Lamb of God (John 1:36). Psalm 23 says, "The Lord is my Shepherd."

God likes what He sees in you too. Do you believe that? _____

What makes you think God doesn't like what He sees when He looks at you?

_____

Ask God to help you overcome the negative thoughts you have about yourself. Remember the shepherds. If He chose them over the "important people" to announce the birth of Jesus, then He will choose you for something important too. You are not a nobody. You are important to God.

Baby Talk

Luke 2:21–40

When a baby is born in America, hospitals have a routine they follow. First, the doctors make sure the baby is alive and can breathe. That's why the doctor sometimes slaps the baby's behind—crying means the baby is alive and breathing. Next, they cut the umbilical cord, separating the mother from the child so the child can live on its own. The nurses then clean the blood and amniotic fluids off the child.

Then, a name tag is attached to the baby. If the parents have not decided on the name yet, the last name is printed along with an ID number so the baby is not confused with other newborns. After Mom has had a chance to hold her new child briefly, the baby is taken away so that the doctors can run a variety of tests to make sure the baby is completely healthy. Hopefully, the doctors will return and announce to the mother and father, "This child is a perfectly healthy baby and will grow up just fine."

Newborn babies of the first century also had a routine. After eight days, the boy was circumcised. After forty days, Mom and Dad took the child into the temple to offer a sacrifice. That's why Mary and Joseph took Jesus to the temple. When they arrived at the temple, two prophets took the child from the mother to announce that this baby was going to grow up in the power of God, cleansing the world from sin. Mary heard that her baby would grow up and change the spiritual health of the nation.

You are still growing up spiritually. You may not have Anna or Simeon to speak encouraging words about you, but you do have the Bible. God's Word is a "pick-me-up" for you. God's Word tells you that He has great plans for your life (Jeremiah 29:11–13). It says that God has chosen you to be a spokesperson for Him (Jeremiah 1:4–7). Every time you read a passage of Scripture, God isn't just giving you a history lesson. He is telling you what He has planned for your life. You have the choice to accept or reject those plans. God's Word can guide you in class at school, at home with your parents, and on a date with someone you care about.

Whose plans do you think will work out better—yours or God's? _____

What do you think God wants you to do as a result of having this quiet time?

_____

Ask God to help you see yourself and your future in the words of the Bible. Let the Bible guide you and encourage you to become a true child of God.

We'll Leave the Light On

Matthew 2:1–12

There is something strange going on in the small Texas town of Marfa. On some nights, if you're lucky, and you face the right direction, the horizon is filled with many inexplicable lights. Sometimes they dance up and down. Sometimes they slide from side to side. Sometimes they do both and leave little light trails like a child's scribbling painted all over the black canvas of night. No one knows what the lights are or where they come from.

Curiosity seekers often come from all parts of the United States and even the world to see the Marfa lights. Some people travel great distances just to see if they can catch a glimpse of the famous lights and guess what source is behind them. Some people guess swamp gas. Some say it's a strange form of lightning. And some say it's other-worldly. The lights haven't been explained yet, but people still keep coming.

Another strange light appeared in the night sky almost two thousand years ago. Wise men, perhaps astronomers, from the Far East saw the light and believed that it signaled the coming of the King of the Jews. So they loaded up gifts of gold, incense, and myrrh (a spice) and traveled a great distance, following the light. These were all very valuable gifts. These men thought Jesus was worth the long journey and the expensive things.

Isn't it strange how much has changed? Today it seems that people expect God to come down from heaven and give *them* expensive gifts. People travel great distances to see the Marfa lights, but how often do people make the effort to go seek God and bring Him gifts?

Are you willing to give up your time, talents, money, dreams, and other important things to God? Are you more of a giver or a taker? Below, place a large dot where you think you stand in your relationship with God when it comes to giving.

Taker   Neutral   Giver

What can you do this week to become more of a giver?

_____

Pray that God will help you to be more of a cheerful giver (2 Corinthians 9:7). Do what the wise men did and seek God by bringing Him all that you have to offer.

Bible Study

Look back through some of the Scriptures you read this week. Write down the one verse or passage that God used to speak to you.

_____

_____

_____

_____

*Memorize this verse or passage. You can do it if you spend just
a few minutes saying it to yourself.*

Now, think of at least one situation you will probably face soon in which you could use this Scripture to help you make the right decision. Write down that situation below.

_____

Quote the Scripture when you face this situation, and live by it.

Prayer Time

*Take a few moments to praise God for who He is.
Now take a few moments to thank God for things He has done for you.
Now ask God to make you into the person He wants you to be.
Ask God to use you to help others become closer to God.*

Below is your prayer list for the week. Keep it updated each week. If your prayer isn't answered this week, carry it over to next week's list.

Request	Date of Original Request	Date Answered
_____	__/__/__	__/__/__
_____	__/__/__	__/__/__
_____	__/__/__	__/__/__
_____	__/__/__	__/__/__
_____	__/__/__	__/__/__
_____	__/__/__	__/__/__
_____	__/__/__	__/__/__
_____	__/__/__	__/__/__
_____	__/__/__	__/__/__

*Pray for the things on your list and trust God to provide.
Forgive anyone you have not yet forgiven.
Ask God to forgive you for any unconfessed sin in your life.
Ask God to keep you out of trouble with sin.
Acknowledge that God is in complete control of your life
and will take care of everything.*

Hired Assassins

Matthew 2:13–18

A Houston woman hires a hit man to kill the mother of her daughter's friend so her daughter will have a better chance at becoming a cheerleader. The leader of a small country publicly executes several men who threaten his power. An ice-skater hires a friend to injure her competitor so that she will have a better chance of winning a national contest. A young teenage girl is pregnant and her boyfriend says he will leave her if she does not have an abortion. Kingpins of drug cartels in Columbia surround their immaculate homes with armed guards twenty-four hours a day to protect them from U.S. agents and competing drug leaders. A high school senior carries a shotgun to a party and attempts to blow away the guy who's trying to steal his girl. A mob boss routinely orders the execution of anyone who stands in his way.

Headlines from our world. Do you see the common thread? Each story explains how one person, so consumed with protecting his or her territory, is willing to take someone else's life.

The Romans called King Herod the "King of the Jews," but the Jews refused to acknowledge him with this title. Herod was insecure about his throne. So when some really smart guys said they heard that the king of the Jews had been born, he became nervous. He tried to get the wise men to divulge Jesus' location, but God directed them to do otherwise. Herod then resorted to mass murder in an attempt to kill the baby he thought would jeopardize his kingdom.

You may have your own "territory" set up. Maybe it's your popularity at school. Maybe it's a certain group of friends that you are unwilling to give up, even though your parents advise you to do so. Maybe it is your grades, and you'll do anything to stay on top. When anyone tries to move in on your territory, you may get angry. You may do things that hurt others. Whatever the case, anger toward another person is the first step toward murder. Hate is just as bad as murder in God's eyes (Matthew 5:21–24).

Have you ever felt angry toward someone who moved in on your territory?

_____

Do you have an earthly kingdom that you have built around yourself that makes you feel secure? What is it? _____

Ask God to help you let go of any hate that you have in your heart toward someone else. Forgive anyone you are holding a grudge against. Learn to love everyone equally, even those who try to move in on your territory.

What's Your Story?

Matthew 2:19–23

Harriet was so close she could taste it. Darkness enshrouded her presence as she slowly crept through the underbrush. Her keen eyes could just make out her destination only a few feet in front of her. She didn't dare to even breathe. She listened for what seemed like hours for her enemy lurking in the shadows around her. Each step was carefully calculated to make no sound whatsoever. Would she make it? She wasn't sure. But she had come this far and now she had to make her move.

She looked and listened once more, just to be safe, and then she leaped onto the path and darted forward. Her heart was pounding as the moonlight exposed her form to any would-be foes. Her lungs were about to burst. She dove across the border and tasted freedom for the first time in her life. Harriet Tubman, former black slave, completed a dangerous course on the Underground Railroad and made it safely into the free states.

Free at last! Do you see the connection between today's passage and the story of Harriet Tubman? Look closer. What seemed like a desperate escape from Herod was actually a living illustration of God's plan for His people. God sent Jesus back to Israel from Egypt to fulfill Scripture (Matthew 2:14–15). He came out of Egypt just like Moses and the Israelites came out of Egypt centuries earlier. It was a living reminder to Jesus' family of how God once delivered His people out of their bondage and into freedom.

God the Father guided this holy trip to show the world that His Son, Jesus, would one day deliver His people out of their bondage of sin and into a land of freedom. He was reliving the deliverance of the Jews. If you are a Christian, you have come out of Egypt (a symbol for sin) into Israel (a symbol for life with Jesus).

Do you remember when you first allowed Jesus to come into your life and to set you free from your slavery to sin? _____

How did you feel? _____

Perhaps today would be a good time to review your first experience with true freedom. Stop right now and relive your salvation by thinking about . . .

- what your life was like before you met Jesus;
- how you realized that you needed Jesus in your life;
- what it was like the moment you gave your heart to Him; and
- what your new life in Christ has been like.

Celebrate your freedom. The story you just relived is called your *testimony*. Ask God to help you remember it and tell someone else. Perhaps your story can help someone realize his or her need for Jesus.

Missing Child

Luke 2:41–52

> You are a prisoner, and now is the moment of escape. You've been in bondage your entire life, but now you have a chance at freedom. The hallway is dark; and the two evil guards sit in the next room taking it easy, unaware of your approach. You crouch low to the floor and stealthily creep on your fingertips into the guard room. There they are—those two hideous figures that for so long have tortured you. You could just scream. But now is not the time. You've got to move. And fast.
>
> The doorway to freedom is so close you can taste it. A wall blocks the guards' view of the door. You make it past the guards and safely to the door. You stand up against the wall, peer back at the evil ones, breathe a sigh of relief, and silently twist the knob that will unlock your misery. Suddenly, a voice comes from behind: "Tammy, are you going somewhere?"
>
> "No, Mom and Dad. I was just trying to clean off this doorknob."

You probably feel sometimes that your house is a prison and your parents are the guards. You think your parents are engaged in a conspiracy to limit your rights and freedom to a wonderful world out there. Let's see how Jesus dealt with this same problem. He had parents too.

Jesus was twelve—the Jewish age of manhood. He had every right to go His own way and do His own thing. And He did. He went to His Father's house and stayed there while His parents were returning home. After all, He had things to do, places to go, people to see. And, of course, He was God.

Jesus was not disobedient when He stayed at the temple. But when His parents explained to Him what they expected, He submitted to their authority and went home with them—for eighteen more years! He didn't leave home until He was thirty (see Luke 3:23)! You may sometimes wish you were God, but you are not. You may think your parents are the evil ones, but they are not. If you have a father, or mother, or both, Jesus has set an example for you to follow.

Have you ever felt like your parents are just there to keep you from having a good time?

_____

Do you honestly think their goal is to make you miserable? _____

Why do you think your parents have set rules for you? _____

_____

Jesus followed the rules His parents gave Him, even though He could have used His power to do otherwise. Jesus wants you to submit to your parents just like He submitted to His parents.

Pray right now that God will give you the desire, patience, and wisdom to obey your parents this week. If you want to be like Jesus, be obedient to your parents.

Taking a Dip

Matthew 3:1–12; Mark 1:1–8; Luke 3:1–18

Steve had his first summer job. He was so excited. The pay was better than minimum wage, and now Steve could afford to put gas in his car, take out a girl now and then, and buy some stereo equipment. Steve had it made.

The only problem was that Steve liked to get his paycheck, but he didn't like to work. He got into a really bad habit of doing just enough to get by. Before long, he wasn't doing anything at all except making sure his time card had all of his hours on it.

Steve's coworkers knew he was sneaking into the back to sleep or goof-off, so they told the boss. The boss couldn't believe someone would be that stupid, so he followed Steve one day to see what he was doing. Steve came in, clocked in, looked around, and tiptoed to the back where there was a cot he had brought from home. He laid down and started to doze off. Needless to say, the boss immediately fired him and told him never to come back.

Can you believe someone would actually do nothing while they were getting paid to do something? John the Baptist used some strong words to explain to people that they must "produce fruit in keeping with repentance." In other words, if you repent of your sin and get baptized, then your life should prove it by how you act and what you do.

Many young people today are doing just what Steve did and just what John the Baptist preached against. They are going to church, playing the game, and then slipping into the back room and going to sleep. John the Baptist said that doesn't cut it. If you're doing that, you're like a tree that won't produce fruit. The owner is frustrated at the fruitless tree and wants to cut it down.

Are you living the life God called you to live, or are you one of those who plays church?

_____

Is there a sin in your life right now that you are involved in that you need to let go of?

_____

What is it? _____

When are you going to walk away from this sin and produce some fruit?

_____

Perhaps now you realize that there are at least a few areas in your life you can change. Go to God right now in prayer and repent of those things that separate you from Him. *Repent* doesn't mean to feel sorry for something. It doesn't mean to simply ask for forgiveness. It means to do an *about face*—renounce your old ways and do a 180° turn and begin doing the right thing.

Gang Leaders Face Off

Matthew 3:13–17; Mark 1:9–11; Luke 3:21–22

Keith was an interim youth minister at a church in southwest Houston. He had been there for seven months, and he was really enjoying working with the young people. He knew he was only there until they found someone else to come full-time, but he gave everything he had to that ministry and really became attached to the youth.

One day the church brought in another young man who had graduated from seminary. He spent the whole weekend at the church getting to know everyone—especially the youth. Keith didn't know what to think. He wanted God's will to be done, but he didn't want to let go of his position. So, he watched and supported the new guy as much as possible.

Sunday night the church voted to bring the new guy on full-time. Everyone seemed to be well pleased with the new "official" youth minister. In two weeks, David would come in, and Keith would be out. David must increase, but Keith must decrease.

That was a tough time for Keith. It was hard watching a ministry that he had built be given to someone else. Keith knew that it would happen, but it was still hard to let go when the time came.

John the Baptist knew that one day someone greater than he would come onto the scene. One day it finally happened. Jesus appeared in a blaze of glory, with the Spirit descending out of heaven and a voice of approval coming from the sky. John's career after that, as you'll read in the future, decreased and led to prison and eventually death. Jesus was only beginning His ministry. John had to decrease while Jesus increased. It was hard for John, but he let go.

Becoming a Christian is a lot like that. When you say "yes" to Jesus, you are basically saying, "Jesus, You must increase while I must decrease." Your will must decrease and even die while His will in your life takes over. Even Jesus faced this in the garden of Gethsemane when He said, "Father, not My will, but Yours." It's hard to let go of what you want and do what God wants (Romans 7:14–20). But the more you become like Jesus, the less you will be like your old, sinful self. Whose will is greater? Yours or His? Who is on the increase? You or He?

Do you ever find it hard to let God have His way with your life? _____

Why does it seem so hard sometimes? _____

What can you change this week in your life to allow Jesus to increase? _____

_____

Perhaps now would be a good time to pray this prayer: "Lord, You increase while I decrease." Let Jesus become great in your life.

I Double Dare You

Matthew 4:1–11; Mark 1:12–13; Luke 4:1–13

It was the weekend, and for the first time in as long as he could remember, Scott had the entire house to himself. Mom and Dad were away at some convention. His sister, Marie, was spending the weekend with a friend over 100 miles away. Scott was a Christian and didn't even think about throwing a wild party. No sir! He was going to stay at home alone tonight just like his parents told him.

Scott sat down to read his Bible when he remembered something. They had cable and no one was here to tell him what to watch. He had never been alone with the remote before. Scott tried to shake the thought, but it kept haunting him. He picked up the cable guide and checked out the movies. Oh no! The movie channels were pretty steamy tonight. Scott had his choice of pornographic films to check out. No one would ever know. Scott closed the shades to the house, making sure no one could see in. He looked at his Bible and then at the remote.

Scott was tempted. He was tempted to feast his eyes on something not meant for him until after marriage. This temptation, or something like it, will one day beg for your submission. What will you do?

How did Jesus deal with temptation? He quoted Scripture. Satan hit Jesus hard with his best temptations, but Jesus quoted Scripture to ward him off. And it worked. The fact that you own a Bible or carry one around means nothing. Your defense against Satan is not in your hands—it's in your heart. The more Scripture you know, the better prepared you will be to handle temptation when it comes.

When you're tempted by pornography, read 1 Corinthians 6:18–20. If drinking is a problem for you, read Ephesians 5:18. If you have a habit of cheating, read Proverbs 11:1. Whatever the temptation, there are Scripture passages that can serve as a flaming sword to defend you against Satan when he attacks.

Are you ever tempted to do wrong? _____

What is one particular sin that really seems to give you trouble? _____

_____

What is a Bible story, verse, or passage that deals with this problem? _____

_____

Using the index to this book, or the one in your Bible, find at least one verse that could help you the next time you are tempted to give in to this particular sin. Memorize it and carry it in your heart. When temptation strikes, quote the verse to yourself and ask God to help you overcome the temptation.

Weekly Bible Study and Prayer Review

Bible Study

Look back through some of the Scriptures you read this week. Write down the one verse or passage that God used to speak to you.

_____
_____
_____
_____

Memorize this verse or passage. You can do it if you spend just a few minutes saying it to yourself.

Now, think of at least one situation you will probably face soon in which you could use this Scripture to help you make the right decision. Write down that situation below.

_____

Quote the Scripture when you face this situation, and live by it.

Prayer Time

Take a few moments to praise God for who He is.
Now take a few moments to thank God for things He has done for you.
Now ask God to make you into the person He wants you to be.
Ask God to use you to help others become closer to God.

Below is your prayer list for the week. Keep it updated each week. If your prayer isn't answered this week, carry it over to next week's list.

Request	Date of Original Request	Date Answered
_____	__/__/__	__/__/__
_____	__/__/__	__/__/__
_____	__/__/__	__/__/__
_____	__/__/__	__/__/__
_____	__/__/__	__/__/__
_____	__/__/__	__/__/__
_____	__/__/__	__/__/__
_____	__/__/__	__/__/__

Pray for the things on your list and trust God to provide.
Forgive anyone you have not yet forgiven.
Ask God to forgive you for any unconfessed sin in your life.
Ask God to keep you out of trouble with sin.
Acknowledge that God is in complete control of your life and will take care of everything.

Denomination Dance

John 1:19–28

Garrett went with a few other friends from his youth group to a Christian concert. He was amazed at the variety of people he saw there. Garrett was a Baptist; but before the concert began he met some people who were Lutheran, Presbyterian, Church of God, Church of Christ, Church of God in Christ, Catholic, Church of the Nazarene, Disciples of Christ, some nonde-nominational Christians, Assembly of God, Episcopalian, Methodist, Pentecostal, and many others he couldn't remember. He used to be "afraid" of these other denominations because he figured they were just way too different in their approach to following Jesus.

But Garrett found out quickly in talking to these people that they were just like him. They had come to the concert to hear about Jesus and to worship God. They were there to have a great time. As Garrett discussed his beliefs with others, he discovered to his amazement that everyone believed basically the same thing: that Jesus Christ is Lord and that He is the only way to a truly satisfying life on earth and to eternal life in heaven. "We just do things a little differently," commented one girl Garrett spoke to that evening.

"Maybe we ought to get together more often and worship God," Garrett suggested as the concert hall doors opened.

Denominations—sometimes the other ones can seem frightening. Sometimes we get so used to the way we do things in our churches that we forget we are not the only ones going to heaven. We have Christian brothers and sisters all across our nation of different denominations who still worship and walk with the same God.

John the Baptist was baptizing people in the desert, and a group of religious people who believed in God came to ask John what he was all about. Instead of advocating a particular viewpoint about how to worship God, John said plainly, "Jesus is the one I follow. How about you?"

What denomination are you? _____

What other denominations are your Christian friends a part of? _____

If we are all on the same team, do you think it's possible that we could work together more often? _____

What would you propose we do to get everybody together? _____

Ask God to help you realize you are a Christian first, and then a member of your denomination second. Ask Him to help you love and work with your Christian friends from other denominations. Perhaps you could have a weekly prayer meet-ing at school for all Christians or a monthly youth rally in your city with every denomination represented. Whatever the case, love each other and work togeth-er. We're all going to spend eternity with each other, so we may as well start get-ting along now.

A Sheepish Grin

John 1:29–34

Imagine yourself back—in Old Testament days. You have committed a sin, and now you must obtain forgiveness—but how? You walk your way through a corral full of sheep, looking for the perfect one. You finally find and pick up a precious, solid white lamb that is barely one year old. The lamb gently licks your face as you carry it toward the tabernacle. It nuzzles its face into your neck and "baas" contentedly. It trusts you. You take your place in line behind other people and wait. A plume of smoke rises ahead, and you are just close enough now to smell the burning flesh. The lamb smells it, too, and begins squirming in your arms. You increase your grip and move forward. Now you're next. The lamb looks at you for comfort, but you offer it none. "Come!" bellows a voice from inside the tent. You step inside the tabernacle. A priest in front of you holds a bloody knife. As instructed, you place the lamb on the ground and kneel down, looking deep into its eyes. You place your hands on the lamb's head and openly confess your sins, symbolically transferring your guilt to the innocent lamb. Then, with tears in your eyes, you take the knife, place it under the lamb's throat, and swiftly pull in and to the right. The innocent lamb who trusted you staggers forward, looks at you unbelievingly, falls to the ground, and drowns in its own blood.

That is not a pretty picture, but it is exactly what you had to do if you lived in the days before Jesus came. Someone has to pay for sin. The only way to be forgiven back then was to confess your sin, transfer it to a completely innocent animal, and let its blood cover your guilt.

John called Jesus the "Lamb of God." He chose that name for a reason. Jesus is the perfect lamb. Everyone who confesses their sin to Him will be covered by His blood and forgiven.

How long has it been since you really thought about what Jesus did for you? He came here, lived a perfectly sinless life, and then died a cruel death. He did it because He loved you enough to provide a way for your sin to be forgiven. His blood covers your guilt.

Can you think of someone you would be willing to die for? _____

Who? _____

Name someone other than Jesus who you think would be willing to die for you. _____

Thank Jesus for loving you enough to die for you. Confess your sins to God, and let Him forgive you through the blood of Jesus. Then make a commitment to live for Jesus. Since He died for you, you can live for Him.

I've Got a Better Idea

John 1:35–51

> *Phil really didn't know what he wanted to do with his life. He was a senior in high school without any real direction. One day, his best friend, Chet, asked him to come to the TV station where his older brother worked as a cameraman. Phil accepted, and he and Chet took off.*
>
> *When Phil stepped into the newsroom, his life was transformed. His eyes followed the spectral blazes cast by the studio lights from one end of the ceiling to the other. He was in awe as Chet's brother stood in front of six different screens and merged different video segments together. He couldn't believe it when he was allowed to sit behind the news desk and pretend he was announcing tonight's high school football scores to the entire Metroplex.*
>
> *Phil left, his life changed and with a new vision. He knew that one day he would work in television. He went home and told his family and friends and began making plans for his career.*

Sometimes if you spend a day around something or someone you've never been exposed to before, it can change your life.

Read today's passage. Do you see the trend? A couple of curious guys spent the day with Jesus, and their lives were so transformed that they began telling everybody else around them. When you have a life-changing experience, you want to tell people.

When is the last time you spent the *day* with Jesus? You're probably thinking, "I'm not going to spend a whole day reading the Bible and praying." That's not what these guys did either. They just spent time with Jesus. You can spend time with Jesus in a unique way too. You could take a bike ride and spend time in God's creation, realizing it was Jesus who made it all. You could spend time helping neighbors or the homeless, knowing that if you help them you are helping Jesus. You could just go to school and take every step asking yourself what Jesus would do.

When is the last time you spent the whole day conscious of Jesus' presence?

_____

What is a way that you could spend time with Jesus (besides reading your Bible or praying)? _____

Ask the Lord to let you spend a day with Him. Be conscious of His presence every moment. It will change your life.

Are you Crazy?

John 2:1–11

> The weary desert traveler was at the point of death. He continued to crawl across the desert sand, but he knew his thirst would not likely be quenched. He reached the top of one more dune, and threw himself over. Down the hill he tumbled until he stopped at an unbelievable sight. Was it a mirage? Was he dreaming? No! It was a bottle full of water sitting next to a hand-operated pump. The water looked old and dirty, but it was better than nothing.
>
> Then he saw a note attached to the bottle. It instructed him to pour all of the water—every last drop—into the pump to prime it. The note said that if he did, the pump would bring an unending flow of cold, fresh, pure water. The traveler thought for a moment. Should he drink the dirty water, which would at least save his life for now? Or should he risk losing it all to get more and better water? He thought for a moment and then decided. He poured out every last drop of water and then began to pump. At first, nothing happened. But then, the water came. He drank freely for an hour. Then he filled the bottle back up with water for whoever might come next.[2]

What would you have done? You've just found water, and the note says to pour it all out. That's crazy! The traveler gave up the old water, but in return he received the new.

In today's passage, you read another story about similar instructions. Jesus told some servants at a wedding to fill up some jars with water and let the banquet master taste it. They needed wine, not water. They could have objected to Jesus' crazy idea; but, at Mary's request, they did exactly what Jesus told them to do. Their obedience produced the best wine ever tasted. Notice that the water did not change to wine until *after* the servants took it to the banquet master.

God wants you to follow Mary's instructions to the servants: "Do whatever Jesus tells you." He wants you to give up every desire, every expectation, and every need over to Him. Then He wants you to wait on Him to provide for your needs. The decision is yours. You can take the small bottle of old, dirty water the world has given you to drink. Or you can pour every last drop of it into the well of God's goodness. Your obedience will produce the best life you could possibly experience.

Have you given every last drop of your life to God? _____

What are you holding back? _____

What do you think would happen if you let go of that and gave it to God?

_____

Ask God to help you give Him every last drop of your old life. Let go of the bad habits. Say good-bye to the worries. Bid a fond farewell to all those thoughts that tell you you're no good. Then wait for God. He is the well of eternal life. After a little while, all the old things you gave to God will turn into a huge waterfall of new life.

Cleaning House

John 2:13–25

Carter had a rough life as an abandoned orphan and a street kid in Chicago, and he was a pretty rough character by the time he reached thirteen. His life had gotten so bad, it seemed that no one cared about him at all. He decided he would kill himself. As he walked down the street plotting his own suicide, he noticed the lights in a church were on. He'd never been to a church in his life. Perhaps, he thought, this was his last chance to see if there was a purpose to life.

He approached the church slowly, in awe of the architecture. It seemed to point to heaven. He gingerly climbed the steps in the front to the massive Romanesque doorway. He took a deep breath and, after almost changing his mind, pulled the door open. A beam of light escaped from the service going on inside. After his eyes adjusted, he slipped inside and sat on the back row, hoping to find the answer to life. The service had just begun. The preacher stepped forward to the pulpit and leaned into the microphone. Carter waited to hear the words of life. Then, the preacher shouted, "If you got a need, plant a seed! Give me all the money you got, and God will change your life!" Carter pulled his pockets out. They were empty, as usual. God wanted money—something Carter didn't have. Carter slipped back out of the church and was never seen again.

Doesn't that make you angry? A preacher should tell others about God's love—not demand money for his own selfish purposes. Money took the place of worship, and Carter couldn't see the real God.

In today's passage, Jesus got angry, too, when money took the place of worship. He was mad because His temple had become a place for the Jews to make money off of travelers. No one could worship because of the noise of money changing hands and the smell of animal dung. Jesus, as you can see, made some changes. In the silence that followed His anger, people finally had the chance to worship God.

Did you know your body is the temple of the Holy Spirit (1 Corinthians 6:19–20)? You are designed to be a place where other people can come and find God—just like the temple used to be. Chances are, though, that you have allowed a few things into your temple that keep people from seeing God. People will not see God in you if you are greedy or selfish. They cannot see God if you lie or cheat. Others will not see Jesus in you if you treat your parents, teachers, or anyone else rudely.

If Jesus walked into your temple (your body) today, would He be pleased with what He found? _____

Name some things that Jesus would throw out of your temple if you gave Him the opportunity. _____

If you have unclean thoughts or habits going on in your heart, ask Jesus to clean house. He may throw a lot of things out, but in the silence that follows, you will see God more clearly.

An Extra Birthday

John 3:1–21

There's a new technique going around to help solve your problems. Doctors call it being born again. Here's how it works. They hypnotize you and supposedly regress you back into your mother's womb. Then they put you between two mattresses and lie you in a fetal position and help you relive your actual birth. Only this time, you get to remember what happened.

One lady decided to try this. She allowed herself to be hypnotized. She was placed between the mattresses, and the process began. While weeping and fighting uncontrollably, she screamed, "Get me out of here!" She seemed to be having the worst nightmare of her life. She fought and twisted until finally the hypnotists pulled her out and woke her up. Now, she claims, she remembers her actual birth. All her previous problems of depression and sleeplessness are gone. She has been born again. She is a new person.

People will try anything to be born again. They want a new lease on life, a fresh start, a clean slate. Humans want to erase their past and start over again. That's because God made us with that need. However, there is only one way to be born again.

In today's passage, we meet a man who needed to be born again. Nicodemus was a man of God, or so he thought. But he found out when he talked to Jesus that he hadn't even begun his life yet because he had not been born again. Nicodemus misunderstood and thought he must go back to his mother's womb. But Jesus explained to him the real way to be born again. The climax to this story is the most famous Bible verse of all time: John 3:16. This is the answer to life—the way to be born again and start over with a clean slate.

In your life, you are going to hear many people talk about many different answers to life's problems. People will tell you the answer to life lies in astrology, scientology, hypnotism, Wicca, money, sex, fame, power, etc. They all think they know how to be born again. Jesus, though, says He is the only way to be born again and experience new life.

Do you remember the day you were born again in Christ? _____

Have you ever told anyone else about what happened? _____

Think of one person you could tell this week about how you were born again. Write his or her name here. _____

Ask God to give you boldness to share your story. Commit yourself this week to be someone who tells others that the answer to life does not lie in all these other popular ideas, but in the simple man from Galilee who offers eternal life to everyone who chooses to trust in Him.

Weekly Bible Study and Prayer Review

Bible Study

Look back through some of the Scriptures you read this week. Write down the one verse or passage that God used to speak to you.

_____

_____

_____

*Memorize this verse or passage. You can do it if you spend just
a few minutes saying it to yourself.*

Now, think of at least one situation you will probably face soon in which you could use this Scripture to help you make the right decision. Write down that situation below.

_____

Quote the Scripture when you face this situation, and live by it.

Prayer Time

*Take a few moments to praise God for who He is.
Now take a few moments to thank God for things He has done for you.
Now ask God to make you into the person He wants you to be.
Ask God to use you to help others become closer to God.*

Below is your prayer list for the week. Keep it updated each week. If your prayer isn't answered this week, carry it over to next week's list.

Request	Date of Original Request	Date Answered
_____	__/__/__	__/__/__
_____	__/__/__	__/__/__
_____	__/__/__	__/__/__
_____	__/__/__	__/__/__
_____	__/__/__	__/__/__
_____	__/__/__	__/__/__
_____	__/__/__	__/__/__
_____	__/__/__	__/__/__

*Pray for the things on your list and trust God to provide.
Forgive anyone you have not yet forgiven.
Ask God to forgive you for any unconfessed sin in your life.
Ask God to keep you out of trouble with sin.
Acknowledge that God is in complete control of your life
and will take care of everything.*

Destroying the Competition

John 3:22–36

> Kyle really liked Laura. She was smart, sweet, and definitely cute. He really wanted to be around her whenever he could. Each morning, Kyle would rush to first period early to make sure he got a seat next to Laura. This morning, however, he was running late. He dashed down the hallway, past the library and around the corner to American History class. He darted through the doorway and immediately headed for his usual side of the room. But, alas! He was too late. Buck, the class stud, had taken his seat next to Laura! Kyle was furious. The only empty seat was on the other side of the room. Glaring at Buck, Kyle trudged to that cold seat.
>
> As he sat across the room, Kyle watched as Laura giggled at Buck's remarks. She really seemed to be enjoying herself. The more he watched, the more furious Kyle became. Kyle began to hate Buck more and more. He wanted Laura, and Buck was moving in on his territory. Later that day, when Kyle saw Laura, he began putting Buck down, making up lies about him. Laura, who thought she was beginning to like Kyle, stomped off. "Kyle, I've never heard you talk about someone like that before. It makes you very unattractive."

Kyle didn't like the idea of another guy moving in on his territory. So he got mad, stewed awhile, and tried to spread rumors about Buck. But his plan backfired. Unhealthy competition always backfires.

People in Israel were beginning to sense competition between Jesus and John the Baptist. They thought Jesus was moving in on John's territory—stealing some of his attention away. They just knew if they went and told John what Jesus was doing that John would get angry—but he didn't. He accepted it as part of God's will.

Competition between humans can get fierce. Candidates for a political office publicly debate and sometimes slander each other. Brothers and sisters fight over who gets what. Children and parents argue about who is right and who is wrong. You may find yourself involved in unhealthy competition with someone else. You have two choices: fight your competition, or turn the whole thing over to God and let Him take care of things.

Have you ever been in competition with a friend, parent, sibling, or someone else? _____

What were you competing over? _____

Did you actually do something to this person? _____

What did you do? _____

Ask God to be the one to solve the problems you have with someone else. The next time you feel like competing, follow John's example and bow out. For further study, read 1 Peter 5:6–7 and Luke 14:7–11. Humble yourself in the sight of the Lord, and *He* will lift you up.

Behind Bars

Luke 3:19–20

Shannon wanted to do what was right. She got up fifteen minutes early (a miracle in itself) and had her quiet time. It seemed to be the best one ever. She read the Bible, and God spoke to her. She prayed, and God listened. She felt at peace. She rose from her knees as a new woman. She opened the door to her room, confident that the day would go perfectly.

"Shannon!" her mother shrieked. "Come here." For ten minutes Shannon's mother griped at her for something she didn't even do. After swallowing her pride and not tattling on her little brother, she finished getting ready for school. She was wearing a new outfit and couldn't wait for Gary to see her. At lunchtime she saw Gary and turned to face him. When she did, her drink tipped over and drenched her clothes. Gary laughed hysterically. Shannon ran outside and sat down on the steps to cry. The vice principal found her and sentenced her to Saturday detention for being out of the lunchroom without permission. Saturday was the day she had planned to go to the beach with her friends.

If you were Shannon, would you wonder why all this stuff happened on the same day that you had a great quiet time? Many young people say that on days when they spend quality time with God, the *circumstances* of the day are worse than ever! Is it a coincidence, or could it be a test?

In today's passage, John the Baptist was going through the test of his life. He had a famous birth. He faithfully devoted himself to God in the desert until his late twenties. He baptized people and proclaimed the way to God for years. He even baptized Jesus Himself. And now, because of his stand against sin, he was thrown into prison at the whim of an evil king. It just doesn't seem fair.

You must remember that God will test your faith when you get closer to Him. He's not being mean. He just wants you to see for yourself how strong your faith really is. When you study at school, you don't get away with just telling the teacher that you studied. You have to take a test and prove it. God is letting you prove your faith. When bad things happen, consider them as a test. Keep your eyes on God and not on the circumstances.

Have you ever had something happen to you that didn't seem fair? _____

What happened? _____

Can you think of one thing God may have been trying to teach you during that time?

_____

Ask God to help you endure and pass whatever test He may send your way. Remember that no test lasts forever. After a little while, it will be over; and your faith will be stronger. For further study, read James 1:2–4 and 1 Peter 1:6–7.

Talk It Out

John 4:1–26

During lunch, Katy usually sat with her Christian friends; but today they had all gone on a field trip, and her lunch was later than usual. She was forced to sit alone in an unfamiliar crowd. As she nibbled her bread in silence, a nerd (as everyone else referred to him) sat across the table from her. He was alone, too, and did not try to start a conversation. Katy wondered if he knew the Lord, but she had no idea how to witness to him. "At least," she thought, "I can start a conversation."

Katy asked him his name. "John," came the simple reply. She asked how school was going. "Fine," he said, avoiding eye contact. Then she noticed his lunchbox with a picture of several characters of a popular television show. Katy commented on the program and mentioned a few of the characters by name. John looked up, surprised she knew anything about his favorite show. A conversation developed. Katy commented that she knew someone who was an even bigger hero than the main character of the TV program. "No way! Who?" John asked. Katy told John about Jesus.

If you want to witness to someone at school during lunch, you don't have to stand up on the table and spout Bible verses.

Jesus showed us in His life that the way to witness to people is to start where they are, discussing familiar things, and then comparing them to what it means to be a believer. Notice how Jesus took the situation He was in and started talking to the woman about water. He took her from that discussion into a conversation about what it meant to be a believer. It changed her life.

You don't have to be a Bible scholar to be a witness to your friends. Jesus wants you to be a *real* witness—someone who can relate to the people around you. If you want to be an effective witness to your friends, you *do* have to study the Bible, but then you have to study the people around you to see what interests them. Then just bring the two together. It can be really fun seeing how many different ways you can tell the story of Jesus based on the situation you're in at the time.

List at least three topics of conversation you have had or will have at school this week (examples include movies, clothes, music, etc.). _____

_____

Pick one of those topics and imagine the conversation. What is a way that you could relate that topic to Jesus and what He has done in your life? _____

_____

Ask God to help you get to know the people around you who need Jesus. Look for opportunities this week and share Jesus in a way they can understand.

Not Another Bite

John 4:27–38

Sunday night meant pizza. After church, the whole youth group was in a frenzy. They were all huddled together trying to decide where to go. Finally they arrived at a consensus: Pizza Shack. As women and children fled from the stampede, the youth stormed through the front doors of the church and into the parking lot. Everyone had a ride. Everyone was included—except Bobby and Amy. These two stood in the doorway and watched everyone leaving without them. Bobby and Amy were outcasts. The youth group never invited them anywhere. As a matter of fact, some youth made fun of them. So, as usual, they went home alone.

When the youth got to Pizza Shack, they noticed a table with four other "misfits" sitting down and having pizza. Several of the youth openly poked fun at the people at the table next to them. After all, it was only fun. The "misfits" at the table realized this was a church youth group. Having never been invited to church themselves, they made a pact with each other to never enter a church building as long as they lived.

This youth group had a problem. They were so concerned with the food that they did not notice the people around them crying out for friendship and acceptance. Pizza took priority over people. Poking fun became a thoughtless game. Without knowing it, people were hurt deeply.

In today's passage, Jesus' disciples wanted Jesus to eat something. After all, it was lunchtime. Jesus tried to get the disciples to take their eyes off the food and place them on the "fields that were white for the harvest." He was saying, "Look around. There are people everywhere who need God's love and acceptance. Take it to them."

If you don't harvest something when it is ripe, it rots. Those four misfits at Pizza Shack would have been drawn to Jesus if some young people had reached out to them. Instead, they dismissed the idea that God was love and continued to go deeper into their world of drugs and gangs.

Have you ever made fun of someone? _____

Have you ever stood by silently while someone else made fun of another person?

_____

Write the name of at least one person to whom you will reach out this week.

_____

Pray that God will show you others who are ripe for His love. It's time to change. It's time to pull the pepperoni off of your eyes, look around, and take God's love to the people who need it most.

Tell It Like It Is

John 4:39–42

Camille's heart was pounding. A tear rolled down her soft cheeks. Her knuckles were turning white as she held on to the pew. God was calling her, and she finally decided to let go. She pushed her way past her startled friends and made her way to the pastor at the front of the church. She explained that she wanted to know Jesus, and that night she knelt and prayed that He would enter her heart.

When Camille got home, she picked up the phone and called her grandparents. "Grandma, I've accepted Jesus." Her grandmother told her that was nice. Then Camille called her best friend. Then she told her older brother, who came home from playing tennis. The next day at school she told her homeroom teacher. She just didn't know any better. She kept telling her brother about it, until he finally came to church just to get her to shut up. He kept coming to church; and finally one night at a Wednesday night youth activity, he gave his heart to the Lord.

Occasionally, you find new Christians who are contagious with their faith. They can't help but tell everybody what has happened to them. Somewhere down the road, though, many Christians lose that enthusiasm and become part of the silent majority.

The woman at the well believed Jesus was the Lord, and she went and told everyone else. This woman had a shady past (five husbands and a live-in at the moment). She was not well thought of in the community. Yet she felt she had to tell everyone in her village about Jesus. Some believed. Some were skeptical. Some came to see for themselves. When they met Jesus and heard Him speak, they, too, became believers.

You may be uncomfortable trying to tell others about Jesus, but you can always invite them to come to church and hear about Jesus there. Like the woman at the well, you can say, "Come with me and find out for yourself." Think about all of the people you know. God has placed them in your life deliberately so that you can seize the opportunity to introduce them to Jesus. Will you be a part of the silent majority, or will you invite others to come and hear more about your God?

When was the last time you invited an unchurched friend to Bible study or a youth activity?

_____

When could you invite someone again? _____

Name one person you can invite to church this week. _____

Pray for this person daily. Make up your mind to invite him or her to an activity at your church where the good news of Jesus is told.

Save It for Sunday

Matthew 4:12–17; Mark 1:14–15; Luke 4:14–15; John 4:43–45

Spit wads sailed past Tiffany and stuck to the chalkboard. It looked like a constellation in the night sky. Wads of paper arched through the air and bounced under her feet. It was home-room, and a young female substitute had lost control. She sat at the front, riveted by intim-idation and waiting for the bell to ring. Everyone except Tiffany was taking advantage of Miss Feldene. After what seemed like an eternity, the bell rang; and class was over. Everyone herd-ed out of the room, leaving a total disaster area behind. Miss Feldene breathed a sigh of relief and began picking up the room.

Tiffany poked her head through the door, came back inside, put her books down, and silently began helping clean up. Miss Feldene was very appreciative. As Tiffany left, barely mak-ing it to her next class, her friend Bill asked her why she had stayed behind. As Tiffany explained, Bill thought she was crazy. Tiffany said she was just doing what Jesus would do. Bill, a member of her youth group, told Tiffany to let go of the Jesus thing. "That stuff is just for Sundays and Wednesday nights. You don't have to take it to school with you."

Do you agree with Bill? A lot of so-called Christians do. They let Jesus have con-trol of part of their lives, but not all.

In today's passage, Jesus went to a rather strange place to preach. For Jesus to go to Galilee was fairly radical. Galilee was miles from the religious center of Jerusalem. Galilee was filled with poor people—people who were worldly. Jesus considered this the perfect place to start His ministry. Jesus went into areas that most people would not have considered. He wanted every part of Israel to be exposed to His message.

You have probably allowed Jesus into some areas of your life, like what you do on Sundays and Wednesdays. However, have you allowed Jesus to be a part of your life in your other activities? Does Jesus direct how you act on the soccer field? Do you make it obvious that you know Jesus in Biology? Is your free time devoted to Him or to something (or someone) else? Are your weekends centered on His will or yours? Jesus wants to be in every part of your life.

Is Jesus in every part of your life, or just a select few areas? _____

List some areas of your life where Jesus is included. _____

Name some areas where Jesus is not included. _____

How can you begin to include Jesus in every part of your life? _____

_____

Ask God to help you make Jesus the center of everything you do. Keep your eyes on Jesus every day, not just on Sunday.

Weekly Bible Study and Prayer Review

Bible Study

Look back through some of the Scriptures you read this week. Write down the one verse or passage that God used to speak to you.

_____

_____

_____

_____

*Memorize this verse or passage. You can do it if you spend just
a few minutes saying it to yourself.*

Now, think of at least one situation you will probably face soon in which you could use this Scripture to help you make the right decision. Write down that situation below.

_____

Quote the Scripture when you face this situation, and live by it.

Prayer Time

*Take a few moments to praise God for who He is.
Now take a few moments to thank God for things He has done for you.
Now ask God to make you into the person He wants you to be.
Ask God to use you to help others become closer to God.*

Below is your prayer list for the week. Keep it updated each week. If your prayer isn't answered this week, carry it over to next week's list.

Request	Date of Original Request	Date Answered
_____	__/__/__	__/__/__
_____	__/__/__	__/__/__
_____	__/__/__	__/__/__
_____	__/__/__	__/__/__
_____	__/__/__	__/__/__
_____	__/__/__	__/__/__
_____	__/__/__	__/__/__
_____	__/__/__	__/__/__
_____	__/__/__	__/__/__
_____	__/__/__	__/__/__

*Pray for the things on your list and trust God to provide.
Forgive anyone you have not yet forgiven.
Ask God to forgive you for any unconfessed sin in your life.
Ask God to keep you out of trouble with sin.
Acknowledge that God is in complete control of your life
and will take care of everything.*

20/20 Vision

John 4:46–54

A young couple really wanted to go on an overseas summer mission trip with their friends, but they were too poor to afford the cost of $2,500. Still, they were certain God wanted them to go. So they continued to plan to go even though they didn't have the money. The day came to actually go to the airport and catch a plane to Africa. This young couple, with no money in sight, packed their bags as if they would spend the entire summer away from home. They arrived at the airport and waited.

Soon, boarding passes were called for, and the couple watched their friends board the plane. Still, they waited, believing in God. One friend who had gotten on the plane was talking about the couple's plight when an elderly gentleman overheard. He quietly wrote a check for the plane ticket and sent it out to the couple. The young couple picked up their packed bags and boarded the plane for Africa and a summer they would never forget.

Some people say, "Just show me a sign, and I'll believe. If God is real, let me see some proof." Other people say, "I believe God is there," and then God shows Himself.

In today's passage, a man approached Jesus and asked for help. He traveled about twenty miles one way (which probably took about five hours) to find Jesus. He was sure Jesus could change the circumstances of normal life, so he asked. Jesus honored that request, and the man believed Jesus at His word. Then he walked twenty miles back. It was an ordinary day with the ordinary sights and sounds of every other day. But because this man chose to go see Jesus, something special happened.

God cares very much about the average, normal things of your life. He cares about your classes at school and the grades you make. He wants to be a part of the friendships you have. He cares about the relationship you have with your parents. He is concerned about the worries and fears you have. He won't force Himself on you, but if you choose to go to Him and ask for help, He will.

Do you ever wonder where Jesus is in the ordinariness of everyday life? _____

Name some places or times when life just seems dull and ordinary and Jesus just doesn't seem to be around (examples: lunch at school, math class, home when parents are arguing).

_____

How can you seek Jesus to help you during these times? _____

Ask God to help you with the everyday struggles and needs of your life. It may take some time, like it did for the man in today's passage; but the results you get will be well worth it.

You're a Riot

Luke 4:16–30

Today was the day. It was early Saturday morning, and most everyone else was sleeping. Jesus, however, was already up. He slipped out before dawn and headed out the door for a quiet stroll through His hometown. As He passed by His old school, He remembered His schoolmates and the friends that He made. He walked through the town, remembering the name of each neighbor as He went. He went to the very edge of town where, abruptly, a cliff prevented Him from going further. He gazed over the magnificent plains below that He Himself had created. He leaned on His staff and watched the sun rise before He headed back to town for synagogue.

Today was the day Jesus would tell His family and friends that He was the Son of God. He was looking forward to it, but He also knew it would be difficult. Inside the synagogue, He stood up, took a copy of the Book of Isaiah, cleared His throat, and in so many words said, "You know, these verses are talking about Me. You're looking at the Son of God."

Jesus was in His hometown with people He loved. He had just visited the beautiful cliffs He created. He just read from the Book of Isaiah, which He wrote. Then, when He shared the truth with those closest to Him, they tried to kill Him. His hometown took offense when He read His own words, and then tried to throw Him off His own cliffs. He really wanted His family and close friends to understand who He was—but they didn't. Just imagine what it must have been like. Those familiar faces He had known so well were now filled with anger. They called Him names. They pushed Him around. They yelled things like, "Who do you think you are? You're a nobody!" Jesus left His hometown that day a reject.

You probably have experienced rejection recently. Jesus knows how you feel. The Bible says, "He was despised and rejected by people. He was a man of sorrows, familiar with pain" (Isaiah 53:3). However, He didn't let what other people thought stop Him from living His life the way God wanted Him to. He just kept on walking. You can do the same thing. When people put you down, look up to God for comfort. Don't fight back. Walk away and let God take care of the rest.

Have you ever felt like a reject? _____

Think about a time recently when someone called you a name, pushed you around, or didn't listen to what you had to say. How did you feel? _____

_____

What did you do to deal with it? _____

When you feel rejected or misunderstood, ask God to help you keep right on walking. He accepts you. He'll help others to do the same.

WWD today? An Offer You Can't Refuse

Matthew 4:18–22; Mark 1:16–20

James was just getting comfortable. He had just graduated from high school and gotten a decent job with his dad (he couldn't afford to go to college). He had made a few friends at the business—friends he could count on and have a good time with. He had met a girl and was thinking about marriage. Yeah, life was OK in James's mind. He was making plans, you see. Plans to save up and build a nice place for him and that pretty girl of his.

Enter Jesus. Boom! Jesus walked right into the family business and said, "Look. I'm heading out. I've got places to go and people to see, and I need a few guys to go with Me. Come with Me now, and you'll see things happen. You'll have a life you never even dreamed of."

James looked at his net. But tomorrow is payday, he thought to himself. He looked at his father. But my dad needs me here. He thought about his girl. But she's so good-looking. Then he looked at Jesus again and . . .

Today's passage is the story of four young men who had decisions to make. The illustration above gives you an idea of what James, the son of Zebedee, might have had to think about when Jesus called him. Look at how they responded. *Immediately* they left the family business and followed Jesus. They knew in their hearts that Jesus knew where He was going. So they followed.

Do you know where you're going? Do you have your own plans for yourself? They'll never work without Jesus. At least, they will never work out to your exact specifications. Something always goes wrong and botches your plans. Enter Jesus. He says, "Hey, I know the way. I'm going places and doing things, and I could use a young person like you. Come with Me, and I'll show you a real life." Now you've got a decision to make. What will you do? Look around. You want to be popular. You want to have a girlfriend or boyfriend. You want to excel in your interests. Will you follow Jesus or your own ideas?

What are some things you want out of life? _____

Do you have a plan to get those things? _____

What would you do if Jesus asked you to let go of those dreams and follow Him—without any idea of where you were going? _____

_____

This is another day. You can do your own thing the way you've planned it, or you can let go of your own plans and follow Jesus to see where He is going with this day. Ask God to show you what He is doing today. Pray that He would let you in on it so you can follow Him.

Try, Try Again

Mark 1:21–28; Luke 4:31–37

When he was only seven years old, he and his family lost their home—he had to go to work to help pay the bills. When he was nine, his mother died. After years of barely any schooling and odd jobs, he lost his job as a store clerk at age twenty-two. A year later, he invested some money with a friend to start his own business. His friend died three years later, and he had to work for years to pay all the debts. He dated a girl for four years and finally asked her to marry him—she turned him down. For several years he tried to get into politics and ran for Congress. He lost. He ran again—and lost. He ran the third time and finally made it, but when he ran for reelection two years later he lost again. He practically had a nervous breakdown.

He married a woman, but the marriage was a struggle from the beginning. When he was forty-one, his four-year-old son died. He ran for Land Officer and lost. Then he ran for the Senate and lost that. A couple of years later he ran for the vice-presidential nomination and lost. He ran for the Senate one more time and lost again. He had crazy ideas, and most people misunderstood him and labeled him a dangerous man.

But two years later, when he was fifty-one, he ran for President of the United States and won. Who was this man? Abraham Lincoln.[3]

Lincoln could have given up long before he became President. He had every right to. He failed miserably at almost everything he ever attempted—but he always got back on his feet and tried again. He kept trying until he became one of the greatest men to ever live.

Jesus went into a synagogue in His hometown just a few days before today's reading and was almost killed in a riot (Luke 4:16–30). Now, perhaps only one week later, we find Jesus entering another synagogue to do the same thing. Why? Was He crazy? Why would anyone try again when He almost lost His life the last time? But He did try again. And this time people believed Him.

You've heard the old saying, "If at first you don't succeed, try, try again." Sometimes, though, that seems like the hardest thing to do. You fail a test. You don't measure up to your parents' expectations. Your basketball coach sits you on the bench. You hurt your best friend's feelings—again. Why not just give up? Why not run away from it all and quit trying? Don't give up. Sometimes you can learn more through failure than success. Some might say that Jesus seemed to fail many times in His life. People refused to believe in Him. He couldn't do miracles sometimes because people lacked faith. And at the height of His career, just when He was becoming great, they killed Him. But He didn't fail. He came out on top.

Have you ever failed at something? _____ *What was it?* _____

How do you feel about that failure? _____ *Do you want to try again?* _____

You can come out on top in spite of your failures. Ask God to turn your failures into victories. Pray that He will show you how to try again and succeed in everything you do.

Can I Take Him Home?

Matthew 8:14–17; Mark 1:29–34; Luke 4:38–41

Church was over (actually, it wasn't what we call church—it was synagogue), and everyone was hungry. They all headed over to Simon's house (Simon was later given the nickname "Peter"). Peter's mother-in-law was there, and everyone was hoping she'd fix one of those great big afternoon meals she was famous for. But when they got there, they discovered that Peter's mother-in-law was sick. She was so sick she was running a high fever and couldn't even get out of bed. "Aw, man!" Peter said. "What are we going to do now?" Everyone began looking at Jesus.

Jesus walked over to the bedside, leaned over Peter's mother-in-law, and placed His hand on her forehead. He felt the high fever inside of her. He closed His eyes and whispered a short prayer. Then, He told the fever to go away and leave the poor woman alone. Miraculously, the fever went away. Peter's mother-in-law hopped up and began making one of her famous meals.

Read today's passage. Disappointment was the big problem. Everybody was hungry, and they were expecting one thing; but unexpected sickness interrupted everybody's schedule and caused problems. Jesus, however, corrected that problem and solved the disappointment.

What would have happened, though, if Peter and his friends had left Jesus back in the church building? Nothing. Everybody would have been disappointed. No one would have eaten. Peter's mother-in-law would still be sick. But Peter and his friends did bring Jesus home with them, and that made all the difference.

Sometimes we forget to take Jesus home with us when church is over. We hear all about Him, but when the services are over we burst through the doors and take off—leaving Jesus and everything we learned behind. Then, sometime that day or during the week, disappointment comes, and we wonder where God is. Jesus really does care about your disappointments, whether it's being sick or having family problems or just not being sure of yourself. He wants to help. But He never forces Himself on you. He wants you to invite Him into every part of your life during the week so He can help.

Have you faced a disappointment recently? _____

What is it? _____

*Have you asked God to help you (besides when you were in church)?*_____

Weekdays without Jesus are just *weak* days. Ask God to help you keep your eyes on Jesus during the week.

God Bless

Matthew 4:23–25; Mark 1:35–39; Luke 4:42–44

The Double Bopper with cheese and large fries looked so good. Gene and David were about to dig in when Gene bowed his head to bless his food. David, out of nervous respect, twiddled his thumbs and looked around until Gene finished praying. When Gene looked up, David fired a question at him.

"Why do you bless your food?"

"I don't know. I just want to pray and ask God to make this food good for me."

"Isn't that kind of hypocritical?" David shot back.

"What do you mean?" Gene inquired.

"Well, I know you pretty well. I know that about the only time you ever pray is when you bless your food. Why don't you pray at other times? Isn't life more important than food? Why don't you bless your day?"

"Bless my day?" Gene asked.

"Yeah. Every day, take the time to pray before you start your day—the same way you pray now before you start to eat. Ask God to make this day what it was intended to be."

That's interesting advice. Many people today say blessings over their food. But how many people say a blessing over their day?

In today's passage, as well as many others, you find Jesus getting up early and sneaking off to find a quiet place to start His day in prayer. Why? Because He wanted God His Father to make the day what it was intended to be—not what circumstances forced it to be. If Jesus had not prayed, His disciples and all the people would have surrounded Him and made Him stay in town and do what they wanted. But after praying, Jesus realized that God wanted Him to go preach and heal in other places.

Prayer is like a time machine. If you pray before you start the day, you are literally changing the future because you are allowing God to be in control of your day. When you don't pray, you are leaving yourself in the hands of whatever circumstances happen to come along that day. Someone once said: "I've got so much to do today that I have to get up four hours earlier so I can pray about it all." That's the attitude Jesus had. It's the same attitude you can have.

Do you ever feel like your day is going to be too hard to deal with? _____

Do you ever have so much to do that you think you just don't have time to pray?

_____

Would five minutes of prayer really disrupt your busy schedule? _____

Commit yourself to begin a time of prayer in the morning before you start your day—even if it's only five minutes. It will make all the difference in the world. Ask God to bless your day.

Weekly Bible Study and Prayer Review

Bible Study

Look back through some of the Scriptures you read this week. Write down the one verse or passage that God used to speak to you.

_____

_____

_____

_____

*Memorize this verse or passage. You can do it if you spend just
a few minutes saying it to yourself.*

Now, think of at least one situation you will probably face soon in which you could use this Scripture to help you make the right decision. Write down that situation below.

_____

Quote the Scripture when you face this situation, and live by it.

Prayer Time

*Take a few moments to praise God for who He is.
Now take a few moments to thank God for things He has done for you.
Now ask God to make you into the person He wants you to be.
Ask God to use you to help others become closer to God.*

Below is your prayer list for the week. Keep it updated each week. If your prayer isn't answered this week, carry it over to next week's list.

Request	Date of Original Request	Date Answered
_____	__/__/__	__/__/__
_____	__/__/__	__/__/__
_____	__/__/__	__/__/__
_____	__/__/__	__/__/__
_____	__/__/__	__/__/__
_____	__/__/__	__/__/__
_____	__/__/__	__/__/__
_____	__/__/__	__/__/__
_____	__/__/__	__/__/__

*Pray for the things on your list and trust God to provide.
Forgive anyone you have not yet forgiven.
Ask God to forgive you for any unconfessed sin in your life.
Ask God to keep you out of trouble with sin.
Acknowledge that God is in complete control of your life
and will take care of everything.*

Trust Me

Luke 5:1–11

It's been a long night. You haven't slept a wink, and in the early morning silence you struggle to stay awake. You groggily fight to pull the weeds from your net. You're an excellent fisherman, one of the best; but last night was the worst. You didn't catch a single thing—except for seaweed and knots. Needless to say, you're in a bad mood, and you don't have a lot of patience. The last thing you want to do is listen to a sermon.

Meanwhile, Jesus sits in your boat and gives a sermon to the people on shore. You hear every word, but it goes in one ear and out the other. Then, after you've finished all the hard work on your nets and Jesus has finished the easy job of preaching, He suggests you get back into the boat and go fishing again.

Um, excuse me, Simon may have thought. I'm the fisherman here—I know what's going on. You don't fish in the middle of a hot morning. You fish at night. And besides, you're a carpenter, and . . . On the argument could go. But Simon agreed with one simple statement. "Because You say so, I will."

Simon (Peter) knew how to fish. Why should he listen to a carpenter tell him what to do? Jesus didn't even help clean the nets! Simon may have been reluctant to do what Jesus said, but look at the incredible results. Simon, the great fisherman, saw the greatest catch of fish he'd ever had in his life.

A lot of times you may be leery about doing what Jesus tells you in His Word. After all, you're the one down here dealing with all the problems. You're the one who barely got out of a fight at the football game Friday night. You're the one who stares at acne every morning in the mirror. You're the one trying to get your parents to pay attention to you. Where is Jesus when you lie awake on your bed at night thinking about all of your own problems? He is there, quietly sitting in your boat, doing what He came here to do—speaking His Father's comforting words. Jesus not only knows what you're going through, He is experiencing it with you and knows every feeling and every temptation.

Do you ever feel like you are all by yourself down here on earth, while God sits disinterested on His throne? _____

If you could tell God how you feel about the way things are going right now, what would you say? _____

Ask God to help you be obedient to His Word. When Jesus tells you to do something that seems pointless or strange, follow Simon Peter's example. Do it simply because Jesus said to.

Best of Friends

Matthew 9:1–8; Mark 2:1–12; Luke 5:17–26

Lance had cancer. He was only in high school—Lamar High School in Rosenberg, Texas. His only choice to fight the cancer was to go through chemotherapy. Not only would it be painful, but it would make all of his hair fall out. He didn't want to be a freak. He didn't want his friends at school to stare at him. Lance really struggled with the decision to have chemotherapy and stay in school. To have cancer and to stick out like a sore thumb (literally) was more than he could bear.

Some of Lance's friends knew what he thinking. They wanted to keep Lance as a friend— and they wanted him to have the chemotherapy. So Lance's friends got together, all eight of them, and made a decision. Every one of them shaved their heads completely bald so Lance wouldn't stick out so much. Imagine nine guys walking down the halls of Lamar High School with shiny little heads—all because of the love of a friend.

Lance's eight buddies were true friends. They paid a price, but it was worth it to them to keep their friend.

In today's passage, four guys did something similar. They carried their sick friend to see Jesus. He surely got heavy after awhile, but no one complained. When they arrived at the house, they didn't let the crowd stop them. They came up with a new plan. They could have stopped to ask, "Who is going to pay for that hole in the roof?" Instead, they did everything to make sure they got their friend to Jesus. No one stopped to consider the cost. Their only desire was to bring their friend to Jesus so they could have him back.

If you really love your friends, you will do all you can to bring them to Jesus. You won't think about the cost. You will spend your last ten dollars buying a friend a new Bible. You might use a little extra gas to pick up a friend and bring her to church. You could spend a little more time on your knees today praying for someone. You might write a note or make a call to someone who needs encouragement. Whatever you do, make time for your friends.

Do you have friends who you would be willing to sacrifice something for? _____

List a few of those friends. _____, _____, _____, _____

If one of these friends were in trouble, would you be willing to help, no matter the cost?

_____

Genuine love comes in actions, not words. Ask God to show you a friend who needs help this week. Sacrifice whatever you can to be a true friend and bring that person to Jesus.

Tax Euasion

Matthew 9:9–13; Mark 2:13–17; Luke 5:27–32

Jesus probed the area, looking for another person who would follow Him and become one of the twelve disciples. So far, He had selected four working-class fishermen, a conceited Bible thumper named Nathan, and a few others. He needed more. He needed someone who was smart and who could perhaps write the very first book of the New Testament some day. He needed someone with a good memory, so His words and deeds could be recorded in a book that the whole world could one day read. He needed someone who was honest and trustworthy, so the words written in that book could be trusted.

As He came to a busy intersection, where travelers from far away passed through the city, Jesus saw Matt sitting there in a little wooden booth. Matt was a traitor to his people because he collected taxes for Rome and probably overcharged everyone so he could get rich quick. To most people, Matt was dishonest, stupid, and the most unlikely candidate of all. But Jesus walked right up to Matt and said . . .

Of all the people to select as a disciple! Of all the people who would end up writing the very first book in the New Testament. What good could Matthew possibly be to Jesus?

You'll find the answer in Matthew 9:12. Jesus was a spiritual doctor. Doctors like to hang around sick people. Jesus liked to spend time with spiritually sick people—sinners, you might say—so He could help them. When He saw Matthew, He didn't see what Matthew *was* (a sinner). He saw him for what he *would be* (a follower of Jesus). He prescribed a new life for Matthew.

No matter what you think about yourself, you are made in the image of God. You may think you couldn't possibly be of any use, but Jesus wants *you*. He is looking for someone real, someone honest, someone who could be a great follower. He sees your weaknesses. He sees your strengths. He looks beyond what you are and sees what you could be—a valuable member of His team.

Do you ever think other people look at you and see very little good? _____

List some of the things you consider weaknesses—things that make you feel inadequate.

_____

List some of your strengths. _____

How do you think God might use both your strengths and weaknesses for His purpose?

_____

Ask God to show you where you fit on His team. Don't let your weaknesses keep you from following Him. He'll show you how to get past them if you let Him.

In with the New

Matthew 9:14–17; Mark 2:18–22; Luke 5:33–39

It was COLD outside. The last thing Steven wanted to do was go to work. He took a long, hot shower, thinking about how nice it would be to stay inside where it was warm.

After getting ready and eating breakfast, he bundled up in his heaviest winter coat and stepped outside. The windshield of his car was completely covered by a sheet of ice. "Great!" he mumbled. "I don't have time for this." He stood there, feeling sorry for himself for a few moments. Suddenly, he had a brilliant idea.

He picked up a bucket from the garage and went into the kitchen. He set the bucket in the sink and filled it to the rim with steaming hot water. He walked back outside to the driver's side of his car. He placed one hand underneath the bucket, and the other on the handle. Then, swinging forward, he threw the entire bucket of water onto his windshield.

CRACK! Steven watched in horror as the entire sheet of glass cracked and then shattered into a million pieces.

Steven learned the hard way that you can't mix hot water and cold glass. The sudden change in temperature is too much for the glass to handle.

In today's passage, Jesus told a story about putting wine into wineskins. When wine ferments, it expands. So if you put new wine into a skin that's already expanded from previous fermentation, it will break because it can't handle the change. New wineskins, however, have room to expand. So, you only put new wine into new wineskins.

Never be fooled into thinking that you can mix Jesus and something else to solve life's problems. Sometimes you pray, but then you try to "help" Jesus answer your prayers. God doesn't need your help. He needs your trust. Sometimes you read the Bible and try to live by its wisdom, but then you add a little worldly advice from a television talk show that may be contrary to what God says. Don't live by God's Word *and* something else. Learn to depend on Jesus alone.

Do you ever depend on other things besides Jesus to get you through your day?

_____

List some of the things you depend on that you probably shouldn't. _____

_____

How can you depend on Jesus more and these other things less? _____

_____

Ask God to help you depend on Jesus alone for all of your needs. Don't look beyond Jesus for the answers—look more closely at Jesus. You just may find something new.

Pool Party

John 5:1–16

The Pool of Bethesda was almost like the Fountain of Youth; but instead of making you young, it made you well. However, there was one catch. The water didn't heal all the time. Now and then an angel would come down and stir the waters. The first person into the water after the water was stirred would be healed. Everyone else was out of luck.

Consequently, lots of people with problems hung out around this pool of water. They would just lie there, waiting for the water to start bubbling. A blind man would have to listen carefully all the time. A deaf woman could never take her eyes off the water. If someone fell asleep, he might miss out. A person who couldn't walk had to stay right next to the pool so he could push himself in with his arms.

Imagine being crippled for thirty-eight years, and lying next to that pool was your only hope. And even the few times you saw the water stirred, other people beat you to it. You are alone, left to rot. And your only hope is what other people say is the cure to your problems.

In today's passage, all kinds of people with different problems flocked to this place that just *might* be of help. The man who had been crippled for thirty-eight long years lay there in front of the pool, staring at the water with hollow eyes. For so long he had waited for things to go his way. He had closed his mind to all other possibilities of finding happiness. Imagine how miserable he must have been.

When Jesus arrived, He changed everything. Notice that Jesus did not focus on the hope of the pool. Jesus tried to get the man to stop looking at the pool and start looking at Him. When the man finally turned his full attention to Jesus, he was healed.

Do you ever feel like the lame man? You sit around your little pool of hopes and dreams, anxiously waiting for something to happen. Then, when it does, someone else gets the breaks. You hope that your job will earn you more money, but the boss fires you. You want your parents to love you, but you feel like they care more about your little brother. You waste a dollar on a lottery ticket, only to see someone else on television holding the big check. It's time to stop trying on your own. It's time to stop hoping that things will work out. It's time to turn to Jesus and let Him show you the way.

What are some of your goals and dreams? _____

How have you tried to accomplish these things on your own? _____

How can you let Jesus be the one to accomplish these things for you? _____

_____

Ask God to help you realize that the key to happiness in this life is not chasing after your selfish dreams and goals. Take your eyes off your dreams and place them on Jesus. Let Him be the one to give you the desires of your heart.

Working Overtime

John 5:17–18

"So what are you going to do for a summer job?" asked Gary. "I've looked everywhere. I don't know what I'm going to do for cash this year."

"I'm going to work for my dad," Tommy said quickly. "He's going to be baling hay all summer and he pays me twice as much as minimum wage."

"Wow, that's great!" Gary chimed. "I don't think I could ever work for my dad, though. He would always be mad at me, and I don't think I could take him telling me what to do."

Tommy responded, "I know what you mean. But, the way I figure it is, my dad is going to be doing this job whether I'm there or not. And somebody's going to make that good money whether I'm there or not. So I decided I will just enjoy being around my dad and doing whatever he says while I'm on the job. Then, when summer's over, I'll have enough socked away for my car, my gas, and my dates for the next school year."

"Good point," Gary commented. "Do you think your dad could use another hand?"

"I don't know. I could always ask. Let's go."

Work isn't everyone's favorite thing. It probably isn't yours. However, work is good for you. You get to accomplish something worthwhile and earn money to live on.

Jesus said that the reason He was working was because His Father was working. Just like Tommy, Jesus went to work with His Father. Why did He do it? Because He accomplished something very worthwhile (helping other people know God) and He earned something to live on (lasting joy and peace).

Have you ever thought about what it is like to work for God? God is going to accomplish His will whether you help Him or not—but He would like to have you join Him. And when you choose to work for Him, you get far more than the minimum wages of the world. You get His blessings.

Do you ever wonder what God's will for your life is? That's really the wrong question to ask. God has a will that He intends to accomplish—with or without you. By reading God's Word and praying and looking around you, you will find out where God is working. If you decide to jump right in where God is working, you will be doing His will.

Think for a moment about what's happening around you. Do you see any place where God might be working? _____ Where? _____

_____

Is there any way you could possibly help? _____

If you see where God is at work around you, pray that God would help you get involved in what He is doing. If not, ask God to *show* you where He is working and how you could join in.

Weekly Bible Study and Prayer Review

Bible Study

Look back through some of the Scriptures you read this week. Write down the one verse or passage that God used to speak to you.

_____

_____

_____

Memorize this verse or passage. You can do it if you spend just
a few minutes saying it to yourself.

Now, think of at least one situation you will probably face soon in which you could use this Scripture to help you make the right decision. Write down that situation below.

_____

Quote the Scripture when you face this situation, and live by it.

Prayer Time

Take a few moments to praise God for who He is.
Now take a few moments to thank God for things He has done for you.
Now ask God to make you into the person He wants you to be.
Ask God to use you to help others become closer to God.

Below is your prayer list for the week. Keep it updated each week. If your prayer isn't answered this week, carry it over to next week's list.

Request	Date of Original Request	Date Answered
_____	__/__/__	__/__/__
_____	__/__/__	__/__/__
_____	__/__/__	__/__/__
_____	__/__/__	__/__/__
_____	__/__/__	__/__/__
_____	__/__/__	__/__/__
_____	__/__/__	__/__/__

Pray for the things on your list and trust God to provide.
Forgive anyone you have not yet forgiven.
Ask God to forgive you for any unconfessed sin in your life.
Ask God to keep you out of trouble with sin.
Acknowledge that God is in complete control of your life
and will take care of everything.

Night of the Living Dead

John 5:19–30

The ancient Egyptians believed that death was not the end. For the most important people, like kings, the Egyptians would go to great lengths to preserve the dead and prepare them for the afterlife. King Tutankhamen, otherwise known as King Tut, was no exception.

He was placed in an elaborate gold sarcophagus worth millions of dollars. His body was specially preserved so that when "resurrection day" arrived, he would still have something left to live in. His tomb was filled with gold and treasures beyond anyone's wildest dreams. All this was done so that one day, when King Tut came back to life, he could have the good life.

The only problem was, a group of men went looking for his tomb in the early twentieth century and stumbled upon it. They became grave robbers, removing all of the treasures and King Tut's body from the tomb. Grave robbers took everything King Tut was looking forward to in the afterlife.

Did you know that Jesus is a grave robber? Only His grave robbing will be on a slightly different scale. One day He will shout, and those people who have believed in Him and died will be reunited with their bodies. They will arise from their graves and go home to be with Jesus forever. Jesus will steal their bodies away.

King Tut never saw the afterlife he was looking forward to. All of the treasures he stored up for himself in his tomb were taken away. If you believe in Jesus and you die, you will see a great afterlife. Your treasures will not be gold and silver from this world. They will be gold in heaven that you earned for giving your life to the grave Robber. You can't take the treasures of this world with you when you die, but you can send a few things on ahead in the form of heavenly treasures. What are *you* stockpiling? Is it stuff you can't take with you? Or is it treasure in heaven that will last for eternity? Are you looking forward to the resurrection day, or just hoping to make it through this day?

Take an inventory of your life and start ditching the stuff that you can't take with you.

What are some things you are trying to hold on to that won't mean anything when you die?

_____

What are some things you are doing that will make a difference in eternity?

_____

Ask God to help you let go of the things that don't matter and start working for the things that do. For further study, read Matthew 6:19–21.

Eyewitness Testimony

John 5:31–47

> *"But Mom, I didn't do it!"* Greg and Jay argued in front of their mother about who broke the glass coffee table. Mom wanted an answer now, but the guilty party was not coming clean. Finally, Mom said she would ground them both if they didn't tell the truth.
>
> Greg and Jay shuffled back to their rooms—practically jail—until the mystery could be solved. Mom sat down on the couch and stared at her once favorite piece of furniture. She thought about which boy could have done this and then denied it, but she couldn't figure it out. She felt guilty for grounding them, but she was just certain it was one of the two.
>
> Just then, the door opened and in walked Dad. He was carrying a large sheet of glass. *"Oh hi, Sally, I didn't figure anyone would be home yet. I guess you saw that mess. The glass broke when I dropped a hammer I was using to fix your couch leg. I've got a replacement piece of glass right here . . ."*

When there are no witnesses and yet there is a crime, it's sometimes hard to know whom to blame when it could be just about anyone—even people you wouldn't expect, like good old Dad.

In Jesus' day, no one could be accused of anything wrong or claim anything supernatural without the testimony of at least two and hopefully three witnesses. There was no such thing as circumstantial evidence. In today's passage, Jesus explained that He had several witnesses to prove He was the Son of God.

John the Baptist testified (vv. 33–34), Jesus' work testified (v. 36), the Father testified (v. 37), the Scriptures testified (vv. 39–40), and Moses testified (v. 46) that Jesus was the Son of God. All of these people pointed to Jesus as God Himself in human flesh, and yet the people whom Jesus was talking to refused to believe it.

Perhaps you are confused at the number of voices telling you what is the truth. You don't know whether to believe the TV or the radio or the preacher or your friends or the Bible or your school books or what! Everyone claims to have the answer. You've got to consider the source of the testimony. Are you going to believe the latest trends in the media and books, or are you going to believe in Jesus?

What do other people you know think about Jesus? _____

What do you think about Jesus? _____

Ask God to help you tell the difference between His voices and the voices of the world. Pray for the wisdom to distinguish the truth from the lies. When in doubt, turn to God's Word. It always tells the truth. It will never let you down.

Corny Rules

Matthew 12:1–8; Mark 2:23–28; Luke 6:1–5

The road sign says, "Stop." Your father says, "No." Your teacher says, "Quiet!" Your test score says, "Try again." Your curfew says, "Now!" Don't taste. Don't touch. Yield. Brush your teeth. Comb your hair. Are you wearing that? Mind your manners. Don't talk with your mouth full. Be quiet. Clean your room. Mow the yard. Wash the dishes. Get off the phone! Get out of bed. Turn that thing down! Do your homework. Where have you been? Come here! Don't talk back to me. Clean your plate. Slow down. Where do you think you're going? Go to your room. What did you do to your hair? Stop whining. Get in the car. Don't lie to me. You're not pulling that stunt again. Don't you have any sense? Well, look again. Don't just stand there. It's your dog. I just washed that. Give that to me. If I have to tell you one more time . . .

Enough already! You may be thinking, I'm sick and tired of the voices that say, "Do!" and "Don't!" Doesn't anybody out there have anything better to do besides tell me how to run my life?

Rules and the people who enforce them are necessary (parents, police, etc.). If you obey the rules, you won't have to deal with all of those voices. But sometimes the rules and the enforcers can get out of hand—especially when you're talking about religion.

The really "religious" people of the day were griping at Jesus for picking corn on the day of rest. They claimed He was breaking the law, but they had made up their own laws about what you could and couldn't do. They made up rules just to make up rules and tell people what to do. Jesus pointed out that the rules were made for people to use, not vice versa.

God is not like the religious people of Jesus' day. He is not just waiting for you to break a rule so He can get angry with you. He loves you, and He wants you to see your relationship with Him as much more than following rules. God doesn't want you to walk around feeling like you have to "do this" and "don't do that." If that's how you live your life, you'll just end up feeling guilty all the time. He wants you to walk with Him and talk with Him, just like Jesus did with His disciples in the cornfield. When you stay close to Jesus, you won't have to worry about rules. You'll do the right thing naturally because you have spent so much time with Jesus that you have learned to do what He would do.

Have you felt guilty lately for breaking rules? _____

What rules have you broken? _____

If necessary, ask God to forgive you.

Don't be overcome by false guilt. If you have sinned against God, ask Him to forgive you, and He will. Remember that your relationship with Jesus is bigger than following rules. For further study, read 1 John 1:9–10; 1 Corinthians 13:4–5; and Psalm 103:12.

Get into the Game

Matthew 12:9–14; Mark 3:1–6; Luke 6:6–11

Dan was late for church. It was raining outside, and he was still dressing himself as he dashed out to the car. He revved the engine and took off down the alley as fast as he could. He entered the road quickly and began his two-mile trip to the church.

As he headed down the barren stretch of winding road, he came across a car with its hazard lights on. A young woman standing in the rain looking woefully at a shredded left rear tire told the story. The woman's right arm was in a cast, making it apparent that she could not change the tire herself. Dan looked at his watch, and then looked at the church steeple just in view ahead. He looked at the woman as he passed and made a quick decision. He pulled in front of her car and got out in the rain. He changed her tire and gave her directions to the nearest gas station. Wet and cold, he climbed back in the car and toward the church.

As Dan slipped quietly into Sunday school, his buddies said, "Well, I guess we know where your commitment to God went this morning. Would you say our closing prayer?"

Some people get so wrapped up in the rules that they forget about the whole point. Serving God is about loving Him and loving other people—in action, not just words.

Can you believe that these religious people were mad at Jesus for healing a man on the Sabbath day? This man had suffered for perhaps years, and these guys were worried about rules and regulations. They couldn't have cared less about the well-being of the man with the withered hand.

It's easy to get caught up in the rituals of your walk with the Lord and forget about the needs of other people. You do need structure: daily Bible study, meeting together in church, and praying. But don't ever forget that these activities are meant to improve your relationship with the Lord so you can get back into the world to express your love for God and for people.

Does your life change because of the Bible verses you read? _____

Do you become a better person because of the prayers you've prayed? _____

Have you improved because of the time you have spent in church? _____

How have you changed, specifically? _____

_____

Spend some time in prayer asking God to show you His will for your day. Get in the huddle, listen to plays called by the Coach, and then get back into the game. The clock is ticking.

Mr. Fix-It

Matthew 12:15–21; Mark 3:7–12

A typical evening newscast. A young girl, head of the drill team, is killed in a car accident as her intoxicated boyfriend loses control. A foreign country threatens to invade another. A plane crash kills 139 people. The President announces that taxes will go up in order to pay for more stuff. A little girl is hit by a police car responding to an emergency. An old man kills himself in the city park. The convenience store near your home is robbed—again. A missing person is found dead in a field.

It's going to turn cold and rain on homecoming. Tornadoes destroy the town square of a historic city. Flood waters demolish crops in Florida. Wildfires rage out of control in California. Your favorite pro football team loses—again.

You turn off the TV and get ready to set your alarm for early the next day so you can take the PSAT, and your electricity goes off.

Doesn't it seem like everything goes wrong? It's just not supposed to be this way. Crime and bad weather and natural disasters and death and sickness seem to scream for attention every day. We're going from bad to worse.

Enter Jesus. Did you see how Jesus healed the sick, and how He forgave their sin, and how He spoke comforting words? Did you catch that part about how Jesus will not snuff out a burning wick?

Your life is messed up too. Face it. You're like a candle that's supposed to burn bright and give light in the darkness; but sometimes you blow it and blow out, and you're nothing but a smoking wick with no flame at all. That's OK. You're going to blow it now and then. Jesus isn't going to write you off and snuff you out. He's going to gently apply His fire to your heart until you burn brightly once again. That's why Jesus came to earth—to fix things. He heals the sick. He forgives sin. He gives hope when there's only despair. He brings joy in the middle of depression. Jesus came into your life to fix you. Let Him take care of you when you're broken. He can fix anything. He'll take care of you.

Have you failed God recently? _____ How? _____

Do you think God can forgive you and still use you? _____

God can solve whatever dilemma you have. Ask God to repair whatever is broken in your life. Turn your sins, your problems, and your cares over to Mr. Fix-It.

A Maker's Dozen

Mark 3:13–19; Luke 6:12–16

Two football teams were about to meet. Jacksonville was the favorite, mainly because of Coach Gilman. Gilman handpicked each player for each position based on a series of tests that determined physical agility, concentration under pressure, and intimidation of the opposing team. Gilman's Eagles were undefeated and were expected to remain that way tonight.

Coach Fundaer had a different approach. His team was 2–1 and a lot less intimidating. The Falcons were expected to lose by 21 points. Fundaer picked his players a different way. He watched each player practice and watched their motivation and drive. He consulted with the assistant coaches and talked it over with the players themselves. Then, after noticing who wanted it the most, Coach Fundaer would assign the first and second strings. The fastest player didn't always make first string—it was the one who wanted it the most. The Falcons wanted to win—and they did. They beat the Eagles 28–7.

Different leaders have different ways of selecting followers. Some coaches are like Gilman, some are like Fundaer, some have other ideas. Some countries have dictators, some have presidents, some have kings or queens. But they all have one thing in common—they fail at some point. They are not perfect.

In today's passage, did you notice what Jesus did before He chose His twelve disciples? He stayed up all night, praying. He went up on a hill and consulted with His Father. Then He picked some of the most unlikely people. Several of these guys were nothing but lowly fishermen, one of whom would one day deny he'd ever met Jesus. One was a political activist who favored the violent overthrow of the government. One was a cheating tax collector. One would sell Jesus for the price of a common slave. Yet, because of those men, two thousand years cannot erase the story they have told about Jesus. If Jesus had chosen His disciples based on appearances, He might have chosen a completely different group. Because He prayed, though, He ended up with the group that God wanted Him to have.

Looks aren't everything. Don't ever base your next decision on the way things *seem* or what things look like. You'll fail every time. The only way to make decisions, whether big ones or small, is to consult with your Father. He knows where you need to go and what you need to do.

Have you made a decision recently that looked good, but in the end turned out to be lousy?

_____

What was that decision? _____

What could you do differently the next time? _____

Ask God to give you the answers you need for all of your decisions. Pray that you will choose His way, not what happens to look good at the time.

Weekly Bible Study and Prayer Review

Bible Study

Look back through some of the Scriptures you read this week. Write down the one verse or passage that God used to speak to you.

_____

_____

_____

_____

Memorize this verse or passage. You can do it if you spend just
a few minutes saying it to yourself.

Now, think of at least one situation you will probably face soon in which you could use this Scripture to help you make the right decision. Write down that situation below.

_____

Quote the Scripture when you face this situation, and live by it.

Prayer Time

Take a few moments to praise God for who He is.
Now take a few moments to thank God for things He has done for you.
Now ask God to make you into the person He wants you to be.
Ask God to use you to help others become closer to God.

Below is your prayer list for the week. Keep it updated each week. If your prayer isn't answered this week, carry it over to next week's list.

Request	Date of Original Request	Date Answered
_____	__/__/__	__/__/__
_____	__/__/__	__/__/__
_____	__/__/__	__/__/__
_____	__/__/__	__/__/__
_____	__/__/__	__/__/__
_____	__/__/__	__/__/__
_____	__/__/__	__/__/__
_____	__/__/__	__/__/__
_____	__/__/__	__/__/__

Pray for the things on your list and trust God to provide.
Forgive anyone you have not yet forgiven.
Ask God to forgive you for any unconfessed sin in your life.
Ask God to keep you out of trouble with sin.
Acknowledge that God is in complete control of your life
and will take care of everything.

Crowd Control

Matthew 5:1–2; Luke 6:17–20

> He had them in the palm of his hand. The people were following him like ants to a picnic. They hung on his every word. They were assembled around him as far as the eye could see. They were everywhere.
>
> He glanced over the crowd. He could ask for money, and he would probably collect enough to spend the rest of his life in the lap of luxury. He could say he was their new leader, and everyone would likely rally to his side and proclaim him as king. He could ask for favors from the people, and they would do whatever he asked. He could take advantage of them in any way he wanted to.
>
> The crowd waited silently, hoping for a word or a miracle. He surveyed the crowd intently one more time in front of him. Then he turned and looked at the steep hill behind him. A hush fell over the entire crowd. He looked at them again, knowing they would do anything he asked. Then he turned away from the people and climbed a hill.

Jesus had a habit of doing and saying the exact opposite of what people expected. Today was no exception. Jesus did not exploit the people. He went up to a more quiet place where He could sit down and teach His disciples.

The crowds and the pressures of each day sometimes got in the way of what Jesus really wanted to do. Spending time with His disciples was more important to Him than becoming the greatest guy of all time in the eyes of everybody else.

Sometimes it's easy to forget what is important, like spending time with the people who love you. We get caught up in the day-to-day stuff of life and get so busy catering to other people and pressures that we lose sight. Never let the urgent crowd out the important. Jesus loves you, and He wants to spend time with you each day. Don't let a busy agenda, a big test, or a stressful schedule keep you from taking time each day to have *a quiet time*—a moment where you spend time quietly with God in His Word and in prayer.

Are you satisfied with the amount of time you spend each day with God?

_____

Why or why not? _____

What could you do to make it better? _____

Put your faith where your mouth is. If you wrote down something you can do to make it better, then start today—right now. Ask God to bless your efforts and give you the strength to keep your commitment.

Opposite Day

Matthew 5:3–12; Luke 6:20–26

One day King Frederick went to visit the prison in Potsdam. He wanted a chance to visit the prisoners and see how the prison was running. He took time to see each prisoner individually—from the robber to the murderer.

Each time the king approached a prisoner and asked how things were going, the prisoner would begin explaining to the king that he was innocent and didn't deserve to be in these terrible conditions. The king would only nod his head as he listened. On and on it went as each and every prisoner looked for pity from the king by making up a sob story about how unjust the system was.

Then, the king approached the last prisoner. This man, however, did not approach the king. He sat on a stool in the corner of his cell and wouldn't even look in the king's direction. "And what is your story?" asked the king.

"Sir, I am guilty in your sight and deserve each and every miserable moment that I spend here," came the simple reply.

"Guards!" yelled the king. "Quick, get this man out of here before he corrupts all these innocent people." The prisoner was released immediately.[4]

The prisoner said the exact opposite of what everybody else was saying, but he was the only one who got what everybody else wanted—happiness and freedom.

Jesus, the King of kings, has a similar attitude about things. Sometimes happiness comes in unexpected places. For instance, read today's passage. If your Bible uses the word *blessed,* substitute *happy* in its place as you read.

Heaven is for those who need to be more spiritual. Comfort awaits those who agonize in tears. The earth will be given to those who give it away. Those starving for spiritual food will be stuffed. People who forgive will be forgiven. Those who remain pure will get to see a pure God. The people who bring peace will be called the sons of God. And those who are persecuted for following Jesus will receive special honor.

Jesus has words like no one else. Listen to what He has to say in these passages. True happiness does not come from popularity, wealth, power, or pleasure. Instead, true happiness is found in things the rest of the world says to avoid. These things Jesus said are called *Beatitudes*—they are attitudes for you to *be.* You'll be looking at these in more detail in the coming weeks.

Would you say your life is truly happy? _____

Why or why not? _____

What is it that you normally think would make you happy? _____

Ask God to help you understand the Beatitudes as you study them. Pray that He will help you to understand how *being* those attitudes will bring you true happiness.

Dependence Day

Matthew 5:3; Luke 6:20, 24

Tarence had everything he ever wanted. He was a professional football quarterback in the NFL. He had a bank account with several million dollars just waiting to be spent. He had girls sending him marriage proposals and provocative pictures. People begged for his autograph wherever he went. He bought two homes—one on the beach and one in the mountains. He had his own private plane. He purchased six of the most incredible cars on the planet—they sat in his twelve-car garage waiting for him to enter. He had as many girlfriends, and each of them gave him whatever he wanted.

Tarence always thought that when he made it to the top he would be happy. But something wasn't right. At night when he went to sleep, he was restless. Something was still missing. He had it all, but he still felt there was something more.

Meanwhile, not ten miles away, was a young man named Hunter who barely made enough money to support himself. He had one girl, one God, and one car that barely ran; and no one ever asked for his autograph. Yet Hunter was the happiest man in the world. Why? Because he was so poor—financially and spiritually—that he had to trust God to provide him with everything he needed.

In today's passage, Jesus says that the poor in spirit are happy. In other words, those who currently have no reason to hope in themselves are fortunate because they can place their hope in God.

Which is better—to have everything you ever wanted or to know the God who will provide everything you'll ever need? Jesus says to be poor is to be happy because when you are in need you are more likely to depend on God. God is probably a big part of your life when you have a problem you can't solve yourself. Only when you are at your lowest point do you look up and see the hand of God reaching down to help you.

Think about it. When do you depend on God more—when you need something or when you are comfortable? _____

What do you do when everything is going well and you have everything you want?

_____

Ask God to help you depend on *Him* for your needs—not your money or your possessions or your circumstances or anything else. Depend on God alone for everything you'll ever need. He will always provide for you.

Good Mourning

Matthew 5:4; Luke 6:21, 25

Janice cried. She cried on the day that she was born because she didn't know what to do in these new and unfamiliar surroundings. She cried on many days as an infant when she needed something and didn't know how to communicate to her parents. She cried when she was four and she hit her head against the wall and it started to bleed. Janice cried the first day her parents made her get on the school bus because she was so afraid to leave home. She cried in third grade when a little boy in her homeroom called her names because it embarrassed and humiliated her in front of her friends.

She cried in sixth grade when her parents got divorced because she thought it might be her fault. Janice even cried the night of the first junior high dance because no one asked her to go. Four years later she cried tears of happiness at the homecoming game when the student body voted her queen. She cried six years later on the day of her wedding because she was filled with so many different emotions. Finally, she cried yesterday when her first baby girl was born and the whole thing started all over again.

People cry. They cry many times during their life for many different reasons. Janice cried on a number of occasions because of certain feelings. Did you notice how many different emotions Janice experienced when she cried? Take a pencil and go back through the illustration above and underline all the different emotions that Janice dealt with on the days she cried. You will find things like "didn't know what to do," "needed something but didn't know how to communicate it," "hurt so bad," "so afraid," "embarrassed and humiliated," "might be her fault," "nobody asked her," "happiness," and "many different emotions."

In today's passage, Jesus says it is OK to cry. As a matter of fact, Jesus says that crying brings comfort. How? When you face a situation that overwhelms you, crying is a way of expressing your helplessness when you feel a certain way. God loves helpless people because the helpless always realize that God is the only one who can help them at a time like this. When you cry, He picks you up and holds you in His lap and tells you everything is going to be OK.

Have you ever cried? _____

During one of the most recent times you cried, what emotion made you cry?

_____

How did you feel after the crying was over? _____

Ask God to help you sense His presence the next time you cry. Don't fight the urge to cry when it hits you the next time—it may just be an opportunity to get closer to God.

Go with the Flow

Matthew 5:5

My mother has the worst timing. I'll be watching my favorite TV program, and right there in the middle of it she will say, "Can you come in here and help me fold these sheets?" I'll say, "Just a minute, Mom." She never understands. She just gets mad. I think I have a right to watch one TV show a week without interruption.

Then there's my father. He never approves of what I wear. Every day before I go to school he tells me to change clothes. I say, "Dad, this is what we wear in the twenty-first century." He just groans. I can't stand that. I have a right to wear what I want.

And traffic—I hate the way some people drive, especially those jerks who tailgate me because they don't like how slow I'm driving. I'll speed up on purpose when they try to pass. That'll teach them to tailgate me! I have a right to punish those idiots.

I have to defend a lot of my personal rights each day. I have a right to privacy from my kid brother. He should never be in my room without permission. I have a right to stay out later than my curfew. I have a right to do my homework when I want. I have a right to date whom I want. I have a right to stay home from church if I feel like it. I have a right to listen to whatever kind of music I want and choose my own friends. I have a right to all these rights and more. Right?

Today's passage may not sound like it has a lot to do with rights, but it does. Jesus says, "Happy are the meek, for they will inherit the earth." Go get a dictionary and look up the meaning of the word *meek*. What did your dictionary say? _____ _____ Your dictionary probably used words like *patient* and *submissive*.

To be meek is to surrender all rights to God and accept everything that happens, whether good or bad, as part of God's plan for you. You go with the flow because God is in control. If you really trust God, you put your entire life in His hands. You trust Him to take care of your rights. You don't demand them yourself. And you know what? When you let go of all your rights and surrender them to God, you will inherit the earth. In other words, you get your rights back when you give them up—only in God's way.

What kinds of rights do you think you have? _____

How do you feel about giving up those rights? _____

Ask God to help you give all your rights to Him. Then the next time Mom or Dad or the driver behind you starts to infringe on those rights, don't demand your rights—just go with the flow.

Can I Take Your Order?

Matthew 5:6; Luke 6:21, 25

"Is dinner ready yet, Mama?" asked freckle-faced Fabian when he bolted through the front door. He had worked hard all day with his father, and he was so hungry he could eat a horse.

"Not yet, Fabe," smiled Mama. "It will be ready soon though. Very soon." The delicate aroma of the approaching meal was almost too much. Fabian went upstairs, cleaned up, and then returned downstairs and into the kitchen. "Not yet," replied his mother before he could even ask.

Fabian sat down in the kitchen to talk to his mother, who was busy stirring. They talked about how the day went, how school was going, and what Fabian wanted for his upcoming birthday. They laughed about a few old memories, discussed how Fabian could bring up his grades just a little, and dreamed about the day that they would have that new car they had been saving for.

"OK, Mama, enough chitchat," Fabian pleaded. "You're killing me with the smell already. When is dinner going to be ready?"

"Actually, it has been ready for thirty minutes," Mama said with a twinkle in her eye.

"Then what are you doing standing there and stirring? Why didn't we eat thirty minutes ago?"

"I love to talk with you, Fabe. But you are gone so much with your friends and your work. But your Mama knows that you will come around when you are hungry."

Fabian and his family then sat down to a fabulous meal. It was worth the wait.

Hunger is a desire that grows. Right after a satisfying meal, you don't think much about food. But the longer you go without something to eat, the more the thought of food begins to get your attention. When you are starving, nothing else matters except food.

In today's passage, Jesus explains that those who hunger and thirst for righteousness (spiritual food) will be as satisfied as Fabian was. And because God likes to spend time with you, He often waits until you are really hungry for Him so that you will go looking for Him.

To be hungry and thirsty spiritually means to have a genuine desire to become more like God—to become more righteous. Sometimes after a good experience with God (like youth camp or a good quiet time), you feel satisfied. But, after a time, the desire begins to grow again, and you must return to God for more.

What are some ways that you would like to be more like God? _____

What specific changes could you make right now to be more like Him?

_____

Ask God to help you become more like Him—more righteous. Be prepared to wait just a little though. He likes to take time preparing the answer so you will sit and talk with Him.

Weekly Bible Study and Prayer Review

Bible Study

Look back through some of the Scriptures you read this week. Write down the one verse or passage that God used to speak to you.

_____

_____

_____

_____

Memorize this verse or passage. You can do it if you spend just
a few minutes saying it to yourself.

Now, think of at least one situation you will probably face soon in which you could use this Scripture to help you make the right decision. Write down that situation below.

_____

Quote the Scripture when you face this situation, and live by it.

Prayer Time

Take a few moments to praise God for who He is.
Now take a few moments to thank God for things He has done for you.
Now ask God to make you into the person He wants you to be.
Ask God to use you to help others become closer to God.

Below is your prayer list for the week. Keep it updated each week. If your prayer isn't answered this week, carry it over to next week's list.

Request	Date of Original Request	Date Answered
_____	__/__/__	__/__/__
_____	__/__/__	__/__/__
_____	__/__/__	__/__/__
_____	__/__/__	__/__/__
_____	__/__/__	__/__/__
_____	__/__/__	__/__/__
_____	__/__/__	__/__/__
_____	__/__/__	__/__/__
_____	__/__/__	__/__/__

Pray for the things on your list and trust God to provide.
Forgive anyone you have not yet forgiven.
Ask God to forgive you for any unconfessed sin in your life.
Ask God to keep you out of trouble with sin.
Acknowledge that God is in complete control of your life
and will take care of everything.

Mercy!

Matthew 5:7

Once upon a time there were two women, Madlynne and Evelyn. Both lived in the same city and were about the same age, but had never met each other.

Each woman shared the same desire: to stop abortion. But Madlynne and Evelyn's tactics were drastically different. Evelyn spent her days like this. Before work each morning, she would put on black clothes to symbolize the death of the unborn, and she would take her sign that read, "Murderers! Don't take your babies into the clinic of death!" Once outside the abortion clinic, Evelyn would scream at the top of her lungs at each young woman arriving for an appointment. She would shove plastic baby fetuses covered with fake blood into their faces and tell them that they would burn in hell if they killed their babies.

Madlynne opted for a different approach. She stood almost unnoticed near the clinic. She silently prayed for each woman who came by. Quietly, and always with a smile, Madlynne would offer a homemade brochure, which some women accepted and some did not. The brochure read, "I know this decision is tough. I know you are scared. If you have doubts about the abortion, please know that I am here to help. I am willing to provide you with a place to stay, food to eat, and all expenses paid to bring your child safely into the world—for your own health and the health of the baby. I will help you put your child up for adoption. I will be the friend you need right now."

Of the two different approaches, which one sounds like what Jesus would do?

Today's passage is not about abortion, but it is about *mercy,* or compassion. The word Jesus uses for "mercy" means to offer assistance to someone who needs it. Madlynne had compassion for the unborn child and for the pregnant mother. Evelyn had no compassion for the mother at all. Jesus says that those who show compassion will get compassion in return. Those who are concerned about the plight of others will receive the same treatment when the time comes.

People need compassion. Jesus spent His life giving it away. Now He wants you to do the same. If you want people to care about you, then care about them. Take the time to listen and understand. Be a friend who is always there. It's easy to condemn people for the things they have done wrong. It's easy to blame people for their own problems. It is difficult to overlook these things and show compassion on people—but that's exactly what Jesus did.

How would it make you feel if someone chose to understand you completely, take the time to listen to you, and never condemn you for your faults? _____

Do you have a friend like that? _____

Who? _____ *Are you this kind of friend to someone else?* _____

Ask God to help you be more compassionate. Look for opportunities to extend a helping hand to someone around you this week.

A Heart of Pure Gold

Matthew 5:8

Stephen never liked going to the dentist. This morning was no exception. It was only after a long argument with his mother in the car along the way that Stephen finally stomped into the waiting area of the torture chamber, as he liked to call it.

After nervously fidgeting through several magazines that he didn't even care for, an assistant called Stephen's name. His heart pounded. He slowly got up, took one last look at Mom as if to say, "Please get me out of this," and trudged into the little room at the end of the hall.

He sat in the chair and stared at all the torture instruments, dreading the thought of even one of them tiptoeing through his two lips. Shortly, the dental hygienist entered the room.

"Good morning, Stephen, and how are you today?" Stephen said nothing. "Let's take a look at those teeth, shall we?"

The next twenty minutes were awful. The hygienist poked numerous utensils into Stephen's mouth, scraped and poked sensitive areas, and sandblasted teeth and gums until they were all sore.

"OK, you are all ready to go. Your teeth are now as clean as they could possibly be."

Who likes the dentist? Not most. But sometimes if you want to get your teeth really clean, a trip into that little room at the end of the hall is the best medicine. It's painful at the time, but those who keep their teeth very clean will one day be glad. They will be glad when others their age are having teeth pulled, getting root canals, and getting twelve fillings recapped.

Today's passage is about that same kind of deep cleaning, only this time it's on the inside. Your heart is where the real you lives—it's who you really are. It's the real you that only you and God know about. This is the part of you that needs a daily cleansing, and occasionally a deep cleaning.

The cleaning won't be pleasant sometimes either. It will be like a trip to the dentist. God may keep you from having something you really want so He can clean out the greed from your heart. He might get your dad to make you do some chores when you could be out with friends, to clean up the disrespect for your parents. He may even reach way back in there and take away something from you to clean up that bad habit you have.

Do you have anything in your heart that needs cleaning? _____

What? _____

Why do those things need to be cleaned out? _____

You may be afraid, but ask God to do whatever is necessary to clean those things out of your heart. The time spent in His chair may be a little painful, but the whole time you get to look up at Him. You'll see God.

The Peacemaker

Matthew 5:9

"Fight, it's a fight!" came the cry from the hallway. "In the cafeteria. It's Sherwin and Glen!" Locker doors slammed, and feet flew across the floor and through the cafeteria doors where C-Lunch was meeting. Over in the far corner, a huddle of students was forming around two large boys who were circling each other and muttering obscenities.

Everyone was yelling. Several teachers struggled to make it through the crowd and stop the fight, but without any luck. It was a mob mentality. Cheers and jeers for the two fighters added to the confusion. A police officer on patrol at the school was shouting for everyone to step back, but nobody listened.

Quietly, though, a young girl who was friends with both Sherwin and Glen slipped to the front of the crowd. Just as the two boys seemed ready to lunge at each other again, she stepped between them. With the calmest expression anyone had ever seen, she stared both of them in the face. She told Sherwin to go take a break, and she told Glen to go walk it off. Because both guys respected her, and because her calmness took the breath out of their anger, they did as she asked. The crowd booed her, but she just got her things and went back to class.

School fights are not uncommon. Any fights are not uncommon, for that matter. Two people or groups of people don't see things eye-to-eye, and tensions rise. Emotions build. Tempers flare. Before you know it, you've got World War III on your hands.

Today's passage deals with this problem and offers a solution: make peace. Jesus was called the Son of God all through the New Testament. According to this passage, you can be a son of God, too, if you just become a peacemaker.

Wars will erupt. Fights will start. Conflict is inevitable. But in the middle of all of these situations, you have two options. You can join the crowd and yell for more violence, or you can choose to do whatever you can to bring the two factions together. Sometimes being a peacemaker means stepping in between two people in a fight and helping them patch things up. Sometimes it means you must take the first step in making peace with someone that *you* are having a problem with.

Can you think of some peacemakers, either famous or just ordinary people you know? List a few. _____

Martin Luther King, Jr. comes to mind. Perhaps you thought of some others. What do you think someone who has the title "peacemaker" should do in the middle of a conflict or fight?
_____

Do you think you could act like that in the same situation? _____

Why or why not? _____

Ask God to help you become more of a peacemaker in the warring world around you. When you do make peace, you prove yourself to be like Jesus—a child of God.

Fate of Hate

Matthew 5:10–12; Luke 6:22–23, 26

> "No, thanks," Ryan said, making his way past the "Safe Sex" booth in the hallway and politely refusing the condom offered to him.
>
> "What, are you one of those abstinence people? Don't you know that condoms promote safe sex? What's your problem? Do you think you're better than the rest of us? You're just . . ." The voice faded as Ryan rounded the corner.
>
> Later that day at lunch, the group of students who were running today's "Safe Sex" demonstration spotted Ryan. They surrounded him and demanded him to explain why he had refused the condom.
>
> Ryan looked up from his sandwich, whispered a prayer, cleared his throat, and said, "I am a Christian. Jesus said sex is only for you and your marriage partner. I am choosing to follow His desire for me. I'll enjoy sex one day with my wife. I have chosen my way, and you have chosen yours. I don't condemn you for your choice. Why do you condemn me for mine?"
>
> With that, the group laughed. The leader yelled, "Hey, look, everybody. Ryan is a 'KuRischun.' He thinks he's better than us. He says if you use condoms you're a pervert."
>
> Eyes from all around the cafeteria rested on Ryan.

Did you notice all the things the group said about Ryan? He never said any of that. He never got angry. He never condemned anybody. The group was convicted by Ryan's righteousness, so they lashed out in anger and humiliation tactics.

When you stand up for what you believe, you may find yourself on the receiving end of some nasty words. Most Christians, to avoid this kind of confrontation, keep their mouths shut and leave well enough alone. Take the condom and then throw it away quietly somewhere. Help someone cheat if she asks you. Write English papers on neutral topics that keep you out of the spotlight. Laugh at that dirty joke even though you know it isn't funny. Don't tell your friends about Jesus because they might think you're crazy. Don't be a Jesus freak.

But real Christians learn to live what they believe. When you live what you believe, you will be persecuted. To persecute means to make fun of or harm others because of their beliefs.

Have you ever been persecuted? _____ *Where and how?* _____

How did you feel? _____

Are there some areas of your Christian life that you have been hiding to avoid persecution? _____ *Like what?* _____

Ask God to help you stand up for what you believe and face persecution when it comes. Jesus knows exactly how you feel because He has been there. According to Him, you will be happy when you are persecuted, because you are living the way He did. See 2 Timothy 3:12 for further study.

Out of the Saltshaker

Matthew 5:13; Mark 9:49–50; Luke 14:34–35

You put it on your french fries. There's a little bit in chocolate chip cookies. Pizza has more than its share of this ingredient. Soup broth requires it. Chips and crackers would be practically inedible without it. That cheeseburger has quite a bit. Garlic bread thrives with it. Canned vegetables always have it.

It preserves meat without refrigeration. It can help melt the snow or help you make homemade ice cream. It can end the life of a slug on contact. Horses often have large blocks of it just to lick.

If you didn't have it on your dinner table or available in little packets at the fast food places, you'd be pretty upset. If suddenly the world ran out, eating would become very bland.

Salt. It's pure and snowy white, and you use some every day. You don't think about it much, but you depend on it because it adds flavor to everything you eat.

Jesus said you are *salt* of the earth. What does that mean? You are the flavor. You are what makes life taste good. You, as a believer, make bland situations so much better because you bring Jesus with you wherever you go.

How do you add flavor? In several ways. First, one grain of salt is not enough to change the taste of much. But when you have a lot of salt working together, it really makes a difference. You must work together with other Christians to change the taste of a situation.

Second, salt must be pure. Have you ever seen or tasted dirty salt? You want white, perfect salt, that has no impurities, on your food. The world will not see a change in taste until it sees pure Christians, undefiled by sin around them.

Third, the salt must come out of the saltshaker! What good is salt if it sticks together and stays inside? It has to come out of the shaker and onto the food to make a difference. Go to church. Depend on your friends. Stick to each other. But, when the time comes, get out of the saltshaker and get into the world and make a difference. After all, Jesus said you are the salt of the world—not the salt of the shaker.

How can you work with other Christians to make a difference in this world?

_____

What can you do to make your life more pure so that others will see Jesus in you?

_____

How can you come out of your saltshaker and share Jesus publicly this week?

_____

Pray for the opportunity to serve God alongside other Christian people. Ask God to forgive you of those things that make you impure. Pray for the courage to come out of hiding, and use your mouth and your life to show others that following Jesus adds real flavor to life.

Got a Light?

Matthew 5:14–16; Mark 4:21; Luke 8:16, 11:33

> Hal needed to replace the lightbulb in the living room, so he went to the garage and found some. He opened a brand-new package containing four bulbs. As he pulled out one of the light-bulbs, it spoke!
>
> "Please, don't take me!" it shouted. "I'm still taking shining lessons. I would probably flick-er on and off uncontrollably. Why don't you take Bob?"
>
> Bob Bulb also complained, "Not me. I'm afraid I would be too bright. I might offend some other electrical appliance."
>
> Tulip Bulb wasn't about to go either. "Look. I don't mind being the light for the hall closet that you only use twice a year. But don't put me there in the living room where I'll have to shine every day. That's giving too much. I don't want to burn out before my time."
>
> The last bulb was silent. "What about you?" asked Hal.
>
> "I'm too scared. I've never done anything like this before. Please get some other bulb."
>
> Hal sighed. Where was he going to find light?

Don't you know God feels a lot like Hal? He goes to a church—where Christians are kept—so He can find someone who will give light to the world. One says, "Hey, not me. I don't know enough about witnessing. Take somebody else." The next one may say, "I don't want to offend anybody, so I'll just keep to myself, thank you." Another says, "I'll invite somebody to church twice a year, but don't expect me to be a witness out there where I live every day." Finally, some say, "I'm just too scared. Please get someone else to do it. Isn't that why we have a pastor?"

Lightbulbs are meant to be put in lamps so they can give off light. Lightbulbs shouldn't complain. They don't need lessons. They were designed to shine. Christians were also designed to shine. They were designed to give off light to a dark world of sin.

Do you regularly share your faith? _____

Why or why not? _____

Have you ever made any of these excuses when you had an opportunity to share your faith? _____ *Are you afraid you won't know what to say?* _____

Are you afraid of offending people? _____

Are you unwilling to take the time and effort necessary to share Jesus with others? _____

Are you just plain terrified of the whole idea? _____

You don't have to be a Bible scholar or a pastor to be a witness. Jesus is looking for ordinary Christians, right out of the box, to be lights in dark places. Ask God to help you share your faith at home, school, work, or when you're just hanging out. Don't make excuses, just let God plug you into His power.

Weekly Bible Study and Prayer Review

Bible Study

Look back through some of the Scriptures you read this week. Write down the one verse or passage that God used to speak to you.

_____

_____

_____

_____

*Memorize this verse or passage. You can do it if you spend just
a few minutes saying it to yourself.*

Now, think of at least one situation you will probably face soon in which you could use this Scripture to help you make the right decision. Write down that situation below.

_____

Quote the Scripture when you face this situation, and live by it.

Prayer Time

*Take a few moments to praise God for who He is.
Now take a few moments to thank God for things He has done for you.
Now ask God to make you into the person He wants you to be.
Ask God to use you to help others become closer to God.*

Below is your prayer list for the week. Keep it updated each week. If your prayer isn't answered this week, carry it over to next week's list.

Request	Date of Original Request	Date Answered
_____	__/__/__	__/__/__
_____	__/__/__	__/__/__
_____	__/__/__	__/__/__
_____	__/__/__	__/__/__
_____	__/__/__	__/__/__
_____	__/__/__	__/__/__
_____	__/__/__	__/__/__
_____	__/__/__	__/__/__
_____	__/__/__	__/__/__

*Pray for the things on your list and trust God to provide.
Forgive anyone you have not yet forgiven.
Ask God to forgive you for any unconfessed sin in your life.
Ask God to keep you out of trouble with sin.
Acknowledge that God is in complete control of your life
and will take care of everything.*

Law School

If you lived in the first century as a male Jew Pharisee, your typical day would be something like this. You rise early and begin putting on your robes. You spend a great deal of time making them look just right. Then you would take these little boxes that had pieces of paper with Old Testament verses written on them and tie them to your wrists and your forehead—that way the Scripture was close to you.

Then you would leave the house and begin your trek to the temple. You would walk through the city and people would look at you in awe with your robes and Scripture boxes. You would frown at the "sin" going on around you. If a beautiful woman came into view, you would turn away from her immediately to avoid any impure thoughts. You would arrive at the temple, enter the courts, and begin praying. You would thank God that you were not born a dog, a non-Jew, or a woman. Then you would go to the marketplace about rush hour and pray there so people would see how great you were. Pharisees were great—at being hypocrites.

The people thought Pharisees were close to God because they were so religious about the law. Jesus says, "Now understand, I'm not putting down the law because I came to fulfill it, but . . ." Then He proceeded to say that unless you are better than people like the Pharisees, you'll never see heaven.

Is that possible? How can you be better than someone who spends his every waking moment thinking about the law? Very simple. Did you notice in today's passage how Jesus said He did not come to abolish (destroy) the law, but to fulfill it? Jesus kept all of the law, and yet He didn't act anything like the Pharisees. Jesus, not the Pharisees, is the model to follow.

A lot of times in your life you come across a situation, and you become a Pharisee when you ask, "What's right or what's wrong with this situation?" If you make a decision just because it doesn't seem to be wrong, you're no better than a hypocritical Pharisee. The right question to ask is, "What would Jesus do?" Jesus fulfilled the law and became everything we were meant to be. Now, when you walk through your day, for every decision and every act you make, ask yourself first, "What would Jesus do?"

Do you ever make decisions by asking yourself, "Is there anything wrong with doing this?"

What is the difference between asking that question and asking, "What would Jesus do?"

Ask God to help you make decisions based on the life of Jesus, not on your own feelings at the time.

If Thoughts Could Kill

Matthew 5:21–26

Rage. Anger. Hatred. You see these every day. Someone's aunt is killed in a senseless drive-by shooting. A motorist cuts another one off because of the way the other was driving. A fight erupts at school, and people form a circle to cheer the rage on until it is fully quenched in victory over the other.

A young person poisons her father with a chemical she found in her chemistry lab at school—and gets away with it for two years. A ten-year-old and an eleven-year-old, furious with a five-year-old for not stealing candy for them, drop him from a fourteenth-story apartment window. It goes on and on. And that's only what we see.

Now look inside of you for a moment. Your parents put their foot down on your independence, and you boil. A friend at school puts you down in front of your friends, and you plot revenge. Someone calls you a name, so you call one right back.

In today's passage, Jesus cut right to the chase. Did you know that in God's eyes hating someone or calling them a name is the same thing as killing them? The reason is because God can read your thoughts. If in your thoughts you hurt or kill someone, then that's the same thing as doing it out in the open for the rest of the world to see. You won't get arrested for killing someone in your mind, but God says you're insane in the membrane if you think you can get away with it.

What's the solution? Every time you come before God to pray (that's what the altar signifies), you must first deal with any relational problems you have with other people. God doesn't want you making yourself out to be a hypocrite by saying you love Him (whom you can't even see) when you hate another human being (whom you can see).

Is there someone you know who is angry with you right now? _____

Who? _____

What is preventing you from straightening out this problem right away?

_____

If you can't think of anyone right now, the next time you go to church or go to God in prayer and remember that there's a problem between you and another person, get it straightened out. Go to that person or grab the phone or make a trip and make things right. Forgive from your heart and then go back to God, where He will accept and forgive you in the same way.

Mind Control

> "Ooowwwww! Yeah!" Howls rose from the guys on the couch as the TV series Beach Bunnies ushered its entourage of scantily clad females past the lens of the camera. "Nothing wrong with window-shopping," said one.
>
> "Yeah, you can look as long as you don't touch," claimed another.
>
> "Oh, yeah," shouted the third. "Man, I wish I was a lifeguard on the beach. That's the life." These three teenage guys were Christians who saw nothing wrong with feasting their eyes on the bodies of several women at once.
>
> The next night the same three guys went to a rally called "True Love Waits." There they listened to a speaker talk about how important it was to wait until you were married to participate in sex. The guys agreed and signed commitment cards, vowing to wait until they were married to have any type of sex with another girl. Then they headed back to the house and sat down to watch another steamy episode of Beach Bunnies.

Read today's passage. Jesus has some strong words here. Remember in yesterday's devotion how it was just as bad to hate someone as it was to kill them? Well, today we find out that it is just as bad to lust for someone as it is to have sex with them. Just window-shopping can get you arrested for shoplifting.

Let's define lust. Lust is not simply an attraction or even a temptation to be with someone. You will have those desires and be *tempted* to cross boundaries. That's OK. Lust is what happens when you use your *mind* to cross those boundaries that you don't cross with your *body*. Lust occurs when you have the chance to turn away from a mind-driven fantasy and you entertain it instead.

Guys, if you deliberately let your eyes "feast" on another woman, whether it be reality or a TV show or a music video or a magazine (even if they have *some* clothes on), you are lusting. It's one thing to be tempted and to fight. It's another thing to say there's nothing wrong with looking as long as you don't touch. Jesus said just the opposite. Ladies, you can be guilty too. Don't dress in a way that leaves little to the imagination—you're giving away your body to their eyes. Save that for your husband. And don't get caught up going too far with a guy in your brain either.

Do you find yourself struggling with lust? _____

What are some things around you that seem to get you into trouble with lust (examples include TV shows, magazines, radio programs, spending too much time alone with a person of the opposite sex, etc.)? _____

How can you stop lust before it starts? _____

Ask God to help you get rid of the things around you that aid your lustful thoughts and habits. And the next time you feel lust taking a hold of your desires, turn away and run. For more information, read 1 Corinthians 6:18–20.

Yes or No

Matthew 5:33–37

"Do you promise to tell the truth, the whole truth, and nothing but the truth, so help you God?" inquires the bailiff. The witness responds affirmatively. Now that she has been sworn in, the jury expects her to tell the truth.

Stacey wants to know Cheryl's secret. "Ooh, come on! You can tell me! I won't tell anybody else. I promise or I'll die and poke a needle in my eye . . ." After a commitment like that, Cheryl decides to confide in Stacey.

"I swear to God I'll be back," the cowboy said, climbing onto his horse. "Just you wait and see." The wife breathes a sigh of relief, watching her husband ride off into the sunset.

"May lightning strike if I am not telling you the truth," Pete said. John wonders whether or not to believe the story he just heard, but figures that Pete is sincere.

There's nothing wrong with a simple oath or vow. Right? Well, for some reason Jesus has a few things to say about this subject.

The main problem in Jesus' day with oaths was the contest going on to see who could make the greatest promise by swearing on the greatest thing. One would swear by the hair on her head, while the next would swear by the temple in Jerusalem. And on and on. It's sort of the same today. People who don't even read the Bible or believe in God swear on the Bible in a courtroom—and that's supposed to make their testimony valid? People swear to God that they'll do something when they don't even know who God is.

Jesus doesn't want us swearing by things because it does two things. First, you have no reason to swear on some things because they don't belong to you. You can't swear to God, or on your life, or on the Bible because those are not even yours. Second, if you swear by something but fail to do what you promised, you are disgracing the object or person you swore by. People swear when their own word isn't good enough.

Are you an honest person? _____ Why? _____

Have you ever broken your word to someone? _____

How did you feel afterward? _____

How can you be sure you will keep your word the next time you have the chance? _____

Ask God to keep you from making empty promises. Pray that you will be a person of your word. Then remember to follow Jesus' example. Don't swear—just say yes or no and leave it at that.

One More Mile

Matthew 5:38–42; Luke 6:29–30

Dean was a soldier. Every night during boot camp he knelt down at his bunk and prayed to God. The other guys in the barracks really gave him a hard time about believing in God. Greg, Dean's bunk mate, gave Dean the worst time. In the middle of Dean's prayers he would taunt him and laugh and make a lot of racket. Dean didn't mind. He just kept on praying.

Late one night while Dean was sleeping, Greg came in drunk. He pulled Dean from his bunk and proceeded to beat the living daylights out of him. Dean was really messed up. Greg just piled in his bunk with his muddy boots on and went to sleep.

Early the next morning, still bruised and weary from his beating, Dean woke up and stood over Greg's bunk. Greg would be sleeping through his hangover for hours. Dean could do anything he wanted. So guess what he did. He took Greg's muddy boots off and shined them up perfectly.

This is a true story. When Greg finally came to and found out that Dean had polished his boots, he broke down and accepted the Lord whom Dean prayed to each night.

Here Jesus goes again making wild and crazy commands on how to live. Now He wants you to not only avoid taking revenge, but He wants you to be extra nice to that person or those people who have hurt you. Isn't that a bit extreme?

No! If you want to get back at someone, do the exact opposite of what they expect. When someone tries to get your goat, they expect you to get upset and fight back. They might even expect you to chicken out and turn away or not say anything. But the last thing they'll be looking for is for you to ask them out to lunch and pay for it. You'll catch them off guard and probably destroy their reason for messing with you again.

Is there someone now you would like to take revenge against? _____

Who and why? _____

What could you do instead of revenge? _____

Ask God to help you keep your cool when someone makes you mad. Pray that you would have the patience and love to go the extra mile. Turning the other cheek is the most powerful weapon you have against your enemy. The next time you get mad at someone and feel like getting even, do the opposite. For further study, read Proverbs 25:21–22.

Hand-to-Hand Combat

Matthew 5:43–48; Luke 6:27–28, 32–36

Nikolas was only doing his job. As a communist in the former Soviet Union, his "job" was to find people meeting illegally for church, bust inside, and beat everybody up. He sometimes got sort of a perverse pleasure out of it.

On one occasion he broke into a meeting and found a very attractive young blonde girl attending church. He and his buddies threw her down on a table and beat her back with her own shoes until she was half dead. A few weeks later Nikolas busted into another meeting and found the same girl. He and his buddies beat her again the same way, reopening the old wounds that had not quite yet healed. Several weeks later, Nikolas found this girl at another Christian meeting. He let her go, shaking in his boots that someone would be so faithful.

During Nikolas's last infiltration, he had a billy club. He found an old woman clutching a Bible and he raised his hand to club her to death over the head. Just before he brought down the final blow, he heard her whisper, "Lord, forgive this boy. He doesn't know what he is doing."[5]

Nikolas never invaded another meeting. In fact, he escaped to Canada, became a Christian, and was eventually assassinated by undercover Soviet agents for defecting.

Nikolas's life was turned upside down because he saw a woman love him while he was trying to kill her. He just couldn't understand. Now he is in heaven with the same woman.

Jesus wants you to realize that to only love the people who love you is easy. Real love kicks in when you deliberately love and pray for someone who hates you and otherwise makes your life generally miserable.

That's hard. But didn't Jesus do the same thing and give us an example to follow? He let the Jews mistreat Him. He let the Romans beat Him. He carried His cross up a hill to die and said nothing to those who jeered Him and spit in His face. Then, after they nailed Him to the cross and hung Him up like a piece of meat and stood back to laugh and watch Him die, He cried, "Father, forgive them, for they don't know what they are doing." Your enemies don't know either.

Who would you consider your enemies (people who dislike or hate you or people you dislike or hate)? Make a list of several here. _____, _____, _____

When is the last time you prayed for them? _____

Do you love them? _____

It's hard to love these people and forgive them. But if you want to be more like Jesus, fall on your knees right now and forgive these people. Put your hands together and pray for them. Ask God to help you love them more each day.

Weekly Bible Study and Prayer Review

Bible Study

Look back through some of the Scriptures you read this week. Write down the one verse or passage that God used to speak to you.

_____

_____

_____

_____

*Memorize this verse or passage. You can do it if you spend just
a few minutes saying it to yourself.*

Now, think of at least one situation you will probably face soon in which you could use this Scripture to help you make the right decision. Write down that situation below.

_____

Quote the Scripture when you face this situation, and live by it.

Prayer Time

*Take a few moments to praise God for who He is.
Now take a few moments to thank God for things He has done for you.
Now ask God to make you into the person He wants you to be.
Ask God to use you to help others become closer to God.*

Below is your prayer list for the week. Keep it updated each week. If your prayer isn't answered this week, carry it over to next week's list.

Request	Date of Original Request	Date Answered
_____	__/__/__	__/__/__
_____	__/__/__	__/__/__
_____	__/__/__	__/__/__
_____	__/__/__	__/__/__
_____	__/__/__	__/__/__
_____	__/__/__	__/__/__
_____	__/__/__	__/__/__
_____	__/__/__	__/__/__

*Pray for the things on your list and trust God to provide.
Forgive anyone you have not yet forgiven.
Ask God to forgive you for any unconfessed sin in your life.
Ask God to keep you out of trouble with sin.
Acknowledge that God is in complete control of your life
and will take care of everything.*

Sleight of Hand

Matthew 6:1–4

The eye of the camera zooms in close, cropping in two men and the large check between them. A rising Christian basketball star has just given a huge sum of money to his small church. Cameras flash. News reporters push and crowd their way to the front for questions. Smiles and handshakes are offered on stage. And everybody keeps talking about that huge, six-digit number on the check. One reporter turns to another and suggests, "I don't know if there is a God; but if there is, this guy is going to heaven."

At the same time, across the country, another Christian basketball player secretly transfers funds from account to account so no one will be able to trace it. Then he withdraws a huge sum in cash. He places it in a paper bag and slips out of the door. He walks across town to the city orphanage, where he grew up, and places it on the doorstep. He rings the door and bolts around the corner, peeking to see what happens. The orphanage administrator opens the door, sees the package, and almost faints when she sees the money inside. The basketball player walks away, happy that the kids will have more needs met.

Do you see the difference between these two guys? Here's one big difference. When they stand before God on Judgment Day, one of them will get a huge reward for everyone to see. The other one will not even get an honorable mention for the money he gave. Can you guess which one is which? If you guessed that the second player will get the big reward, you are right. You see, the first guy was great for giving the money; but his reward came from the people on earth and in front of the cameras. He already has his reward.

Jesus wants you to give some of what you have back to those who are needy. But He doesn't want you to do it for the sake of being noticed and getting attention. If, or *when,* you help someone out with money or with a helping hand, Jesus wants you to do it in secret so there will be no question as to the real reason you gave. Don't even let your left hand know what your right hand is doing.

Do you know of anyone right now who could use a little help with money or possessions? _____ *Who?* _____

What can you do to help? _____

There may be a family near you whose house has burned down. Maybe during the holidays a family needs help with food. Maybe someone at school just needs some lunch money.

Ask God to help you be aware of people around you who need help. Pray that you will be willing to give your time, money, or possessions in a quiet way—so your reward will come from heaven.

What Did You Say?

Matthew 6:5–6

"Let us pray," said the young man who had been asked to close the morning worship service. People all over the entire room—most people, anyway—bowed their heads to listen to these words . . .

"Our Most Gracious Honorable Majestic Heavenly Supreme Being of a Father figure, we humbly bow before Thy nebulous presence to seek Thy will in our miniscule excuses for lives. You, almighty Lord and God and Father, are our Father. We ask You, Father, to be our Father. Father, find us faithful and fearful in our faith, Father. As we go now to partake of our Sunday bounty, bless our food to the nourishment of our bodies and keep us from waiting too long in line. Amen." As people filed out of the church, several people commented on the young man's prayer.

"It was very good. He should pray more often," someone said. One woman told the young man he was a saint.

Later that evening, when the same young man was at home getting ready for bed, he prayed again. While shaving and looking in the mirror, he said, "Dear Lord, You are so awesome. Please make me more like You. Thank You for giving me my home and my wife and my children. And please help me to figure out this problem I'm having at work. Thank You, Lord. I ask these things not for myself, but so that Jesus may be more a part of my life. Amen."

Look at the two prayers, offered by the same person. They sure are different. What do you think made the difference? _____ Probably because the first prayer was in public, the man felt like he had to make a show for the people in his church. The second prayer, though, was much more natural because the man was only talking to God. He wasn't talking to a room full of people.

You may be asked to pray in public occasionally. But whether you pray in public or private, the language of your prayer should be the same. Don't be a hypocrite—hypocrites change depending on who is around. A true Christian will be the same in front of thousands of people as he or she is in front of a few.

For a moment, let's forget about the public prayers. Do you pray on a regular basis in private? _____ Why or why not? _____

What time of day do you pray? _____

Where do you go when you pray? _____

What do you pray for? _____

Take time to go to the Lord right now in prayer. Ask Him to help you set aside a time and place each day where you can be free of distractions and have a time to genuinely talk to and listen to God. Jesus suggested a closet, but if it's too small or dirty, feel free to use the edge of your bed.

A Beautiful Model

Matthew 6:7–15; Luke 11:1–4

_____

_____

_____

_____

_____

_____

In today's passage you see what most people call the Lord's Prayer. It's more of a model prayer—an outline to follow rather than something to quote. Compare it to the letter you wrote to your big boss. You might see some similar elements.

First, you see an address to the Father in heaven (the boss) and some things about how great He is. After you address the boss and say some good things about Him and what He is doing, then you finally get to the things you want (like the model prayer); then you close with a big finish (like the model prayer).

Use the model prayer as an example to follow when you pray. Follow the suggestions below.

Model Prayer	Suggestions for Your Prayer
Our Father in heaven,	God, You are my Father and my Lord,
Hallowed be Your name.	Your name is great—help me to make it more great.
Your kingdom come.	Help me to be a Christian, a spiritual being, before I am anything else.
Your will be done on earth as it is in heaven.	Show me Your will. Help me to do Your will. Make me more like You.
Give us today our daily bread.	Please provide me with the things I need for today.
Forgive us our debts, as we also have forgiven our debtors.	Please forgive me of my sin as I forgive those who have sinned against me.
Do not lead us into temptation,	Help me to make it through my trials and temptations.
But deliver us from the evil one.	Keep me from giving in to Satan's will.
For Yours is the kingdom and the power	You are God. I know that everything happens according to Your will.
and the glory forever and ever.	Thanks for hearing my prayer.

Go Fast

Matthew 6:16–18

> Jesus looked at the hill. There was not a tree in sight. Dust and rock were all it had to offer—as well as the heat. The sun blazed down relentlessly during the day, offering no relief to anyone exposed. Jesus breathed a deep sigh. This hill would be His home for the next six weeks. He would be all alone. He checked His provisions. Yes, they were all there—the clothes on His back. No food. No water. Jesus began to climb.
>
> On this barren hill Jesus met with His Father. Not just once a day or even several times a day, but all day long. Jesus never ate a single bite. He prayed, and He prayed, and He prayed. Finally, almost six full weeks since He ascended that hill, Jesus descended. He was stronger than He'd ever been before.

Jesus fasted for forty days and forty nights. Why? What was His purpose? When He fasted, He gave control of His bodily desires to the Lord so He could pray and focus on His Father.

In today's passage, Jesus pointed out that some people fast so they can walk around all sad-looking and say, "Woe is me, I'm so hungry. I'm fasting for God." True fasting is an important part of the Christian life—and an often forgotten one. Fasting is like giving a percentage of your food to God. When you fast, you can feed the hungry with the food you don't eat. Imagine if every Christian fasted one day a week and gave that food or money to the poor and needy.

Another reason for fasting is to give your desires back to God. You will get hungry when you fast. But when you fast and pray, you are committing your whole body to God even when hunger tries to call you away.

Have you ever even considered fasting? _____

Do you know anyone who does? _____

Try starting out by skipping one meal and praying during that time. Give the money or food you would have used to someone else. Do you think you could do that? _____

Before you run out and fast, make sure you are healthy. Jesus was healthy, and He doesn't want you to fast if you have health problems that would prevent it. Check with your parents and doctors first. Then fast once a week or month. Try it and see what happens. Pray that God would use this activity to draw you closer to Him. For further study, read Isaiah 58:1–14.

Heart Transplant

Matthew 6:19–21; Luke 12:33–34

Somewhere in the deepest, darkest jungles of the Congo lies an undisturbed tribe of natives who have lived the same way for thousands of years. They live in a city-state with a king.

Any man can be king, as long as he is between the ages of sixteen and thirty. If a new king is needed, and you want to be king, you just sign up. If no one wants to compete against you, then you are the new king. If others want a shot at the top, there will be a contest of strength. The strongest man becomes king.

Here are the rules to being king: your term as king is seven years to the day. You can do, say, and eat anything you want. You can have all the women you want—just say the word, and they are yours. You can seize anyone's property and make it your own. You can make everyone in the city-state your personal slave, if you want. Anything your heart desires is yours, for seven years.

Is there catch? Yes. At the end of your seven years, your head is chopped off, and your body is placed on a tree for the birds to eat. Even considering the rules, every seven years men sign up for the opportunity to live in the lap of luxury.[6]

Would you sign up to be king or queen if this kind of opportunity were offered today? If you would take this chance, you probably are thinking about the seven years of "fun." If you would not take this chance, you probably don't want to die in seven years.

You might have plans for your life to get a fun job making lots of money so you can get a good house, car, and spouse because you are told these things make you happy. You may think having the best stereo, the nicest clothes, or the best-looking boyfriend or girlfriend is all you need. Keep in mind, though, that God says if you choose to run after all these things, one day—maybe seven years, maybe longer—you will lose it all. Why? Because everything that exists will be stolen or will eventually rot. That's just the way it is.

Jesus says that there are certain things that will never be stolen or rot. They are eternal rewards in heaven for living an unselfish life for God while down here on earth. Think about the difference. You can enjoy the stuff of earth for maybe up to seventy or eighty years, if you're lucky. Or you can experience the things of heaven for eternity.

Which one do you want? _____

What are you going to spend your time doing to make sure you get it? _____

_____

Make a conscious choice to transplant your heart from this world to the next. Ask God to help you set your heart on the things above.

Looking Up

Matthew 6:22–23; Luke 11:34–36

> "I can't see!" Terry shouted frantically.
>
> "Shhhhhh!" urged Michelle. "This flashlight isn't that powerful. You just have to stare at the ground where I shine it and make sure your feet are on the path. If you do that, we'll be OK. Now, keep quiet or we're goners for sure!"
>
> Stealthily the two cadets foraged their way along the path through the dense woods. Their objective was to travel from point A to point B without getting lost or captured by the enemy. There was no moon out and blackness enveloped the duo. When they were halfway there, they noticed that the flashlight started growing dim. Finally, it just went out.
>
> "Michelle! What are we going to do now?" Terry complained. "What is wrong with that stupid thing? We haven't used it long."
>
> In a frenzy, Michelle shook the flashlight, but nothing happened. Then she remembered. "I forgot to put in new batteries," she whispered hesitantly.
>
> "What!" Terry screamed. "How could you possibly—"
>
> "Freeze!" came a deep voice from behind them. The enemy had found them.

Lights don't work well without power. Forget the power source, and you have no lights.

Jesus said that your eyes are the flashlights of your body. That means that your eyes see the world around you and tell your brain how to respond. You see a delicious meal on your plate, and your body responds by eating it. You see a car coming right at you, and your body gets out of the way. You see a swimming pool when you're hot, and your body wants to jump in.

If you point your eyes at something you shouldn't, your body will still respond. If you stare too long at somebody else's stuff, you might find yourself wanting to steal. If you look longingly at a model on television, you might find yourself working to look just like her. If you open up a pornographic magazine, you could find yourself battling sexual desires you can't control.

God is the power source for your eyes. If you choose to let Him control where your eyes roam, then you will always be able to see how to stay on the path of life. But if you decide for yourself what you are going to look at, you might find yourself in the darkness of sin with the enemy right behind you.

What have you looked at recently that you shouldn't have? _____

How did you respond when you looked? _____

What could you do differently the next time you are tempted to look? _____

_____

Ask God to help you keep your eyes where they ought to be. Keep your eyes on Jesus by looking up to Him. You may not have enough light to see everything, but He'll give you just enough to take the next step.

Weekly Bible Study and Prayer Review

Bible Study

Look back through some of the Scriptures you read this week. Write down the one verse or passage that God used to speak to you.

_____

_____

_____

_____

Memorize this verse or passage. You can do it if you spend just
a few minutes saying it to yourself.

Now, think of at least one situation you will probably face soon in which you could use this Scripture to help you make the right decision. Write down that situation below.

_____

Quote the Scripture when you face this situation, and live by it.

Prayer Time

Take a few moments to praise God for who He is.
Now take a few moments to thank God for things He has done for you.
Now ask God to make you into the person He wants you to be.
Ask God to use you to help others become closer to God.

Below is your prayer list for the week. Keep it updated each week. If your prayer isn't answered this week, carry it over to next week's list.

Request	Date of Original Request	Date Answered
_____	__/__/__	__/__/__
_____	__/__/__	__/__/__
_____	__/__/__	__/__/__
_____	__/__/__	__/__/__
_____	__/__/__	__/__/__
_____	__/__/__	__/__/__
_____	__/__/__	__/__/__
_____	__/__/__	__/__/__

Pray for the things on your list and trust God to provide.
Forgive anyone you have not yet forgiven.
Ask God to forgive you for any unconfessed sin in your life.
Ask God to keep you out of trouble with sin.
Acknowledge that God is in complete control of your life
and will take care of everything.

Money Talks

Matthew 6:24; Luke 16:13

There once was a man with millions of dollars. He lived all of his life in luxury. One day, though, the time came for him to die. As he lay on his deathbed, he called his son to him.

"Son, I want you to promise me that when I die, you will take the $3 million in my savings account and bury it with me."

Shocked, the son, who was very loyal and devoted to his father, exclaimed, "But I can use that money!"

"No, son. You must bury all of it with me. Promise me!"

The son reluctantly promised. His father soon died and funeral arrangements were made. The son agonized over whether to keep his promise or the money. He knew that if he broke his promise, he would be miserable all of his life—even with the money.

Finally, he had an idea. His father was buried, and the son did put $3 million in the casket before it was lowered into the ground. A friend asked, "Did you keep your promise to your father?"

"Yes!" the son replied. "I wrote him a check."

You can't take it with you. This old man tried to take it with him, but all he got was a check that will never be cashed. Some day the son will die too, and he will lose whatever he has left.

Jesus has some tough words to say about money. You cannot serve both God and money. It's one or the other.

So which is it? Which master are you serving? Think about it for a moment. You can usually take the following test to determine which master is in charge. Circle the correct answer.

Do you give a portion of your earnings to God?	Y	N
Are you willing to help people with your money?	Y	N
Do you realize that all your money belongs to God?	Y	N

Did you answer "N" to any of the questions above? _____ If so, you have some work to do.

Pick one of the questions you answered no to and think of one thing you could do today that would change the answer to yes. Did you think of something? What are you going to do? _____

_____

Money talks. It will speak volumes if you start giving it away. Ask God to show you what He wants you to do with your income. If you don't already, start giving a certain percentage of your income or allowance to the Lord through your church. Give this week if you can. Be willing to give some of your money to people who need it—or spend a little extra on the next birthday present you buy. Finally, commit all of your money to the Lord and realize it belongs to Him. Spend it the way He would.

Wings and Petals

Matthew 6:25–34; Luke 12:22–32

Enter the classroom. Look around. The teacher is lecturing, and everyone is looking in her direction; but take a peek into the minds of what these young people are thinking.

Emily, the dusty blonde there in the third row, is hoping that Mike, the super stud to her left, will ask her out this weekend. She is so worried about it that her stomach hurts.

Terry, that redhead up front with freckles, is afraid the teacher will call on him to answer a question. Terry didn't read the chapter last night, and he is avoiding the teacher's gaze.

Cat, the gorgeous brunette on the last row, is worried she might be pregnant. She's a cheerleader and very popular; and she's writhing in her seat, afraid of what her parents, her teachers, her boyfriend, and everyone else will think if she's pregnant. Cat is so worried that she is considering taking her own life to avoid the possibilities.

Worry. It plagues all of us. It wraps its ugly tentacles around our brains and squeezes until it hurts. None of us are immune from this deadly monster. What can you do to escape?

Jesus has a few words to say about worry—don't do it! But how? Jesus points to nature. Birds and flowers don't worry, and they seem to do OK. Jesus points to your head. How much worrying does it take to add hours to your life or inches to your height? Answer: it can't be done.

Worry accomplishes nothing toward the goal of what you worry about. Worry is directionless hope. When you trust God to provide you what you need, that is faith and hope in Him. When you just hope things will work out without having a God to ask for help, that is worry—directionless hope. Hope without someone to hope in is no hope at all—it is despair.

What is the first thing that comes to your mind when you think about your worries?

_____

Be honest, and write down one thing that your worry has accomplished toward taking care of this problem. _____

From now on, when worry begins to wrap itself around your brain, channel the hope that you have toward God. Trust in Him to provide the things you want and need. Ask God for a date with the right guy. Confess to God that you didn't study and you will do better next time. And when you get into trouble over your head and worry eats at you until you just want to die, lay all your troubles at Jesus' feet. First Peter 5:7 says it all.

Jury Duty

Matthew 7:1–5; Mark 4:24–25; Luke 6:37–42

> Twelve people have been selected to serve on the jury, and you are one of them. The man who stands accused of double murder claims he is innocent. You will decide his innocence or guilt. You will determine if he should spend his life behind bars or be free to walk away. You are the deciding vote.
>
> What if the judge in this case told you to be very careful how you decide because whatever method or standard of judgment that you use to convict this man, that same method and standard would be used against you?
>
> For instance, if you thought the man was guilty because of his color, you would stand trial for being your color. If you assumed the man was guilty because of the look on his face or a remark he made in the courtroom, then you, too, would be judged based on your facial expressions and careless remarks. And if you only convicted the man because it was proven to you beyond a reasonable doubt, then you would only be judged for what you did.

Be really careful how you judge other people, because every standard and method that you use to judge someone else will one day be used against you—on Judgment Day.

Are you prejudiced? Do you judge people quickly and easily in your mind? Think about it. Does someone's color affect the way you think that person will treat you or the way you treat them? Does the clothing someone is wearing affect whether or not you would be willing to be seen with them? Do you avoid people who don't fit your idea of what a normal person is?

On a scale of 1–10, with 10 being the worst, how prejudiced do you consider yourself?

_____

Are you satisfied with that rating? _____ What particular issue do you find yourself most prejudiced about (color, clothes, etc.)? _____

What can you do to change this attitude? _____

If you write people off because of a bad standard of judgment, look out. One day God will have a chance to judge you. And He will judge you based on the same mercy that you showed to other people. If you are willing to give others the benefit of the doubt, God will do the same for you. But if you have a habit of ignoring or mistreating people whom you are prejudiced against, don't expect God to ignore your prejudice. He will, out of love to teach you a lesson, treat you the same way you have been treating others. Stop right now and ask God to eliminate all prejudices from your heart. Read Psalm 139:23–24.

Pigs and Pearls

Matthew 7:6

Derrick's family told him he could go out for pizza on his birthday. He misunderstood, though. As the family stepped outside to get in the car, Derrick took off running with his hands held up high and looking over his shoulder. "Throw it. Throw it!" he yelled. Derrick was going out for pizza.

Victoria was driving home from college one weekend. As she passed a new gas station on the side of the road she glanced up at the sign, "Grand Opening. Clean Restrooms." With a sigh, Victoria pulled over and got out of the car. She went into the gas station bathroom, got down on her hands and knees, and began scrubbing. It took her over an hour, but she managed to clean those restrooms.

Eric returned to school after the summer. It was the first day, and he wasn't in the school mood yet. His teacher assigned everyone to write a two-page paper that night entitled, "How to Be Lazy over the Summer." Eric moaned about the assignment, but he went home and wrote his paper. A few days later, after the papers were graded, Eric's teacher asked him to stay after class. Apparently Eric had written his two-page paper with only one word on each page, right in the middle. On the first page he wrote, "LIKE." On the second page he wrote, "THIS." His teacher was not amused.

Some people just don't get it. They hear or see something, and they misunderstand it so completely that they end up doing something crazy.

Jesus said not to throw pearls to pigs. Well, of course not. Pigs don't understand pearls. All they would end up doing is stomping on them and maybe coming after you for giving them pearls instead of food. So, what in the world does this mean? Well, don't be like Derrick, Victoria, and Eric. Don't go throwing your mom's pearl necklace at your neighbor's pigs.

The point here is to not take something holy and give it to someone who doesn't understand what it's for. You don't give your church's money to an immoral business. You don't open up a restaurant where you serve Communion (the Lord's Supper). And you don't take your body, the place where Jesus lives, some place that it shouldn't be.

Have you ever been in a situation that you knew you shouldn't be in? _____

Where was this? _____

Why shouldn't you have been there? _____

Pearls don't look good in the mud. You don't make your faith in God look good when you place yourself in situations you know you shouldn't be in. Ask God to help you make the right decisions when you have a choice about what to do and where to go—this may include friends you choose to be with, what parties and places you choose to go to on the weekends, and the person you want to date.

All You Have to Do Is Ask

Matthew 7:7–11; Luke 11:9–13

Rick was a roadie for a popular Christian rock band. He volunteered to tour with the group, to help them set up for concerts, and do whatever else he could. Music was Rick's life, and he wanted to be around people who used music to minister to other people for the Lord.

One day, the lead singer left the band. The group began praying for their next lead singer. They held auditions and began looking for the right person for the job. Rick, who had a good voice, was churning inside. He wanted to try out, but he was afraid everybody else would just laugh. After all, Rick was just a roadie.

Finally, Rick got up the nerve and went to the group. "Guys, I want to try out. I don't want any special treatment, but please just let me sing. Listen and see what you think."

Rick did sing, and the group was so overwhelmed that they hired him on the spot. Now, the band Whiteheart continues to tour the country proclaiming the good news of Jesus, and Rick is their spokesman.

Sometimes all you have to do to get something is get up the nerve to ask. If you don't ask, you won't have a chance.

Jesus is giving you an open invitation to ask. Whatever it is, whatever you need, whatever you want to go away—ask God. He is there to listen and to give.

Do you really believe that God will listen to you and give you what you ask for? Sit down, grab a pencil, and make a list of some things you really need right now.

_____

_____

_____

_____

_____

_____

Now, this is your prayer list. Take this list right now to God and honestly explain to Him your needs. He already knows what you need, but He wants you to trust Him enough to ask. Keep asking (that's what the verses say) until you receive your answer. God can't answer until you ask.

Do What You Want

Matthew 7:12; Luke 6:31

Gary rounded the corner, late again for his third period class. He was staring at the floor as he ran, thinking about the homework he forgot to do and the girl he wanted to see. Then, suddenly, it happened.

BOOOOOM! The next thing Gary knew he was sprawled out on the floor with his papers everywhere. He looked up and saw Vance in basically the same position, and he didn't look very happy. Vance, captain of the wrestling team, got up and began walking toward Gary very angrily. Gary slithered his way to the wall and sat up. Just then, Principal Stevens walked by. "You two boys get to class!" he commanded without waiting for an explanation. Both boys slowly walked to their respective classes, in opposite directions, thank goodness.

All afternoon Gary worried himself sick over what Vance would do to him. Gary wanted Vance to forget about it, but he was afraid that just wasn't going to happen. He managed to make it through the day without seeing Vance at all. He went home and plopped down on the couch, thankful to be alive.

Just then the doorbell rang. Without thinking, Gary opened the door. There stood Vance and two of his wrestling buddies. Vance said, "Gary, I have something I want to give you." Gary took a step back, his eyes as big as saucers. "Here," said Vance, handing him two tickets to a wrestling match. "I felt real bad about running into you and thought this would help make it up. Bring your girlfriend and enjoy tonight's match."

All day Gary just knew Vance was going to kill him. What Gary expected was trouble. What he got was totally unexpected. That is what the Golden Rule (today's passage) is all about—doing to others the unexpected—doing to them as you would have them do to you. Most people want good things to be brought to them on a silver platter. The Golden Rule, though, gives those good things to others.

Think about all the things you want other people to do for you. You want people to care for you and respect you for who you are. You want them to like you and go out of their way to call you by name and invite you to spend time with them. You want someone to make you feel accepted. Do the same for that person across the cafeteria table from you today. Do the same for your third period teacher who wonders if you really pay attention. Do the same for your parents.

It takes guts to live the Golden Rule. It takes courage to treat people the way you want to be treated. Do you agree with that? _____

Why is it more courageous to live by the Golden Rule than not to? _____

_____

Can you think of a time recently when you lived the Golden Rule? _____

Pray that God will give you the courage and wisdom it takes to really live the Golden Rule. Memorize it. Practice it. Live it.

Weekly Bible Study and Prayer Review

Bible Study

Look back through some of the Scriptures you read this week. Write down the one verse or passage that God used to speak to you.

_____

_____

_____

_____

Memorize this verse or passage. You can do it if you spend just
a few minutes saying it to yourself.

Now, think of at least one situation you will probably face soon in which you could use this Scripture to help you make the right decision. Write down that situation below.

_____

Quote the Scripture when you face this situation, and live by it.

Prayer Time

Take a few moments to praise God for who He is.
Now take a few moments to thank God for things He has done for you.
Now ask God to make you into the person He wants you to be.
Ask God to use you to help others become closer to God.

Below is your prayer list for the week. Keep it updated each week. If your prayer isn't answered this week, carry it over to next week's list.

Request	Date of Original Request	Date Answered
_____	__/__/__	__/__/__
_____	__/__/__	__/__/__
_____	__/__/__	__/__/__
_____	__/__/__	__/__/__
_____	__/__/__	__/__/__
_____	__/__/__	__/__/__
_____	__/__/__	__/__/__
_____	__/__/__	__/__/__
_____	__/__/__	__/__/__

Pray for the things on your list and trust God to provide.
Forgive anyone you have not yet forgiven.
Ask God to forgive you for any unconfessed sin in your life.
Ask God to keep you out of trouble with sin.
Acknowledge that God is in complete control of your life
and will take care of everything.

Where Do You Draw the Line?

Matthew 7:13–14; Luke 13:23–24

Where do you draw the line? Imagine for a moment that there is a line running down the middle of your neighborhood. Which side of the line you live on depends on where you stand on certain issues. For instance, let's say your house is on the Agree side of the neighborhood, and other houses are on the Disagree side. Now, would you live in your own house or move somewhere else if the issue was . . .

Abortion		*Euthanasia*
Homosexuality		*Evolution*
Your chores	*Your curfew*	*Your allowance*

Notice that where you live now is on the Agree side. Would you actually move to show your position on these issues? Or would you just stay put and say, "It doesn't really matter. I'll just keep quiet and go about my business."

Most people view life like a neighborhood with a line that divides people based on their opinions. You can live wherever you want to, but it will always be on one side of the line or the other. People will treat you differently based on where you live with respect to the line.

But what if all this time the line itself was drawn in the wrong place?

Jesus has drawn the line for your life. It stretches as far as the eye can see. It's very straight and very narrow. Only, instead of demanding that you stand on one side or the other, He simply asks that you walk *on* the line. The line is the path of life, and He is the leader. If you choose to follow Him, you will always know where you stand on every issue—you stand with Jesus.

Following Jesus on this path is not easy. Quite often it becomes steep and dark and even scary. From time to time there are forks in the road, and Jesus takes the more difficult fork. You are left to make the decision to follow Him or take the more "interesting" road. The other road is often much wider with a lot more people and what seems to be a lot more fun going on. But the point is not what the road you're on is like—it's where the road is going.

Do you ever find it difficult to keep following Jesus? _____ Why? What is it that makes you want to turn back or take a different path? _____

You've probably been down other paths before. Is it worth it? _____

Why or why not? _____

Following Jesus can sometimes get difficult. The temptation to just quit and give up is sometimes very great. Take a few moments to evaluate where you draw the line. Is it along the path of Jesus or is it down some other road? Pray that God will give you the power from His Spirit that you need to continue following Him in spite of the other roads that often come your way. Ask Him to help you make the right choice.

Rotten Fruit

Matthew 7:15–20; Luke 6:43–45

> *"The Lord Jeeeezus is waiting for you to trust in Heeim. When you have a neeeed, plant a seeeeeeed! You jist got ta tell Satan that he's gonna have ta give it up, cuz Jeeeeezus is gonna give you evre thang you neeeed. All you got to do is sit down right now and write out a check for $100, or $500, or $1000. If the money's not in that bank right now, git yer credit card and sind us money thataway. When you sind me your money, you're tellin' Jeeeeezus that you luv Heeim.*
>
> *"Those phonz have got ta start a' ringin'. I don't hear 'em. Have you called in yer pledge yit? Have you given your money to tha Lord? If you call right now, I'll send you one of theez here pitchers of me. You kin put that thar pitcher in a frame on yer fireplace and all your sicknesses'll be healed and go sailin' out cher house through the chimnee! Call now! Give to Jeeeeeezus."*

How many times have you heard someone like this on the radio, the television, or maybe in real life? It's all too common. Somebody who claims to be a Christian is leading people astray for his or her own selfish gain.

Jesus said there is a simple test to determine the true prophets from the false prophets: their fruit. Some TV preachers have recently been shown to have collected money and thrown away prayer requests. Some claim to be poor and in need when they own houses and cars. Some say they preach Jesus when they purchase prostitutes in private. What do you think? Sounds like a bunch of rotten fruit.

True believers don't produce bad fruit. They produce good fruit—like kindness and love and gentleness and mercy and joy and stuff like that. They are quietly living out what they say they believe. They are changing people's lives. Are you producing good fruit that lines up with what you believe, or is your fruit rotting because you don't practice what you preach? Now is the time to check your branches and see what kind of fruit is growing.

Now, the inevitable question. What kind of fruit do you produce? Is it fresh and ready for someone to eat, or do you find it rather mushy and smelly?

_____

What kind of life would you have to live for other people to see good fruit? List some specific things you would do. _____

_____

Ask the Lord to help you produce the right kind of fruit. Do those things that you listed above and prove to people through your actions that you are a follower of Jesus. For further study, read Galatians 5:22–23.

Have We Met?

Matthew 7:21–23; Luke 6:46, 13:25–27

Cheryl really admired the President of the United States. She knew his full name, where he lived, what his policies were for foreign and domestic issues, and what his favorite food was. She often dreamed of meeting him. She mailed him a letter once a week, hoping for a response, but one never came.

Finally, when she graduated from high school, she packed her bags and told her mom and dad that she would be back in a few days—that she had to go see a very important person. She got on a bus and rode all the way to Washington D.C.

When she arrived, she got off the bus at the White House and walked up to the front gate. There a fence and a posted guard prevented her from going any further. She walked straight up to the guard and announced, "I'm here to see the President." The guard didn't even acknowledge her statement. She persisted, "You don't understand. I've watched him on TV for several years. I've read all about him in magazines and books. I even know his full name and why his mother named him. You've just got to let me in."

"Ma'am," the guard responded. "You say that you know the President. But the real question is, does he know you? Have you ever met him?" The question caught Cheryl off guard. She backed up, sat down on her bags, and stared at the pavement.

"No, he doesn't know me," she muttered.

"Then I'm sorry, Miss. I cannot disturb the President if he does not know or is not expecting you."

You probably know the President's name. You probably know where he stands on certain issues and whether or not you would vote for him. If you walked into a room and the President were there, you could probably identify him immediately. There's no question, you know who the President is.

But if the President walked into your house, would he have any clue who you are? In most cases, probably not. Why? Because you've never met him before. Just because you know who he is doesn't mean he knows who you are.

It may surprise you, but the same rules apply to you and God. Oh, sure, He knows who you are because He created you. But does He *know* you—*know* means you've met before because you asked Him into your heart. There are a lot of churchgoing people who know a lot about God, but they've never met Him because they've never taken the time to ask Him to be their Lord.

Have you ever asked Jesus to be your Lord? _____ *When?* _____

How did your life change after that? _____

If you've never asked Jesus into your life, pause right now to do so. He wants to know you in this life. If you have asked Jesus into your life, thank Him for His love for you and spend a few moments imagining what it will be like the day you get to go to heaven for the rest of eternity.

Home, Sweet Home

Matthew 7:24–27; Luke 6:47–49

In the beautiful California neighborhood of Malibu, luxurious homes are prominent. Huge, beautiful homes pepper the hillsides overlooking the spacious landscape below. Celebrities, wealthy businesspeople, and others took great pains in designing and building their showplaces.

In the early 1990s, a forest fire, blazing out of control, swept through Malibu, destroying every home in one hillside neighborhood. A few weeks later, torrential rains, too late to douse the fires, caused treacherous mudslides, eroding the scorched earth and sweeping away the remnants of the burned-out homes.

In this entire section of Malibu, only one home remained standing—surviving the fires, the rains, and the mudslides. It was not the most beautiful home, nor the home of the most famous person. It was a home made completely of solid concrete with deep foundational supports into the hillside. It did not burn or fall because it was built out of rock and into the rock.

In today's Bible passage, two men built two houses with different architectural schemes. One saved a lot of money by skipping the expensive foundation and starting with the good part. Another spent much more money making sure the house was built on a firm foundation. Like the home in Malibu, only the home supported by the rock could withstand the storms.

Imagine that house is your life. The storms are like the bad things that happen to you. The foundation represents what you depend on every day during good times and bad. If you have chosen to build your life on the firm foundation of Jesus, then when things beyond your control try to blow you down, you will survive because you are on the rock. If you do not depend on Jesus, then when things beyond your control blow up in your face, you will fall with a great crash.

What do you turn to when times get rough for you? Your choices might include music, money, TV, video games, or friends. Some choose drugs and alcohol to run away from their problems.

The storms of life are going to come. They may not be fires, rains, and mudslides, but they will seem just as bad to you when they happen. Your parent(s) and you may not get along. Someone you know may get sick or hurt or even die. You might feel rejected by other people your age. Someday you may get so depressed that you feel like ending your own life. All of these storms test what you're made of and what your life is built on.

Are you facing a rough time in your life right now? _____

What is it? _____

Try depending on God for this problem. Go to Him right now in prayer and ask Him to take care of that problem. Then ask Him to help you depend on Him when the next storm comes. He will always be there for you.

You Know What They Say

Matthew 7:28–29

> They say that you can cure hiccups by eating a tablespoon full of sugar.
> They say there is a pot of gold at the end of the rainbow.
> They say if you have a dream in which you die, you will die in reality from the stress.
> They say that eating an apple a day will keep the doctor away.
> They say it is impossible to sneeze with your eyes open.
> They say it is absolutely impossible to travel at the speed of light.
> They say if you cross your eyes too much they may get stuck that way.
> They say that a bird in your hand is worth two in the bush.
> They say you should never look a gift horse in the mouth.
> They say if you imagine something you want long enough and hard enough then it will become yours.
> They say that practice makes perfect.

OK, wait a minute. Time out. Excuse me, but who are *they?* People are always talking about this invisible group of wise people who seem to have an answer for everything. Some of those things up there sound true; some sound a little iffy; some sound downright crazy. How are you supposed to know what is true and what isn't anymore?

In Jesus' day, when the religious *they* taught about the Bible, they would always say, "Well, Rabbi so-and-so says it means this, and Teacher what's-his-name says that, and . . ." No one ever came along and just said, "Here's what's true and what's not." That is, not until Jesus.

Jesus had just finished the famous Sermon on the Mount. He had been explaining to people how to live from the Old Testament. Only Jesus didn't say what someone else thought. He basically said, "Here's what it means—and let Me add some to it. After all, I am the author." The people who heard Him were amazed.

Jesus wants to help you with your decisions about right and wrong. How? Two ways. First, He left you an example to follow. He lived the perfect life. So, if you imitate His life, you will be certain to be on the right track. Second, He left us a love letter, called the Bible, to show us the way.

Sometimes it is difficult to know right from wrong. When you are faced with a decision about right and wrong, how do you choose? _____

How do they (other people) say you should decide what is right and what is wrong?

_____

Ask God this week to help you turn to Him whenever you face a decision between right and wrong. Ask yourself what Jesus would do and what the Bible says. Then do it.

Reach Out and Touch

Matthew 8:1–4; Mark 1:40–45; Luke 5:12–16

Susan had AIDS. She had all the classic symptoms of someone with only a few months left to live. She was frail and weak, with purple lesions on her face. Her neighbors in the apartment complex could tell she had AIDS, so they avoided her like the plague. They quietly whispered about her punishment for being homosexual and it serving her right for choosing that lifestyle.

The only problem was, Susan got the HIV virus from a blood transfusion back in 1984, before anything was really known about AIDS. Nevertheless, she was an outcast. She had no family, and her few friends had left her long ago when she was first diagnosed. Susan sat curled up on her couch as tears streamed down her face. She could not remember the last time someone had looked at her and smiled. She could not remember the last time someone touched her. People were so afraid of her that she was entombed in a living grave. All she wanted was for someone to hug her and tell her everything was OK.

It's happened throughout the centuries. Someone gets a weird disease that might be contagious, and people avoid that person at all costs. Leprosy was that disease in the first century. If you had it, you had to live outside the city on your own or with other lepers. And if you dared approach the city, you had to yell, "Unclean!" as you approached so everyone could flee in disgust.

Notice what Jesus did when the leper approached Him. He did not recoil in terror. He did not chastise the man for coming close. Instead, He had compassion and reached out His hand and touched the man—touched him! Imagine what that must have felt like! Years had passed since someone had cared enough to forget the social stigma and the possibility of catching the disease and simply touch him.

There are people around you who are hurting. They have been ostracized from your peer group for one reason or the other. They are looked down upon, and no one wants to be near them. Can you imagine how they feel? Do as Jesus would do this week, and when you see one of those people, touch his or her life. If you happen to feel like you are an outcast yourself, then go immediately to the Lord. He will have compassion on you and touch your life.

Have you noticed people in your school, your youth group, or around your neighborhood who people avoid for one reason or the other? _____

Can you name one person? _____

What about you? Have you ever felt like the person everyone is avoiding? _____

If you have felt like that, what could someone do to make things better? _____

_____

Ask God to help you touch a hurting life this week. Your kindness may help someone in a way you could not possibly begin to imagine.

Weekly Bible Study and Prayer Review

Bible Study

Look back through some of the Scriptures you read this week. Write down the one verse or passage that God used to speak to you.

_____

_____

_____

_____

Memorize this verse or passage. You can do it if you spend just a few minutes saying it to yourself.

Now, think of at least one situation you will probably face soon in which you could use this Scripture to help you make the right decision. Write down that situation below.

_____

Quote the Scripture when you face this situation, and live by it.

Prayer Time

Take a few moments to praise God for who He is.
Now take a few moments to thank God for things He has done for you.
Now ask God to make you into the person He wants you to be.
Ask God to use you to help others become closer to God.

Below is your prayer list for the week. Keep it updated each week. If your prayer isn't answered this week, carry it over to next week's list.

Request	Date of Original Request	Date Answered
_____	__/__/__	__/__/__
_____	__/__/__	__/__/__
_____	__/__/__	__/__/__
_____	__/__/__	__/__/__
_____	__/__/__	__/__/__
_____	__/__/__	__/__/__
_____	__/__/__	__/__/__
_____	__/__/__	__/__/__
_____	__/__/__	__/__/__

Pray for the things on your list and trust God to provide.
Forgive anyone you have not yet forgiven.
Ask God to forgive you for any unconfessed sin in your life.
Ask God to keep you out of trouble with sin.
Acknowledge that God is in complete control of your life and will take care of everything.

Just Say the Word

Matthew 8:5–13; Luke 7:1–10; John 4:46–54

An elderly woman, tired with age, sits down on a folding chair. Across town, two business-women board a passenger jet bound for another state. Nearby in the airport terminal, a man hands his money to someone behind the fast-food counter.

Meanwhile, a sixteen-year-old with a new driver's license puts the key in the ignition and turns it. A young woman behind the wheel calmly goes through an intersection when the light turns green. A teenager grabs the remote and hits the power button. His sister turns on the computer to do her homework.

Amazingly, at the same time next door, a young man with the day off pulls the cord to start his lawn mower. His wife opens the refrigerator to find cold drinks for them both. Across the street, Mr. Gustaffson walks out front to get the mail. A young girl wobbles past on her new bicycle.

Can you think of what all of the above examples have in common? If you guessed that each of these instances required some degree of faith, then you are correct.

Every day you place your faith in a variety of things. You sit down in the chair with the faith that it will hold you up. You open the refrigerator and expect the drinks to be cold. You punch "Power" on the remote, confident that the TV will come to life.

A centurion—a commander of 100 soldiers—asked Jesus to heal his servant. When Jesus offered to come help, the centurion calmly requested that Jesus just say the word and the servant would be healed.

Jesus was amazed. Did you catch that? God was amazed that someone could have such great but simple faith. You have faith every day in ordinary things.

Faith is believing in what you cannot see. You can't see that the chair will hold you up, but you sit down anyway. You don't know that the refrigerator is cold inside, but you open it up expecting chilled drinks. Why can't we trust God as simply? Isn't He much more reliable than refrigerators and chairs and televisions and lawn mowers and computers? Trust God this week with your parent problems, pop quizzes, boyfriend/girlfriend troubles, emotional needs, and every other need you may have. Stun God by asking Him for help, believing wholeheartedly in Him.

Is your faith in God simple enough to trust in Him for your every need? _____

List the last three things you can remember asking God for.

_____ , _____ , _____

Ask God to help you have a faith like the Roman soldier. Take Jesus at His word and expect great things to happen.

The Funeral Is Over

Luke 7:11–17

All her hopes and dreams seemed to come true the day she said, "I do." She was happy. She just knew she would live happily ever after when she and her husband gave birth to a beautiful baby boy. It would be the only child she ever had. Still, life seemed complete to the woman, who grew to love both her husband and her son with all of her heart.

Then, tragedy struck. Her husband was killed in a tragic boating accident during a raging storm. The woman was crushed. Where was God in all of this? She retreated to herself in great sadness and despair. Only the presence of her son, who had become the man of the house, brought a smile to her face.

Unbelievably, her son was tragically killed in a similar accident a few years later. The woman was utterly devastated. She was too old to bear children, and she had no one to protect her in a society where widows were low-class citizens. She wept bitterly as the pallbearers carried her son toward the cemetery. Where was God? She prayed earnestly for a miracle to save her.

The woman in today's passage, who could have experienced circumstances similar to those described above, was hopeless. Her only son had died, and her husband was already dead. God was there, even if the widow thought He was not. Not only was He there, but He had compassion on her and raised her son from the dead and gave him back to her.

Jesus is concerned about you right where you are. Although bad things happen, they won't stay that way forever. At just the right time, when things seem to be at their very worst, Jesus will come and take away your grief. He will give you new hope. He will help you feel better again.

Have you ever experienced despair or tragedy? Briefly describe a recent experience.

_____

_____

How would you like God to comfort you in this difficult time? _____

_____

Call on God now and ask Him to rescue you from your plight. Wait for His timing and His comfort. He knows just what to do.

Out of Doubt

Matthew 11:1–6; Luke 7:18–23

He was the greatest man of God for all time. When he was a child in his mother's womb, he was filled with the Holy Spirit. When he was young, he left his parents to go live in the desert and prepare for his ministry. While living in the desert, he developed an appetite for locusts—finger-licking good. After the crunchy but juicy main course, he would have a golden desert dessert of wild honey. Then he would put on his animal skin clothes and go preach waist-deep in the muddy Jordan River while thousands of people came to hear his message and be baptized.

He even had the opportunity to baptize the Son of God and watch the Holy Spirit descend on Him in the form of a dove. John was really cooking. He couldn't wait to see what would happen next. Jesus even said he was the greatest man who ever lived.

John was summarily thrown into prison, isolated from friends and family, his ministry was stripped away, and through all of this came the most dreaded feeling of all—a feeling he had never known before in his life—doubt.

John the Baptist, the greatest prophet in the world according to Jesus, was in prison wondering whether or not Jesus was even the Messiah. He was plagued with doubt.

Did you know that it is OK to doubt? Did you know that you probably will doubt many times in your life as a Christian? You will want to ask questions. You may even doubt that Jesus is real or that He is the only way to heaven. You may doubt that He has called you to be a servant in His kingdom. It's OK.

Look at today's passage again. Do you see any place where Jesus condemned John the Baptist? No! As a matter of fact, Jesus said John was the greatest man who had ever lived. Quietly, though, Jesus sent word back to John in prison. "John, the blind see, the lame walk, the deaf hear, the dead live." He told John that God's work was going on and would continue. He gave John the message he needed to hear.

Have you ever faced doubt? Write down a recent bout with doubt and what you think caused it. _____

_____

Does it upset you when you doubt God? _____ *Why?* _____

When you doubt, feel free to approach God and explain your doubts openly. He will give you words of praise and comfort.

Get Real

Matthew 11:7–15; Luke 7:24–30

Alisha had never faced a decision like this in her life. Two guys were asking her out to the prom, and she had to choose one of them by tomorrow. She agonized over what to do but finally decided to make a list of pros and cons for each guy. She grabbed a pencil and a piece of notebook paper from her school binder and wrote . . .

Rodney		Troy	
Pro	Con	Pro	Con
Nice car	Stuck on himself	Really nice	Older car
Lots of money	Not a Christian	He's a Christian	Not much money
Good dancer	Sometimes fake	He's real	Average dancer
Very good-looking	Cheats a lot	Honest	Decent looking
Captain of football team	Tells dirty jokes	Sense of humor	Not popular

Alisha poured over her list for a few minutes, and then suddenly it became clear to her. All of Rodney's positives were external and all of his negatives were internal. Troy was just the opposite. All of his positives were inside—making up who he is. All of his negatives were external. Alisha called Troy to accept his invitation. Then she called Rodney and politely turned him down.

Sometimes—actually a lot of the time—we fall into the trap of going after what looks good instead of going after what really *is* good. We want the most money, the best-looking date, the hottest car, and the biggest house. But all of those things are external—they have no meaning in and of themselves.

John the Baptist wasn't much to look at, but the entire country went out to see and hear this man. Why? Because he spoke the truth. People are starving for the truth—for what is real.

The same is true for you and for the people around you. If you are a Christian—and your family and friends know that—they are watching you. And they don't care about all the external stuff. They want to see and know if you are living an honest life of conviction. They want to see you living your life like Jesus would live it. They want to know that you are real, or *authentic*.

Do you consider yourself an authentic person? _____

Why or why not? _____

What is one thing about you that you know is fake? _____

Decide now to get rid of those things in your life that aren't authentic. Ask God to forgive you, and begin to live your life as the person God created you to be. Let people around you see the real you, not the you that you want them to see. When you're authentic, Jesus will shine through, and people will want to know what makes you so real.

Excuses, Excuses

Matthew 11:16–19; Luke 7:31–35

> *"But, officer, I didn't see the red light. Honest."*
> *"I was going to take out the trash right after my show was over, but then the phone rang and . . ."*
> *"Yes, Mrs. Thompson, I know it's due today. But my dog really did eat my report."*
> *"Sorry I'm late. My alarm clock didn't go off this morning."*
> *"I would love to go out with you Saturday, but my long lost sister is coming into town that morning."*
> *"Mom, I didn't practice piano today because I hurt my hand washing dishes."*
> *"I was going to call you back, but my dad was using the phone all night."*
> *"God, I was going to have my quiet time today. Honest. But I was real busy and . . ."*
> *"Lord, I know that person needs help, but I've got my own problems, you know?"*
> *"I know I ought to get up and go to church in the morning, but I was out real late. I need to rest."*
> *"This is the last time, I promise. Then I'll kick this bad habit once and for all."*

Excuses, excuses. They can get you out of one jam after the other. The only problem is, they're mostly half-truths. Police officers, parents, teachers, and God have probably heard them all. And you know why? These are the authority figures in our lives—they are the ones who tell us what to do. There is something about being told what to do that gets all of us a bit uptight.

So, instead of listening to the authority figures in our lives, from time to time we try to explain why we should be exempt from doing what we are told because there were "special circumstances."

In today's passage, Jesus explained to the people of His day that they were no different. John the Baptist came and told people to repent and turn to God, and many said, "But John is crazy. He's demon-possessed. He doesn't eat right, and he dresses funny. And he's out there in the desert away from everybody. Who could take him seriously?" Then Jesus, who was very different in style, came with the same message. Then people said, "He eats too much, and He hangs around with all sorts of sinful and weird people. He doesn't fit our picture of a Messiah."

Do you ever make excuses to God about why you don't do something that you should?

_____

Write down your most classic excuse. _____

In all honesty, is that a valid excuse? _____

Then what do you intend to do about it? _____

Ask God to help you start doing the things that you have learned about in His Word. Then, the next time you feel an excuse coming on, do the opposite—do what you know you should so you won't have to make any more excuses.

Opportunity Knocks

Matthew 11:20–24

> *Once upon a time a rich man died. He left no will, so the state planned to auction off the items in his home. People came from many miles to the auction because the man was very rich and had many luxurious things. As the auction was about to begin, the room was filled with excited whispers about the value and beauty of the man's things.*
>
> *Soon the auctioneer stepped to the front and began the bidding. The first item up for sale was a picture of the rich man's only son. The picture was not very striking—the son was born with a disease that caused him to die at a very young age. Nevertheless, the auctioneer started the bidding. "What will you pay for this picture of the dead man's one and only son?"*
>
> *No one in the room raised a hand or said a word. No one cared to have an ugly picture of a person they didn't even know or care about. They wanted to hurry up and move to the better things. Just when the auctioneer thought he would have to give up on the picture, an old woman in the back raised her hand, bidding a very modest amount. Since no one else even placed a bid, the picture was hers.*
>
> *The woman returned to her seat, admiring the picture. She happened to notice a bulge under the paper in the back of the frame. She carefully made a slit in the paper and pulled out a long document. It was the rich man's missing will! In the will, the man emphatically stated that whoever bought the picture of his son was worthy to receive his entire estate. The old woman, who years before had been a nurse to the dying boy, inherited the man's entire estate simply because she loved his son.[7]*

Opportunity knocked once, and everyone had a chance to bid. Only one woman responded.

Jesus explained that opportunity might knock only once for the crowds around Him as well. Jesus had been to the cities of Bethsaida, Capernaum, and Korazin and performed many miracles and proclaimed the good news about God. But these cities refused to believe the truth—they rejected God's Son. Now Jesus explained that on the Day of Judgment, it will be more bearable for the cities that repented than it will be for those who did not.

God will often move in your heart so that you will do something He wants you to do. But, perhaps just as often, you find reasons not to take hold of the opportunity. Maybe you refused to witness to a friend, or to do what your parents told you, or to get up this morning for quiet time. Don't refuse God when He prompts you. The more you ignore God, the easier it gets. Today may be your last chance to have a quiet time, witness, obey your parents, or just live an honest life.

Have you ever felt God prompting you to do something, and you ignored it because you were afraid or you just didn't feel like it? _____ What did He want you to do? _____

What do you plan to do the next time God prompts you to do something? _____

Pray that God will help you listen and obey His will for you. Then, when you hear His voice, don't delay. See Revelation 3:20 for further study.

Weekly Bible Study and Prayer Review

Bible Study

Look back through some of the Scriptures you read this week. Write down the one verse or passage that God used to speak to you.

_____

_____

_____

_____

Memorize this verse or passage. You can do it if you spend just
a few minutes saying it to yourself.

Now, think of at least one situation you will probably face soon in which you could use this Scripture to help you make the right decision. Write down that situation below.

_____

Quote the Scripture when you face this situation, and live by it.

Prayer Time

Take a few moments to praise God for who He is.
Now take a few moments to thank God for things He has done for you.
Now ask God to make you into the person He wants you to be.
Ask God to use you to help others become closer to God.

Below is your prayer list for the week. Keep it updated each week. If your prayer isn't answered this week, carry it over to next week's list.

Request	Date of Original Request	Date Answered
_____	__/__/__	__/__/__
_____	__/__/__	__/__/__
_____	__/__/__	__/__/__
_____	__/__/__	__/__/__
_____	__/__/__	__/__/__
_____	__/__/__	__/__/__
_____	__/__/__	__/__/__
_____	__/__/__	__/__/__

Pray for the things on your list and trust God to provide.
Forgive anyone you have not yet forgiven.
Ask God to forgive you for any unconfessed sin in your life.
Ask God to keep you out of trouble with sin.
Acknowledge that God is in complete control of your life
and will take care of everything.

Easy Does It

Matthew 11:25–26

Mr. Vickson, an electrical engineer for a national company, sat droopy-eyed in front of his home computer, weary from trying to install his new Internet software. Every time he tried to log on, he just got noise from his phone and a blank screen. He was losing his patience fast.

"What are you doing, Dad?" thirteen-year-old Jimmy Vickson asked his father as he strolled into the room with his roller blades on.

"No blades in the house, son," said Dad. "I'm stuck here trying to get logged on to the Internet. I think the software is messed up. I probably ought to take it back."

"Wait, let me see." Jimmy stood over his father's shoulder and grabbed the mouse. His father's head spun just trying to keep up with what Jimmy was doing. "There, that should do it," Jimmy said with a final click.

Like magic, the screen came alive, and Mr. Vickson was suddenly surfing the World Wide Web. "How do you know all this, son?" asked Mr. Vickson incredulously.

"It's a piece of cake. Anybody could do it. You're just too smart to see how easy it really is."

"Too smart to see how easy it really is." Lots of people have that problem when it comes to things like computers, video games, and other stuff.

Lots of people in Jesus' day had the same problem. They analyzed Jesus from every conceivable angle: where He was from, what He looked like, whom He hung around, what kind of miracles He performed, what He said, etc. Yet the really "smart" people refused to accept Jesus because they couldn't figure Him out. They were so smart that they couldn't see how easy Jesus' message really was.

But the "unwise" people—like unschooled fishermen, prostitutes, lepers, poor people, and little children—all believed Jesus and His message with great ease. Why? Because they didn't analyze it to pieces. They took Him for what He was: the Son of God, a friend to sinners and people with problems. They took His message for what it was: "If you believe in Me, then you have eternal life."

Sometimes you may feel that the Christian life is complicated—all these "rules." Do this, don't do that, and *never* do that. But you don't have to walk a tightrope of rules all your life. All you have to do is walk with Jesus. Practice His presence by talking with Him wherever you go, talking about Him with everyone you know, and depending on Him to take care of your every need.

Look at it this way. If you really want to get to know a person, reading books about her or listening to others talk about her is great. But how much more can you get to know someone by actually spending time with her? _____ Would it make a difference? _____

Why? _____

Read your Bible and pray. Then live what you read and spend time with the Author. Ask God to help you practice His presence every single second today. The difference may surprise you.

The Yoke's on You

Matthew 11:27–30

Dina was about to explode. She thought she would die if one more problem crept up. Her mother was diagnosed with cancer only two weeks earlier, leaving Dina as the oldest child in the house. She had to pick up major chores while her mother suffered the awful chemotherapy. Dina's mom depended on Dina emotionally, and Dina didn't dare ever seem down. She always seemed cheerful and pleasant in an attempt to cheer up Mom.

Whenever night fell and the time came to finally plop into bed, Dina would cry herself to sleep. She was drained emotionally, physically, and intellectually. She couldn't balance school, youth group, homework, Mom, sister, Dad, chores. Aaaaaahhh! It was too much for a young teenager to handle.

Dina's life went from pleasantly peaceful to unbearable over the next few weeks. Her burdens were just too heavy to carry anymore. She didn't know where to turn.

Have you ever been overwhelmed with problems? Have your burdens ever been so great that you just had to drop all of them for awhile?

Did you catch what Jesus said? Everyone with heavy burdens is invited to come to Him for rest and peace. He knows life gets tough, but He promises to take your burdens and give you lighter ones that are much easier to bear.

A lot of Christians who begin to carry burdens think God would be upset with them if they took their problems to Him. Some people have the attitude that you have to get your life straight before you can go to Jesus. Jesus said to come to Him, burdens and all, and just lay them at His feet.

God knows and cares about the burdens you carry and the problems you face. Remember that Jesus openly invites you to come and lay all your burdens on Him. He will take care of them—every one of them. Below, write down some burdens you need to give over to Jesus. Lay them at His feet and just walk away. Trust Him to take care of them.

_____

_____

_____

_____

_____

_____

_____

_____

_____

Everything Is Gone

Luke 7:36–50

Gretchen's mom died when she was four, and her father left when she was six. Gretchen, or "G" as her friends called her, was left to survive in the streets downtown.

She made friends with several rough characters; and by the time she was twelve years old, "G" became a prostitute. She sold her body to men in order to have enough food to eat. She hated every minute of it, but she didn't know what else to do. Periodically, "G" would be walking home from her "job" and would pass the home of a prominent religious leader. He would notice her from his doorway as he came out in the morning and begin harassing her. He condemned her for her sins, told her she was going to hell, and told her to stop walking by his house because God might strike her with lightning and catch his house on fire.

One day, "G" heard that a visitor was at the religious man's house. She had heard about him and just had to meet him. So, while the visitor was having lunch with the religious man, she came right through the front door without even knocking and . . .

While "G" has had her past and name made up to help with the story, she may not be too different from the woman in this passage. Do you see the difference in the way the Pharisee (religious man) and Jesus thought about her? How did each man treat her?

Pharisee: _____

Jesus: _____

Jesus said that the prostitute was forgiven of all her sins. The religious man just couldn't stomach that. He got mad. Why do you think he got mad? _____

_____

Jesus forgives. There is nothing that you have ever done or said that He can't forgive. The only thing you have to do is be genuinely sorry for your sins, ask for forgiveness, and turn away from those sins completely. The woman in the passage offered Jesus all she had, weeping for her sin. Jesus had great compassion on her. He did not condemn her as the religious man did—He forgave her.

Make a list on another sheet of paper (this is important) of all of the sins you can think of that need to be forgiven. Look it over. Realize the depth of your sin. Then ask for forgiveness for each sin and throw away the paper. When you genuinely asked for forgiveness, your sins went into the same place as that paper—the trash can. They are gone forever.

Need Some Cash?

Luke 8:1–3

Brook really wanted to go to ZYU, but it was a private school, and she knew her parents couldn't afford it. Her grades were great—she was in the top percent of her class—and her SAT scores would allow her acceptance into any major university in the country. In spite of her good grades, though, she didn't seem to have much of a chance at an academic scholarship. She played basketball as well and was very good. But an athletic scholarship didn't seem very likely either.

Brook began racking her brain. "What can I do to get enough money to go to ZYU?" She really felt like God wanted her to go to this university, but she thought maybe the lack of money was God's way of closing the door. Several days passed, and Brook began to be depressed when nothing turned up—no scholarships, no grants. That left taking out a loan that would take a lifetime to pay back, or going to another university.

Then, when Brook was at her lowest point, she fell down on her knees before God and begged for His help. "God, please, if it is Your will, grant me the money I need to go to ZYU."

God smiled. He thought, Finally, she chose to come to Me. Immediately He set the plans in motion for Brook's funds to be provided.

In this case, God always wanted Brook to go to her favorite college, but He deliberately withheld the money from her sight so she would trust in Him to provide.

Did you ever wonder how Jesus afforded to wander the countryside, preaching the good news? We never hear of Him earning money after He left home. How did He and twelve disciples make it? They had to eat and find places to stay.

The answer is in today's passage. It wasn't just Jesus and the disciples traveling around—there were several women, some of them apparently wealthy, who chose to give some of their money to Jesus to take care of His needs. Jesus trusted His Father to provide the money He needed.

If God wants you to do something, He will provide the money you need to do it. The Father wanted His Son to preach and travel, so He brought some women who would help. God never asks you to do something without providing everything you need to do it.

Are you struggling with a financial need right now? _____

Have you asked for God's help? _____ *If not, write down a very specific prayer about what you need and why you need it.* _____

_____

If this need is part of God's will for your life, then you have no worries. He will take care of you. And if you don't have any financial needs right now, just wait. You will. Always ask God for help *first*. For further study, read Proverbs 3:5–6.

A New Do

Matthew 12:22–37; Mark 3:20–30

"Oh, so you're a Christian?" Matt asked curiously. "So what do you do?"

Julia squirmed in her seat. She hadn't realized Matt would be so interested in her faith. "Well, I go to church several times a week, and I—"

"No, that's not what I mean," Matt pressed. "I assumed you went to church. Tell me what you do. What does a Christian do differently from everybody else?"

"I pray and read my Bible. I walk with God, I guess you could say," replied Julia.

"OK, we're still not getting anywhere," commented Matt. "Besides church and prayer and Bible reading, how do you live? What things do you do in normal life that make you different from me?"

Julia bit her bottom lip and thought for a moment. "I don't drink or do drugs or lie or cheat. And I don't—"

"Julia, now you're telling me what you don't do. Can't you think of anything that you do?"

Julia picked up her books and left the library table. "No, actually I can't right now. Let me get back to you, OK?" Julia walked away, trying to figure out just what a Christian really does.

Thousands of Christians in this country think the extent of being a Christian is going to church, reading your Bible, praying to God, and staying away from certain evils. But they never stop to think that Jesus spent most of His life *doing* things to help people.

In today's passage, Jesus was taking evil spirits out of people. What He did made some people so angry that the teachers of the law (religious people who read the Scriptures all the time) accused Jesus of being possessed Himself. Then Jesus said something amazing: "If you are not with Me, you are against Me. And if you aren't gathering with Me, you're scattering." In other words, "Hey, you Bible readers. Reading your Bible doesn't mean anything if you don't *do* what's written inside."

Can you think of things you do *as a Christian? Make a list of several things.* _____

_____

Was making that list difficult? _____ *Why or why not?* _____

Going to church, reading your Bible, and praying to God are things you must and will do if you are a Christian. But the reason you do these things is to become more like Jesus. Jesus spent His time telling other people about God, helping people who were in trouble, and giving His life away so other people could know God. Does this describe you? _____

Ask God to help you start living your Christian life. Start doing the things you hear about on Sundays, and take them with you to your school campus, your room, and the hallways where you talk to your friends. Be a doer of the Word. For further study, see James 1:22–25.

Prove It

Matthew 12:38–42

The rain just wouldn't stop. The floodwaters were rising so fast that city officials were evacuating local residents. One man, a Christian, refused to leave. He said God would rescue him.

While the man prayed for a miracle, the flood waters rose to the second story of his home. From upstairs he prayed. A boat came by and offered to rescue him. "No, thanks. God will rescue me." Then the waters rose to the roof of his home. From the top of his house he prayed. Another boat came by and offered to take him to safety. "Thanks, but God will rescue me."

Finally, the waters rose to the man's neck. As he stood on his toes and prayed for a miracle, a helicopter threw down a lifeline. The man refused it, declaring that God would show him a miracle and rescue him. Two hours later the man drowned.

As he entered heaven, he approached God and asked why He had not answered his prayers and rescued him. God replied, "I tried three times to rescue you. I sent you two boats and a helicopter."[8]

God did answer this man's prayers. Only the man was looking for a big miracle. God had already worked miracles by causing the boats and helicopters to come by to rescue the man.

The Pharisees had seen Jesus heal people, raise people from the dead, and say and do things only a man of God could do. Yet they still stubbornly refused to believe in Jesus and asked Him to prove Himself with another miracle. Like the man about to drown, they kept praying for miracles when God had already given them everything they needed to believe.

Jesus has already given us everything we need to believe and trust in Him. Sometimes we can't see Him, though, because we are too busy being busy. Get alone with God under the stars or out by a lake or stream and see Him in His creation. Read the stories from the Bible and experience God through His Word. Listen to some worshipful music and know God through His Son who lives inside you.

Do you sometimes wonder where God is? _____

Have you ever asked God to perform a miracle or give you a miraculous sign to show you which way to go? _____

List some ways that God is at work around you every day. _____

Ask God to help you see Him in His creation, His Word, and in His Son. Keep your eyes open for the creative way your Creator might speak to you this week.

Bible Study

Look back through some of the Scriptures you read this week. Write down the one verse or passage that God used to speak to you.

_____

_____

_____

_____

*Memorize this verse or passage. You can do it if you spend just
a few minutes saying it to yourself.*

Now, think of at least one situation you will probably face soon in which you could use this Scripture to help you make the right decision. Write down that situation below.

_____

Quote the Scripture when you face this situation, and live by it.

Prayer Time

*Take a few moments to praise God for who He is.
Now take a few moments to thank God for things He has done for you.
Now ask God to make you into the person He wants you to be.
Ask God to use you to help others become closer to God.*

Below is your prayer list for the week. Keep it updated each week. If your prayer isn't answered this week, carry it over to next week's list.

Request	Date of Original Request	Date Answered
_____	__/__/__	__/__/__
_____	__/__/__	__/__/__
_____	__/__/__	__/__/__
_____	__/__/__	__/__/__
_____	__/__/__	__/__/__
_____	__/__/__	__/__/__
_____	__/__/__	__/__/__
_____	__/__/__	__/__/__
_____	__/__/__	__/__/__

*Pray for the things on your list and trust God to provide.
Forgive anyone you have not yet forgiven.
Ask God to forgive you for any unconfessed sin in your life.
Ask God to keep you out of trouble with sin.
Acknowledge that God is in complete control of your life
and will take care of everything.*

We're Not Alone

Matthew 12:43–45

Eerie chants filled the old red barn. The glow of the red candles illuminated shrouded figures huddled around a pentagram drawn on the floor. One figure, with an emblem sewn into his hood, led the chants.

Next to the leader about waist-high was a makeshift altar. On top was a young calf that the group had stolen from a nearby field. The calf was struggling to free himself from the ropes, but to no avail. Suddenly, the leader brandished a sharp knife that sparkled in the candle light. With a cry of victory from the others, the leader killed the calf unmercifully. The blood from the altar ran out of a homemade spout on the side and into a large cup.

One by one, everyone in the satanic ritual drank the blood of the calf. They then called upon the demons—Satan's angels—to destroy a local Christian church body. Unseen by anyone but the leader, from the pentagram on the floor arose a ghastly figure—a fallen angel. The demon angrily denounced those who called on him and reluctantly went to organize a force to cause the local church to fail.

Early the next morning, before Sunday school, Sheila and Stacey arrived early to set up for a drama they were going to perform. For some reason the quiet room seemed unusually cold. "Do you ever get the feeling we're not the only ones here?" asked Sheila.

Demons are real. They were once angels who served God, but then followed Satan in a rebellion against the Lord. They were cast out of heaven. Their mission is to thwart God's plan for humans on earth. Their abilities range from just annoying someone to possessing them completely. They have limited power that God allows while we live here on earth.

Jesus made it very clear that Satan's forces are real. They are not something to be trifled with. Any form of satanism can open a door for demons to influence you in some way. These include Ouija Boards, horoscopes and astrology, séances, fortune tellers (palm readers, psychics, etc.), witchcraft, channeling, New Age religions, and reincarnation regression, to name only a few. Each of these things look to a force other than God to provide answers only God should provide.

Have you ever been involved in any of these or other satanic activities or beliefs? _____

_____

If so, what should you do? _____

Ask God to help you avoid and get out of all activities and beliefs that involve any form of satanic influence. Ask Him to give you the wisdom to sense when you are getting too close to these influences. Make a commitment to seek God and God alone for all the things that you need. For further study, see Acts 16:16–18 and Deuteronomy 18:10–13.

Thanks, Mom!

Matthew 12:46–50; Mark 3:31–35; Luke 8:19–21

Waldo ducked out of sight in the after-school crowd. He held his breath and prayed for deliverance. As he peaked from his hiding place, he could see that the woman continued to stalk him ruthlessly. She searched the crowd for his familiar red-striped shirt, but she could not see him.

Waldo slipped past the cheerleaders and the jocks and huddled for awhile with the nerds. Still, the woman got closer, as if an infrared beam guided her search. Waldo dashed from his hiding place and darted for cover behind the band hall. Just before he disappeared around the corner, the hideous evil tormentor that sought his body spotted him. She called his name aloud for all to hear, "Waldo! Where's Waldo?!"

Laughing hysterically, the crowd began to chant Waldo's name. "Where's Waldo, where's Waldo? Your mother is here, Waldo!" Embarrassed, Waldo came around the corner, head drooped to the ground. He had been found.

Isn't it embarrassing when your parents show up unexpectedly at one of your most vulnerable moments: lost in a crowd of other teenagers whose mothers are not looking for them?

Jesus knows exactly how you feel. Read today's passage. Jesus' mother and His brothers were outside looking for Him, and some people in the crowd let everybody know about it. "Oh, Jesus. You think You're so great. Well, Your mother is here, and she wants to talk to You." You would think Jesus would come out, head hanging low, and say, "Gee thanks, Mom. I just about had everyone in the palm of My hand."

No, Jesus would never do that. And He didn't. He responded to the taunt with a bold statement. "Hey guys, look around. My real mother and brothers—my real family—are those who listen to My words and then obey them." Then He went out to see His mother and brothers.

Are you part of God's family? _____ *Would Jesus call you a brother or a sister?* _____

Do you spend time listening to Jesus' words and then putting them into practice? _____

How do you practice God's Word? _____

In what ways do you not practice God's Word? _____

Now is a good time to ask God to help you continue doing the things you are doing right, and to help you change the things you are doing wrong. You are part of His family. He will help with whatever problem you are struggling with. Thank God for allowing you to be His child. Then go and live like royalty—you are a child of the King.

You're Grounded

Matthew 13:1–12, 18–23; Mark 4:1–9, 13–20; Luke 8:4–18

> The green grass was fading as summer beat down on the local golf course, so the manager asked Zach to fertilize all eighteen holes with the fertilizer in the storage shed. Zach set up the machine and prepared to load it.
>
> Zach emptied bags and bags of stuff into the machine and began distributing all of it into the soil on the golf course. It took most of the day, but by quitting time he had covered every square inch of grass on the course. Zach put up the machine and went home for the weekend.
>
> All weekend long it rained, but Monday morning was nice and sunny. Zach arrived at the golf course and stared in disbelief. The entire course was an ugly brown. The grass was dying. Zach hopped out and ran to the storage shed just in time to find the infuriated manager. "Zach, you put weed killer into the fertilizing machine and killed the whole course. You're fired."

You get out of the ground what you put into it. Zach found out the hard way. It was an innocent mistake—but he should have paid more attention to what he was putting onto his course.

Jesus tells a story of planting seed. Some seed was eaten, some died, but some actually grew the way it was intended. What was the main difference between the seed that never grew and the seed that did?

The seed that grew fell on good soil. Good soil is moist, plowed, and well taken care of by the farmer. It is rich in nutrients that will supply growth to the seed.

The seed is God's Word. If you heart is soft (willing), plowed (submissive), and well taken care of by God, then you will hear God's Word, and that seed will sprout and grow into something magnificent for your life. If, however, you resist God's Word and don't spend time with the Farmer, your life will never grow into what it was intended.

What are some things you have been putting into your life lately that you know you shouldn't? _____

Is your heart willing to follow everything God says? _____

What can you do to become more willing to follow God? _____

You can either put fertilizer or weed killer into your soil. The fertilizer symbolizes the good things God has given you. The weed killer represents the things that harden your heart—they come from Satan. Ask God to make you well-grounded in your faith. Be careful what you put into your heart.

Growing Pains

Mark 4:26–29

Felicia was so excited she couldn't stand it. It was her birthday, and she was about to open her last present. It was from her brother. Aaron brought in the box and sat it down in front of her. Felicia lifted the lid off the box and squealed as a tiny puppy yelped for attention. Felicia picked it up and said, "Mom, can I keep it?" Mom was too nice to say no.

Aaron was in college and had to leave, but he said a sweet good-bye to Felicia and the puppy. It would be six weeks before Aaron could come home again. During those six weeks while he studied, Aaron imagined Felicia and the puppy playing and having a great time. He couldn't wait to see the two of them again.

Finally, Aaron went home and walked through the front door. He was shocked to see Felicia and this huge dog by her side. "Oh, Aaron, look at Max. He's so wonderful!" Aaron wasn't thinking wonderful, he was thinking BIG. He couldn't believe how big that dog had become.

It's amazing how your mind plays tricks on you. If you don't see a puppy for awhile, your mind has memories of a small dog. Before long, though, that puppy is a full-grown dog.

Jesus compares your life to that of a stalk of grain. At first, when you accept Christ, you are nothing but a little seed buried in the ground and trying to come out into the world. Time passes and you grow into a ripe plant ready to be harvested by God.

Time passes so slow for you sometimes that you don't see your own growth. Your mind plays tricks on you and tells you you're still this tiny little unimportant seed when you are actually a growing child of God.

Do you think you have grown spiritually in the last year? _____

In what areas? _____

In what areas would you like to grow? _____

Don't let your mind put you down. Your memory of where you have been is sometimes not accurate with where you actually are. Never forget you are growing. God is watering you, fertilizing you, and seeing to it that you continue to grow until the day that He returns.

Weeding the Garden

Matthew 13:24–30, 36–43

Why, God? Why? Why did Bobby have to have leukemia and die before he reached his sixteenth birthday? Why did a guy drive his truck into a Luby's at rush hour and blow away twenty-three people? Why do so many drive-bys happen in my neighborhood that I see a funeral procession every day? Why did a drunk driver kill my girlfriend?

Why, God? Why? Why are my parents getting divorced? Why is my dad such a jerk to my mom? Why does my best friend spread rumors about me and deny it to my face? Why did the dog eat my English paper?

Why, God? Why? Why do I have a zit smack-dab in the middle of my forehead on prom night? Why do my friends have more money and clothes than I? Why can't I make good grades when I study just as hard as my brother? Why can't my life just be like I want it to be?

In today's passage, Jesus gave one answer to the question, Why? with an analogy about weeds. In the natural world, we understand that if weeds are growing side by side all through a crop, you can't uproot the weeds or you'll damage the good stuff too. That we understand. Perhaps, though, the wheat doesn't understand why they have to put up with these annoying weeds that damage and sometimes kill the wheat.

As Christians, we are the good plants—the wheat. We don't understand why we have to put up with evil things right next door. For whatever reason, God says to leave good and evil side by side until the time of harvest. Bad things continue to happen. Your car gets a flat tire during a traffic jam. You drop your tray of food in front of everyone. Someone that you love gets sick and dies. Your parents argue and fight all the time. For whatever reason, as long as you live on this planet, evil will continue to thrive. It may not make sense now, but God is still in control of the garden. He will take care of you no matter how bad things look.

Perhaps you have your own question you would like to ask God. Go ahead. Why, God? Why? Why is it that _____

Don't you sometimes wish God would answer you? _____

Ask God to help you trust in Him, despite the evil all around you. Remember that Satan, not God, is the author of evil. Be patient when evil strikes and wait for the day when God will rescue you from its clutches.

It Won't Be Long

Matthew 13:31–32; Mark 4:30–32

Minh Luc was eleven years old when he got in serious trouble with his father. His punishment was to take care of and grow a Chinese bamboo tree in his family's backyard. His father said, "On the day that your tree reaches eighty feet tall, you will be a man and you may do as you like. But until that day, you must obey everything your mother and I ask you to do."

Minh received one small bamboo seed from his father and followed the instructions. He buried it and proceeded to water it each day. "How long does it take to grow, Father?" Minh would ask each week.

"It will grow, my son. Be patient," was the only response that his father would ever give.

Minh watered the spot where he buried the seed for one year, but nothing ever happened. Two years passed, but still nothing. Minh was beginning to think this was a cruel joke. Three years passed, then four, then five. Finally, when Minh was sixteen, he walked into the backyard one morning and saw a small sprout. He was excited, but he thought, "At this rate, I will never be considered a man."

Two months later, however, that tiny little sprout had reached eighty feet in height. Minh's father explained that Chinese bamboo trees grow like that. The seed drinks water for five years and finally explodes into life.

Jesus told His disciples about a mustard seed. The point of both stories is the same: your relationship with God is like a tiny, insignificant-looking seed that will one day become full of life.

It's hard to see yourself growing spiritually. Sometimes you pray really hard for something, and God just seems to ignore you. You may have a really good devotional in your room, and then walk out into the face of angry parents that ruin the rest of your day. You might even think sometimes that you are worse now than you were when you first became a Christian—you feel like you've gone backwards.

Do you ever feel like you're going nowhere in your walk with God? _____

In what ways have you grown? _____

In what areas would you like to see improvement? _____

Don't give up. It may take years of daily devotions, many prayers, and constant care before suddenly God sprouts life into areas that you thought were hopeless. One day—perhaps soon, perhaps not—you will become the person you really want to be.

Ask God to help you keep following Him even when it seems like you're going nowhere. Make a commitment to spend time daily with Him. Trust Him to make you into the person He wants you to be.

Weekly Bible Study and Prayer Review

Bible Study

Look back through some of the Scriptures you read this week. Write down the one verse or passage that God used to speak to you.

_____

_____

_____

_____

*Memorize this verse or passage. You can do it if you spend just
a few minutes saying it to yourself.*

Now, think of at least one situation you will probably face soon in which you could use this Scripture to help you make the right decision. Write down that situation below.

_____

Quote the Scripture when you face this situation, and live by it.

Prayer Time

*Take a few moments to praise God for who He is.
Now take a few moments to thank God for things He has done for you.
Now ask God to make you into the person He wants you to be.
Ask God to use you to help others become closer to God.*

Below is your prayer list for the week. Keep it updated each week. If your prayer isn't answered this week, carry it over to next week's list.

Request	Date of Original Request	Date Answered
_____	__/__/__	__/__/__
_____	__/__/__	__/__/__
_____	__/__/__	__/__/__
_____	__/__/__	__/__/__
_____	__/__/__	__/__/__
_____	__/__/__	__/__/__
_____	__/__/__	__/__/__
_____	__/__/__	__/__/__

*Pray for the things on your list and trust God to provide.
Forgive anyone you have not yet forgiven.
Ask God to forgive you for any unconfessed sin in your life.
Ask God to keep you out of trouble with sin.
Acknowledge that God is in complete control of your life
and will take care of everything.*

Home Alone

Matthew 13:13–16; Mark 4:10–12, 33–34

It was dark, and young Kevin was home alone. His parents had accidentally left him unattended for several days, and he was a little scared. To top it off, he overheard two thieves plotting to break into his house the next night at exactly 9:00 P.M. So, what did Kevin do? He made a plan.

Kevin booby-trapped the house all day. He used ice, paint cans, broken Christmas tree ornaments, irons, and many other household items to protect himself and his house from the thieves. Thanks to his quick thinking, he saved his home and got the thieves arrested.

As two teenagers—one a Christian and the other a non-Christian friend—were leaving the theater after watching this Christmas comedy, the Christian spoke up. "You know, the plot for that movie came out of the Bible."

"No way!" the non-Christian friend shot back. "The Bible could never think up something that good."

"I'll show you." When they got into the car, the Christian pulled his Bible out of the glove compartment and read Matthew 24:42–44 to his friend. This sparked an intense discussion, and before the evening was over, there were two Christians sitting in the car.

Sometimes the best way to teach someone something is to tell a story. The movie *Home Alone* is a story that one young man used to lead his friend to Christ. Stories just have a natural way of drawing people in, creating curiosity and interest.

Jesus told a lot of stories (parables) when He was alive on earth. Why? Because stories make the Bible come alive—spiritual things make more sense when you tell a story to illustrate the point. Stories also create curiosity—they draw you in. Then, when you're hooked, you learn the moral of the story before you even realize it.

Stories can be a great way to witness to your friends. How? Suppose you go with a non-Christian friend and see a movie that reminds you about something you have learned from the Bible. You could relate the story to the Bible. Or you tell jokes (funny stories) or use illusions (visual stories) to share Jesus. You could use the newspaper, movies, magazines, books, or even current events to help you tell the story of Jesus through a modern-day story.

Do you like stories? _____ Why? _____

Can you think of one way that you could share Jesus through stories? _____

_____

Ask God to help you use your head and your heart to share Jesus with at least one person today through some kind of story. Remember you're not alone. God is always with you.

It Doesn't Take Much

Matthew 13:33–35

Joel was in trouble. His clothes were really dirty, and he couldn't let his mom see them that way. So, since he got home early, he decided he would wash them himself.

He threw the soiled clothes into the washer in the utility room and then found the washing detergent. He thought for a moment about how much to put into the big washer. The back of the bottle said to put in one cup for a normal load. "Normal load?" Joel thought to himself. "This stuff is really dirty. I better put in about five cups." Joel did just that. He closed the lid and walked into the living room to relax.

Two minutes later, and unknown to Joel, the washer's churning had worked up the soap into a dense lather. The lid to the washer began to levitate as the machine began belching bubbles into the utility room. For ten full minutes, white foam slithered down the sides of the washer and onto the floor, creating a five-foot-high cloud.

Joel walked in to check on his load and was engulfed in soap. He could barely see. Boy, he had been in trouble before, but now he was really going to get it.

Sometimes people think if a little bit of something works, then a lot of it will work even better. This is not always the case—as it is with washing detergent, vitamins, medicines, or yeast. Just a little dab'll do you.

Jesus illustrated this by telling His own story about yeast. You don't put too much yeast in bread dough, because a little is enough for a lot of bread. Bread without yeast is flat—like a cracker. Bread with too much yeast is out of control, but bread with just the right amount of yeast is perfect.

What does all this mean? Look at it this way. If Jesus is the yeast, and your life is the bread, then all you need to do is get Jesus worked into every part of your life. If you don't include Jesus in your life at all, your life on earth will be flat and boring. If you go too far and try to be "religious," you could get out of control, like the Pharisees in Jesus' day. But if you simply take the life of Jesus and apply it to every part of your life, you will come out just right. In other words, take what you have learned in the Bible and apply it to every part of your life.

Is Jesus the Lord of your eating habits? _____ *What about your school work?* _____

Have you obeyed the Bible by honoring your parents? _____

Do you choose your friends and dates according to what the Bible says? _____

Do you avoid gossip and cursing as the Bible plainly teaches? _____

Do you witness regularly to your friends? _____

Ask God to take your life and work Jesus into every part of it. Place yourself in His hands and let Him work you thoroughly—like a big ball of bread dough—until every part of your life is affected. Be patient, and your life will rise higher than you ever thought possible.

Eureka!

Matthew 13:44

He didn't have much money in his pocket, but he always enjoyed going to the country flea markets in Pennsylvania. Today was no exception. While browsing around, the man took special note of an old painting. It was torn, but the frame looked like something he could use. He bought the whole thing for a grand total of four dollars.

When he returned home, the man took his purchase to his shop and began his work. He carefully removed the old painting. While doing so, however, he noticed that something lay hidden behind the painting. It was a folded piece of parchment. He unfolded it carefully and began reading these words: "When in the course of human events, it becomes necessary for one people to dissolve. . ." He gasped. It was a copy of the Declaration of Independence!

At first, the man did not think the document could be very old because it was in such good condition. Later, however, he had it evaluated. To his surprise, he discovered that it was one of the first twenty-four copies ever made, printed in July of 1776. The document was so valuable that he sold it later for $2.42 million—all for an investment of four dollars.[9]

This man's life just wasn't the same after that day. He used the money to buy some things that he always wanted. He made lots of changes in his life. Wouldn't you?

Jesus compares becoming a Christian to someone finding buried treasure. The man in the story wasn't looking for anything in particular—he was just busy working in someone else's field when he found treasure. Maybe you weren't really looking for God when you found Him, but when you stumbled across the good news about Jesus, it changed everything.

Have you made changes in your life since you met Jesus? _____

Like what? _____

How have you looked at life differently? _____

How have you taken advantage of God's wealth of life? _____

If you had a struggle answering some of those questions, here are some ideas. Make changes in the way you treat people. Respect your parents. Love your brothers and sisters. Help people around you. Look at life like a temporary place to stay before you get to go home to heaven forever. Look at your troubles as if they were small compared to what you'll get in heaven (2 Corinthians 4:17). Take advantage of God's wealth. He owns everything, so you can ask Him for anything. Trust Him to provide everything you'll ever need, whether it be college tuition, lunch money, or a new friend in a strange place.

Ask God to help you see your life in Jesus like buried treasure. If you dig down far enough, you'll find more than you ever dreamed possible.

Digging Deeper

Matthew 13:45–46

It was a strange hobby, and sometimes people gave him a hard time about it; but Brad didn't mind. He had a good time—just him and his metal detector.

He bought a nice model that didn't pick up much junk, and he hunted the historical sites in the area: old schools, courthouses, town squares, etc. Fairly often, he would find a dime, quarter, or half-dollar made before 1964 that was silver. He added these to his coin collection. It wasn't worth much, but it was fun.

One day, though, while searching along the banks of an old creek, the metal detector made quite a noise. Often Brad would ignore these big signals because they were probably just a pile of copper or aluminum. But since he had some extra time, he decided to dig. He carefully poked deep into the ground with a long screwdriver until he felt something hard. He began to dig; and after over an hour, he managed to scrape away enough dirt to make out the outline of a small, old wooden chest. He pulled it out, opened it, and to his amazement found a cache of more than fifty $20 gold pieces. They would later turn out to be worth more than a million dollars.

Brad had been looking for buried treasure, but he never thought he would hit it this big. He figured all he'd ever find were a few small coins. Now he was rich. His dreams were small, but the payoff was huge.

Jesus compared being a Christian to finding unexpected treasure. This merchant had bought lots of pearls before, but this one was different. It was huge, perfectly round, and beautiful! He just had to have it. So he sold everything he had so he could get it. His dreams were small, but the payoff was huge.

Being a Christian is not meant to be dull. We often make it that way because we're not looking in the right place. We look for things on the outside to make us happy, like money, popularity, physical pleasure, etc. But God wants you to look on the inside to your heart, where Jesus lives, and to trust Him for everything. You may think this is boring, but if you really started digging deep into your soul and letting God have control, you might hit pay dirt. Don't wait for youth camp or a revival to be on fire for God. Make it happen now—today.

Have you ever thought being a Christian was dull? ____ *Why?* _____

Have you ever experienced God in way that just blew you away? _____ *How?* _____

_____

What was different about this event? _____

Ask God to help you experience a truly awesome Christian life. Don't be a casual Christian. Be a radical Christian—one who sells out to Jesus and lives every day walking with Him.

A Fishy Story

Matthew 13:47–52

Two young soldiers carefully made their way through the underbrush. Scott, the brown-haired seventeen-year-old whispered to his freckle-faced friend Jim, who was eighteen, "Something's awfully fishy about this."

"You can say that again," said Jim. "It's too quiet." The two continued to advance. Scott was a Christian, and many times he had tried to tell his friend about Jesus. Jim would always push him away and tell Scott that he didn't want to join his little Christian club. Even now, Scott prayed for Jim.

"Look there!" Jim pointed. High above them in the treetops was a white rag tied to a branch. "I wonder what that means." Before Scott could answer, they found out. To the enemy, it meant that a mine lay directly below underground. To Scott and Jim, it meant death. They never knew what hit them.

Instantly both young men stood before the Lord. Scott was escorted into heaven because he had asked Jesus to forgive him of his sins and be Lord of his life. Jim, on the other hand, was taken to hell because he had always refused God. He wanted a life without God, and now he had his wish for all of eternity.

Scott and Jim were just minding their own business when suddenly, BOOM! It was all over. They were caught. Both received exactly what they had requested: life with or without God.

Jesus compares the day you stand before God to a little fishing expedition. A fisherman catches some fish, keeps the good ones, and throws away the bad ones.

When you ask Jesus to forgive you and you commit your life to God, you become a fish worth keeping. Those who refuse God are like the bad fish—God just can't use them. Sometimes this may seem awfully unfair, but keep in mind you have a choice. If you choose to live with God on earth, you will live with Him for eternity. If you live your life without God, your eternity will be the same—hell is the only place in the universe where God is not.

Do you know some friends who do not know Jesus? _____

Have you taken the time to tell them the good news? _____

Why or why not? _____

Do you value them enough to at least give them the opportunity to accept Jesus? _____

What will you do about it today to make a difference? _____

Ask God to remind you daily that your days are numbered (Psalm 39:4) and that life is precious. Don't wait to tell your friends about Jesus. Today may be the last chance you have. You may be the only Jesus someone else ever sees today.

Tender Care

Matthew 8:23–27; Mark 4:35–41; Luke 8:22–25

Chelsea was forced to work a dead-end job she didn't like to help support her family. Her mother, twice-divorced and an alcoholic, changed jobs about every other month. Often, late at night, Chelsea would stare up at the ceiling and ask God, "Don't You care about me? Why is this happening?"

One night, during the long walk home through back alleys in the inner city, she noticed a man watching her from behind a garbage dumpster. She gasped as she realized he was holding a large knife. She prayed desperately, "God, please! Help me. Don't You care? Please get me out of this!" Trembling, she kept walking past the man. For some reason, he never came after her.

Later, the man was arrested for several rapes and murders in the same area over a four-month period. Chelsea wanted to know why the man had not attacked her, so she arranged a jail visit with a local newspaper reporter. She sat face to face with the man who could have killed her and asked, "I was the girl in the alley that night. You let me walk right past you. Why?"

"Lady, are you crazy? You had that big, tall man dressed in white clothes walking next to you. There was no way I was going to fight him for you."

Chelsea then realized the Lord had answered her prayer. He did care about her, and He helped her when she called on Him. An angel had protected her.

Do you sometimes feel like God has abandoned you in the middle of your problems? Do you ever ask Why? when certain things happen? We all do. Even Jesus' disciples asked that question.

Jesus went to sleep in the boat, and a horrible storm came up. For a long time the disciples tried to fight it themselves. Finally, they woke Jesus up and said, "Hey. Don't You care about us? We're going to die!" Jesus gave them a little lecture about faith and then stopped the storm dead in its tracks.

What's the point? The disciples tried to solve their own problems first—without God. Then, only after everything else had failed, they finally called on the Lord. If they had only trusted God to begin with! Jesus wanted the disciples to trust Him—even when it seemed like He was asleep and unaware of their problems.

Jesus is aware of your problems. He cares. But sometimes He waits before stopping the storm to see if you'll call on Him instead of trying to solve things yourself.

Do you ever try to solve your own problems? _____ Why? _____

Who do you think can solve your problems better, you or God? _____

Who are you going to call on the next time you face a big storm? _____

Go wake God up. Surprise Him. Ask Him to help you with all of your problems. Make a list of each one; and then give the whole thing to God, and wait on Him to take care of you. Step back and watch Him work.

Weekly Bible Study and Prayer Review

Bible Study

Look back through some of the Scriptures you read this week. Write down the one verse or passage that God used to speak to you.

_____

_____

_____

_____

Memorize this verse or passage. You can do it if you spend just
a few minutes saying it to yourself.

Now, think of at least one situation you will probably face soon in which you could use this Scripture to help you make the right decision. Write down that situation below.

_____

Quote the Scripture when you face this situation, and live by it.

Prayer Time

Take a few moments to praise God for who He is.
Now take a few moments to thank God for things He has done for you.
Now ask God to make you into the person He wants you to be.
Ask God to use you to help others become closer to God.

Below is your prayer list for the week. Keep it updated each week. If your prayer isn't answered this week, carry it over to next week's list.

Request	Date of Original Request	Date Answered
_____	__/__/__	__/__/__
_____	__/__/__	__/__/__
_____	__/__/__	__/__/__
_____	__/__/__	__/__/__
_____	__/__/__	__/__/__
_____	__/__/__	__/__/__
_____	__/__/__	__/__/__
_____	__/__/__	__/__/__

Pray for the things on your list and trust God to provide.
Forgive anyone you have not yet forgiven.
Ask God to forgive you for any unconfessed sin in your life.
Ask God to keep you out of trouble with sin.
Acknowledge that God is in complete control of your life
and will take care of everything.

Who, Me?

Matthew 8:28–34; Mark 5:1–20; Luke 8:26–39

> "Please let me go, Dad!" Donovan pleaded for the fifth time. For the fifth time his dad responded the same way that he had before.
>
> "Don, you can't. You need to stay here in the apartment with your sister and take care of her. I need you to do this for me. Now, I have to go. Bye." Dad slipped out of the door, leaving sixteen-year-old Donovan muttering near-obscenities under his breath about his father and his little sister. His sister, two-year-old Savannah, just smiled and danced around the room, oblivious to Donovan's sorrow over missing a chance to go to the NBA championship game with his dad.
>
> Later that night, after Savannah and most people in the apartment complex were asleep, Donovan thought he smelled smoke. He stepped outside and noticed flames leaping from the roof of the building. He hurried inside, got his little sister out, and began running from door to door, waking sleeping tenants and yelling, "Fire!"
>
> As it turns out, the smoke detector system had failed, and only Donovan's quick thinking had saved more than 100 lives from certain death in the blazing inferno that destroyed the entire complex. Donovan realized that because he stayed home, he got to be a hero.

Sometimes we just want to go, and God tells us to stay—not because He doesn't want us to join in on the fun, but because He has a special plan in store for us. For instance, in today's passage, a man who had been healed of demon possession really wanted to go with Jesus. Jesus said, "No, I want you to go home to your family and tell them how much God has done for you." So the man went home, to a metroplex of ten cities where he lived, and told everyone there the good news of Jesus. You see, that man had a special ministry in his own hometown and the surrounding areas.

Have you ever wanted to do big things for God? You've asked God to show you His will for your life out there in the future. You want Him to make you into something big—something that will make a difference. In your mind, you figure that will mean going some place other than where you are now. You figure life doesn't really begin until you graduate from high school or get out of the house.

But what if God's plan for your life right now is to minister where you are—in your family, in your school, in the area where you live?

Do you believe God has a ministry for you right here, right now? _____

What could you do for God right where you are now that you haven't done before?

_____

God isn't just training you for something big later. He wants you to have a ministry right where you are. Ask God to show you what your specific ministry is and what you can do for Him.

If I Could Just . . .

Matthew 9:18–26; Mark 5:21–43; Luke 8:40–56

The youth group was returning home from a ski trip in the mountains, exhausted from several fun-filled days on the slopes. Each car in the caravan was filled with a mixture of laughter from the stories of the week and complaints of pain in arms, legs, and backs. Suddenly, however, everyone forgot about both.

A jeep in the caravan struck a patch of ice and skidded off the road, tumbling down the steep mountainside, flipping many times before coming to rest upside-down below. Someone called 911 from a cell phone, and everyone jumped out of their cars. Soon, help arrived. Everyone was unhurt for the most part and accounted for—all except for one fourteen-year-old girl. Jenna was missing, and despite all search attempts, no one could find her. Finally, however, rescue workers pushed over the crumpled jeep and found Jenna underneath, crushed by the vehicle. She was immediately rushed to a nearby hospital with the youth group in tow. X-rays showed Jenna's body to be so mangled that bones and organs would perhaps never be the same. She was life-flighted to another hospital. But the youth group chose to stay in the waiting room of the first hospital to pray. They prayed to God and refused to give up hope. They prayed during Jenna's entire flight on the helicopter.

When the helicopter arrived at the other hospital and the helicopter doors opened, Jenna walked out on her own two feet, with no broken bones and no permanent injuries.[10]

God heard the prayers of that youth group. Because of their faith, Jenna was healed.

This story is not very different from a story about a woman in Jesus' day. She had tried for twelve years to stop a bleeding problem she had. She spent all her money, and the doctors gave her no hope. But when she heard that Jesus had come to town, she told herself, "If I could just touch the edge of His clothes, I know that I will be healed." Her faith in Jesus healed her completely—and God did what money, doctors, and years of energy could not.

You may now, or sometime soon, find yourself in a seemingly helpless situation. Your parents want to divorce. Someone abuses you. A close friend hurts you. A disease grips you. You think your present situation will be left to run its own course. However God is more powerful than your circumstances.

Is there something in your life that really needs to change but seems impossible? _____

What is it? _____

Do you believe that God can change this situation and that it is His will to do so? _____

Then take this problem right now to God, and give it to Him. Let go. Let Him have it. Touch the edge of heaven with your voice, and let God do as He sees best.

It may not be easy. The woman had to fight her way through a huge crowd to reach Jesus. Don't give up. Keep praying. Fight your way through the doubt that begs you to quit. Trust God and let Him do what only He can do. He won't let you down.

Dead and Gone?

Matthew 9:18–26; Mark 5:21–43; Luke 8:40–56

> Kelsey was trying out his new pickup truck and enjoying every minute of it. He had the window down, the radio on, and his fishing gear in the back. He headed up a small mountain on a winding road out in the country, on the way to his favorite fishing spot. Everything was perfect.
>
> Suddenly, as Kelsey neared a dangerous curve, a convertible careened around the curve, kicking up a cloud of dust and pebbles. It swerved into his lane, and for a brief moment Kelsey just knew that he was going to die. At the last possible moment, the convertible darted out of his lane and back into the other. As the two vehicles passed each other, the female driver of the convertible shouted at Kelsey, "Pig!"
>
> Kelsey was dumbfounded. Here he was, minding his own business, when suddenly this idiotic woman nearly runs him off the mountain; and then she has the gall to call him a pig. Kelsey's temper lit up like a match; and before the woman got out of earshot he leaned out of his pickup window, turned back to face her, and yelled at the top of his lungs, "Cow!"
>
> Satisfied, Kelsey turned his attention back to the road and rounded the dangerous curve. Just as he rounded the bend, the rest of the road came into view and he saw it. It was huge. Massive. Monstrous. Pink! It was too late. With a thunderous crash, Kelsey slammed into the pig, destroying the front of his truck and creating enough bacon to feed Rhode Island.

Kelsey had a mental block. He made two assumptions: (1) the car is driving recklessly, so the driver must be an idiot, and (2) because the driver yelled "Pig!" she must be calling me names. Kelsey was wrong on both counts, and it cost him dearly.

In today's passage, a lot of people made the assumption that Jairus's daughter was dead and gone for good. It's dangerous, though, to assume things when Jesus is present. He tends to change things. He dismissed the assumptions of the crowd and healed the little girl. She was alive, and everyone else was wrong.

Have you been to a funeral lately? Most people assume the person is gone for good, but it's not true. The person who died has graduated from this life and moved on to the next—fully alive. If that person is a Christian, he or she is now in heaven, walking with Jesus on streets of gold and living an unbelievably happy life. Don't assume that just because the body doesn't move anymore that the person is gone—he or she is now with Jesus.

Have you ever lost someone you love to death? _____ *Who?* _____

How did you feel when this happened? _____

Do you realize that this person, if a Christian, is now with the Lord? _____

Don't lose hope. No matter what the tragedy, Jesus cares for those who have accepted Him and then die. He greets them and escorts them into heaven for all of eternity. Pray that God will give you the peace to continue on in your life until one fine day when you are reunited with this person in heaven.

It's Up to You

Matthew 9:27–34

Warren had worked all morning long on his bulldozer, tearing up a section of road in order to install an underground pipeline. He had carefully placed signs announcing, "Detour—Road Closed" several hundred feet ahead in both directions. After four hours of hard work, Warren finally cleared enough dirt to be able to install the pipeline. He decided to rest and take a lunch.

While munching on his PBJ sandwich, an ambulance approached the work site, sirens blaring and lights flashing. The driver hopped out and yelled at Warren, "I've got to get through! There's a baby choking about two minutes from here, and if I take the detour it will be too late. Can you get me through?" Warren tried for a moment to talk the ambulance driver into taking the detour because it would be so difficult to redo his work, but the ambulance driver was insistent. Finally, at the thought of helping a small child, Warren quickly undid four hours of work, sending the ambulance driver through.

Later that evening, when Warren arrived home, to his surprise his wife met him at the door in tears. "Our baby almost died today! He was choking to death, but the ambulance arrived just in time and saved his life."

Warren didn't realize it, but he had saved his own child's life. He made a conscious decision to help someone, and the outcome was a direct result of his decision.

Many stories about Jesus are about someone getting healed. Today's passage is no exception: Two blind men received sight and a demon-possessed mute was set free. Notice particularly, though, verse 29. Jesus, being the Son of God, has unlimited power and can do anything. But to the two blind men whom He healed He said, "To the degree that you have faith in me you will be healed." Both were healed completely.

This means one thing: The two blind men trusted Jesus completely. They believed in Him and His power to heal. *As a result of that faith,* they received their sight. The outcome was a direct result of their decision.

Where does this kind of faith come from? The Bible answers that question clearly in Romans 10:17. Faith comes from listening to the word of Jesus. Did you notice that the men who were healed by Jesus were blind? They had never seen Jesus. So where did their faith come from? They had obviously made their decision to believe in Him by *listening* to Him with their ears. They believed His message, and so their faith grew.

Do you have a lot of faith? _____ *Do you want to increase your faith?* _____

What can you do today to increase your faith just a little? _____

You may not be able to see Jesus, but you have an entire Bible full of words to listen to and grow in your faith. Ask God to increase your faith, and pray that He will keep you listening to His Word on a daily basis.

Out of the Ordinary

Matthew 13:53–58; Mark 6:1–6

The phone rang in Misty's room. She pounced on the bed, rolled over, flipped the long, brown hair out of her deep blue eyes, and calmly picked up the phone.

"The President is coming to our town?" Misty screamed. "Why?" As she listened intently to her friend's explanation, she couldn't believe her ears. The President would be visiting the First Community Church of Smithville as he passed through on another assignment. "What am I going to wear?" Misty wondered aloud.

The First Community Church normally had a Sunday attendance of 45. However, news of the President's visit had spread so rapidly that preparations were being made to accommodate more. They set out extra chairs inside and outside the church building—perhaps to hold 200 total. It still wasn't enough.

When Sunday came, over 1,500 people tried to crowd in and around the small church as the President attended the service. It was their highest attendance in history.

A week later, the small sign out in front of First Community Church read, "The President isn't here this week, but God is." They had 42 people in attendance.

Amazing, isn't it? People will flock to see or hear someone famous, just so they can say, "I went to church with the President." But what happens when God shows up? Does anyone care?

In today's passage, Jesus went to His hometown to the synagogue. There He preached. They had heard about His miracles, and now they heard His extraordinary words. But they knew Jesus. They watched Him grow up—playing with the other boys and girls in town. They knew His mother and father and His brothers. So they assumed He couldn't be great because He seemed so ordinary.

Sometimes we get used to God—it's sad but true. We get used to going to church, meeting with youth, praying over our food, and we assume God isn't really that big of a deal anymore. We put God and His power into a little box. We lose our faith in Him. We expect Him only to do a few, simple things. And, like the people of Jesus' hometown, God is unable to do many miracles because of our lack of faith.

Do you ever feel like you get so used to God that you forget He's there? _____

What causes you to feel that way? _____

Have you ever had a big problem or need that you assumed God wouldn't handle, because it was out of the ordinary? _____

Do you really think God is incapable or uncaring when it comes to your life? _____

Ask God to help you get to know Him—again. Pray that you will realize His power and His love. Remember all that God has done in your life. Thank Him and praise Him for being the God that He is.

Windows of Opportunity

Matthew 9:35–38

They were in love. They wanted to get married. And, since they both went to the same university, what better place to seal their vows than in one of the two beautiful little chapels on campus?

On the day of the wedding, the florist arrived early and set up the immaculate flower arrangements, as planned. It was a beautiful sight—pink and white arrangements scattered throughout the little chapel. The florist thought to herself, This is my best job ever. The bride will be so pleased.

Later that day, however, when the bride's party arrived at the chapel an hour before the wedding, there were no flowers. The bride frantically called the florist to find out why she had not come, but the florist said that everything was all set up. One of the bridesmaids called to the bride and said, "Hey, the flowers are in the wrong chapel. They're over here!" The second chapel on campus had indeed been set up with the flowers, but the doors were locked and there was no way to get inside. The bride began to scream and pound on the door. The minister who was to do the wedding arrived and heard the bride crying about her flowers.

"What's the matter?" the minister asked. "Don't you have enough flowers?"

"Yes," she cried. "There are plenty of flowers, but there's no one here who will get them for me! Will you get someone to unlock these doors and send some people inside to help me get them?"

The flowers were ready, but there was no one to help get them. How horrible.

Jesus had a similar problem. He looked at the crowds of people—people who were ready to hear from God and follow Him—but who would go out into the crowds and help bring them to God?

Jesus still has the same problem today. All around you are people who, though you may not know it, are ripe for hearing the gospel. God's Spirit is drawing them to Him. Without Christians, though, to go to work and spread the message, they will stay where they are. Like the flower arrangement, if someone doesn't help in time, it will be too late.

Do you know anyone around you who is not a Christian? _____

Are they ripe for hearing God's Word? _____

If you responded "Yes," then who do you think God wants to share His Word? _____

That's right, you. You are the one God has chosen to be His witness.

The time is short. The time is now. Ask God to send you into His harvest field and be one of His workers. He will give you everything you need to succeed. For further study, read Romans 10:14–15.

Weekly Bible Study and Prayer Review

Bible Study

Look back through some of the Scriptures you read this week. Write down the one verse or passage that God used to speak to you.

_____

_____

_____

Memorize this verse or passage. You can do it if you spend just
a few minutes saying it to yourself.

Now, think of at least one situation you will probably face soon in which you could use this Scripture to help you make the right decision. Write down that situation below.

_____

Quote the Scripture when you face this situation, and live by it.

Prayer Time

Take a few moments to praise God for who He is.
Now take a few moments to thank God for things He has done for you.
Now ask God to make you into the person He wants you to be.
Ask God to use you to help others become closer to God.

Below is your prayer list for the week. Keep it updated each week. If your prayer isn't answered this week, carry it over to next week's list.

Request	Date of Original Request	Date Answered
_____	__/__/__	__/__/__
_____	__/__/__	__/__/__
_____	__/__/__	__/__/__
_____	__/__/__	__/__/__
_____	__/__/__	__/__/__
_____	__/__/__	__/__/__
_____	__/__/__	__/__/__
_____	__/__/__	__/__/__
_____	__/__/__	__/__/__

Pray for the things on your list and trust God to provide.
Forgive anyone you have not yet forgiven.
Ask God to forgive you for any unconfessed sin in your life.
Ask God to keep you out of trouble with sin.
Acknowledge that God is in complete control of your life
and will take care of everything.

One Dozen Do-Nuts

Matthew 10:1–16; Mark 6:7–13; Luke 9:1–6

"I need one dozen donuts, to go, please," Teresa said politely to the man behind the counter.

"What kind would you like?" the donut man asked.

Teresa's heart pounded. She forgot to ask her friends what kind of donuts they liked. There were so many to choose from—chocolate iced, chocolate filled, glazed, cake, eclairs, twists, bear claws, cream filled, fruit filled. It was too much to choose from. Then Teresa suddenly remembered that she forgot her purse. She had no money! There were fifteen people in line behind her, and the man behind the counter was growing impatient.

"Miss, what kind of donuts would you like?"

"Why did they send me?" Teresa screamed, turning away from the counter and running toward the door. "I can't do it! I just can't do it!"

Buying donuts isn't as tough as Teresa was making it out to be. It's really very simple. Wouldn't you agree?

Being a witness for Jesus isn't as tough as we make it out to be either. It's really very simple. It's not like we have to choose from among the various types of people and pay a toll every time we witness. Jesus makes it easy on us because He gives us everything we need.

Jesus told His disciples to go, and He spent some time giving them specific instructions. Where were they to go? _____

How much money could they take? _____

Where were they supposed to stay? _____

What were they supposed to say? _____

Jesus not only gave them instructions, He gave them what they needed to accomplish their task. What does it say that Jesus gave them in Matthew 10:1? _____

Jesus gave specific instructions to the disciples at this particular place and time because He had a job for them to do. He didn't just expect them to go out in their own power and do it—He gave them everything they needed. The disciples listened to Jesus and went out, telling others about the good news. Are you a *do*-nut? Do you *do* whatever Jesus tells you to *do?* Did you know that when He has a job for you, He will give you clear instructions on what to do, and He will equip you with everything you need to do it. Your life can be filled with the excitement of following Jesus if you will simply do what He tells you to do.

Ask God to show you exactly what He wants you to do—at home, at school, everywhere. Then, trust Him to provide you with the strength and wisdom you need to do what He tells you. Take a risk. Get out of your comfort zone—be a do-nut.

Speak Up

Matthew 10:17–20

Biology class was normally fun for Rachel, but today things had taken an unexpected, nasty twist. The teacher said resolutely, "The Bible is a bunch of myths. Science clearly tells us that God does not exist, that we could never have come from two humans named Adam and Eve, and that evolution proves that the Bible is historically inaccurate."

Rachel's heart pounded, and several classmates looked directly at her, knowing that she was a Christian. She muttered a quick prayer to the Lord and chose to speak rather than remain silent.

"Mr. Thompson, I disagree." Rachel posed. "I think there is another possibility."

The room grew strangely quiet, and Mr. Thompson politely said, "Please explain, Rachel. I think the class would love to hear your perspective."

Rachel suddenly felt a peace she had never felt before. For the next five minutes, she very eloquently stated why science and Christianity did not conflict—but rather supported each other. She gave numerous examples from the Bible, some that she didn't even think she knew until she found herself talking about it. It was like God was speaking through her, and she just let Him take over.

Have you ever faced a time at school, home, or out with friends when suddenly your beliefs were attacked and your faith was on the line? _____

What did you do? _____

Jesus said that times like this would come. You will face persecution. And there is only one way to get ready for these difficult circumstances—don't worry about what you're going to say. Jesus said that during persecution, He will give you the words that you need to say to defend God and your faith in Him. Don't worry about it. Don't plan it. Just trust God to give you what to say, because He will be doing the speaking—not you.

Wow! No other time in the Bible is an instruction like this given. Don't plan. Don't worry. Do absolutely nothing, and God will be there for you when you need Him.

How does it make you feel to think that you may actually be persecuted for being a Christian someday? _____

What can you do now to prepare for that day? _____

Ask God to help you prepare for that day by simply trusting in Him now. If you trust in Him today, then you will be able to trust Him to give you the words in the future—whether it's tomorrow in the school cafeteria or ten years from now in another country.

Tolerating the Intolerable

Matthew 10:21–23

> "Tolerance is the most important virtue we can have as human beings," Anthony insisted. "I believe everyone else's beliefs, values, and lifestyles are just as important as mine, even though they may be very different. For instance, I'm not a homosexual, but I think homosexuality is just as normal and valid as my own choice of being a heterosexual."
>
> Bonnie thought for a moment and said, "I disagree. The most important virtue I can have as a human being is love. Love is quite different from tolerance. For instance, I love my baby brother, Pete. He's so cute and cuddly. But he gets himself into trouble. The other day, he picked up a rock in the yard and started to put it in his mouth. If I 'tolerated' his choice, he would have choked to death and died. But, because I love him, I chose to stop him from harming himself. I think tolerating bad decisions is actually the opposite of love."
>
> Anthony couldn't believe his ears. His anger had reached the boiling point. "Who do you think you are? Babies are one thing, but I'm old enough to make my own choices, and there's not a person alive, including you, Miss Goody Two-Shoes, who can tell me I'm making a bad decision. People like you are what's wrong with our country."
>
> "What's the matter, Anthony?" Bonnie asked with a grin. "Can't you tolerate my beliefs?"

Tolerance is being touted as the highest virtue—over and above love. But, as Jesus pointed out two thousand years ago, tolerance leads to the hatred of Christians. Where is the love in tolerance?

If you do not already, you will begin to find yourself intolerable among the tolerant crowd. Why? Because you choose to love. And love means believing in a God who loves. And believing in a God who loves means believing in a God who loves us so much that He sent His only Son Jesus to free us from the horrible effects of sin. God cannot tolerate sin, but He loves us so much that He sentenced Himself to death to win us back.

Have you heard the word tolerance *recently?* _____

Have you found yourself intolerable by those who claim to be tolerant? _____

How should you respond to them? _____

The Bible says not to lash out in return. Walk away from it. Shrug it off. Love the person anyway.

Ask God to help you to have the highest virtue of all—love. Pray that you will be able to love even when times get so bad that you find yourself being hated for loving.

Awesome Fear

Matthew 10:24–31

It was December 15, 1989, in Timisoara, Romania. The secret police had come to arrest Pastor Laslzo and his wife, Edith. Word of this impending arrest had spread like wildfire, and Christians from Pastor Laszlo's church and many other congregations gathered together in a peaceful protest around the church building and the pastor's home. Soon, thousands of people formed a wall of protection for the pastor and his family. The secret police were unable to penetrate the wall.

The people remained there for two days, until finally the secret police had enough. They broke through the wall, arrested the pastor and his wife, and disappeared. The Christian crowd then moved in protest to the city square. Romania's government sent in tanks and armed soldiers to dispel the crowd, but the Christians were not afraid. In rage, the soldiers began to fire their machine guns into the crowds. Many people fell to the ground, killed instantly. Others fell in agony as their legs were shot. Still, the people of Timisoara stood in faith without fear and without retaliation against the soldiers.

Eight days later, Communism fell in the country of Romania, and Christians once again had the right to meet and worship God."

It's hard to imagine that a story like this took place so recently in our world. Yet there are Christians who are willing to stand up for Jesus and not be afraid—even when it seems that death could be the consequence.

Jesus encouraged us not to fear humans who persecute us, for they can only kill our bodies, but our spirits will go on to live with Jesus forever. Rather, we are to fear God Himself, who has the power to determine our eternal destiny.

Have you ever been afraid to take a stand for Jesus? _____

What were you afraid of? _____

Do you think this fear is justified when you consider that Jesus died for you, and that others, like the Romanian people of Timisoara, died for their faith? _____

Our God is an awesome God. When someone is awesome, we hold him or her in a reverent fear. Do you fear God? _____

Can you name at least five attributes of God that He has that make Him worth holding in awe? _____ , _____ , _____ , _____ , _____

Take time to worship God by holding Him in awe. Consider His love, mercy, and grace. Meditate on the price He paid for your soul. Thank Him for taking care of you and providing for your needs. Praise Him for being who He is. Ask this great and mighty God to help you not to be afraid of people the next time you are given the opportunity to stand up for Jesus.

I'd Also Like to Thank . . .

Matthew 10:32

When his name was called over the loudspeaker, Jeff couldn't believe it. Trembling, and with tears in his eyes, Jeff rose from his seat and made his way down the long aisle amidst thunderous applause. He climbed the stairs to the stage, took the award from the hostess, and turned to face the auditorium.

Clearing his throat, Jeff began to speak in a shy, crackled voice. "I'd like to thank the academy for considering me for this incredible award. I'd like to thank my producers, directors, and fellow cast members who made all of this possible. I'd like to thank my wife and children for their loving support while I was away making this movie. And, most of all, I'd like to thank my Lord Jesus Christ for making this day possible. Without Him, I could do nothing. Thank you."

Jeff backed away from the stage, bowed slightly with a weak grin, and disappeared behind the curtain. In the audience, a young woman leaned over to her husband and said, "Why do people insist on acknowledging a dead man like Jesus for their successes in life?"

Her husband replied, "I don't know. Perhaps he knows something, or someone, we don't."

Odds are that you will never stand before thousands of people to give acknowledgments to those who have helped make you who you are. However, the odds are great that today you will have the opportunity to acknowledge or deny Jesus in everything that you say and do.

Take a look at a related passage of Scripture, Proverbs 3:5–6, which says, "Trust in the Lord with all of your heart, and do not depend on your own thinking. *Acknowledge* the Lord in all you do, and He will make straight paths for you."

What does *acknowledge* mean? Take a look at the word. It contains the word *knowledge,* which simply means "to know." It also has the two-letter prefix *ac-* in front of it. That prefix means "to make." So, *acknowledge* simply means "to make known." To acknowledge Jesus is to make Him known to others.

All throughout your day, you will have the opportunity to let others know that Jesus is your Lord. If you do not acknowledge the Lord in all you do, then you are not acknowledging Him at all. How can those around you know that Jesus is Lord unless you take the time to somehow acknowledge Him?

List some ways that you can acknowledge Jesus with your mouth: _____

Does it make you nervous to think about doing that with people you know who are not Christians? _____ *The more you get to know Jesus, the more natural it will be and the more willing you will be to acknowledge His hand in everything that happens in your life.*

Ask God to help you acknowledge Jesus with your mouth in front of everyone you know at least once this week. Pray that God would give you the opportunity and the boldness to do so.

Long Division

Matthew 10:34–39

Standing on the edge of a thousand-foot cliff were five people, each of them with various beliefs. The first stated confidently, "I believe that if I jump off this cliff I will float to the bottom." The second boasted, "I believe that if I jump off this cliff I will be caught by angels just before I reach the rocks below." The third asserted, "I believe that if I jump off this cliff a bird will snatch me up with his talons and fly me to the bottom on his wings." The fourth said, "I believe that if I jump off this cliff I will land on the rocks below, but they will not hurt me." Finally, the fifth person said, "I believe that if I jump off this cliff my parachute will save me and that the rest of you will die unless you wear a parachute."

A look of horror broke out on the faces of the first four. They could not believe their ears. They said, "Look, we're all going to the same place. How dare you tell us how to get there. We can all choose our own way. The most important thing here is unity—that we all accept each other's beliefs." The fifth person continued to disagree, offering parachutes to the other four. The other four refused.

Finally, they all jumped off the cliff simultaneously. One of them could be seen floating lazily above the rocks below on his parachute. The other four plummeted straight to the bottom and were killed instantly.

Suppose the fifth person in this story had chosen to "convert" and believe someone else. Would he have survived? No. Suppose the other four had "converted" and taken parachutes. Would they have survived? Yes.

Today, millions of people claim that we are all going to the same place, and that we should all accept everyone else's theory of God. *Unity* is touted as the ultimate goal, and for someone like a Christian to come along and say that Jesus is the only way is considered downright wrong.

Jesus said that He did not come to the earth to bring peace, but division. He wants us to be loyal to Him and to make disciples of others. If they choose not to believe, however, there will undoubtedly be division and conflict. *Unity* is not the ultimate goal. *Faithfulness* to Jesus is the ultimate goal.

Have you ever felt like your faith in Jesus has caused division between you and your friends or family? _____

Describe one such situation. _____

Have you ever felt like you should be more tolerant of someone else's beliefs to keep division from occurring? _____

Jesus says that loyalty to Him is more important than peace and unity. Ask God to help you be faithful and loyal to Him—even when conflict from friends and family makes it difficult.

Weekly Bible Study and Prayer Review

Bible Study

Look back through some of the Scriptures you read this week. Write down the one verse or passage that God used to speak to you.

_____

_____

_____

_____

*Memorize this verse or passage. You can do it if you spend just
a few minutes saying it to yourself.*

Now, think of at least one situation you will probably face soon in which you could use this Scripture to help you make the right decision. Write down that situation below.

_____

Quote the Scripture when you face this situation, and live by it.

Prayer Time

*Take a few moments to praise God for who He is.
Now take a few moments to thank God for things He has done for you.
Now ask God to make you into the person He wants you to be.
Ask God to use you to help others become closer to God.*

Below is your prayer list for the week. Keep it updated each week. If your prayer isn't answered this week, carry it over to next week's list.

Request	Date of Original Request	Date Answered
_____	__/__/__	__/__/__
_____	__/__/__	__/__/__
_____	__/__/__	__/__/__
_____	__/__/__	__/__/__
_____	__/__/__	__/__/__
_____	__/__/__	__/__/__
_____	__/__/__	__/__/__
_____	__/__/__	__/__/__
_____	__/__/__	__/__/__

*Pray for the things on your list and trust God to provide.
Forgive anyone you have not yet forgiven.
Ask God to forgive you for any unconfessed sin in your life.
Ask God to keep you out of trouble with sin.
Acknowledge that God is in complete control of your life
and will take care of everything.*

Help Your Brother

Matthew 10:40–42

Roger was traveling through the Dallas area of Texas in his old car. It wasn't much, but it was what God had given him, and he was grateful. Roger was grateful for a lot of things. Though he was deaf, he was grateful he could see and walk—and live.

When Roger got to DeSoto, Texas, his car broke down. Roger had no money, and he knew nothing about how to fix his car. Undaunted, though, he prayed to God for help and walked into a nearby grocery store. There he said the following to the clerk, "Please call a local church. Tell them that a Christian was passing through and his car broke down and he needs help." The clerk opened the yellow pages, selected the first church she found, and called.

The secretary of the church who answered the call told the pastor. The pastor called a church member who was also a mechanic. The mechanic drove out to Roger, fixed his car, and sent him on his way—all at no charge.

Though Roger was deaf, he could hear the message loud and clear: "God's people love me and take care of me."

According to today's passage, the mechanic who helped Roger will receive a reward in heaven for his kindness. Everyone will receive a reward in heaven if they choose to be kind and do something special for another person because he or she is a Christian—one of God's children.

Is this favoritism? Shouldn't we be nice to everyone? Yes, you should be kind to everyone. However, Jesus is saying here that if a Christian is in need, other Christians should respond immediately to help out of love and compassion.

Think for a moment. Is there anyone in your youth group who has a genuine need?

_____

Who is this person and what does he or she need? _____

What can you and your youth group do to help? _____

Get with some of your friends and do your best to meet this need as quickly as possible.

After you have helped with this need, don't stop there. Be on the lookout for other Christians who have needs—youth, adults, senior adults, children, etc. Learn to develop an attitude that says, "I will get out of my comfort zone and help people around me."

Pray that God will show you daily how you can help the Christians around you. And, when your time comes and you are in need, pray that God will send some Christians your way to help you.

Don't Lose Your Head

Matthew 14:1–12; Mark 6:14–29; Luke 9:7–9

What better way to celebrate my birthday than to throw a party with lots of my friends and plenty of booze? thought the king. So he sent out the invitations.

Herod's friends and VIPs from the government, army, and upper class showed up to celebrate. Soon the party was in full swing. There was laughing, joking, and plenty of drinks. Herod, wanting to show his guests how beautiful and amazing his stepdaughter was, called for her to come and dance.

Her dance so mesmerized the guests and pleased Herod that he called her over and said out loud for all the guests to hear, "My daughter, ask whatever you want and I will give it to you—up to half my kingdom."

Not knowing what to ask for, the girl rushed out to consult her mother, Herodias. Herodias hated a man in prison named John the Baptist, so she told her daughter to ask for his head on a platter.

The girl returned to Herod and made her request. The room fell silent. Herod liked John very much, but he was afraid of embarrassing himself in front of his friends, so he gave the order. John the Baptist was immediately executed and his head brought to the girl on a platter.

Notice that the sole reason John the Baptist was killed was because Herod was afraid of what people would think. Herod did something he did not want to do because of peer pressure.

You have already faced many situations where you were pressured into doing something you didn't want to do by the crowd. Think for a moment about what happens in this type of situation. You want to be accepted, so you do something you don't want to do. You act *fake* so that others will like you. The fake you is the one being accepted by the crowd—not the real you. So, in reality, you aren't being accepted at all. The real you has been rejected—by you.

Have you ever given in to peer pressure? _____

Describe a recent time when you did something you didn't want just to be accepted by the crowd. _____

Does the crowd you hang around with accept the real you or the fake you? _____

One of the things that made Jesus so famous was that He *never* cared what people thought. Jesus always presented His true self in every situation. Some accepted Him. Others rejected Him. But those who accepted Him (His disciples) loved Him so much that most of them died for Him.

Don't be fake to gain friends. Be real and God will give you true friends, just like He did for Jesus (John 15:13–15). Ask God to help you stop pretending to be someone you are not for the sake of the crowd. Pray that He will make you more like Jesus and give you true friends who accept the real you.

Leftovers Are Great

Matthew 14:13–21; Mark 6:30–44; Luke 9:10–17; John 6:1–14

"Mom! Nobody else carries his lunch around. I don't want to take my lunch. Everyone will make fun of me." But after Mom put her foot down, Josh reluctantly walked out the door with his sack lunch.

"Why me?" thought Josh, kicking up the dust as he walked down the road. "It's summer, for crying out loud. I'm just going out to play with the guys. They are going to think I'm such a freak." Josh opened the sack and peeked inside to see what his mother had packed. He managed a grin when he saw the five fresh pieces of bread and the freshly cooked fish, seasoned just how he liked it. Josh realized his mother loved him and was only trying to take care of him.

As Josh's day went by, he tried to hide his lunch. His friends never noticed, and before long no one cared. Suddenly a huge crowd of people showed up where the boys were playing. A stranger was in front of the crowd speaking. The boys tried to see what was going on, and they were so enthralled by the stranger's words that the whole day passed by before they knew it. Suddenly, Josh and everyone else realized that it was time for supper. Josh was embarrassed that he had a lunch, but that all changed when a man named Andrew walked up to him and said, "Hey, are you going to eat that?"

Read the rest of the story in today's passage. One young boy among five thousand men (counting the women and children, this number could have been as high as fifteen thousand) had a lunch. Before his very eyes, Josh watched the Son of God take his little lunch and feed all those people with it. It was a day Josh would never forget.

Notice that the disciples didn't have the faith to come up with a way to feed all these people. Notice at the end, though, how many baskets of leftovers they picked up—twelve. Have you ever wondered why there were twelve baskets of leftovers? Perhaps it was so that each of the twelve disciples could see and feel the weight of all that food so that they would never forget what Jesus had done with such a little bit of food.

Do you ever feel like you are a nobody? _____

Do you ever feel like you have little or nothing to offer God? _____

Can you think of at least one or two things, no matter how insignificant, that you do have or that you can do that God might be able to use? _____

If God can use a little boy's lunch to feed all those people, then He can certainly use what little you have to offer to do great things for Him. Ask God to show you how He can use you this week to do great things for Him. Be prepared, though—it may be in a way you never expected.

Row, Row, Row Your Boat

Matthew 14:22–33; Mark 6:45–52; John 6:16–21

After receiving distressing news about his daughter, the pastor caught the first late-night flight out of town.

There weren't many people on the flight, and no one at all was in first class. The pastor, seated in coach, asked a flight attendant if he could sit in first class. The flight attendant, dressed in a pink uniform with blue trim, explained that the rules did not allow this—even though first class was empty. The flight attendant then moved on.

A moment later, however, a flight attendant in a blue uniform with pink trim came and told the pastor to come with her. The pastor, noticing the different uniform, assumed that this was the head flight attendant and followed her. She led him to first class and brought him some food and made conversation with him for some time. The pastor never mentioned his daughter, though inside he still worried.

Suddenly, the flight attendant leaned forward and said, "Listen, man of God, your daughter will not die. She will be fine. Do not worry." Then, she left.

The first flight attendant, dressed in a pink uniform with blue trim, walked through first class and was surprised to see the pastor. "What are you doing up here?" she asked. "I told you that you could not sit here."

The pastor quickly explained about the "head" flight attendant in a blue uniform and pink trim. He even showed her the packages and crumbs from the food he had eaten. She explained that no one had a blue uniform with pink trim. The pastor realized that an angel had comforted him. God had been with him all along.

This is a true story. It is not very different from today's passage. The disciples just had a very long day, and Jesus told them to row to the other side of the lake and He would meet them there later. Then Jesus went up on a hill to pray. But a strong wind came up, and the disciples ended up rowing for at least nine hours against the wind. The disciples probably thought Jesus didn't know or care about their struggle. Notice, though, that Mark 6:48 says that Jesus could see His disciples struggling. Jesus did know. Jesus did care. And He came to them at just the right time.

Do you ever feel like God doesn't know or care about a struggle you have? _____

Name a struggle or two that you wish God would help you conquer. _____

_____

God does know about your problems. He does care about what you are going through. And, though it may not seem fair, He is waiting for just the right time to come to you and take care of you. Ask God to give you the faith and strength to wait for His timing in this struggle. For further study, see Isaiah 40:30–31.

Closer, Closer

Matthew 14:34–36; Mark 6:53–56

CRACK! It was the sound Dan had been waiting for—the sound of a bat hitting a home run. Dan had lousy seats in the back of the baseball field, but that all changed when the ball began to head toward his section of the bleachers. Dan hopped up, tore off his baseball cap, and began running toward the ball's final destination.

Everyone else in the crowd wanted the ball too, and Dan had a terrible time making his way through the crowd around him. By now the ball was descending, but Dan was not yet where he needed to be. "Closer, closer—if I could only get a little closer!" Dan thought to himself as he tried to squeeze between the others.

Finally, as the ball was about to land, Dan stood up on the bleachers and leaped in the air, holding his baseball cap high overhead as a glove. He leaned and stretched, and just managed to slip his cap underneath the ball. He felt a satisfying tug as the ball landed in his cap.

The TV cameras managed to catch the elated look on Dan's face as he victoriously pulled the ball out of the cap and held it up for everyone to see.

Dan's hot dog and drink were no longer important. His seat was no longer important. All he could think about was getting close enough to the ball to win the prize.

In today's passage, people were straining to get close enough to Jesus to touch the edge of His cloak and be healed. They left everything to get close enough to Jesus to experience His power and be changed.

Do you ever feel like God is far away? _____ Why? _____

What can you do to change that? _____

The people in Jesus' day left everything to get close to Jesus. They went where He was and left everything else behind. Here are some ideas to follow to get closer to God:

- Spend time in *worship*—together with friends at church and alone at home by yourself. Get some quiet Christian music and spend time focusing on God and His qualities. God inhabits the praises of His people.
- Spend time in *prayer.* Leave your worries and thoughts behind and simply get alone with God and pour out your heart to Him in prayer. God hears the cries of His people.
- Spend time *reading God's Word.* Get away from the TV and the radio and read the words of your Creator. God wrote the whole book just for His people.

Don't wait another moment to get closer to God. Spending time in His presence always changes you for the better.

Undeniable Proof

John 6:22–40

> A teenage atheist walked into a convenience store late one night to buy a snack. As she went up to the counter, she noticed that the guy in front of her had a very nice leather jacket. She liked it so much that she spoke up.
>
> "That is one awesome jacket!" she exclaimed.
>
> The man in front of her turned around, looked at her, and smiled. "You like it?"
>
> "Yes, very much," the girl said. "That's the best-looking jacket I have ever seen in my life."
>
> "You're serious? You really like it that much?" the man asked.
>
> "Yes, I do," she insisted.
>
> Without another word, the man took off the jacket. The girl was expecting the man to show her how nice the inside of the jacket was as well. She was expecting to get a "tour" of all of its features. Instead, when the man took off the jacket, he handed it to her and said, "It's yours."
>
> The girl could not believe her ears. "You are giving this jacket to me? No kidding?"
>
> "No kidding," the man said as he walked out of the store. "Enjoy it."
>
> The girl stood there, dumbfounded. She paid for her snack, went back to the car, and climbed in where her friends were waiting. "I believe in God," she told them suddenly. "There must be a God because of what just happened."

This is a true story about an atheist who suddenly found herself without an argument against God's existence. No one proved it to her through scientific evidence or a miraculous sign, but she believed because one man unselfishly gave her a gift with no questions asked.

Something similar happened to a group of people who spent a day with Jesus. They were given an unselfish gift—Jesus fed all five thousand of them. Yet these people chose not to believe that Jesus was who He said He was.

God doesn't expect you to prove that He exists to people with scientific evidence or miracles. Instead, He wants you to introduce Jesus to them through your actions—your love for them and your Christian brothers and sisters (John 13:35).

Do you know of anyone who does not believe Jesus is the Son of God? _____

Write down the names of at least one person whom you come into contact with on a regular basis who is not a Christian. _____

Now, write down something totally unselfish *that you could do for this person during the next week.* _____ *Don't expect anything in return. Don't expect the person to suddenly believe in God. Just love that person unselfishly and see what happens.*

Ask God to give you an opportunity to be a witness to this person this week through an unselfish act. If the person asks you why you are doing this, explain, "Because it's what Jesus would do." Then use that opportunity to tell the person about Jesus.

Weekly Bible Study and Prayer Review

Bible Study

Look back through some of the Scriptures you read this week. Write down the one verse or passage that God used to speak to you.

_____

_____

_____

_____

*Memorize this verse or passage. You can do it if you spend just
a few minutes saying it to yourself.*

Now, think of at least one situation you will probably face soon in which you could use this Scripture to help you make the right decision. Write down that situation below.

_____

Quote the Scripture when you face this situation, and live by it.

Prayer Time

*Take a few moments to praise God for who He is.
Now take a few moments to thank God for things He has done for you.
Now ask God to make you into the person He wants you to be.
Ask God to use you to help others become closer to God.*

Below is your prayer list for the week. Keep it updated each week. If your prayer isn't answered this week, carry it over to next week's list.

Request	Date of Original Request	Date Answered
_____	__/__/__	__/__/__
_____	__/__/__	__/__/__
_____	__/__/__	__/__/__
_____	__/__/__	__/__/__
_____	__/__/__	__/__/__
_____	__/__/__	__/__/__
_____	__/__/__	__/__/__
_____	__/__/__	__/__/__
_____	__/__/__	__/__/__

*Pray for the things on your list and trust God to provide.
Forgive anyone you have not yet forgiven.
Ask God to forgive you for any unconfessed sin in your life.
Ask God to keep you out of trouble with sin.
Acknowledge that God is in complete control of your life
and will take care of everything.*

You Are What You Eat

John 6:41–59

> The Israelites were wandering in the desert with no food to eat, and they were hungry. So God decided to provide them bread from heaven called manna, which means, "What is it?"
>
> The bread would appear on the ground like frost in the morning. The Israelites would leave their tents and gather just enough manna to provide them with food for the day. If they gathered more than they needed for one day, the next morning the manna would be rotten and full of maggots. However, on Friday the Israelites were instructed by God to gather enough manna for two days, because Saturday was a day of rest. When the Israelites gathered enough manna for two days on Friday, it would not rot the next morning—it would still be good for the day.
>
> Every day for forty years the Israelites went out Sunday through Saturday to find manna. They could bake it, boil it, or cook it in any number of ways. God did this so that the Israelites would realize that the food came straight from Him. He wanted His children to know that He was their Father, and that He cared enough for them to provide for their needs.

If you want to read more about this story, you can find it in the Bible in Exodus 16:1–36. This story is important to know for today's passage because Jesus claimed to be *manna*—true bread from heaven. This was a radical thing for Jesus to say, and it made a lot of people mad.

What Jesus was really saying was (1) I come straight from God; and (2) You must eat My flesh (believe in Him and His death on the cross where His body was sacrificed for you) or you will die. We earthlings are wandering around on this planet like the Israelites were wandering in the desert. God has provided us with Jesus to give us what we need to really live—His death on the cross, where His flesh was offered for you. God cared enough for us that He provided us with exactly what we needed—Him.

What's the longest you've ever gone without eating anything? _____

What's the longest you've ever gone without reading your Bible? _____

Praying? _____

Jesus Christ is real food, meaning you must choose to put Jesus inside you every day through prayer and Bible study. And don't worry, He tastes good (Psalm 34:8). He is exactly what you need. The longer you go without Him, the weaker you will get. The more of Him you eat, the stronger you will get.

Ask God to help you put Jesus inside of you every day. Plan on having breakfast with God with an early morning quiet time. Have a late-night snack with God by praying before you go to bed. Spend some time right now with God by thanking Him for providing you with all that you need—Jesus Himself.

Taking the Easy Way

John 6:60–71

Marvin watched with fascination as the little cocoon in front of him began to wiggle and roll over. Inside was an unborn butterfly ready to see the world and fly to far-off places. Soon, a tiny hole appeared in the end of the cocoon as the insect began to work its way out.

Slowly and steadily the butterfly enlarged the hole and began to squeeze through. As Marvin watched, it seemed as if the struggle would never end. The hole seemed too small for the butterfly to fit through. At one point, the butterfly seemed to give up entirely.

Marvin decided that the butterfly needed help, so he gently reached down and tore the hole in the cocoon open completely. Now the butterfly could escape with ease, Marvin thought.

The butterfly did come out of the cocoon, but something was dreadfully wrong. The butterfly's head was too large and the wings were too small and brittle. It could not fly at all.

Marvin discovered later that he had made a serious mistake. God had designed the cocoon to be difficult to climb out of so that as the butterfly squeezed through the hole, the pressure forced fluids in the insect's body back into the wings.

Sometimes life gets tough, and we want to ask God, "Why is this happening to me?" What we don't realize is that God has a plan for us, and the struggle we go through is actually making us into something better. Many people give up on God during tough times though, like those in today's passage.

Jesus said some things that made many of His disciples turn away from Him, but the original twelve disciples did not, because in the words of Peter, "Where else are we going to go? You've got all the answers." The ones who walked away were taking the easy road—back home where it was comfortable.

Do you ever find it difficult to be a Christian? _____

In what way(s)? _____

Do you ever feel like giving up? _____

Where do you go or what do you do when God doesn't seem to be the answer? _____

_____

People turn away from God and to other ways of life because they think it is easier. Drugs, alcohol, sex, music, TV, popularity, and money are only a few things that people turn to when following God seems too hard. Can you think of other things? _____

_____

The butterfly struggles to get out of the cocoon, but in doing so is given wings to fly. You struggle to follow Jesus, but in doing so you are given wings to fly (Isaiah 40:31). Don't ever give up on God, even when the going gets tough. Ask God right now to help you follow Him when times get tough or you don't understand what He is doing. Wait on Him, and He will give you wings to fly.

Stop Your Lion

Matthew 15:1–9; Mark 7:1–13

Gar had gone without work for several months, and he was completely broke. As he strolled down the street one day pondering his plight, he noticed a sign at the city zoo: HELP WANTED.

The zoo's gorilla had recently died, and they needed someone to dress up in a gorilla suit for a few days and eat bananas, sit around, and sleep. The pay was good, so Gar took the job.

Gar did as he was told for awhile, but he started to get bored. So he began walking around, hopping, and otherwise acting like a good gorilla should. Soon, a crowd began to gather. Gar liked the attention and really began playing the part. He jumped up and down, hung from a tree, and made gorilla noises. The crowd loved it. Gar climbed a tree and began swinging from a vine. As the crowd cheered, the vine broke and Gar landed a few feet in front of a lion in the pen next door.

Gar panicked and began running around, screaming, "Help! I'm going to be eaten alive! Help!" As Gar went "bananas," the lion tackled the gorilla and said, "We are both going to get fired if you don't shut up!"[12]

The zoo had a habit of employing fake animals. They dressed the part and fooled the crowd, but they were just people in animal suits.

Jesus had a problem with fakes in His day. Some men were accusing Jesus and His disciples of sinning for not ceremonially washing their hands before they ate. The Bible says nothing about such a rule, but these men thought it was necessary to please God. Jesus disagreed with them and accused them of being fakes—pretending to be religious by following rules without reason.

It's easy to become a fake Christian without realizing it. You can wear the "suit" by wearing a Christian T-shirt, carrying a Bible, and showing up at church. You can make Christian "sounds" by saying the right things, singing during worship, and praying magnificent prayers out loud. However, if you don't truly read your Bible, pray, worship, and live your faith, then these actions mean nothing. How can you avoid being a fake? By letting Jesus, who lives in you, live *through* you. Jesus was never a fake, so if you let Him control your life then you won't be either.

Have you pretended to be a good little Christian when really you were not walking with God the way that you should? _____

Have you ever noticed someone else being a hypocrite? _____

How could you tell? _____

If it was easy for you to spot a hypocrite, don't you think others will spot you? _____

Will God spot you? _____

Ask God to help you be true to yourself, to your faith, and to Him. When you suffer, pray about it and tell someone—don't pretend everything is OK. When you sin, don't hide it—confess it to God and walk away from it.

Losing Your Marbles

Matthew 15:10–20; Mark 7:14–23

Manuel often made money for his family by traveling from his small Mexican village into Arizona and collecting scrap metal. On one such occasion Manuel picked up a large amount of scrap metal and piled it into the back of his pickup truck and headed back to Mexico.

Inside this pile of scrap metal was an old X-ray machine that bounced around as Manuel drove. Soon, from inside the machine, shiny little metal balls the size of marbles came rolling out into the bed of the pickup truck. Manuel did not notice this. Soon he arrived at a scrap metal dealer, sold his cargo, and returned to his home in a small village.

The children in the area soon discovered the marbles in Manuel's truck and began playing with them. No one noticed or asked where the marbles came from. The marbles soon were spread out all over the village. A few weeks later, many people in the village began to get sick. Some people even died after a time. The whole village seemed to have a curse hanging over it, and no one could explain why.

Finally, when specialists were called into the village to find the source of the plague, they discovered that the little "marbles" were radioactive. Those tiny little steel balls had caused the entire village to be affected by a very bad case of radiation poisoning.[13]

The source of the problem was very difficult to find. No one ever suspected the true source until many people had died. Sin is a lot like that—we wonder what the source of it is. When people choose to become addicted to alcohol, people call it a disease. When people choose homosexuality as a lifestyle, society says they are born that way. When a normally sane person commits murder, he can often plead "temporary insanity" as a defense.

The truth is, as Jesus stated in today's passage, the source of sin is clear: it comes from the heart. Sin is a choice. Nothing that comes from the outside (temptation, circumstances, the devil, etc.), can cause sin. Sin is caused by evil desires that come from within the heart. This is difficult to swallow because it means that we are ultimately responsible for our own sin. We can't blame the devil or our situation. We made a conscious choice and have to face the consequences.

Have you ever blamed someone or something else for the sin(s) you commit? _____

Why? _____

What was the true source of the sin? _____

If your heart is the true source of your sin problem, what can you do to solve it? _____

_____

Ask God to help you cleanse your heart from sin. Concentrate on giving Jesus your whole heart so there isn't any room in there for anything else.

For further study, read Psalms 119:9–11, 139:23–24; Proverbs 4:23; and James 1:14.

The Answer Is Obvious

Matthew 15:21–28; Mark 7:24–30

During the Civil War a father and son were killed in the Battle of Gettysburg, leaving only the youngest boy as the man of his family. His mother and sisters could not survive without him to plant the crops that year, so the soldier went to Washington, D.C. to ask President Lincoln to receive a hardship discharge.

When the soldier arrived at the White House, a guard met him at the front gate. The soldier explained his plight, but the guard would not let him pass. Discouraged, the soldier sat down on a park bench nearby.

A young boy noticed the soldier's sadness and sat down next to him. He asked, "What's wrong?" The soldier told the little boy. The little boy hopped up and said, "Come with me."

The soldier followed the young boy, who led him right past the guard at the front gate of the White House. Then they walked into the White House past several guards who didn't even glance their way. The soldier was amazed. Finally, the little boy led the soldier to the Oval Office and without even knocking walked right in to see the President. President Lincoln looked up from behind his desk and said, "Good morning, son. Introduce me to your friend."

The soldier explained to President Lincoln his problems and promptly received a hardship discharge. [14]

The reason the soldier was so successful is that he found a way—the only way—into the White House. That way was through President Lincoln's son.

In today's passage, Jesus was trying to take a little break from all His work and get some rest. Suddenly, an unexpected woman showed up and began asking Jesus for help in healing her daughter from demon possession. At first, it looked as though Jesus was telling her to go away. The woman persisted in her pleas, and her faith was so great that Jesus answered her request. Jesus knew all along that He would answer the woman's prayer, but He tested her faith to see if she would seek Him as the only answer.

Sometimes it may look as though God is ignoring your prayers. You ask and ask and ask and it seems as though God just doesn't care. The woman could have thought this and walked away, but instead she became even more humble and even more persistent in her prayers. She is an example for you to follow.

Have you prayed for something that God has yet to answer? _____

What is your request? _____

How do you feel when you don't see the answer? _____

Do you really believe Jesus is the only hope for you, or have you decided to look elsewhere?

_____

Don't give up. Place all of your hope in Jesus. Become more persistent in your prayers. Humble yourself even more before God. He loves you and wants to help you, but He wants to make sure you are seeking Him and Him alone for the answer.

Youth Ministry

Matthew 15:29–31; Mark 7:31–37

Miss Thompson was a schoolteacher. She tried her best to treat every child the same, but often she did not. Teddy was especially hard to like. He wasn't interested in class. He was messy. He was unattractive.

When Miss Thompson graded Teddy's papers, she would get satisfaction out of putting X's on his paper. If he failed, she would put a bright red "F" at the top. Miss Thompson knew better. She had seen Teddy's records. His mother died two years ago, and his father never helped him with schoolwork.

Just before Christmas, Teddy brought a crudely wrapped gift. Miss Thompson was afraid to open it, but she did. Inside was an old bracelet with missing rhinestones and some cheap perfume. The other kids in class giggled, but Miss Thompson put on the bracelet, dabbed on some perfume, and pretended to really enjoy the gift. Teddy stayed after class to tell Miss Thompson that she looked and smelled nice—like his mother.

When Teddy left the room that day, Miss Thompson begged God for forgiveness. She became a new person, dedicated to helping everyone in class—including people like Teddy.

Teddy went on to graduate second in his class in high school, first in his class in college, and then went on to become a doctor. When he got married, he asked Miss Thompson to sit in the pew where his mother would have sat. She did.[15]

Sometimes it's easy to do good for a group of people, like a class of students, but harder to do good for an individual like Teddy. In today's passage, both Matthew and Mark are telling stories from the same time period. Matthew talks about a large group of people that Jesus healed. Mark, however, tells the story of just one man. Jesus ministered to both groups and individuals.

If you are going to do what Jesus did, you've got to be a minister to both groups and individuals. What is a minister? A minister is a person who chooses to do good for people without any expectation of repayment. A minister is a person who goes to people where they are and meets their needs. A minister is a Christian—God has called all of us to be ministers (Acts 26:16). When you do these things, you are doing ministry that helps people see God as a loving, caring God.

Name a group of people around you that needs ministry. _____

Name one person around you that needs ministry. _____

What can you do to minister to the group? _____

What can you do to minister to the individual? _____

Ask God to show you what your ministry is to the people around you—both groups and individuals. Keep your eyes open for opportunities, and never turn anyone away. You never know what kind of impact you can have on other people's lives, including the Teddys of the world.

Weekly Bible Study and Prayer Review

Bible Study

Look back through some of the Scriptures you read this week. Write down the one verse or passage that God used to speak to you.

_____

_____

_____

_____

*Memorize this verse or passage. You can do it if you spend just
a few minutes saying it to yourself.*

Now, think of at least one situation you will probably face soon in which you could use this Scripture to help you make the right decision. Write down that situation below.

_____

Quote the Scripture when you face this situation, and live by it.

Prayer Time

*Take a few moments to praise God for who He is.
Now take a few moments to thank God for things He has done for you.
Now ask God to make you into the person He wants you to be.
Ask God to use you to help others become closer to God.*

Below is your prayer list for the week. Keep it updated each week. If your prayer isn't answered this week, carry it over to next week's list.

Request	Date of Original Request	Date Answered
_____	__/__/__	__/__/__
_____	__/__/__	__/__/__
_____	__/__/__	__/__/__
_____	__/__/__	__/__/__
_____	__/__/__	__/__/__
_____	__/__/__	__/__/__
_____	__/__/__	__/__/__
_____	__/__/__	__/__/__
_____	__/__/__	__/__/__

*Pray for the things on your list and trust God to provide.
Forgive anyone you have not yet forgiven.
Ask God to forgive you for any unconfessed sin in your life.
Ask God to keep you out of trouble with sin.
Acknowledge that God is in complete control of your life
and will take care of everything.*

For God So Gloved the World

Matthew 15:32–39; Mark 8:1–10

Jason threw open the door and ran outside to the mailbox expectantly. The bright July sun made him squint as he opened the mailbox and reached inside. His fingers felt what he was looking for—a package.

"Yippeee!" Jason screamed as he ran back inside the house. He threw the other mail onto the coffee table and ran into his room and closed the door. Every year, Jason couldn't wait for his birthday. Every year, Aunt Clara sent a mysterious, expensive gift inside a small box wrapped in plain brown paper and tied with kite string. Barely able to contain himself, Jason tore open the wrapping and pried open the box.

Immediately his face fell. Inside was a pair of winter gloves and nothing more. "Gloves!" Jason groaned. "What am I going to do with gloves in the middle of July?" Disappointed, Jason put the gloves into his closet on the top shelf and forgot about them.

Nine months later, Jason was packing for a ski trip with his youth group. He noticed the gloves Aunt Clara had sent him in the closet and decided to try them on. Something was stuffed into the fingers, however, blocking Jason's hand from sliding into the gloves. Investigating further, Jason began to pull out $10 bills from each of the fingers. Aunt Clara had given him $100 in cash, but Jason hadn't noticed because he didn't think the gloves were of any use to him.

For nine months Jason had $100 that he didn't even know about because he didn't take the time to look carefully at his gift. As Christians, we can often make the same mistake. Just look at the disciples in today's passages. If you remember, Jesus had once fed more than 5,000 people with only five loaves of bread and two fish. Now, there were more than 4,000 people who needed food, and Jesus suggested to the disciples that they feed the crowd themselves. Did the disciples remember the time that Jesus fed the 5,000? No! Instead, they asked, "Where in the world could we find food to feed all these people?"

Has God ever helped you with a problem or need? _____

How? _____

Do you have any needs in your life right now that you are worried about? _____

What are they? _____

Don't you think God is just as able to help you with these needs as He did before? _____

When you became a Christian, God stuffed Himself inside of you just like Aunt Clara stuffed those $10 bills into the gloves. Sometimes, though, it's easy to forget that Jesus is inside, waiting to take care of your every need. Look on the inside at the gift God has given you. Take time right now to do two things: (1) thank God for all of the things He has done for you in the past, and (2) ask God to help you with the needs and problems you have in the present.

I Saw the Sign

Matthew 16:1–4; Mark 8:11–13

This is a true story. The resurrection of Jesus was a sign to these two men that Christianity was true. In today's passage, some men wanted Jesus to perform some miraculous sign to prove that He was who He claimed to be. Jesus said that no sign would be given except the sign of Jonah. Jonah spent three days in the belly of a fish. People assumed he was dead, but Jonah turned up alive. Jesus said that the only sign He would give to humans was His resurrection. Much like Jonah, Jesus was assumed to be dead permanently, but He turned up alive a short time later.

Why do you think God doesn't just appear to people miraculously to prove He exists?

_____

Is it fair for God to expect us to believe in Him when we can't see Him? _____

Why or why not? _____

Two brilliant atheists became Christians when they took the time to look at the facts. God doesn't want to force Himself on us and give us no choice to believe. He wants us to seek *Him* (Hebrews 11:6). Those who actually take the time to seek Him will find that He is real.

Perhaps at times in your Christian walk you doubt the existence of God. Your emotions and circumstances cause you to wonder if He is really there. Don't lose hope. Turn to some close Christian friends and tell them how you feel. Ask them to pray for you. Spend some time reading the Bible—examining the facts. Ask God (even if you wonder if He's there to hear you) to help you overcome your doubts and see Him again. If He's real—and He is—then He will hear your prayer and answer you.

Beauty and the Yeast

Matthew 16:5-12; Mark 8:14–21

Sir William Osler eyed his new class of medical students at Oxford University with hope that they would listen carefully to his lectures and learn the concepts he would teach this semester. He began his first class with a lecture on the importance of paying attention to details.

He said, "I have in my hand a bottle of urine. By tasting it, we can often determine what is wrong with the patient." He then put a finger into the urine. Then, to the disbelief of everyone, he put his finger into his mouth. The class shuddered in disgust and low "ooohs" echoed across the room.

Sir William then said, "Pass this bottle around the room, and each of you do exactly as I did." With much reluctance, each student took the bottle of urine, dipped a finger inside, and tasted the liquid. Each student reacted differently—some with twisted facial expressions, others with audible gags, some with silly giggles. All of them, though, hated the idea and decided that Sir William was someone they would not like very much.

When the bottle made its way back to Sir William, he announced, "Perhaps now all of you will understand what I mean when I lecture you about paying attention to details. If you had watched me carefully at the beginning of class, you would have noticed that I put my index finger into the urine, but I put my middle finger in my mouth."[17]

Details *are* important. There is a big difference between putting a clean finger into your mouth and putting a urine-soaked finger into your mouth. In today's passage, Jesus explained the importance of details as well. He mentioned three people who taught false rules, and that we should be detailed in avoiding those teachings. What were they? The Pharisees taught that following God was all about observing rules and traditions. The Sadducees and Herod taught that there was no afterlife—that's why they were sad, you see. Just as a little yeast can make a lot of bread rise, so also can a little false teaching take a true disciple of God and turn him or her into something else.

Have you ever heard someone teach something that is false when compared to what God says? _____

For instance? _____

Every day you are faced with false teachings. You hear things like (1) There is no God, and humans evolved from nothing; (2) Abortion isn't murder—it's a woman's right to choose; (3) All religions are equal as long as you are sincere—everyone will go to heaven. If you aren't careful in paying attention to details, you may start to believe these things and stop living your life like Jesus would.

Ask God right now to help you discern true and false teachings around you. Pray for the courage to stand up for what is right even when you may be the only one. Make a commitment to stay in God's Word, where all true teaching is found.

Got Milk?

Mark 8:22–26

> Three-year-old Brandon loved his daddy. One day as he passed through the living room, he saw his dad eating chocolate chip cookies. Brandon noticed that Dad didn't have any milk.
>
> Brandon ran into the kitchen, pulled up a chair, and climbed up to the cabinet with the glasses. As he opened the door, he smashed it against the adjacent cabinet, leaving a hole. Then, as he reached for a glass, he knocked several others off, and they fell to the floor and shattered. Brandon didn't notice, though, because all he wanted to do was get his dad some milk. Brandon's dad could see all of this, but decided to watch his son instead of interrupting.
>
> Brandon climbed down, avoiding the broken glass, and ran over to the refrigerator. He jerked the door open so violently that it almost came off the hinges. He put the glass on the floor, reached for the milk, and began pouring it into the glass on the floor. Most of the milk spilled on the floor.
>
> Excited, Brandon picked up the glass of milk and ran into the living room to his father, screaming, "Daddy, guess what I did for you?" Just before Brandon reached his father, he tripped, breaking the glass and spilling milk on his dad and everything else.
>
> Brandon started to cry and looked up at Daddy, expecting to be punished. Instead, Brandon's daddy picked him up, held him tight, and said, "This is my son!"

Brandon tried very hard, but he really didn't do anything right. And yet his daddy loved him anyway. This is called *unconditional* love—it's the kind of love God has for you. Look at today's passage. A blind man came to Jesus to be healed. Jesus touched him, and when the man opened his eyes he could only see a little bit. Instead of condemning the man for his lack of faith, Jesus touched him *again* so that he could see perfectly. Jesus loved the man and was patient with him in spite of his failure.

God loves you in spite of your failures, just like Brandon's daddy loved him and just like Jesus loved the blind man. Sometimes the way that you feel and the circumstances around you make you think that God has abandoned you. However, even when you fail He picks you up and holds you and says, "This is My child!"

Have you ever failed a test? _____ Have you ever lost a game? _____

Have you ever let your parents down? _____ Have you ever failed at doing what God wants you to do? _____ Describe your greatest failure. _____

Do you ever feel like God doesn't love you because of your failures? _____

Ask God to help you be aware of His unconditional love for you. And the next time you fail at something, don't run away from God in fear—run toward Him and let Him hold you in His unconditional love.

Pop Quiz

Mr. and Mrs. Beasley, an older American Christian couple, moved to a country in the Middle East. Mr. Beasley had found work there and was trying to make his fortune. Mrs. Beasley spent her days at home taking care of their large, luxurious house. To assist her, Mrs. Beasley hired a local young boy to become her servant.

Mrs. Beasley liked things to be perfect, and she pushed the servant boy hard to clean and make things just right. Often she would be harsh with him when he did not do things exactly the way she wanted them. But the servant boy never complained and always did what Mrs. Beasley said.

After five months, the servant boy showed up one morning and announced, "I am quitting today."

"But why?" asked Mrs. Beasley. "I need you to help me with all of the housework."

The boy responded, "Ma'am, I want to find God. I chose to work with you for five months because I heard you were a Christian. You have shown me by your actions who Jesus is. I do not like what I see. Now I shall go work for a Muslim woman for five months and see what Allah is like."[18]

The young servant boy saw Jesus as a harsh, uncaring perfectionist because that is what he saw in Mrs. Beasley. In today's passage, Jesus wanted to know how other people saw Him, so He asked His disciples to tell Him what people were saying. Many of the people who had seen Jesus from a distance said He was just another prophet. But the disciples who had spent time with Jesus, especially Peter, saw Jesus as the *Christ*—which means the Messiah, or the Son of God Himself.

Do people see Jesus for who He really is when they look at you? Imagine for a moment that someone placed a hidden camera on your head yesterday and taped everything you did. This tape was then played on the national news with the headline, "The day in the life of a Christian." If everyone in America saw this, who would they say that Jesus is?

_____

Are you satisfied with this answer? _____ What can you do tomorrow to make sure that you live your life in a way that would help others see Jesus? _____

When you ask yourself, "What would Jesus do?" in every situation in life, and then you live the answer to that question to the best of your ability, people around you will begin to see Jesus. However, if you fail to answer that question (or if you just fail to ask the question in the first place), people around you will not see Jesus for who He really is.

Ask God to help you live your life today like Jesus would. Pray that you will never forget to ask yourself, "What would Jesus do right now if He were me?" Then ask for the wisdom and power to live the answer.

Denial Is Not a River in Egypt

Matthew 16:21–28; Mark 8:31–9:1; Luke 9:21–27

Ivan the Terrible was the ruler of Russia more than five hundred years ago. His sole desire was to conquer the countries around him and make them his own. He was so busy fighting that he didn't have time to find a wife and produce an heir to the throne. His advisors urged him to find a good wife. Ivan did—Sophia, the princess of Greece.

The king of Greece agreed to allow Ivan the Terrible to marry his daughter on one condition—Ivan must become a Christian and be baptized. Ivan agreed and traveled to Greece with five hundred soldiers to be baptized and get married.

The five hundred soldiers decided that they wanted to be baptized with Ivan. Before the baptism took place, the priest of the church in Greece explained that to be baptized, everyone must agree to the articles of the Christian faith of the church of Greece—which included no fighting. Ivan and the soldiers wanted to join the church, but they did not want to give up fighting. They came up with a plan.

At the baptism, Ivan and his five hundred soldiers walked down into the river. As the priests motioned for them to go under the water, Ivan and the soldiers all pulled out their swords and submerged themselves in the water—except for one arm and the sword pointed toward the sky.[19]

The story of the unbaptized arm says that becoming a Christian doesn't require full commitment. Jesus says just the opposite. In today's passage, He said there are three things that a committed Christian will do to follow Jesus. What are they?

1. _____

2. _____

3. _____

The answers are to deny yourself daily, take up your cross, and follow Jesus. To deny yourself is to do what God wants and not what you want. Name something that you know God wants you to do that you haven't been doing recently. _____

To take up your cross daily means to finish what you started, even when things get tough. Jesus came to the earth to die on the cross, and it got awful tough when He finally started carrying it up the hill. Name something that you once did for the Lord but quit because it got too tough. _____

To follow Jesus means, well, to follow Jesus. And you can't follow someone you're not looking at. You've got to keep your eyes on Him at all times and go where He leads. Name something that you feel God is leading you to do. _____

Look back at the last three blanks you filled out, and spend the rest of your quiet time praying that God will help you to deny yourself, take up your cross, *daily*, and follow Him in these areas.

Weekly Bible Study and Prayer Review

Bible Study

Look back through some of the Scriptures you read this week. Write down the one verse or passage that God used to speak to you.

_____
_____
_____
_____

*Memorize this verse or passage. You can do it if you spend just
a few minutes saying it to yourself.*

Now, think of at least one situation you will probably face soon in which you could use this Scripture to help you make the right decision. Write down that situation below.

_____

Quote the Scripture when you face this situation, and live by it.

Prayer Time

*Take a few moments to praise God for who He is.
Now take a few moments to thank God for things He has done for you.
Now ask God to make you into the person He wants you to be.
Ask God to use you to help others become closer to God.*

Below is your prayer list for the week. Keep it updated each week. If your prayer isn't answered this week, carry it over to next week's list.

Request	Date of Original Request	Date Answered
_____	__/__/__	__/__/__
_____	__/__/__	__/__/__
_____	__/__/__	__/__/__
_____	__/__/__	__/__/__
_____	__/__/__	__/__/__
_____	__/__/__	__/__/__
_____	__/__/__	__/__/__
_____	__/__/__	__/__/__

*Pray for the things on your list and trust God to provide.
Forgive anyone you have not yet forgiven.
Ask God to forgive you for any unconfessed sin in your life.
Ask God to keep you out of trouble with sin.
Acknowledge that God is in complete control of your life
and will take care of everything.*

Go Figure

Matthew 17:1–13; Mark 9:2–13; Luke 9:28–36

Once upon a time three businessmen came to a hotel to find a place to stay. The hotel manager had only one room. He charged them $30 for the room. The men paid and went to their room.

An hour or so later, the hotel manager felt he overcharged the men. He decided $25 was a fairer price for the room. The manager gave the bellboy $5 to return to the men. As the bellboy made his way upstairs, he said to himself, "I will keep $2 for myself and give them the other $3."

Question: Each man received $1 back, so they paid $9 each, or $27 total for the room, and the bellboy kept $2 for himself. $27 plus $2 is $29—but they originally paid $30! Where is the missing dollar? Take the time to consider the details of the story, and see if you can find the missing dollar.

Answer: Each man paid $27. SUBTRACT (don't add) the $2 the bellboy kept and you arrive at the correct total of $25—the amount the hotel manager actually charged!

In today's passage. Jesus had taken three men (Peter, James, and John) with Him to the top of a mountain. Suddenly, Jesus was transfigured (or dramatically changed in appearance). Moses and Elijah, two prophets from the Old Testament, appeared and talked with Jesus. A cloud enveloped them, and a voice from heaven spoke. Question: If three men go to the top of the mountain and hear a voice from heaven say, "This is My Son, the one I have chosen—listen to Him," then what should they do?

The answer to this question is easy—*listen to Jesus.* Many times in life you will face situations and circumstances that seem to have no answer—like the word problem above. You struggle over what to do, when to do it, how to do it, etc. Sometimes you listen to sources of advice that you shouldn't—bad advice from non-Christian friends, horoscopes, something you saw on TV, etc. You don't have to face decisions on your own. You already have the answer living inside your heart: Jesus. He has things to say to you that will take care of any problem you face. Just listen to Him.

Do you ever struggle with decisions? _____

What is one decision you are struggling with right now? _____

How can you "listen to Jesus" for the answer? _____

Making right choices is part of the Christian life. Each time you face a decision, you can choose to find out what Jesus wants, or you can go your own way. What will you do?

Spend some time in prayer asking the Lord to show you which way to go in this decision and any others you face. You may not think Jesus cares about your problem, but be patient and wait. Jesus will be transfigured before you (meaning you will see Him in a new light) as He reveals the answer to you.

The Axe of the Apostles

Matthew 17:14–21; Mark 9:14–29; Luke 9:37–43

The big, rugged lumberjack walked up to the foreman at the lumber mill and asked if he could have a job cutting down trees. The foreman said, "We could use someone else, and you look plenty strong enough. Let me see you cut down this tree here first."

Using his own axe, the lumberjack quickly and easily chopped down the tree. "You're hired," the foreman said. "Show up bright and early Monday morning and get started."

On Monday morning, the lumberjack showed up and began working. That day he cut down more trees than anyone else. In fact, he broke the lumber mill's record for the most trees cut down in one day by one person. On Tuesday, though, the lumberjack only cut down about the same number of trees as everyone else. He couldn't figure out why because he worked just as hard. By the end of the day Wednesday, the lumberjack had fallen into last place and could only cut down a few trees.

The foreman was threatening to fire the lumberjack, but first asked a very important question. "Hey, have you been sharpening your axe?"

Suddenly the lumberjack realized why he had not been able to cut down many trees. "I got so busy that I just forgot!" he exclaimed.[20]

If you don't sharpen your axe, you won't be able to chop down many trees. Prayer is like sharpening your axe—it's easy to forget, but it's the most important thing you can do. If you don't pray, you won't be able to chop down many obstacles that come your way. In today's passage, Jesus' disciples were unable to cast the demon out of a boy. Jesus expressed frustration over their lack of faith, and then cast out the demon Himself. Later the disciples asked Jesus why they were unable to tackle this problem, and Jesus said, "This kind comes out only by prayer." If you review the passages from yesterday, you will remember that Jesus went up on a mountain to pray. The three disciples who were with Him fell asleep, but Jesus was in prayer. When Jesus came down the mountain, He was "prayed up" and easily able to take care of the problem that faced Him. Notice that Jesus didn't necessarily have much time to pray about the specific problem at hand, but He had already spent a good deal of time in prayer with His Father, which empowered Him to take care of anything.

Are you prayed up? _____

What is the one thing that keeps you from spending more time with God in prayer?

_____

What could you do to get past this problem and pray anyway? _____

Take the time right now to pray. Remove all distractions. Get alone. Get quiet. Be still and know that He is God. Forget the clock, and just begin talking to God. Tell Him what He means to you. Tell Him what you need. Rest in His presence.

This Is for the Birds

Matthew 17:22–23; Mark 9:30–32; Luke 9:44–45

> It was 1942. World War II was taking its toll on American lives, and Eddie Rickenbacher was afraid he would be next. He and his eight crewmen on The Flying Fortress crash-landed into the ocean with no help in sight. They scrambled into two rafts and began to wait for someone to rescue them.
>
> The men carefully rationed what little food they had salvaged from the plane. After eight days, the food was gone. Still no one came. The sun continued to beat down on them relentlessly, and starvation seemed to be the only thing that awaited the men. Nine-foot-long sharks often circled the eight-foot-long rafts hungrily, waiting for their chance to feast. Days went by.
>
> In spite of this, every day in the afternoon the men would have a Bible study and prayer time. One day, right after the devotion, Eddie pulled his hat over his head and leaned back to try and get some sleep. A few seconds later, something landed on his head. Eddie didn't move—he realized that a seagull had landed on him. All the men were very quiet. Eddie moved suddenly and grabbed the seagull. Everyone had a chance to eat part of its flesh to survive. They used the guts of the bird for fish bait, caught some fish, and were able to survive until help arrived. They spent thirty days at sea.[21]

Eddie Rickenbacher did not understand why he was going through this painful trial. He was a Christian. Why were times so tough? Suddenly, a seagull came out of nowhere. Where did it come from? They were miles from land. It came from God, who did not forget Eddie and his men. He provided food so they could survive.

The disciples had just come from two days of victory. Three of them saw the transfiguration of Jesus on the mountaintop, and all of them saw Jesus cast a demon out of a boy. Things were looking great. Then Jesus announced that soon He would be arrested, tortured, and killed. The disciples didn't understand. They were filled with grief. They were afraid to talk to Jesus about what He meant. Suddenly, things didn't seem so great anymore.

Circumstances often dictate how we feel. When things are going great, we feel good. When things are not so great, we feel bad. Isn't that true? Name something that happened recently that made you feel good. _____

Now name something that happened recently that made you feel hurt or confused.

_____

Regardless of what you are going through, God has a good plan for your life. Don't get discouraged by the circumstances. Keep praying and asking God to see you through it.

Ask God right now to give you the strength to make it through whatever difficult times you currently face. And keep your eyes open for the amazing way that God will work.

Getting out of a Jam

Matthew 17:24–27

As Peter walked through his hometown, two men spotted him. Peter knew them—they had gone to school together. He knew they collected the annual temple tax. Peter squirmed, knowing he had not paid yet. He tried to avoid their gaze and pass by, but to no avail.

"Hey, Peter!" they said. "Long time no see. Listen, we don't have any record that you or this Jesus guy you follow has paid the temple tax this year. What's the deal? Doesn't Jesus support the temple?"

Peter opened his mouth without thinking and said, "Of course He does." Peter kept walking and said nothing further, leaving the two men murmuring behind him. The whole way home Peter thought about what he would say to Jesus. He paced back and forth in front of the house before finally going inside. As he walked through the door, Jesus spoke.

"So, Simon. Tell Me. When the king collects taxes, does he charge his own sons or everyone else?"

Amazed that Jesus already knew his situation, Peter mumbled, "Everyone else."

"Right," Jesus said. "But we don't want to offend the tax collectors, so go to the lake and take your fishing line with you. The first fish you catch will have a coin inside. Use that to pay My tax and yours."

Peter was always opening his mouth without thinking and getting himself into a jam. He had no idea whether or not Jesus had paid the tax. Peter probably anguished over what to say to Jesus. Notice, though, that Jesus was already aware of Peter's plight before Peter had a chance to say a word. Jesus explained patiently to Peter that he and the disciples were all exempt from the temple tax because they were sons of the real King—Jesus. Peter was then given a rather odd solution to his problem—which worked.

There is an important lesson here. You will make mistakes and get yourself into trouble. God knows that. And when you do, you'll pace around and wonder how to explain yourself to God. Realize, however, that before you ever go to Jesus to confess your plight, God has already worked out a solution.

Have you ever made a mistake that got you into trouble? _____

How did you feel? _____

Did you try to get out of trouble yourself, or did you ask for God's help? _____

Don't let your mistakes worry you or make you feel like you blew it and all hope is lost. Jesus understands that you make mistakes, and He will provide a way for you to get out of trouble if you will just go to Him for the answer. Ask God right now to give you a solution to the problems that you face. Wait for the answer. It may seem bizarre when it comes, but it will work.

Won't You Be My Baby?

Matthew 18:1–6; Mark 9:33–37; Luke 9:46–48

Two-year-old Collin ran to his toy box and pulled out a book. He ran over to Uncle Brian, handed him the book, and jumped up in his lap. He began clapping and squealing, waiting for Brian to read the book to him.

Collin didn't want Brian to just read the words of the book entitled, Animals on the Farm. Collin wanted Brian to point to each animal and make the right noises. "There's a horse," said Brian. "It goes . . ." Brian then proceeded to do his best horse imitation. As Brian turned each page, Collin sat mesmerized with glee, listening intently to every word and sound. He loved to hear about the dogs, cats, cows, ducks, frogs, chickens, and other animals.

When Brian finished with the book, Collin ran back to the toy box and pulled out a ball. "OK, Brian," he said, cocking his arm back and preparing to throw the ball to his uncle. He didn't even come close, but Brian didn't mind. He just laughed, went after the ball, and threw it back to Collin.

Young children like Collin have no jobs. They don't get paid. The government doesn't cease working if they die. They have yet to offer anything of real significance to society. Yet Jesus said that if we want to become great in the kingdom of heaven we must become like little children.

What do little children do that Jesus said we should imitate? One thing about children is that they love to spend time with their relatives. They crawl up in our laps, beg us to read books, ask us to play ball, and want us to hold them when it hurts. God likes that. He wants His children to come to Him for everything—when times are good and when times are bad. Another thing about children is that they love to practice doing "grown-up" things: playing ball, pounding hammers, dressing dolls, etc. God loves to see His children practicing their faith, even though they may make lots of mistakes along the way. When you drop the ball, God just goes over, picks it up, and throws it right back. Children also trust their parents to take care of them. God wants you to trust Him to take care of you.

What are ways that you could be more like a child in your walk with Jesus? _____

_____

What are some areas in which you could practice being more "grown-up"? _____

Do you love to spend time with God? _____

Do you really trust God to take care of all your needs? _____

Ask God to help you be more like a child in your faith. Lay all of your needs at His feet, and trust Him to take care of you. Crawl up in His lap and just spend a few minutes sitting with your Father. He'll hold you tight and let you know that He loves you more than anything in the world.

You're Not from Around Here

Mark 9:38–41; Luke 9:49–50

Shepherd Baptist Church and Shepherd Community Church were both located on the same street. Their youth groups would often compete against each other in basketball, volleyball, and softball. They were always trying to outdo each other.

One Saturday after a youth Bible study on serving, the Shepherd Community Church met together to go out and serve others. The youth pastor divided them into groups, sent them out, and told them to go serve others, all the while asking themselves, "What would Jesus do?" One group washed cars for free. Another group provided full service at a self-serve gas station. One group went to a nursing home and sang songs to the people there.

One group, though, went to a woman's house and pulled weeds, raked leaves, mowed, and picked up dead tree limbs. When they were done, the woman invited them inside, where she gave them some treats and prayed with them. As the group left, the old woman waved good-bye and said, "You young people from Shepherd Baptist Church are wonderful."

Everyone in the youth group looked at each other, debating whether or not to tell the woman that they were from Shepherd Community Church. They decided not to, because they believed that is what Jesus would have done.[22]

Though these two churches were of different denominations and their youth groups were rivals in sports, this youth group decided that they were not rivals in the kingdom of God—they were allies.

In today's passage, the disciples were offended when they saw another man who was not part of their group doing some work in Jesus' name. Rather than be glad that someone else was imitating Jesus, they became upset and told him to stop. Jesus said, "Wait a minute. Don't stop them. If they are not against us, then they are for us."

Jesus' statement has much to say about how Christian churches and denominations should treat each other. We are not enemies or rivals, we are allies fighting the same fight as we try to win the world to Jesus. We may not all be part of the same little group, but when we come into contact with someone else doing the work of Jesus we should support them.

How many other Christian denominations have churches nearby? _____

Can you name them? _____

What could you or your youth group do to show your support for these other churches?
_____ *Could you ask your youth pastor about a joint youth service among different denominations?* _____

Ask God to help you look beyond denominational labels and into the heart. Love your Christian brothers and sisters from other churches by supporting them and even joining them in what they do. Make a commitment to be united with everyone who claims Jesus Christ as Lord and Savior.

Weekly Bible Study and Prayer Review

Bible Study

Look back through some of the Scriptures you read this week. Write down the one verse or passage that God used to speak to you.

_____

_____

_____

_____

Memorize this verse or passage. You can do it if you spend just a few minutes saying it to yourself.

Now, think of at least one situation you will probably face soon in which you could use this Scripture to help you make the right decision. Write down that situation below.

_____

Quote the Scripture when you face this situation, and live by it.

Prayer Time

Take a few moments to praise God for who He is.
Now take a few moments to thank God for things He has done for you.
Now ask God to make you into the person He wants you to be.
Ask God to use you to help others become closer to God.

Below is your prayer list for the week. Keep it updated each week. If your prayer isn't answered this week, carry it over to next week's list.

Request	Date of Original Request	Date Answered
_____	___/___/___	___/___/___
_____	___/___/___	___/___/___
_____	___/___/___	___/___/___
_____	___/___/___	___/___/___
_____	___/___/___	___/___/___
_____	___/___/___	___/___/___
_____	___/___/___	___/___/___
_____	___/___/___	___/___/___
_____	___/___/___	___/___/___

Pray for the things on your list and trust God to provide.
Forgive anyone you have not yet forgiven.
Ask God to forgive you for any unconfessed sin in your life.
Ask God to keep you out of trouble with sin.
Acknowledge that God is in complete control of your life and will take care of everything.

Cut It Out—I Mean, Off!

Matthew 18:7–9; Mark 9:42–48

Big Cypress Swamp in Florida was the home to an old woman who lived in a makeshift shanty next to a pond. The pond was home to an alligator, and the old woman knew it. She didn't seem to mind though. Every day she would go down to the pond and dip her bucket to get her daily supply of water. Occasionally the woman saw the alligator, but she paid him no mind.

One day the woman came down to the pond as usual to draw water. As she bent down and dipped her bucket, the alligator suddenly lunged from underneath the water and locked its teeth on the old woman's right hand. She screamed and began trying to free her hand from the alligator's mouth, but she couldn't. The alligator rolled over, painfully twisting the old woman's hand until finally it came off completely. The woman, dazed and bleeding, ran into the house to call an ambulance.

The next day the authorities caught and killed the alligator. They cut open the alligator and found the old woman's hand inside. The park ranger told the newspaper, "Alligators are even more dangerous when they lose their fear of humans. Allowing them to stay near you actually increases the likelihood that they will attack."[23]

It's easy to say, "That woman was asking for it. I would never let an alligator live in my pond." However, we do the same thing every day. How? We allow the temptation for sin to live so close to us that it is bound to attack us sooner or later. Jesus said in today's passage that if your hand causes you to sin, then cut it off. What does He mean—that I have to cut off my hand?

Jesus is saying do whatever it takes to remove something that leads you to sin. For example, if you have satellite TV "living" in your home, perhaps you should stay away from it when your parents aren't around or you may end up watching something you shouldn't. When you go out on a date, plan in advance to make sure that you and your date don't go anywhere that would give you the opportunity of compromising your sexual purity. The next time you and your parents get into an argument, bite your tongue and don't say anything in the heat of the moment—count to ten and speak respectfully.

Do you have sin "living" near you? _____

What are some sins with which you particularly struggle? _____

What can you do to remove the opportunity for sin to attack? _____

Don't leave the alligator of sin in the pond of your life. Remove any and all opportunities for sin to reach out and grab you. Don't make the devil's job any easier. Ask God right now to help you identify sin around you and to give you the wisdom and strength to protect yourself in advance from temptation.

Someone Is Watching

Matthew 18:10–14

Cheryl was four years old, and she loved to go with her father to his little grocery store in the country. She would help him stock the shelves and tell the customers "Thank you," when they left the store. She loved to help.

Every day the milkman came into the store. Each time he saw Cheryl, he would say, "How is my little Miss America doing this morning?" Cheryl always turned red and giggled, hiding behind her father. As time went by, however, and Cheryl got older, she began to enjoy the milkman's encouraging words. She really looked forward to seeing him every time he came through the door. Sometimes she found herself staring through the window waiting for the milkman's truck to pull into the parking lot.

By the time Cheryl was a young teenager, she had a fantasy about becoming the real Miss America. She watched every pageant and dreamed of the day when she would be crowned. Eventually Cheryl's fantasy turned into a passionate vision. When she was old enough, Cheryl entered the local pageant. She went all the way to the national pageant, and in 1980 she became Miss America.[24]

The milkman probably had no idea how his simple daily greeting impacted the life of one little girl. Young people are like that though. They grow up to be what they see and hear around them. They watch and listen to others around them, even when they don't realize it.

Jesus knows the importance of the way we act around young people. In today's passage, He encourages us not to look down on them, but in fact to do everything we can to influence them in a godly way so that they will not grow up without hope. Whether you realize it or not, someone younger than you is watching you. They analyze your words and your actions, and they are imitating you.

The things you do and say around young people may affect them the rest of their lives—just as the milkman's words affected Cheryl. Once you realize this, you must be very careful to do what Jesus would do, which is to live your life for the kingdom of God so that those watching you will learn to do the same.

Does it scare you to know that others are watching you? _____

Why? _____

Think about the best and worst things you have ever done or said in public. Write those down: Best _____ *Worst* _____

Now suppose someone just a few years younger than you saw you do one or the other of these two things. How do you think it might affect that person for the rest of his or her life?
_____

Don't ever think that what you do goes unnoticed. God notices, and people younger than you notice. Ask God to help you live your life for Him at all times—even when you think no one is watching.

I've Got Something to Say

Matthew 18:15–20

Krista said some mean, hurtful things to Alice during lunch. Alice hoped that Krista would apologize to her before the end of the day, but she didn't. That night Alice couldn't concentrate on her homework, and she didn't sleep well. The next day Alice again waited for Krista to make the first move; but by lunch, it became obvious that Krista was ignoring her altogether.

Alice's thoughts then turned to revenge. Maybe she could start a rumor about her. Maybe she could say something just as hateful. Then Alice came back to her senses. No, I can't hurt Krista, she thought. But what do I do?

Alice decided to confront Krista on the phone that evening. She called Krista and explained how hurt she was, but Krista just hung up the phone. Then Alice called another friend and told her what happened. The two of them decided to confront Krista together the next day at lunch. Krista would not listen and simply walked away.

Two days later, during Sunday morning Bible study, Alice told the entire class what had happened with Krista sitting right there. Everyone looked at Krista to see what would happen. Krista began crying, offered an apology, and the two girls became friends once again.

Sometimes friends, or just two Christians who happen to know each other, can have a falling out. Jesus knew this kind of thing would happen, and He provided a plan of action in today's passage. If a Christian sins against you, it is your responsibility to make the first move. You should go to that person privately and explain the situation. If things aren't settled, you should then take a friend along and confront the person again. If the situation still doesn't get resolved, you are to take the problem to the church—perhaps your Sunday school class or your entire youth group. By then, hopefully, things will be resolved. If not, you have done your part—now you just leave the other person alone until she decides to admit fault and ask for reconciliation.

Do you have an unresolved conflict between you and another Christian? _____

Who is the person and what is the situation? _____

Have you taken the biblical steps to become reconciled to this person? _____

What step can you take next to resolve this problem? _____

_____

Ask God to reveal what you need to do to resolve any ongoing conflicts between you and another Christian brother or sister. Pray for the strength you will need to be bold enough to confront this person and take the necessary biblical steps to see it resolved. God wants the two of you to be reconciled together. Do what Jesus would do and make things right.

Paint and Suffering

Matthew 18:21–35

> Leonardo da Vinci is the famous artist who created the painting The Last Supper, which shows Jesus and His twelve disciples seated around a table about to have a meal on the night before He was crucified. While da Vinci was creating his masterpiece, the time came to paint the face of Judas Iscariot, the one who betrayed Jesus. As da Vinci pondered how to create a face that would represent pure evil, he thought of someone he knew—a fellow painter who had become his enemy. Da Vinci smiled at the thought that his enemy would be represented as Judas in his painting and created a perfect likeness of his face. Satisfied, he moved on to the rest of the disciples.
>
> The time came to paint the face of Jesus. After days of careful deliberation, da Vinci just couldn't seem to create Jesus' face. He paced. He pondered. He tried numerous times but still could not paint the face of Jesus at the center of the Last Supper table.
>
> Finally, da Vinci realized his problem. He could not paint the face of Jesus because he was blinded by unforgiveness for his enemy in the face of Judas. Da Vinci quickly changed the face of Judas, forgave his enemy, and found that he was then able to paint the face of Jesus.[25]

Leonardo da Vinci, one of the most famous artists of all time, recognized that he could not see the face of Jesus without first forgiving his enemy. In the same way, the unmerciful servant in today's passage learned the same thing the hard way.

Can you think of at least one person who has done something to you that you have not yet fully forgiven? If so, write down that person's name. _____

What did this person do to you? _____

Now, write down your own name. _____

Write down a sin that you committed recently that you have not yet asked God to forgive you for. _____

Do you want God to forgive you for your sin? _____ Then take the time right now to forgive this person from your heart. It may take some time, but ask God to give you the strength and the love to do so. Realize that Jesus died for this person the same way He died for you. Then, once you have forgiven this person completely from your heart, ask the Lord to forgive you as well.

What did Jesus do when people beat Him, spit on Him, pulled the hair of His beard out of His face, and crucified Him to suffer a cruel death—He forgave them. In your attempts to imitate Jesus and do what He would do, you must learn to forgive others no matter what they may do. He left you an example to follow. Ask God to give you an attitude of forgiveness toward those who sin against you.

The Runt of the Litter

Luke 9:51–56; John 7:1–9

Seven-year-old Mark walked into the pet store, spying a bin full of Beagle puppies for sale. Mark found the owner and said, "Hey, Mister. How much are those puppies?"

The pet store owner said, "Oh, it depends. They cost $50 to $100 each."

"I've got two dollars and eighty-five cents," Mark stated confidently. "What will that get me?"

"I'm afraid I don't have anything for that price," the man said.

Disappointed, Mark said, "Well, could I at least see them?" The man agreed and let all of the puppies out on the floor. Mark laughed as he played with them and chased them around the room. One of the puppies, though, did not run. He just sat there.

"What's wrong with that puppy?" asked Mark.

The man said, "Oh, he's not for sale. One of his back legs is crippled. We'll probably just put him to sleep."

Mark quickly said, "Would you take $2.85 for him?"

The store owner said, "You don't want that dog, boy. He'll never be able to run and play."

Quietly Mark pulled up his jeans on his right leg to reveal a badly crippled leg with a brace. He said, "I do want that dog, Mister. I understand him."

Mark walked out of the pet store without any money but with a new friend.[26]

The store owner and most other people saw no use for a dog with a crippled leg. But Mark saw a puppy he could understand. Normally, that puppy would have been rejected by everyone and put to sleep. God and Mark had other plans.

In today's passage, Jesus was facing rejection on every side. He wouldn't go to Jerusalem because the people there wanted to kill Him. Jesus' brothers didn't believe that He was the Messiah and made fun of Him, teasing Him about going to Jerusalem. When Jesus did decide to go to Jerusalem at the right time, some Samaritans refused to offer Him a place to stay. Jesus was a reject.

You face rejection sometimes too. Your friends turn on you. People at school think you're weird. You feel that your parents don't understand. Rejection hurts, and sometimes it causes us to do desperate things to get attention. Jesus didn't give in to the pressure of teasing, and He didn't get angry with those who rejected Him.

Have you ever felt rejected? _____

By whom and how? _____

What did you do to deal with your feelings? _____

God does not reject you. He understands you, just like Mark understood the puppy. And, when the time is right, God will pick you up out of the box of rejection you are feeling and take you to a place where you will experience total acceptance. Ask God to help you wait on His timing for acceptance from others.

Are You a Chicken or a Pig?

Matthew 8:18–22; Luke 9:57–62

Once upon a time a chicken and a pig were walking around the barnyard together. They were discussing the hard times that had fallen on the farmer and his eight children. They needed money desperately, or they would lose the farm. Neither the chicken nor the pig liked the idea of being forced to live somewhere else.

"I've got an idea," said the chicken. "Let's have a huge breakfast for the whole town. We'll invite everyone out, and we'll charge two dollars per plate. Then we'll give the farmer and his family all of the money, and they can save the farm."

The pig really liked the idea as well, so he and the chicken began planning. The chicken made the invitations, and the pig cleared the barnyard and set up a table. Finally, the night before the big breakfast arrived.

"OK," said the chicken. "It's time to begin cooking the food."

"Right," said the pig. For the first time, the pig picked up an invitation to see what was on the menu the next morning. The invitation said in big, bold letters, "BACON AND EGGS."

"Hey!" screamed the pig. "This only requires a small sacrifice from you, but for me it requires total commitment!"[27]

Many Christians are chickens. They haven't really committed themselves to follow Jesus. They just make small sacrifices here and there. Jesus wants Christians who are like pigs—willing to give their life for others.

In today's passage, three people had excuses about why they couldn't offer Jesus total commitment. One couldn't stomach the idea of sleeping outside—he wanted to be comfortable. Another wanted to wait until his father was dead so he could use the inheritance money—he wanted financial security. One wanted to hear the opinions of his friends and family first—he cared about what other people thought. Not one of them followed Jesus as far as we know, because they weren't willing to make a total commitment.

Would you say your Christian walk is more like the chicken or the pig? _____

What kind of excuses have you offered to God when the time came to do something for Him? _____

Perhaps you have said things like, "I'm too tired. I don't have enough time. I don't have enough money. What will people think? I've got some other things I need to take care of first."

All of these excuses will paralyze you and keep you from making a total commitment to Jesus Christ. Ask God right now to help you deal with each excuse that stands between you and total commitment to Jesus. Pray for the strength to overcome the excuses so that you can walk with Jesus wherever He goes.

Weekly Bible Study and Prayer Review

Bible Study

Look back through some of the Scriptures you read this week. Write down the one verse or passage that God used to speak to you.

_____

_____

_____

_____

Memorize this verse or passage. You can do it if you spend just
a few minutes saying it to yourself.

Now, think of at least one situation you will probably face soon in which you could use this Scripture to help you make the right decision. Write down that situation below.

_____

Quote the Scripture when you face this situation, and live by it.

Prayer Time

Take a few moments to praise God for who He is.
Now take a few moments to thank God for things He has done for you.
Now ask God to make you into the person He wants you to be.
Ask God to use you to help others become closer to God.

Below is your prayer list for the week. Keep it updated each week. If your prayer isn't answered this week, carry it over to next week's list.

Request	Date of Original Request	Date Answered
_____	__/__/__	__/__/__
_____	__/__/__	__/__/__
_____	__/__/__	__/__/__
_____	__/__/__	__/__/__
_____	__/__/__	__/__/__
_____	__/__/__	__/__/__
_____	__/__/__	__/__/__
_____	__/__/__	__/__/__
_____	__/__/__	__/__/__

Pray for the things on your list and trust God to provide.
Forgive anyone you have not yet forgiven.
Ask God to forgive you for any unconfessed sin in your life.
Ask God to keep you out of trouble with sin.
Acknowledge that God is in complete control of your life
and will take care of everything.

Lord, Liar, or Lunatic

John 7:10–13

The following quote is taken from C.S. Lewis in his book Mere Christianity.

I am trying here to prevent anyone saying the really foolish thing that people often say about Him: "I'm ready to accept Jesus as a great moral teacher, but I don't accept His claim to be God." That is the one thing we must not say. A man who was merely a man and said the sort of things Jesus said would not be a great moral teacher. He would either be a lunatic—on a level with the man who says he is a poached egg—or else he would be the Devil of Hell. You must make your choice. Either this man was, and is, the Son of God: or else a madman or something worse. You can shut Him up for a fool, you can spit at Him and kill Him as a demon; or you can fall at His feet and call Him Lord and God. But let us not come with any patronizing nonsense about His being a great human teacher. He has not left that open to us. He did not intend to.

In today's passage, people were discussing who they thought Jesus was. One group said He was a liar, deceiving the people. Another group said He was a "good man." This group of people had only heard about Jesus from a distance. When they would hear Him claim to be God, their tune would change—they would either accept Him as Lord, liar, or lunatic.

When you have the opportunity to witness to other people, you might often use this technique. Ask someone, "Who do you think Jesus was?" Allow them to respond. Most people will say, "Oh, He was a good man with some good teachings." When they say this, you have the opportunity to ask, "But would you believe that anything good could come from a man who claims to be God?" Most often, the answer is no—which leaves them to either believe that Jesus is who He claimed to be, or to just believe that He was a liar or a lunatic. Your question can open up a frank discussion about Jesus.

Have you ever asked someone else (a non-Christian) what they think about Jesus? _____

Why or why not? _____

Are you willing to be bold enough to do this if God asks you to do so? _____

_____

Jesus talked about Himself a lot because He is what all of us need. If you plan to imitate Him, then you will need to talk about Him a lot to others. Ask God to give you the boldness you need to be a witness to your friends at school. Then ask everyone you know who they think Jesus is, and share with them what you know about Jesus.

Monkey See, Monkey Do

John 7:14–18

Deep in the jungles of Africa, a wide variety of monkeys roam the forest. African natives hunt the monkeys for food and other purposes. The monkeys are very quick and difficult to catch or shoot, but one tribe has developed an ingenious method of capturing them.

The natives remove a coconut from a tree, cut it in half, remove the milk, and make a hole in one of the halves. They then take a fresh orange, slice it open, and place it inside the coconut. The two coconut halves are then sewn back together. The hunters then take a rope, tying one end to a tree and the other end to the coconut. Then they hide and wait.

Before long, a monkey approaches and smells the orange. He finds it inside the coconut and reaches his hand inside through the hole to take it. The orange is too big to fit through the hole, though, and the monkey cannot get it out. The hunters then simply walk out from their hiding place toward the monkey. The monkey sees the humans approaching, but rather than let go of the orange and flee, he continues to try in vain to remove the orange until he is captured. His own selfishness leads to his demise.

We allow our own selfishness to get us into trouble all the time. We would rather get into serious trouble than let go of what we want.

In today's passage, Jesus explained that when someone is giving a defense of himself, then his words cannot be trusted because he is testifying on his own behalf. However, you can trust the words of someone who does not defend himself, but instead defends the one who sent him. In other words, people are intrigued and inclined to believe a person who doesn't appear to be selfish.

Jesus was far from selfish. He did not seek to be popular. He did not seek money. He did not seek power. He did not seek pleasure. Jesus sought to reveal God to people so they would understand clearly who He was. This was His purpose. Because of that, people did see God in Him and chose to believe.

If you were to ask your friends at school what their purpose in life is, what do you think they would say? _____

What do you think your purpose in life is? _____

Do you ever find yourself distracted by the attractions of popularity, possessions, power, or pleasure? _____

What can you give up so that you are able to better fulfill your purpose? _____

_____

Your purpose in life is to know God and reveal God to others. It's that simple. Ask God to help you to know and understand Him better, and then to be able to spend your time and effort on making Him known to others.

Tough Cookies

John 7:19–24

> While waiting for her plane at the airport, a woman bought a small package of cookies to eat on the flight. She sat down and began reading the newspaper. A man sat down in the chair next to her, with a small table between them. The woman didn't notice him at first, but then she heard a very distinctive sound: crinkle crinkle.
>
> She lowered the newspaper and saw to her amazement that the man had opened the package of cookies and was eating one. Rather than say anything, the woman reached over and took a cookie herself to establish ownership. She continued to read the paper as she nibbled on the cookie.
>
> She heard the sound again! Crinkle, crinkle, crinkle. She lowered the newspaper and saw that the man was eating more cookies. In anger and frustration, she grabbed all but one cookie and ate them feverishly. She watched the man to see what he would do. He looked back at her with a frown, took the last cookie, broke it in half, and slid the packaged remains over to her. Then he got up and left.
>
> In total astonishment, the woman grabbed the package just as her flight was called. She opened her purse to deposit the half-eaten cookie when she saw something that shocked her senseless. Inside her purse was the original, unopened package of cookies she had purchased earlier.[28]

Oops! The entire time the woman had assumed that the man was eating her package of cookies. In reality, the man had bought his own package. The woman had made a false judgment based on appearances and not on fact.

We do the same thing, and it gets us into trouble every time. In today's passage, Jesus had been judged by the people around Him. He had sometime earlier healed a man on the Sabbath day, and the people judged Him for doing "work" on the day of rest. If the people had gotten past their hang-up about the Sabbath, though, they would have realized God loves people enough to heal them on any day of the week—including the Sabbath. Jesus told them to stop judging by appearances so they could make a righteous judgment.

Have you ever judged someone about something and later found out that you were wrong?

_____

Has anyone ever judged you and been wrong? _____

What problems resulted because of either one of these situations? _____

What can you do differently the next time you are tempted to judge someone else? _____

_____

It's easy to judge people and make assumptions about them. It is more difficult to do what Jesus would do and love them anyway, giving them the benefit of the doubt. Pray that God would help you to have a loving, nonjudgmental attitude toward everyone around you. Pray that He would help you to look past appearances and into the heart.

Can You Stand the Test?

John 7:25–31

The end of the semester had finally arrived, and Tom was in dire straits. In his first semester as a freshman, he had done well in all of his classes except Philosophy. He was barely passing the class, and the final test would determine his fate.

During the last class period before the final, the professor explained to the terrified class, "You may take a single sheet of paper and place anything on it that you like to use during the test."

The class breathed a sigh of relief to know that they were allowed to bring along a legal cheat sheet. Tom struggled for hours trying to think of what to put on his piece of paper. Then he had a brilliant idea.

On the day of the final, the students filed into class and sat down. The professor passed out the tests, and everyone began working feverishly. Tom, however, was simply sitting in his seat with a smile on his face. He calmly took out one blank sheet of paper and placed it on the floor next to his desk. Then, on cue, the philosophy professor's assistant walked in and stood on the paper next to Tom, giving him the correct answers to every single question. Tom passed with flying colors.[29]

This class was a major struggle until the professor provided a way out. Rather than depend on his efforts, Tom realized that his only hope was to have the professor's assistant give him all the answers.

Sometimes life can seem like a major struggle. In today's passage, Jesus was going through some struggles of His own. If you look at things at face value, it may look as if Jesus was failing. He had given His all and told the truth, and yet few people believed in Him and some were even thinking of killing Him. Notice that Jesus did not panic. Instead, He said calmly that He knew who He was and the Father who had sent Him.

God doesn't want you to fail at anything. And though at times it may seem like you are, it is only a test. And, like the philosophy professor, God has given you a way out. The way out is not positive thinking, or better planning, or running away from your problems. The way out is Jesus. You can go to Him and talk to Him and ask Him to give you all the answers.

Are you facing any struggles in your life that you fear failing? _____

Describe one or two. _____

What do you normally do when you seem to be failing or losing a battle? _____

What should you do? _____

Ask God to help you depend on Him to get you out of your struggles and failures. Don't lose heart when things seem to be sliding downhill. Ask Jesus to give you all the answers. If you do, you'll never fail. You'll pass the test with flying colors.

A Little Slice of Heaven

John 7:32–36

"When you die, you die," Casey asserted. "That's it. You cease to exist. You're fertilizer. How could you possibly believe in some mythical heaven?"

Dawn thought about her response carefully and replied, "I believe it because the Bible says so. And besides, how could you possibly believe that there is no afterlife? What about all the stories of people dying in the hospital and then coming back to life with stories about heaven?"

Casey retorted, "Those are all fairy tales! People's brains dream up all that stuff simply because that's what they've been taught all their lives."

Dawn responded, "Casey, we obviously disagree about this. I seriously doubt that we'll change each other's minds by arguing. If what you are saying is true, then when we die we will have no existence and no memory of our existence. There is no reason to live except to please yourself, and you won't even remember that pleasure after you die. If what I'm saying is true, and I know that it is, then I invest my life in things that will matter after I die."

"I just can't comprehend that," Casey said, shaking his head.

Dawn smiled. "I know. I wish you could. Life is a lot better when you know it will never end."[30]

People who think life is over when we die can't comprehend eternal life in heaven. Christians, however, can't comprehend what this life would be like without knowing we will go to heaven. People in today's passage didn't understand what Jesus meant when He said He was going to heaven—back to the one who sent Him.

Sometimes life can seem so ordinary. We can't see heaven or see God, so we slowly begin to assume that what we see is all there is. God, however, wants us to keep our eyes focused on Him and the knowledge that we are strangers here for only a short time. We should develop "forever eyes"—eyes that see beyond the ordinary and into eternity.

There are only two visible things on this planet that will last for eternity. Can you name them? (1) _____

(2) _____

The only two things that will last forever are people and the Word of God. What does this tell you about how you should spend your time? _____

Jesus spent His entire life helping people and spreading the Word of God. What can you start doing today that would make you more like Jesus? _____

Close your eyes for a moment and try to imagine how beautiful heaven will be. Picture pearly gates, golden streets, tearless eyes, marvelous mansions, and Jesus walking by your side. Try and grasp just how long eternity really is and how wonderful it will be to be in heaven forever. Now picture your friends, neighbors, and family. Will they be in heaven with you?

Ask God to help you spend your days investing in what matters most: people and God's good news.

Enjoy the Ride

John 7:37–44

A tightrope stretched its way across the entire length of Niagara Falls. An excited crowd gathered to watch the man who claimed he would walk across it. He did just that, walking across and then back.

The man then asked, "How many people think I can push a wheelbarrow across the Falls?" The crowd roared with applause, certain he would make it and eager to watch. The man successfully walked back and forth on the high wire while pushing the wheelbarrow.

Then he shouted, "How many of you think I can load this wheelbarrow full of bricks and push it all the way across?" The crowd cheered, jumping up and down and shouting their vote of confidence. They watched as he pushed the wheelbarrow full of bricks all the way across and back. They couldn't wait to see what he would do next.

The man asked, "How many of you think I can push this wheelbarrow all the way across with a person sitting inside?" At this the crowd went wild, jumping up and down and cheering their approval. The man then asked, "Could I please have a volunteer?"

The cheering suddenly stopped. Nothing could be heard except for the sound of the roaring falls. Not one person volunteered. They were not willing to take their supposed belief that far.

The people claimed to have faith in the tightrope walker's abilities. However, when the time came to put their faith where their mouth was, no one said a word. The truth is, the people did not have as much faith as they thought they did.

A lot of people followed Jesus around and listened to the words He said. They seemed to have some measure of faith in Him. However, when Jesus asked everyone to "get in the wheelbarrow," so to speak, and come with Him, many refused to go that far. They preferred to remain at a distance and simply listen and observe.

You obviously believe in Jesus, but how far are you willing to go with Him? Have you put your faith where your mouth is? Do you always follow Him no matter what the cost? What sinful habits have you not given up yet? _____

What attitudes do you have that need to be adjusted? _____

What worries do you need to give up and turn into prayers? _____

How could you improve your relationship with your parents? _____

You filled in the blanks above. They represent the wheelbarrow. It's one thing to acknowledge the need to change with your mind. It's quite another to actually do something about it. Ask God right now to lead you to make these changes in your life that you know you need to make. Don't put it off any longer. God's Spirit will make the changes when you actually get into the wheelbarrow. Go to Jesus and trust Him to walk the tightrope for you. You won't fall. Just relax and enjoy the ride while He does all the work.

Weekly Bible Study and Prayer Review

Bible Study

Look back through some of the Scriptures you read this week. Write down the one verse or passage that God used to speak to you.

_____

_____

_____

_____

*Memorize this verse or passage. You can do it if you spend just
a few minutes saying it to yourself.*

Now, think of at least one situation you will probably face soon in which you could use this Scripture to help you make the right decision. Write down that situation below.

_____

Quote the Scripture when you face this situation, and live by it.

Prayer Time

*Take a few moments to praise God for who He is.
Now take a few moments to thank God for things He has done for you.
Now ask God to make you into the person He wants you to be.
Ask God to use you to help others become closer to God.*

Below is your prayer list for the week. Keep it updated each week. If your prayer isn't answered this week, carry it over to next week's list.

Request	Date of Original Request	Date Answered
_____	__/__/__	__/__/__
_____	__/__/__	__/__/__
_____	__/__/__	__/__/__
_____	__/__/__	__/__/__
_____	__/__/__	__/__/__
_____	__/__/__	__/__/__
_____	__/__/__	__/__/__
_____	__/__/__	__/__/__

*Pray for the things on your list and trust God to provide.
Forgive anyone you have not yet forgiven.
Ask God to forgive you for any unconfessed sin in your life.
Ask God to keep you out of trouble with sin.
Acknowledge that God is in complete control of your life
and will take care of everything.*

Hear, Here

David had been praying for his friend Melissa for most of the semester. He wanted to witness to her, but every time he tried, the words just wouldn't come out right.

One Saturday night, David's youth group planned a coffee-shop concert and rally. David invited Melissa, and she accepted the invitation. Melissa thought it would be fun to sit around, drink coffee, talk, and see the show.

Melissa was surprised at how good the music was. The lyrics really spoke to her heart about God. The speaker afterward gave a brief message on how to become a Christian. Melissa listened quietly and carefully, and for the first time in her life she prayed.

After the concert, as David was taking Melissa home, he said, "So, what did you think about the concert?"

Melissa turned to David and said, "I asked Jesus to come into my heart after it was over. Can you tell me what I should do next?"

David had no idea that taking Melissa to the concert would result in her salvation. It did, though, for two reasons: (1) David provided an environment for Melissa where she would be comfortable, and (2) the message of Jesus was proclaimed clearly.

In today's passage, the Jews were tired of Jesus speaking in the temple, so they sent Roman temple guards to arrest Him. The temple guards were in their own territory—they were comfortable in their environment. While fighting their way through the crowds, though, the guards had the opportunity to hear Jesus speak. Jesus caught them off guard on their own turf.

When you witness to other people, make sure that (1) the environment is comfortable for them, and (2) the message of Jesus is spoken clearly. If the environment is comfortable but you don't make Jesus clear, then witnessing doesn't really take place. Or, if you try to present Jesus in an environment where people are uncomfortable, chances are they will not hear you.

Do you have friends who need to meet Jesus? _____

In what kind of environment are they most comfortable? _____

How could you present the message of Jesus to your friends in that type of environment?

_____

Jesus wants to meet people where they are. Ask God to help you witness to your friends in their own territory—where they are comfortable and free from distractions. Pray that God will empower you to speak the message of Jesus clearly in that environment. Then, when God gives you the opportunity, catch them off guard and let them hear about Jesus.

Getting to Know You

John 7:50–52

Joy walked the halls of her new school with anxiety, never quite sure where her next class was. Sometimes a student would offer her help, but most of the time she was on her own.

Everyone around Joy whispered about the new girl in town. "Who is she? Where is she from?" These were the most common questions people asked. "I hear she is from Iowa and her father is a pilot," said one student.

Another said, "No, she's from Texas and she's got a strong, Southern accent."

During lunch in the cafeteria the rumors continued. "Joy was kicked out of school in another district, and this is the only place left for her to go," suggested someone.

"No. You're all wrong," insisted James. "Debbie told me that her mother committed suicide, and she has come here to live with her grandparents."

Just then Joy sat down near the group and began eating her lunch. One of the guys shouted, "Hey, Joy. Where are you from?"

Joy smiled, glad to have someone talk to her. "Oh, I'm from Washington, D.C. My mother is a retired secretary for the President. This is her hometown, so we decided to move here."

A lot of times we make assumptions about people from a distance that turn out to be dead wrong once we actually meet them. In today's passage, people were spreading rumors about Jesus without taking the time to investigate the truth for themselves.

Some religious leaders heard that Jesus was from Galilee. Since the Bible says that the Messiah would come from Bethlehem—not Galilee—the religious leaders rejected Jesus as the Messiah. Nicodemus, one of the leaders, said, "Now wait just a minute. Are we going to condemn this guy without first listening to Him for ourselves?" If these guys had taken just a few minutes to talk with Jesus for themselves, they would have discovered that Jesus was born in Bethlehem, but then He moved to Galilee. Perhaps then they would have seen things differently.

Making assumptions about people without getting to know them first is called passing judgment. *Have you ever passed judgment on someone?* _____

Has anyone ever passed judgment on you? _____

How did it make you feel? _____

What can you do the next time you are tempted to pass judgment on someone else?

_____

The solution to the problem is simple: Get to know the person and talk to him or her personally. Perhaps God has created a natural curiosity in you so that you will get to know that person better. Who knows? You may discover a lifelong friend or someone you can win to the Lord.

Ask God to help you overcome the tendency of passing judgment on others. Pray that He will give you the wisdom and courage to find out the truth about others and get to know them better.

Drop Your Weapon

John 8:1–11

While traveling in Hawaii, popular author and youth speaker Tony Campolo found himself battling jet lag. One morning at 2:00 A.M., he decided to take a walk and get something to eat.

The only place open at this hour was a bar. He went inside, sat down, and ordered a sandwich. Shortly afterward, a group of prostitutes walked in from their evening's "work" and sat at a table behind him. Tony overheard them talking about another prostitute named Julie, mentioning that her birthday was tomorrow and she would be in the bar.

Tony quietly arranged for a cake to be made, and he returned to the bar the next morning at 2:00 A.M. The prostitutes came in shortly afterward with Julie and sat down at their usual table. The bartender took the cake to Julie, with candles on top and her name written in icing.

Julie began to cry. "Who did this? Who gave me the cake?"

Tony walked over to her and responded, "I did."

Julie said through her tears, "Who are you?"

"I'm a minister," Tony replied.

"A minister!" Julie gasped. "What kind of church do you belong to?"

Tony answered, "The church that throws birthday parties for prostitutes."

Why in the world would a minister be so nice to a prostitute? Perhaps it is because Tony was doing what Jesus would do.

In today's passage, a woman caught in the act of adultery was brought to Jesus. The Jews wanted to kill her, as the law required. If Jesus said to kill her, it would contradict the fact that He spent time with prostitutes and sinners. If He said not to kill her, He would be contradicting Old Testament law. Jesus answered by saying, "If you have no sin in your life, then go ahead and throw the first stone."

When someone sins against us, our first reaction is to get even—to throw some stones. Yet when this woman broke one of the Ten Commandments—which Jesus Himself wrote—He forgave her, releasing her and telling her to change her ways.

Do you ever find yourself wanting to harm someone who has sinned against you? _____

What "stones" are you tempted to throw (examples: hurtful words, physical harm, rumors, etc.)? _____

Why don't you have the right to throw these stones? _____

Jesus forgave others who sinned against Him. We must learn to do the same. Ask God to help you forgive the people who hurt you. Drop your stones, and step away from the situation. Practice forgiveness the way Jesus did.

Never Alone

John 8:12–20

The Armenian earthquake of 1989 leveled hundreds of buildings and killed more than thirty thousand people. Immediately after the quake, a young man left work and ran to the school where his son was. The building was demolished.

The young man had once promised that he would always be there for his son. That promise drove the man to begin digging in the rubble for his son. For hours he scraped and dug and pulled until his fingers began to cramp and bleed. People all around him told him to give up—that the children were all dead. He refused to listen and kept digging.

He dug for forty hours with no help from anyone. He was exhausted and losing hope. Then, after removing a large piece of rubble, he heard the voice of his son calling his name.

"Dad! I knew you would come. I told all the other kids not to worry because you would find us." The thirteen children were safe and sound in a natural pocket formed by the walls when the building fell.[31]

Even after forty hours in a dark, silent hole, the young boy held on to his father's promise. In today's passage, Jesus seemed all alone when a crowd of people began to ridicule Him. But, in spite of how hopeless His situation seemed, He said, "I am not alone. I stand with the Father who sent Me."

Many times in your life you will feel like you are the only Christian, and you will feel alone and powerless. Perhaps you feel alone at school because you don't have lunch or classes with Christian friends. You might feel alone at home because no one else in your family knows Jesus. Your job may be a place where God seems far away. You may even feel alone in your youth group because no one else seems to want to grow like you do. It's not easy to take a stand for God when no one else does. Jesus knows that firsthand. He had confidence, though, because He knew His Father would be there for Him.

Do you ever feel like you are alone when you try to live like Jesus? _____

When do you feel alone the most? _____

What do the people around you do or say that makes you feel so alone? _____

Do you ever wonder if God is really there? _____

God is always with you. He will never let you down. Ask Him to give you faith to depend on Him during those times and in those places where you feel alone the most. Remember His promise to always be with you. With God in your heart, you are never alone.

Not of This World

John 8:21–30

Ricky and Sally carefully and cautiously made their way through the dark corridors of the old mansion. They were investigating unexplained phenomena reported by the residents of this small town.

"Look!" Sally uttered in a guarded whisper, pointing toward a cobweb-wrapped staircase that ascended into darkness. A shadowy figure made its way up the staircase and quickly disappeared. Ricky looked at Sally as if to ask, "Do you want to keep going?" They each took a deep breath and put their feet on the first step, piercing the darkness with their flashlight.

As they reached the top step, Ricky felt something brush by his leg. His heart pounded as he whirled around and aimed his flashlight. What Ricky and Sally saw made them gasp. "Raccoons!" he shouted. "It's just a bunch of raccoons."

The unexplained noises were caused by nothing more than a large family of raccoons who had taken shelter in the old mansion.

Were you expecting aliens or ghosts? We seem to have a fascination with things that are not of this world. We want to know more about possible beings from beyond. In today's passage, you get to meet an alien who has invaded earth.

Jesus said that He is not of this world—that He came from above. The people around Him didn't understand His alien behavior. The people of earth were saying that the purpose of living is to please yourself. Jesus said that kind of living is called sin, and if you continue to live that way you will die in your sin. He said the purpose of living is to please God. How bizarre!

Like Jesus, you are not of this world. You are an alien. Your purpose is not to please yourself or others but to please God. Often, while you are trying to live your alien life, the earthlings around you will make fun of you or intimidate you into becoming more like them. They try to convince you to live life according to their purpose—to please yourself. They use "peer pressure" to get you to act like them. If you give in to peer pressure, you start doing things you normally wouldn't just to be accepted by the crowd.

Do you ever face peer pressure? _____

Have you ever done something you normally wouldn't do just to be accepted by the crowd?
_____

Name some things you have done because of peer pressure. _____

What can you do the next time you find yourself under pressure by the crowd? _____

Jesus never let the crowd pressure Him into changing His purpose or doing something just to be accepted. Ask God to help you be like Jesus. Pray that you would be able to keep your mind set on your purpose the next time you face peer pressure. Remember that you are an alien and stranger to this world.

Fat Chance

John 8:31–37

In the fourteenth century there was a very large man named Raymond. He loved to eat more than anything else in the world. If it were up to him, he could spend his entire day eating.

Raymond was a royal official in his kingdom. During a revolt, his younger brother captured and imprisoned him. Raymond was placed in an unusual prison cell. The window and the door had no bars on them, but they were too small for Raymond to fit through. All Raymond had to do to get out was to lose enough weight to become a normal size. Then, he could simply walk through the door.

Each day, though, the prison officials brought Raymond a smorgasbord of delicious and fattening foods. Each day Raymond would stare at all of the tempting morsels in front of him and agonize over his choice. He could eat a lot of food and remain in his cell, or he could eat sensibly and escape to return to his place as a servant in his kingdom.

What did Raymond do? He ate. And he never escaped his prison cell.[32]

Most of the time when you think of prison, you think of people who are forcefully kept under lock and key against their choice. In this case, however, Raymond held the key to his own cell. All he had to do was choose to eat right.

In today's passage, Jesus described sin as something that imprisons us—just like Raymond's gluttony. We can choose to participate in sin for the sake of temporary pleasure, but we will not be able to serve in God's kingdom in our rightful place. On the other hand, we can choose to reject the temporary pleasures of sin and instead serve God in His kingdom and be truly free.

The word *freedom* today is often defined as "being able to do what you want, when you want, and how you want, without anyone telling you otherwise." That isn't really true. True freedom is being able to become all that God intended you to be without being hindered by sin.

Do you have any sinful habits? _____

List the top three sins that enslave you. _____, _____, *and* _____

How do these sins imprison you and keep you from becoming all that God wants you to be?
_____

Do you want to be free from these habits? _____ *What are you willing to do to conquer them?* _____

Only a close relationship with Jesus will help you overcome these habits. You cannot do it yourself, but He can. Keep your eyes focused on the freedom you will have when these habits no longer control you. Ask God for His Spirit to give you the discipline you will need to become free. Jesus will set you free, and when He does, you will be truly free.

Weekly Bible Study and Prayer Review

Bible Study

Look back through some of the Scriptures you read this week. Write down the one verse or passage that God used to speak to you.

_____

_____

_____

_____

*Memorize this verse or passage. You can do it if you spend just
a few minutes saying it to yourself.*

Now, think of at least one situation you will probably face soon in which you could use this Scripture to help you make the right decision. Write down that situation below.

_____

Quote the Scripture when you face this situation, and live by it.

Prayer Time

*Take a few moments to praise God for who He is.
Now take a few moments to thank God for things He has done for you.
Now ask God to make you into the person He wants you to be.
Ask God to use you to help others become closer to God.*

Below is your prayer list for the week. Keep it updated each week. If your prayer isn't answered this week, carry it over to next week's list.

Request	Date of Original Request	Date Answered
_____	__/__/__	__/__/__
_____	__/__/__	__/__/__
_____	__/__/__	__/__/__
_____	__/__/__	__/__/__
_____	__/__/__	__/__/__
_____	__/__/__	__/__/__
_____	__/__/__	__/__/__
_____	__/__/__	__/__/__
_____	__/__/__	__/__/__

*Pray for the things on your list and trust God to provide.
Forgive anyone you have not yet forgiven.
Ask God to forgive you for any unconfessed sin in your life.
Ask God to keep you out of trouble with sin.
Acknowledge that God is in complete control of your life
and will take care of everything.*

What Lies Ahead

John 8:38–47

Jessica knew she wasn't supposed to be at this party. But it wasn't her fault—not really. She was on her way to the movies, just like she told her parents, when she and Kathryn ran into a group of friends who invited them to the party. "Let's go!" Jessica said to Kathryn. "I've always wanted to go to one of these parties." Jessica was surprised at how easily the lie left her lips. At Jessica's insistence, the two followed their friends to the abandoned warehouse. The party was already in full swing.

Later, when it became apparent that Jessica was going to be late getting home, she found a pay phone and called her parents. "Mom? Kathryn and I decided to stop for pizza after the movie and ran into some friends. I'll be late, OK? Oh, yes, the movie was great. You need to see it. Yes, I'll see you soon. Bye."

It was just a little white lie. What could it hurt? And what could it hurt to take her first drink of alcohol? She hated the taste, but the lie in her smile said she loved it. And what could it hurt to dance with this great-looking guy? And what could it hurt to take another drink that he offered her?

When Jessica woke up the next morning, still groggy from the drug the cute guy had slipped into her drink, she realized that her lies had hurt more than she could have ever imagined.

Jessica found out the hard way that lies are a stairway that goes only one way: down. She lied to herself. She lied to her friends. She lied to her parents. She lost the trust of her parents and her best friend, and she lost her innocence to a guy she never saw again.

In today's passage, Jesus explained that Satan is the father of lies. His tactics are so sly. If he can just get you to tell one little white lie today, then tomorrow he can take you one step further down the stairway with a bigger lie. Before you know it, you find yourself someplace where you never intended to be, and Satan is laughing all the while.

Have you ever told a lie? _____

To what people have you lied? _____

What is your most recent lie? _____

Do you want to continue lying? _____

What can you do right now to reverse your pattern of lying? _____

Ask God to help you run away from the father of lies the next time you hear him calling. Whenever you are tempted to lie, you can be sure that Satan has nothing but catastrophe in store for you. Don't hold Satan's hand and start down that stairway. Run to Jesus, hold His hand, and always speak the truth.

I Am

John 8:48–59

"Grandpa, what is God's name?" Moses looked down into the deep, sparkling blue eyes of his grandchild. He stroked his beard, leaned back in his chair, and smiled.

"One day while I was tending my sheep, I saw this bush—on fire—but it wasn't consumed by the flames. I stood there for a moment, scratching my head, when suddenly I heard God speak. He called my name and told me to take off my shoes because I was standing on holy ground. Then He told me to rescue the people of Israel from Pharaoh and lead them out of Egypt and into the Promised Land. I didn't think I was capable of doing such a thing. I gave God a whole lot of excuses about why I couldn't do it.

"I said to God, 'Look, if I go and tell the Israelites that I've been sent by You to rescue them, they may ask me which God I'm talking about. What will I tell them? What is your name, God?

"God said, 'Tell them that I AM has sent you, for that is My name.'"[33]

The Jews of Jesus' day knew the story of Moses. They knew God's name. In Hebrew, "I AM" is "Yahweh." With this in mind, you can imagine their shock when Jesus said what He did in today's passage in verse 58. He said, "Before Abraham was born, I AM." By saying this, Jesus was claiming to be God. That's why the people picked up stones to kill Him. Their view of God did not match what they saw in such a common, ordinary man like Jesus. Because the people rejected Jesus' claims, they missed the chance to experience God.

We often miss the opportunity to experience God, too, because we don't notice Him working around us. A soft sunset full of brilliant colors says, "I AM your Creator, and I love you." In the middle of a painful trial, God sends a friend to comfort us as God says, "I AM your Counselor, and I care about what you are going through." When our parents tell us we can't go somewhere we really want to go, God is saying, "I AM your Father, and I care about your safety."

When was the last time you remember really experiencing God? _____

What did God say to you? _____

Is there a situation recently where God may have spoken to you, but you just missed it?

_____

Describe that situation. _____

God is always at work in your world. He is always there for you. Ask God to make you more aware of His presence. Pray that you would be sensitive to His voice as He speaks to you. Look for Him in places you normally wouldn't look. Remember, no matter where you are or what you are doing, in some way God is saying to you, "I AM." He is. For further study, meditate on Psalm 46:10.

Help Wanted

Luke 10:1–16

In 1271, two brothers named Nichelo and Matteo Polo (Marco Polo's father and uncle) traveled to the East from Europe as missionaries. There they met Kubla Kahn, ruler of the entire Far East. The brothers shared the story of Jesus with Kahn.

Kahn was so interested in the message of Jesus that he told the brothers, "Go back to your country and get permission from your high priest to send my country one hundred missionaries to spread this good news. When they return, I will accept your message and be baptized. The men who govern under me will also hear your message, accept it, and be baptized. Then your missionaries will go throughout our entire country, sharing the good news of Jesus until everyone here accepts it and is baptized."

With great enthusiasm, the Polo brothers returned to Europe and asked the pope to send one hundred missionaries to the Far East. The pope said, "Those barbarians do not deserve to hear about Jesus. We will send no one." For thirty years no one returned to the Far East. In the meanwhile, people of another religion came to the Far East and converted everyone to Buddhism, which is still the dominant religion there to this day.

If only the pope and people of that day had recognized the need for missionaries, literally billions of people today might know Jesus. Instead, they place their faith in the empty, false religion of Buddhism.

Jesus recognized the tremendous opportunity to share the gospel in His day, but He needed missionaries to help Him. In today's passage, He sent out about seventy-two people in pairs ahead of Him into various cities to spread the good news and prepare the way for Him to pass through. Jesus said to these people, "The harvest is plentiful, but the workers are so few. Ask the Lord of the harvest to send workers into His harvest field." Jesus needed people to go into specific areas to share His story.

The harvest is just as plentiful today as it was in the days of Jesus and in the days of the Polo brothers. The Lord is still looking for workers to go into His harvest field. He needs young people who will take the gospel to parents, teachers, coworkers, cheerleaders, football players, band members, convenience store cashiers, mail carriers, and many others.

Think about the people in your world. Where do you see the greatest opportunity for sharing Jesus? _____

Have you done your part in taking advantage of this opportunity? _____

What can you do to share the good news of Jesus to this group of people? _____

Notice that Jesus sent the missionaries of today's passage out in pairs. He doesn't expect you to be alone as you witness. Ask God to send *you* into His harvest field with a friend. Pray that He will help you see the tremendous opportunities to share Jesus with others.

Regeneration

Luke 10:17–24

"On the outer edge of the second millennium, there has been born a generation through whom God is moving in a special way." These are the words that open a video entitled Generation that highlights how God is using young people to bring about spiritual awakening in America and the world. Consider how God has used young people since 1990 in the following areas.

1. Prayer. The worldwide prayer movement known as "See You at the Pole" was born in a small Texas town during a weekend retreat. Since then, millions of students gather annually in September on their school campus to pray. Hundreds of thousands meet weekly or daily to pray.

2. Sexual Purity. The "True Love Waits" emphasis started in one youth group in one church. Now millions of Christian young people have pledged to remain sexually abstinent until marriage.

3. Campus Evangelism. Bible clubs have sprung up in thousands of schools across the nation, and many non-Christian students have found Jesus because of the testimony of their friends.

4. Global Missions. More young people than ever before are taking short-term mission trips to share the gospel around the world with others.

5. Imitating Jesus. In 1899, Charles Sheldon wrote the book, In His Steps from which the "What would Jesus do?" movement was born. Almost one hundred years later, a church asked a local bracelet maker to create the WWJD bracelets for its young people. Those bracelets have since united the Christian world and challenged them to become more like Jesus.

This is a spiritual awakening of unprecedented proportions. The seventy-two missionaries Jesus sent out returned in today's passage with stories of spiritual awakening. Jesus even said that He saw Satan falling like lightning from heaven. Truly, as Jesus said, the kingdom of heaven is near.

You can be a part of this spiritual awakening. Here's how: (1) pray daily and fervently; (2) commit to remain sexually pure until marriage; (3) become involved in winning others to Jesus on your school campus; (4) go on a short-term mission trip with your youth group; and (5) ask yourself "What would Jesus do?" in any and every situation, and follow through with the answer to the best of your ability.

Take a sheet of paper and write down a specific commitment to God that you will strive to keep in each of these five areas. Place this paper in a prominent place so that you will see it every day and be reminded of your commitments.

Pray that God will use you in a special way to bring about spiritual awakening in your world. Perhaps you and your youth group will give birth to a movement that changes the world.

Life Savers

Luke 10:25–37

Kevin was walking home from school when he noticed the guy ahead of him trip and fall, dropping all of his books along with two sweaters, a baseball bat, a glove, and a small tape recorder. Kevin helped the guy pick up his things and walked home with him, sharing the load.

As they walked Kevin discovered the guy's name was Bill, that he loved video games, baseball, and history, that he was having a lot of trouble with his other subjects, and that he had just broken up with his girlfriend. They arrived at Bill's home first, and Kevin was invited in for a Coke and to watch TV. The afternoon passed pleasantly with a few laughs and some small talk. Then Kevin went home. They continued to see each other around school and talked occasionally. They ended up at the same high school where they had brief contacts over the years.

Just before graduation, Bill asked Kevin if they could talk. Bill reminded him of the day years ago when they had first met. "Do you ever wonder why I was carrying so many things from school that day?" asked Bill. "You see, I cleaned out my locker because I didn't want to leave a mess for anyone else. I was going home to commit suicide. But after we spent some time together I realized that if I had, I would have missed that time and so many others that might follow. Kevin, you saved my life by helping me pick up my stuff."

Kevin didn't realize that his simple act of kindness would save Bill's life. He was just helping out—being a "Good Samaritan." In today's passage, Jesus told the original story about the good Samaritan. A man walking along a road was beaten, robbed, and left for dead. Two religious guys walked right by and ignored the man in need. But a Samaritan—who was considered racially inferior by many Jews—stopped to help the man. He cleansed and bandaged his wounds, took care of him overnight, and paid an innkeeper to look after the man while he was gone. The Samaritan saved the man's life by a few simple acts of kindness.

Notice the sacrifices the Samaritan made: time, effort, and money. These are three things the world says should be spent on ourselves. However, Jesus says that when the opportunity comes, we should sacrifice these three things to help others.

List some areas where your time, money, and effort are spent: _____

When is the last time you sacrificed one or more of these things to help someone else?

_____

How could you sacrifice these things this week to minister to someone in need?

_____

Ask God to make you aware of the opportunities around you to help others. Then, when He answers your prayer and you see those opportunities, don't just walk on by like the religious guys in the parable. Be the good Samaritan and give your time, effort, and money to minister to someone else. You never know when you might be saving someone's life.

Listen Up

Luke 10:38–42

> I knelt to pray, but not for long, I had too much to do,
> Must hurry off and get to school, for homework soon was due.
> And so I said a hurried prayer, jumped up from off my knees;
> My Christian duty now was done, my soul could be at ease.
> All through the day I had no time to speak a word of cheer,
> No time to speak of Christ to friends—they'd laugh at me, I feared.
> No time, no time, too much to do—that was my constant cry;
> No time to give to those in need—then came the time to die.
> And when before the Lord I came, I stood with downcast eyes,
> God looked at me and said to heaven, "Goodness, how time flies.
> Your mansion isn't ready yet—looks like we fell behind.
> It seems that your construction crew just never found the time."
>
> Author Unknown

Our lives can get so busy. Sometimes twenty-four hours isn't enough for school, homework, extracurricular activities, chores, fun, food, and whatever else you have to do today. Oops! It looks like we left God out of our list. That's exactly what Martha did in today's passage.

Jesus was staying at the home of two sisters named Mary and Martha. Martha felt she should spend her time cooking, cleaning, and making other preparations to make Jesus' stay more comfortable. Mary, on the other hand, simply sat at the feet of Jesus and listened to His words. Martha was uptight about the lack of assistance from Mary and complained to Jesus. Jesus responded that Mary had chosen what was better.

Like the poem above, we often find ourselves so busy tackling our schedule that we don't take time to sit at the feet of Jesus and just listen. How do we listen to God? There are several ways: (1) read your Bible during your quiet time; (2) study your Bible with friends or at church in a class; (3) listen to a message from your pastor, youth pastor, or other speaker; (4) read a Christian book.

Which of the above four areas have you allowed your busy schedule to crowd out? _____

What could you adjust in your schedule to allow you more time to sit at the feet of Jesus and listen to Him speak to you? _____

Don't leave Jesus out of your schedule. Nothing is more important to your day than listening to Jesus and finding His will for your life. Ask God to forgive you for crowding Him out of your day, and pray that you will be able to modify your schedule to include time listening to God each day in a variety of ways.

Weekly Bible Study and Prayer Review

Bible Study

Look back through some of the Scriptures you read this week. Write down the one verse or passage that God used to speak to you..

_____

_____

_____

_____

Memorize this verse or passage. You can do it if you spend just
a few minutes saying it to yourself.

Now, think of at least one situation you will probably face soon in which you could use this Scripture to help you make the right decision. Write down that situation below.

_____

Quote the Scripture when you face this situation, and live by it.

Prayer Time

Take a few moments to praise God for who He is.
Now take a few moments to thank God for things He has done for you.
Now ask God to make you into the person He wants you to be.
Ask God to use you to help others become closer to God.

Below is your prayer list for the week. Keep it updated each week. If your prayer isn't answered this week, carry it over to next week's list.

Request	Date of Original Request	Date Answered
_____	__/__/__	__/__/__
_____	__/__/__	__/__/__
_____	__/__/__	__/__/__
_____	__/__/__	__/__/__
_____	__/__/__	__/__/__
_____	__/__/__	__/__/__
_____	__/__/__	__/__/__
_____	__/__/__	__/__/__
_____	__/__/__	__/__/__

Pray for the things on your list and trust God to provide.
Forgive anyone you have not yet forgiven.
Ask God to forgive you for any unconfessed sin in your life.
Ask God to keep you out of trouble with sin.
Acknowledge that God is in complete control of your life
and will take care of everything.

The Prayer Room

Luke 11:1–13

Perhaps it isn't set up quite like this, but God does have so many things He wants to give His children if they would only ask.

Imagine this. It is midnight and suddenly a good friend of yours comes over. He's traveled a long way without food, and your refrigerator is empty. You go next door and wake up your neighbor. You ask your neighbor if you can borrow a frozen pizza and a couple of soft drinks. Your neighbor says, "Leave me alone. I don't want to get dressed and turn on the lights just so you can have a late-night snack. Go away." You continue to pound on the door, though, and your neighbor finally gives you what you ask for—not because you are his neighbor but because he figures you must really need this if you were bold enough to wake him up.

Jesus tells us to be just as bold when going to God in prayer and asking for the things that we need. Notice two things from this parable: (1) the man asked for something he genuinely needed, and (2) he wouldn't take no for an answer. God wants you to ask Him for your needs and continue asking even if the answer doesn't come right away.

Do you currently have genuine needs? _____

Make a list here or on another sheet of paper of those needs that come to your mind.

_____

Have you asked God to meet these needs? _____ *Have you continued to ask God even though you haven't yet received an answer?* _____

Spend time asking God for each need and explaining to Him why you need it. If you don't have an answer by tomorrow, knock on God's door and ask again. Be bold and knock, and the door will be opened.

The Touch of the Master's Hand

Luke 11:14–28

The auction was nearing its end, and the sun was about to set. The auctioneer looked at the last item—an old, battered violin. *It doesn't look worth much,* thought the auctioneer, *but I guess we should sell it too.*

The auctioneer started the bidding, asking for one dollar or maybe two. No one seemed interested at all in the old, dusty, scarred violin. During the awkward silence, though, a gray-haired man stepped out of the crowd and picked up the violin. He wiped away the dust, picked up the bow, tightened the strings, and began to play. The sound of the tent was filled with the purest, sweetest melody that anyone had ever heard. The old man finished his song and returned to the crowd.

The auctioneer quietly picked up the violin. Holding it high, he began the bidding again. He started the bidding at $1,000. After several moments, the violin sold for $3,000. Many people in the crowd did not understand why the violin suddenly changed in value. One man replied, "It was the touch of the master's hand."

This story, based on a poem by Myra Brooks Welch, illustrates how the battered and scarred life of someone can be drastically changed by the touch of the Master's hand. The Master is Jesus.

In today's passage, we are presented with the horrible reality that Satan has the power to bring misery to people's lives. A man who could not talk because of a demon was in the crowd. For perhaps years this man had been unable to speak. Most people of his day didn't read or write, so communicating on paper wasn't really an option. People probably made fun of him and shunned him. His life was a wreck. One day, though, Jesus touched him, driving Satan away and giving him his voice back. His life was new all over again.

Satan and his army of demons have nothing better to do than to make your life miserable. You may face trials and temptations that seem utterly hopeless. Some of your difficulties may have led you into depression or thoughts of suicide. You feel as if there is no way out. Contrary to what you may think, Jesus is very aware of what you are going through. He is much more powerful than Satan and your circumstances. Just one touch from His hand can change your life completely.

Do you feel that Satan is causing pain in your life? _____

In what way? _____

What do you wish would change about this situation? _____

Jesus knows, understands, and cares about the pain you feel because of Satan's schemes. He does not, however, intend for Satan to have the final victory. Jesus is the Master, and He wants to touch you in a way that will make you new all over again. Ask God to take away the pain or difficulty that you face. Let Him touch you where it hurts.

You-Turn

Luke 11:29–32

> The battleship eased its way through the midnight fog. The captain, Jonathan Bright, would not allow himself any rest until the fog lifted or the night ended. He carefully watched the area in front of the ship for hazards unknown.
>
> Suddenly, his keen eyes spotted a faint light directly ahead. Desperate to avoid a head-on collision, he grabbed the radio and announced, "This is Captain Jonathan Bright. Please turn and alter your course ten degrees to the east."
>
> A voice immediately returned and said, "Sir, this is Private Bill Jones. You turn. Please alter your course ten degrees to the west."
>
> The captain was furious. He shouted, "Private, I am a Captain. You turn! I order you to alter your course ten degrees east."
>
> Private Jones responded again, "Sir, you turn. Please alter your course ten degrees west immediately."
>
> By this time the captain was in a complete rage. He screamed into the radio, "By the authority vested in me by the United States Government, I command you to turn and alter your course ten degrees east. I am a battleship."
>
> Private Jones spoke quietly in reply, "Sir, please turn and alter your course ten degrees west. I am a lighthouse."[34]

Captain Bright decided that he would turn. If he hadn't, he would have surely crashed on the rocks. This is a picture of repentance—turning away from sin.

In today's passage, the crowd around Jesus had refused to repent. Jesus contrasted the crowd with Ninevah, a huge city that long ago repented of its sin because Jonah the prophet told them about God. Now, here God was standing among the people, and they refused to repent of their sinful lifestyles and turn to Jesus.

A ship that refuses to make a U-turn away from the rocks is going to be ship-wrecked. If you don't turn away from sin, you will face negative consequences. Some consequences of sin are obvious. Premarital sex often results in sexually transmitted diseases. Using drugs or getting drunk can cause you to do something you normally wouldn't. Disobeying your parents may lead you into a dangerous situation from which they tried to protect you.

All sin has consequences. Can you think of a consequence you suffered as a result of sin?

_____

Describe that situation. _____

What can you do to avoid the negative consequences of sin? _____

Think about how your future can be changed right now by your decision to turn away from sin. Pray that God would (1) help you to give up any existing sins and (2) help you to avoid giving in to any future temptations. Make a *you-turn* from sin; alter your course to head in God's direction.

Inside Out

Luke 11:37–41

Travis and Sara could not believe their luck. They had practically stolen this beautiful country home nestled in the piney woods only a half hour from Travis's job. Travis whisked his new bride off her feet and carried her across the threshold and into their new home.

It wasn't long, though, before things started going wrong. While preparing breakfast one morning, the electrical wiring in the kitchen caught fire. Not long after repairing that, a furious rainstorm revealed more than thirty leaks around the house. A few days later the railing on the spiral staircase simply fell off. Travis spent all of his evenings after work trying to keep up with repairs. Before he finished one problem, another would start.

Over the next year, the front door fell off the hinges. Several holes appeared in the floor. Both bathrooms had plumbing problems. The paint on the walls and ceiling peeled completely off and floated down to the floor in big, ugly flakes. Travis and Sara realized that they had made a huge mistake. The house looked so nice on the surface, but underneath it was nothing more than junk.

It's easy to make a house look good on the outside, but the inside is what really counts. The same holds true for your life. It's easy to fool people and appear like a decent person on the outside, but the inside is what matters.

Jesus tried explaining this to a Pharisee in today's passage. The man didn't understand why Jesus didn't ceremonially cleanse His hands before dinner. Jesus, impatient with the Pharisees' obsession with outward religious displays, began a stern lecture. He compared the Pharisees to a cup that is clean on the outside but dirty on the inside.

The world can pressure you into being obsessed with your outward appearance. Models, body builders, celebrities, and even others at school can demand that you look a certain way to be accepted. As a result, you spend your time making yourself look good on the outside. You stare at the mirror, dissatisfied with what you see, and try again. Meanwhile, on the inside you cry out to be accepted just the way you are.

Do you try to make yourself look good on the outside because of pressure from your peers or the media? _____

What do you hate most about your appearance and why? _____

What extremes have you gone to in order to make yourself look different? _____

Obsession with your appearance can lead to eating disorders like anorexia or bulimia. It can also lead to a self-centered lifestyle, in which you spend all your time worried about how you look on the outside. Jesus doesn't want you to live in such a frantic world. He wants you to know that you are valuable to Him just the way you are.

Concentrate on making the inside of your life clean. Ask the Lord to fill you with His Spirit on the inside and build your character. After all, once people get past the front door to your life, they'll like you better if they find good things on the inside.

Put Your Two Cents In

Luke 11:42

> Mr. Johnson signed his year-end tithe check to his church, sat back in his comfortable leather chair, and smiled. *This will give me a good tax break,* he thought to himself, *as well as raise a few eyebrows among the other members.*
>
> He placed the check in an envelope, sealed it, and placed it in his pristine, black leather Bible on the coffee table. Just then, his wife called him into the dining room for dinner. After the long and well-worded blessing, Mr. Johnson lifted the fork to his mouth—and the doorbell rang. "Who could that be at supper time?" he fumed, rising to answer the door.
>
> "Yes?" Mr. Johnson asked impatiently.
>
> "Um, sir," the poorly dressed young man said. "My family and I are traveling. Our car broke down, and we spent all we had for the repairs. We need food and perhaps some gas money. Can you help us?"
>
> "No!" screamed Mr. Johnson, slamming the door. He walked back into the dining room, and his wife asked him who was at the door. "Some bum," muttered Mr. Johnson as he buttered his roll.

Mr. Johnson may have given a lot of money to his church, but he forgot that God is more concerned with how we treat the people around us. The Pharisees in today's passage got a stern lecture from Jesus for having the same problem. They followed the letter of the law by giving ten percent of everything they had to God, but they did not honor God by helping people in need.

If we aren't careful, we can end up being just as insensitive. We sometimes feel like we earn our "points" with God by attending church, giving our offerings, and carrying a Bible. However, God is just as interested in how we react to the man holding the sign that reads "Will work for food." He looks to see how much we tip the waitress and how clean we leave the pizza place after the youth fellowship. He wants to know how we treat our parents when we don't get our way. God listens to see what we say about the new, weird-looking guy at school.

People matter to God, and He wants us to treat them with love. What could you do to love your parents better? _____

Your brother or sister? _____

Your schoolteachers? _____

Strangers in need? _____

Pray that God would show you specific ways to love the people He has placed in your life. Then look for opportunities to treat others with love and respect.

Be Yourself

Luke 11:43

> Once upon a time, in a magnificent country far away, an emperor decided to choose his own successor to the throne. He called for all of the teenage boys in the kingdom to gather before him. He gave each of them a seed and said, "Plant this seed in a pot. One year from today, bring me what you have grown, and I will select the boy with the best plant to be the next emperor."
>
> One of the young boys named Karan tried in vain over the course of the year to get his seed to sprout. While the other boys were talking about how well their plants were doing, Karan had no luck at all. At the end of the year, he had nothing. His mother encouraged him to return to the emperor anyway and simply explain that he had done his best.
>
> Karan carried the empty pot back to the emperor's palace. Hundreds of other young boys had gathered, each with tall and beautiful plants of various kinds. Karan hid in the rear of the crowd because he was so ashamed.
>
> The emperor arrived and walked through the crowd carefully, examining each plant. He finally stopped in front of Karan and stated, "Young man, you will be the next emperor of my kingdom." Karan was astonished and the crowd began to murmur. The emperor said, "I gave each of you boiled seeds that could not grow. All of you planted something else when you saw that your seed wouldn't grow. All of you tried to impress me with lies, but this young man came to me as he was."[35]

Karan became the next emperor because he didn't try to be popular. The Pharisees of Jesus' day spent most of their time trying to be popular by being seen in all the right places, and in today's passage Jesus reproved them for doing so.

The pursuit of popularity can often lead you to pretend to be something that you are not. You find yourself putting on a mask to impress others in hopes that they will like you better. You may not really care to try the latest drug, but when it is offered to you at a party, you take it anyway. You might not normally speed in your car, but when you're following a friend whose doing 100 mph, you floor it anyway so you won't seem uncool.

Do you want to be popular? _____

Why? _____

What have you done recently that you know is wrong just to be noticed? _____

_____

Jesus says, "Woe to those who seek popularity." There's nothing wrong with being popular, but seeking popularity causes lots of problems. Ask God to help you be honest about who you are at all times, whether you are alone or in front of a crowd. Whether you realize it or not, people will like you if you simply be yourself.

Weekly Bible Study and Prayer Review

Bible Study

Look back through some of the Scriptures you read this week. Write down the one verse or passage that God used to speak to you.

_____

_____

_____

_____

*Memorize this verse or passage. You can do it if you spend just
a few minutes saying it to yourself.*

Now, think of at least one situation you will probably face soon in which you could use this Scripture to help you make the right decision. Write down that situation below.

_____

Quote the Scripture when you face this situation, and live by it.

Prayer Time

*Take a few moments to praise God for who He is.
Now take a few moments to thank God for things He has done for you.
Now ask God to make you into the person He wants you to be.
Ask God to use you to help others become closer to God.*

Below is your prayer list for the week. Keep it updated each week. If your prayer isn't answered this week, carry it over to next week's list.

Request	Date of Original Request	Date Answered
_____	__/__/__	__/__/__
_____	__/__/__	__/__/__
_____	__/__/__	__/__/__
_____	__/__/__	__/__/__
_____	__/__/__	__/__/__
_____	__/__/__	__/__/__
_____	__/__/__	__/__/__
_____	__/__/__	__/__/__
_____	__/__/__	__/__/__

*Pray for the things on your list and trust God to provide.
Forgive anyone you have not yet forgiven.
Ask God to forgive you for any unconfessed sin in your life.
Ask God to keep you out of trouble with sin.
Acknowledge that God is in complete control of your life
and will take care of everything.*

I Smell a Rat

Luke 11:44

Emily walked home from school on Friday, climbed the stairs to her room, and tossed her books into the corner. She took off her shoes and plopped on the bed, totally exhausted from the long week at school. She knew she only had ten minutes to rest before getting ready for the football game, but she savored every moment.

As she lay there, she became aware of a faint, pungent odor in the air. "Yuck! What is that?" she thought to herself. Before she had time to think, it was time to go. She headed out the door for the football game.

When Emily returned later that night and went up to her room, the smell almost made her sick. She couldn't even go in her room. Her dad came and tried to find the source of the smell, but he couldn't. Emily slept downstairs on the couch that night, and the next morning they tried to find the source of the smell again. This time it was unbearable. Emily's dad went up into the attic with a flashlight, and before long he yelled, "I found it! There's a dead rat between the walls next to your room, Emily." Emily shuddered at the thought that a rat had been lying only a few feet from her and she didn't even know it.

Emily smelled a rat—something unseen but very wrong—in her room. In today's passage, Jesus smelled a rat. He told the Pharisees that they were like unmarked graves that people walk over without knowing it. In other words, just beneath the surface—out of view—lay something rotten.

We all have a private side to our lives that no one else sees. There's nothing wrong with that. However, if we have a private life of sin that no one else knows about, it can become a big problem. For instance, you may be nice to your parents with your words and facial expressions, but then when your bedroom door is closed you mutter words that would break your parents' hearts. Or perhaps when you are home alone you flip on the satellite TV system and watch things you shouldn't. Maybe you have a secret sin so hidden and so shameful that you have developed a rotten lifestyle, and you don't know how to stop.

Do you have any secret sins? _____

What are they (if you are afraid to write them down, just write down a letter or two that symbolize the sin)? _____

Would you like to give up these sinful habits? _____

What will you have to do to quit? _____

Jesus doesn't want you to have a secret sin life. He wants you to be true to Him when everybody is watching *and* when only God is watching. Confess each one of your secret sins to Him right now, and ask for forgiveness. Then pray for the strength to resist the urges you will feel to commit those sins again.

The Tangled Web We Weave

Luke 11:45–46

"The Internet is pure evil," claimed Robert. "There's so much bad stuff going on that for you to use the Internet or E-mail at all is wrong." Abbie shook her head to disagree, but before she could get a word in edgewise, Robert continued. "The Bible says we are not to take part in the things of this world. The Internet is the World Wide Web."

Abbie could stand it no longer. "Robert, you're crazy. Sure, some people use the Internet for evil, but a lot of people use it for good. I E-mail my aunt who is a missionary in Zimbabwe. I also go to Web sites that will help me with my schoolwork."

Robert cut in. "It doesn't matter. It's worldly, and it's wrong. You're living in sin. I can't believe you get on the Web, Abbie. How can you say you are a Christian?"

"Robert, look. You don't even own a computer, so you couldn't surf the net if you wanted. You've never seen all the good things out there, so it's wrong of you to say that Jesus would never get on the World Wide Web."

Robert had a problem called *legalism*. He tried to say that something was evil all of the time, even though it wasn't. In today's passage, Jesus condemned legalism.

Some of the teachers of the law—the "preachers" of Jesus' day—were adding things to the Bible that weren't there. The Bible says in the Old Testament not to work on the Sabbath day. The teachers of the law made up six hundred rules on top of that biblical command to define what "work" was. These rules said you couldn't carry certain things or walk more than a certain distance. They made up so many rules that the people couldn't keep up with them, and they felt guilty all of the time.

Jesus does not want us to make up extra rules to go along with the Bible. The Bible is all we need. If the Bible says that something is a sin, then it is a sin. There's no need to make up extra rules or exceptions to the rule to fit our personal preferences. For instance, the Bible says in Hebrews 10:25 that Christians should meet together for church as often as possible. However, does this mean you should feel guilty if you are sick or go out of town and miss a Sunday or Wednesday? Of course not.

Do you have any rules you follow that really aren't in the Bible? _____

Like what? _____

Has anyone ever tried to make you feel guilty for not following a rule that is not found in the Bible? _____ *Explain.* _____

_____

Don't be a legalist, and don't let legalists make you feel guilty for not obeying their rules. Ask God to help you look to the Bible alone as your source for what is right and wrong. Then, to the best of your ability, follow what the Bible says.

Dying for Change

Luke 11:47–51, 53–54

Have you ever wondered what happened to the disciples of Jesus? The best records indicate that all but one were killed under persecution. James, the brother of John, was beheaded with a sword. Ten years later, Philip was beaten, imprisoned, and finally crucified.

Andrew, the brother of Peter, was crucified on an X-shaped cross. He was tied to it, rather than nailed, so that the suffering lasted longer. He apparently hung there for several days, and the entire time he continued to tell the good news of Jesus to everyone who came near. James the son of Alphaeus was dropped from a great height, and when that did not kill him, someone crushed his head with a large hammer.

Thomas traveled to India to spread the gospel, where he was stabbed repeatedly with spears and thrown into the flames of an oven. Peter was crucified upside-down at his own request because he did not feel worthy enough to die in the same way as Jesus. John was thrown into a pot of boiling oil but escaped unharmed. He was exiled to a deserted island for many years before being released.

The disciples of Jesus didn't just become average, ordinary people after Jesus ascended to heaven. From what we can tell, all of them but John were persecuted and killed for their beliefs.

In today's passage, Jesus condemned persecution. He also made it clear, though, that persecution would be part of life for His faithful believers. Notice that when Jesus finished speaking a woe to those who persecute others, the Pharisees turned right around and began persecuting Jesus. They publicly opposed Him and tried to catch Him in His words to make Him look bad.

If you live your life like Jesus did, you will face persecution. Often, because we fear public opposition, we keep our mouths shut. Don't let the fear of persecution keep you from saying and doing what you know is right. Yes, you may suffer—but when you suffer persecution and still love the people who are hurting you, they see Jesus more than ever before.

Have you ever kept your mouth shut for fear of what others would think? _____

Have you ever held back from doing what was right because you were afraid of what people would say? _____

What is something you feel strongly that you ought to say or do in spite of the possibility of persecution? _____

Jesus Himself and eleven of His own disciples were tortured and killed for doing what is right. Pray that God would give you the same amount of courage as they had to face persecution. Then, when persecution comes, stand your ground and take it. When you do, others will see Jesus in you.

Clowning Around

Luke 11:52

Once upon a time, a traveling circus stopped near a large village. They set up the tents about a mile from town in the middle of a dry field of grass and began advertising their presence to the villagers. Many people came to see the circus acts, and the ringmaster was quite pleased.

One afternoon, however, one of the circus performers threw a cigarette on the ground and started a fire. The fire quickly spread through the circus tents, engulfing it in flames. The dry grass ignited and began burning toward the village. The ringmaster, fearing that the village would catch fire, sent a circus clown running to warn the people.

The clown, fully dressed for his act, sped away on a bicycle to the village. Upon his arrival, he began running through the streets, jumping up and down, and screaming—warning the villagers to evacuate and escape the coming inferno. The crowd, rather than run, began to gather around the clown in curiosity. Soon they were rolling with laughter. The more insistent the clown became, the more the crowd laughed.

Moments later, the flames reached the village and burned it to the ground. Many people died because no one took the clown seriously.[36]

Nothing the clown said mattered—his costume communicated comedy, not concern. A mismatch between words and appearance can completely destroy a message.

In today's passage, Jesus offered His final woe to the teachers of the law for taking away the key to knowledge. What does that mean? It means that these guys said one thing with their mouths, but their actions told a different story. They taught the law, which required them to love their neighbors, and yet their actions were devoid of love altogether. As a result, people could not take them seriously.

When you make it public that you are a follower of Jesus, you become the key to knowledge to those around you. You become the avenue through which others will have a chance to see what Jesus is really all about. If your actions line up with your words, you will create a genuine curiosity in people to know more about Jesus. If you wear a clown suit, so to speak, and your actions communicate something other than Jesus, then you take away the key of knowledge and others will miss the chance to see Jesus in you.

Can you think of one person or a group of people around you who is not aware that you are a follower of Jesus? Who are they? _____

How can you use your words this week to let them know about your relationship with the Lord? _____

What action can you take that will support your words and draw that person closer to a knowledge of Jesus? _____

God longs to bring others to a saving knowledge of His Son. Pray that God will give you the opportunity and the courage to use your words and actions to share Jesus with others. Don't clown around—there are people in your village to save.

A Good Hair Day

Luke 12:1–12

Ethan had studied all night long for his final in animal science, and he was tired. He had spent about seven hours carefully learning about all of the different types of rodents in North America. The final was at 8:00 A.M. and Ethan uncharacteristically skipped his shower so he could use the time to study. At 7:52 A.M., Ethan put on a baseball cap and darted out of his dorm room toward the class.

When he arrived, he noticed that the front of the room had three long tables with twenty plastic containers on the top. Inside each container were hair samples from twenty different North American rodent species. The test paper had twenty blanks on it. The professor said, "Your final is to identify each rodent species from its hair sample. You have one hour. Begin."

Ethan sat speechless, not believing his eyes or his ears. He walked past the hair samples and realized that he didn't stand a chance. He began to get angry—so angry that he wadded up the test and threw it into the trash can. He began storming out of the room, until he heard the professor's voice, "Excuse me, young man. What is your name?"

Ethan took off his baseball cap and tilted the top of his head toward the professor, pointing at his hair, "You tell me, Professor! You tell me!"[37]

Ethan could have used a little more tact, but he made his point. He couldn't identify the rodents from their hair samples any more than the Professor could identify Ethan by his.

Jesus mentions in today's passage that He knows you so well that He knows how many hairs are on your head. He says you are worth more than all the rodents and sparrows in the world. Why? Because He loves you more than you could ever imagine.

If you stop and think about it, you spend most of your time looking for love. You look for friends who will love you and accept you. You want your parents to love you for who you are. You spend hours dreaming about that cute boy or girl, longing for him or her to notice you and return your affection. All of these people can let you down, but God's love is perfect and unconditional. He will never let you down.

Have you ever been hurt by people who say they love you? _____

Describe the most recent situation. _____

Have you ever hurt someone that you love? _____ *How?* _____

God will never hurt you. He wants you to know and experience His deep love for you. Spend some time right now counting your blessings—remembering all of the ways that God has shown you His love. Close your eyes, rest in His presence, and think about all He has done for you.

Have a Beach Ball

Luke 12:13–21

A businessman, tired of staring at his laptop computer, walked out of his hotel room and sauntered out the back door, down a long, wooden pathway, and onto the beach.

He came upon a young man sitting casually in the sand and reeling a fishing pole. The businessman looked him over and decided that the fisherman was lazy. He said, "It's Tuesday afternoon, young man. You should be at work!"

The young man asked, "Why?"

"So you can make lots of money!" replied the businessman.

"Why?" was the only response.

"So you can build yourself a good retirement," the businessman insisted.

"Why?"

By now the businessman was getting angry, "So you can retire in wealth and afford to come out to a nice beach like this and fish all day."

The fisherman finally looked at the businessman, smiled, and cast his line back into the ocean.

The businessman was so busy making money to be happy someday that he didn't even realize the young fisherman was happy now—without wealth. In today's passage, Jesus told the story of a successful businessman. This man did so well that he was finally ready to retire and enjoy life, depending on his wealth to provide him with happiness. However, what the man didn't know was that he was going to die on the evening before his retirement began.

True happiness does not come from having a lot of money in the bank. We spend so much time running after money, thinking it will make us happy, when in reality we can be truly happy right now without all the green stuff. How? By being rich toward God, as Jesus said. You do this by seeking your happiness in the things of God—not in money or possessions. Think about it. If you knew you only had twenty-four hours to live, would you spend one minute of it hoarding money? Of course not. And if you were lying on your deathbed, would you regret not earning more money? No way.

Do you ever want to have more money and buy expensive things to make you happy?

_____

If you had all of the money in the world, what is the first thing you would buy?

_____

How can you be happy in the Lord right now with what you already have? _____

Don't waste your time walking over dollars, trying to find another dime. Trust God to provide you with the money you need. Ask God to help you find your happiness in serving Him, not in material things.

Weekly Bible Study and Prayer Review

Bible Study

Look back through some of the Scriptures you read this week. Write down the one verse or passage that God used to speak to you.

_____
_____
_____
_____

Memorize this verse or passage. You can do it if you spend just a few minutes saying it to yourself.

Now, think of at least one situation you will probably face soon in which you could use this Scripture to help you make the right decision. Write down that situation below.

_____

Quote the Scripture when you face this situation, and live by it.

Prayer Time

*Take a few moments to praise God for who He is.
Now take a few moments to thank God for things He has done for you.
Now ask God to make you into the person He wants you to be.
Ask God to use you to help others become closer to God.*

Below is your prayer list for the week. Keep it updated each week. If your prayer isn't answered this week, carry it over to next week's list.

Request	Date of Original Request	Date Answered
_____	__/__/__	__/__/__
_____	__/__/__	__/__/__
_____	__/__/__	__/__/__
_____	__/__/__	__/__/__
_____	__/__/__	__/__/__
_____	__/__/__	__/__/__
_____	__/__/__	__/__/__
_____	__/__/__	__/__/__
_____	__/__/__	__/__/__

*Pray for the things on your list and trust God to provide.
Forgive anyone you have not yet forgiven.
Ask God to forgive you for any unconfessed sin in your life.
Ask God to keep you out of trouble with sin.
Acknowledge that God is in complete control of your life
and will take care of everything.*

The Cold Shoulder Treatment

Luke 12:32–34

The snowstorm caught the two travelers by surprise. They bundled up their coats tightly, shuddering from the cold, and continued to walk across the Himalayan pass.

Before long, the two travelers came across another man who was hurt and lying in the snow by the pathway. One of the two travelers, a Christian, wanted to carry the man to safety. The other traveler refused, and instead went on alone. The Christian bent down, picked up the half-frozen man, and began carrying him on his back. Soon, the traveler's body heat provided much-needed warmth to the man he was carrying, and he revived. The two men walked side by side, keeping each other warm as they walked.

As they walked and talked, suddenly they both tripped over something lying on the ground and covered in snow. When they brushed the snow away, they discovered the first traveler who had refused to help. He was frozen solid and quite dead.[38]

This is a true story. The dead man thought if he took the time to help someone else, he might endanger his own life, so he went ahead alone. If he had taken the time to give, he would still be alive.

Jesus said in today's passage to "Sell your possessions and give to the poor so that you can have real treasure in heaven." He also says in Acts 20:35, "It is better to give than to receive." These are verses we like to skip over. We think that if we spend money on others, we won't have enough for ourselves. The truth is, when we spend money on those who need it, the warmth we receive from giving will make us happy.

God loves the poor, and He calls on Christians every day to share and sell their possessions and give to the poor to help them. Yet, in today's world, we have forgotten to help the poor. Do you realize that if every Christian decided today to give about one dollar per day to the poor that we could wipe out homelessness and hunger completely? Now, the important question: What can you do to help? Go on a mission trip with your youth group or church to help the poor. At Christmastime, buy a gift for someone your age who wouldn't otherwise get any presents. If your church collects a special offering for the poor, make sure you contribute. Skip lunch one day and give the money you would have spent to the person holding the sign at the street corner.

Do you have any money at all, even pennies, you could give to someone less fortunate?
_____ *Do you have one thing, no matter how big or small, you could sell and give that money to the poor?* _____

Who can you help with this money? _____

When are you going to help them? _____

Don't turn a cold shoulder to the poor. Ask God to show you opportunities to give, and then give like Jesus would give. Don't hold back. Your reward in heaven will be worth far more than you can ever imagine.

I'm on My Way

Luke 12:35–48

The boss said his good-byes to his employees and walked out the door for a long, much-needed vacation in the Bahamas. He was nervous about leaving the entire company in the hands of his one hundred employees, but he decided to trust them as he went away to rest.

Three days into his vacation, here was the scene back at his office. Most of the employees came in an hour or two late. Half of them were taking two-hour lunch breaks. During what remained of the work day, many of the employees simply leaned back in their chairs and relaxed. Ten or so of the employees worked as diligently as they always did.

Meanwhile, back at the beach, the boss was busy worrying about his office. Suddenly, a thought came to his mind. He grinned. He took out his cell phone, called the office, and said, "Hey, how is everybody? I decided to cut my vacation short. I'll be in the office in about ten minutes. Bye." Then he hung up and didn't worry anymore.

Back at the office, it was mayhem. Ninety people screamed and scrambled, trying to clean up the place and catch up on work left undone. The other ten simply continued to work at the same pace, without worry or fear.

When the boss is away, the employees will play. That's often the case. Some people, though, work hard whether or not the boss is in the office. That's the way it should be.

Jesus, our boss, left us with instructions on how to run the business after He ascended into heaven. He has promised us that He will come back soon. In the meanwhile, He asks us to be dressed and ready for service—meaning we should always be ready and willing to do whatever God calls us to do. If we don't stay ready, we can become apathetic—lazy and self-centered.

The literal definition of *apathy* is "without passion." Someone who is apathetic about eating Chinese food just isn't passionate about having an egg roll. Someone who is apathetic about Jesus may show up at church, but isn't interested in passionately sharing the gospel with others. Apathy is so rampant among Christians today that we look like the servants Jesus described in today's passage. We say to ourselves, "Jesus won't be back today. I can relax and do what I feel like."

On a scale from one to ten, with ten being the highest, where would you rate your passion for following Jesus? _____

Think about a Christian you know who has a genuine passion for God. What makes this person stand out in your mind? _____

How can you conquer the sin of apathy and ignite the flames of passion for Jesus in your own life? _____

Jesus is looking for some passionate young people to do His work. Ask God to help you overcome any apathy in your life as you begin to seek Him more. Jesus is coming back soon. When He does, let Him find you busy doing His will.

Family Feud

Luke 12:49–53

> Though Bruce attended church with his family, he did not meet Jesus until a friend shared the gospel with him. By his bed one evening, Bruce gave his heart to the Lord and became a Christian. Bruce told his parents about his salvation, expecting them to be excited. Instead, they became angry. Bruce's dad said, "Do not ever speak of this again. Is that clear?" Bruce couldn't believe it. Why didn't his parents understand? Later, at his next youth group meeting, Bruce shared his story with the youth pastor and his peers. Once again, Bruce was shunned. The other youth group members labeled Bruce a freak.
>
> After high school, Bruce felt called to be a missionary to the tribal Indians of South America. He shared this vision with his parents, who still did not understand. They ridiculed his calling and told him he was crazy. Bruce knew he wasn't crazy. He knew God had called him to South America. Without any support from his family, he purchased a one-way plane ticket to South America. He had seventy dollars in his pocket and nowhere to go when he arrived on an unknown continent.

Bruce Olson tells his story in the book *Bruchko*. After many trials and tribulations, he became a missionary in Colombia and has since led hundreds of Indians to the Lord.

In today's passage, Jesus explains that often our commitment to Him will cause division between us and our friends and family. He tells us this so that we will not be surprised when the people around us do not understand what God is doing in our lives. We shouldn't think it strange when some of our friends and family ridicule or shun us for following Jesus.

Why does God allow this to happen? Why can't we all just get along? The answer to this question lies in one simple gift that God has given us: the freedom to choose. God will not force Himself on anyone. If you have two people in the room, and one has chosen to give her life to Jesus completely and the other has rejected God, you will have division. It is not desirable, but it is inevitable. Your response to this division is never to argue or fight back. Instead, your response is to love those who disagree with you and gently continue to share the message of Jesus with them (1 Peter 3:15–16).

Has your commitment to Jesus caused division between you and someone else? _____

Who? _____

What problems have resulted because of this division? _____

Have you done your best to imitate Jesus by loving these people unconditionally in spite of their confusion about your commitment to God? _____

How might you go the extra mile in sharing Jesus with these people? _____

Division will come if you are committed totally to Jesus. Ask God to help you face that division with patience and love. For further study, meditate on Romans 8:31.

Life Sentence

Luke 12:54–59

I knew this day would come, but that didn't take away the knot of pure worry in my stomach. I stood up as the Judge made his entrance, terrified of my impending fate.

I glanced at my lawyer. How could he be so calm? He was almost smiling. I looked over at the prosecuting attorney. His eyes were filled with hate and determination. I don't stand a chance, I thought helplessly.

The prosecutor stepped toward the bench with a list—a very long list. He began to prance around the courtroom, reading each item on the list slowly but loudly. I hung my head in shame. I was guilty of each and every charge, and I knew it. After what seemed like hours, the prosecutor sat down with a grin. "Your honor, I rest my case," he thundered.

Quietly, my lawyer stood. He knelt on the floor and said to the Judge, "This man is innocent because he placed his faith in Me." The prosecutor immediately rose in objection, pointing to the list he held in his hand. My lawyer, Jesus, took the list and held it near His head. He seemed in pain, and then I saw blood. It dripped onto the list, and suddenly every accusation disappeared. The list was white as snow.

While the prosecutor stared in disbelief, the Judge brought His gavel down and declared my sentence. "Life!"

We all will stand before God one day and face judgment (see Hebrews 9:27). Our fate will depend on whether or not we settled with God. Our accuser is the devil—Satan. He keeps a list of every sin we ever commit, and he stands before God with that list to accuse you of the evil you have done (Zechariah 3:1–2 and Revelation 12:10). The list is accurate and truthful. You are guilty of everything on the list. You're going to need a great attorney to get out of this jam.

Enter Jesus. He knows the penalty for sin is death, so He paid that price Himself. His blood becomes a covering for your sin. All it takes is one drop of that precious blood to make your list of sins as white as snow. Satan is left without a case, and your sentence is *life—eternal life* in heaven. Now, during the course of your Christian life, you will sin. Satan will then stand before God again to accuse you of that sin. You, however, need to settle matters and go to God for forgiveness, asking once again for the blood of Jesus to cleanse you and make you whole.

If Satan were in heaven right now to make accusations, what would he have to say against you? _____

Settle this matter quickly. Remember the old, rugged cross and the price that Jesus paid. Confess your sins to God, and allow the blood of Jesus to cleanse you. Case dismissed.

Untimely Death

Luke 13:1–5

On November 22, 1963, President John F. Kennedy arrived in Dallas, Texas, at Love Field on Air Force One. He and his wife, Jackie, shook hands with well-wishers at the airport and then took their places in the presidential limousine that would carry them through downtown on their way to a special luncheon at the Dallas Trade Mart.

As the motorcade neared the end of its route, Kennedy's limousine turned right off Main Street onto Houston Street, and then made a hairpin turn to the left onto Elm into what is called Dealey Plaza. The limousine slowed to eleven miles per hour. Kennedy waved to the crowd with a smile, looking directly toward an area known as the Grassy Knoll.

Suddenly, the President stopped waving and raised both arms, putting his hands to his throat. He leaned toward his wife, who had no idea that her husband had just been shot. A few seconds later, in front of dozens of witnesses, President John F. Kennedy was struck in the head by a fatal bullet. He collapsed into his wife's lap. Less than thirty minutes later, he was pronounced dead at Parkland Hospital.

The nation grieved that day. Why did it happen? Did God cause the President to die because He was angry with him? Did President Kennedy do something to deserve such a horrible death?

God does not take away human life arbitrarily to punish us for sin. Jesus explained in today's passage that people whose lives are cut short by crime or accidents are not singled out by God to die because of their sin. He points out that *all* of us will die because of our sin. God told us way back in the garden of Eden that if we ate from the wrong tree we would die—someday, somehow.

If you have not already, you will experience the untimely death of someone that you love. Your first question will be, "Why, God?" The answer to this question is not that God assassinated this person because he or she was a greater sinner than someone else. All of us will die—someday, somehow. Knowing this helps us to keep perspective. Eternity is what matters. The few days we have on this planet should be used to prepare ourselves and others for eternity.

Have you experienced the loss of a loved one to an untimely death? _____

Who? _____

What happened? _____

How did you feel? _____

Do you blame God? _____ *Do you think you can learn to take the blame off of God and accept the fact that we all must die because of our sin?* _____

It's OK to grieve for losing a loved one, but don't let this death cause you to blame God. Let it remind you that your own days are numbered. Ask the Lord to help you number your days and make each one count for Him. Live each moment as if it were your last.

I Know You Can Do It

Luke 13:6–9

"Ellen, would you be willing to sing a solo during the youth-led evening service next month?" the youth pastor asked. Ellen's mouth dropped open.

"Me?" she stammered. "Can I think about it?"

"Sure," Debbie said. "Just let me know by next Sunday." As Debbie walked away to do other youth pastor things, Ellen leaned against the wall in a daze. She felt a mixture of fear and inadequacy. She had a good voice, and she sang all the time in choir at church and school. But a solo! In front of all those people? Ellen decided that she just couldn't do it.

When the next Sunday arrived, Ellen's stomach churned with acid when she walked into the morning Bible study. She tried to avoid Debbie, but to no avail. The inevitable question came.

"So, Ellen, are you going to sing in the youth-led service?" Debbie posed.

"Um, well," Ellen fought to get the words out. "I don't, I mean, I . . ."

Debbie, sensing Ellen's fears, said, "Ellen. You have a great voice. You can keep it to your-self or use it to serve God. I know you can do it, and people will be drawn to the Lord because of you. Now, what do you say?"

You may not be able to sing the solo, but God wants you to use the talents you do have to serve Him. When you do, you do what the Bible calls *bearing fruit*.

In today's passage, Jesus told a parable about a tree that wasn't producing fruit. After three years of nothing, the owner was going to cut the tree down but decided to give it one more chance to produce fruit. Jesus is the owner, and you are the tree. He wants to see obvious signs of fruit in you. In other words, He wants to see you using your God-given talents, interests, and abilities to serve Him.

You were created uniquely by God to do certain things. He equipped you with the ability, and now He waits to see what you will do. Your talents might include any or all of the following: singing, teaching, physical strength, organizing, coming up with great ideas, playing a musical instrument, intellectual abilities, or any number of other things. It doesn't matter what you can do, but it does matter whom you are doing it for.

What talents do you have? _____

How are you using them now? _____

How are you, or how can you, use each of these talents to serve the Lord? _____

What do you think the results would be if you began to give God more of your time and talents? _____

What do you think the results might be if you refuse to use your talents for God's purposes?

_____

Don't look now, but here comes God—looking you over for some fruit. What will He find? Ask the Lord to show you how you can best use your talents to serve Him.

Weekly Bible Study and Prayer Review

Bible Study

Look back through some of the Scriptures you read this week. Write down the one verse or passage that God used to speak to you.

_____

_____

_____

Memorize this verse or passage. You can do it if you spend just
a few minutes saying it to yourself.

Now, think of at least one situation you will probably face soon in which you could use this Scripture to help you make the right decision. Write down that situation below.

_____

Quote the Scripture when you face this situation, and live by it.

Prayer Time

Take a few moments to praise God for who He is.
Now take a few moments to thank God for things He has done for you.
Now ask God to make you into the person He wants you to be.
Ask God to use you to help others become closer to God.

Below is your prayer list for the week. Keep it updated each week. If your prayer isn't answered this week, carry it over to next week's list.

Request	Date of Original Request	Date Answered
_____	___/___/___	___/___/___
_____	___/___/___	___/___/___
_____	___/___/___	___/___/___
_____	___/___/___	___/___/___
_____	___/___/___	___/___/___
_____	___/___/___	___/___/___
_____	___/___/___	___/___/___
_____	___/___/___	___/___/___
_____	___/___/___	___/___/___

Pray for the things on your list and trust God to provide.
Forgive anyone you have not yet forgiven.
Ask God to forgive you for any unconfessed sin in your life.
Ask God to keep you out of trouble with sin.
Acknowledge that God is in complete control of your life
and will take care of everything.

Take a Wild Guest

Luke 13:10–17

First University Church was packed for the morning service. The first two Sundays after college started in the fall were always full, but today not one empty seat could be found. The congregational singing was over, and the offering plates had been passed. Everyone was seated as the choir began singing a magnificent special. All eyes faced forward.

From the back of the auditorium, a college freshman entered. He wore a dirty T-shirt, jeans full of holes, and no shoes. Before anyone even noticed him, he was walking down the aisle in search of a place to sit. The eyes of the choir were as big as saucers. As the young man passed each pew, the congregation could not help but stare. The young man made it all the way to the front, and finding no seat, he simply sat down on the floor beneath the pulpit.

As the choir neared the end of its song, a deacon rose from his seat and made his way down front toward the student. Everyone shifted restlessly, wondering what was about to happen. The deacon reached the front, crouched down toward the boy, and took a seat right next to him.

The old deacon offered compassion toward the freshman. Rather than pass judgment and ask the student to leave, the deacon went down to where the boy was and joined him.

Jesus illustrated compassion in today's passage when He healed a woman who had been crippled for eighteen years. What is unusual about this event is that it took place in the middle of a worship service in the synagogue. Many people were upset, thinking this healing interrupted God's teaching and should have been done some other time. Jesus claimed that the service was the perfect time to illustrate God's compassion for people.

You probably attend church regularly. Sometimes it's easy to get in a routine of sitting in the same place with the same people in a Bible class or worship service. You may not even notice that new face—another teenage guy or gal who feels awkward and out of place—looking for a place to sit. This is a perfect opportunity for you to show compassion by getting out of your seat—and your comfort zone—and going to where this person is. As Jesus illustrated, when God's people meet, it isn't so we can just sit and listen—it's also an opportunity to show compassion to others.

When you attend Bible study and worship services, do you usually sit in the same place? _____ *Do you usually sit with the same people?* _____ *Do you ever notice strangers or guests?* _____ *What have you done in the past to make these guests feel welcome?* _____ *What is something you could do next time you notice someone new?* _____

Ask God to help you be sensitive to the needs of others the next time you go to church. Follow Jesus' example and show compassion to those who need it. For further study, read Colossians 4:5.

Just a Little Bit

Luke 13:18–21

> The Sunday school teacher was nervous. In fact, he was terrified. He took a deep breath, cleared his throat, and walked into the shoe store to talk to a teenage salesman there about the Lord.
>
> The teacher thought about just making small talk and inviting the boy back to Sunday school, but decided instead to share the gospel. As he spoke, he stared at the ground, thinking that the young man was probably disinterested. When he finished, he looked up and to his surprise found the shoe salesman in tears. There, in a Boston shoe store, Dwight L. Moody gave his heart and life to Jesus.
>
> Dwight L. Moody became an evangelist and had a profound influence on a young preacher named Frederick B. Meyer. Meyer began to preach on college campuses and there led a student named J. Wilbur Chapman to the Lord. Wilbur Chapman asked a former baseball player named Billy Sunday to come to Charlotte, North Carolina, for a citywide revival. Charlotte community leaders were so impressed that they planned another revival and asked Mordecai Hamm to come to town to preach. In that revival a young man named Billy Graham stepped forward and gave his life to Christ.

Because one scared Sunday school teacher decided to share Jesus with a shoe salesman, millions of people have come to know Jesus through men like Dwight L. Moody and Billy Graham.

Jesus explained in today's passage that it only takes one mustard seed to grow a thirty-foot tree full of branches where birds can build their nests. It only takes a little bit of yeast to make an entire batch of bread dough rise to the occasion. In the words of the old song "Pass It On," "It only takes a spark to get a fire going, and soon all those around can warm up in its glowing."

You may often feel that the things you can do for God are small and insignificant. You may not be the world's greatest evangelist. You might not be able to sing in front of thousands. Perhaps your grades are not the best. Maybe you have less money than most. Maybe you think, "I'm not going to change the world. What could I possibly do?" Jesus says that small things can cause big things to happen. You can change the world, even with what you perceive to be limitations, if you simply do what He leads you to do.

If God could ask you to do one small thing for Him this week, what might He ask you to do at home? _____ *At school?* _____

At church? _____ *During free time?* _____

Don't ever miss out on serving God by thinking that what you do is too insignificant. Ask God to lead you to serve Him in little ways at home, school, church, and everywhere else you go. When you sense God's leading, take a deep breath and follow through. You never know how big the results might be.

Down in the Mouth

John 9:1–5

It was a beautiful summer day, and Joni thought it would be fun to take a swim. She dove headfirst into Chesapeake Bay, not realizing how shallow the water was. She broke her neck and became paralyzed from the neck down for the rest of her life. She was only seventeen.

Why did this horrible thing happen to such an innocent, young girl? Was God punishing her for something? People all around Joni asked these questions. Joni asked some herself, but then decided to stop asking questions. Joni stopped asking why she couldn't move from the neck down and decided to start working with what she had from the neck up.

She learned to draw and eventually paint with a pencil in her mouth. Her spirit and her artwork caught the attention of the world. She wrote eleven best-selling books, played herself in a full-length movie about her life, and spoke on her own radio show heard by millions across the world. In 1987, President Reagan appointed her to the National Council of Disability.

If you ask Joni why God allowed this to happen to her, she will tell you that it happened so that the work of God might be displayed in her life.

Joni realized and now teaches the world that tough times and disabilities are not the end—they are the beginning of an opportunity to allow God to display His work.

In today's passage, Jesus corrected a long-held misconception that accidents and disease are the result of sin. The disciples noticed a man born blind and asked Jesus if the man or his parents sinned to cause this disability. Note Jesus' answer. He said that this man was not blind because of sin. He said this happened so that the work of God could be displayed in his life.

You may feel you have some sort of unfair disadvantage compared to others. Maybe you have a disability. Perhaps you think you are not as smart or as nice-looking as your friends. Maybe you don't have the athletic skills to make you the most valuable player. Regardless of your disadvantage, Jesus wants you to know that your problem is not your fault. Neither is the problem a random case of genetics or circumstances gone awry. Instead, God has allowed you to possess this disadvantage in order to use it for His glory. Instead of a disadvantage, you actually have an advantage because God has a very specific purpose for your weakness.

What do you feel is your greatest disadvantage? _____

How have you let this "problem" affect your attitude about God? _____

About life? _____

How might God use this disadvantage for His purpose? _____

Don't view this so-called disadvantage as a problem or a limitation. Ask God to show you specifically how you can serve Him and give Him glory in your weakness. This will require you to stop looking at what you don't have and start working with what you do have. For further study, read 2 Corinthians 12:7–10.

Here's Mud in Your Eyes

John 9:6–12

Indiana Jones stepped carefully through the cobwebs, knowing that the two who had tried to pass before him were beheaded. The words of his only clue ran through his mind over and over, "Only the penitent man will pass." Suddenly, he solved the puzzle, realizing that a penitent man must kneel. Indiana knelt just in time as the sharp, steel blade swung above his head.

The second clue was even more difficult, "Only in the footsteps of God will he proceed." Indiana stared at the mosaic floor, each odd-shaped piece with a letter of the Latin alphabet. After making a near-fatal mistake, Indiana stepped forward carefully on only those letters that spelled out the name of God.

The third and final clue seemed impossible, "Only the leap from the lion's head will prove his worth." Indiana stood next to the lion's head and stared into a bottomless pit. He realized that the clue was telling him to take a leap of faith. With his eyes nearly closed, Indiana took one step into nothingness and found, to his surprise, an almost invisible bridge over the chasm.

Indiana safely made it through three potentially deadly booby-traps because he listened carefully to the clues and then did exactly what they suggested.

In today's passage, Jesus gave a blind man a clue that could restore his sight. He spit on the dirt, made a little mud, and then spread the mixture onto the blind man's eyes. Jesus then told the blind man to go wash his eyes in the pool of Siloam. The blind man could have asked, "Hey, why are you putting mud in my eyes? And how can I find the Pool of Siloam when I can't see?" Instead, he did exactly as Jesus said, and his sight was completely restored.

Sometimes it seems like Jesus asks us to do some crazy things. We want to ask questions. We might say, "God, wait a minute. I don't see anybody else doing what you're asking me to do." God's response is probably, "That's right, and that's exactly why I'm giving you this assignment." Another objection might be, "God, I don't see how to get where You're telling me to go." Like the blind man, once you decide to go where Jesus tells you, you will be able to see.

Do you ever sense God asking you to do something that seems too crazy or difficult? ____

Explain. _____

What are your questions or objections to following through with God's request? _____

What do you think might happen if you just obeyed God's prompting without getting more information first? _____

Think of God's daily instructions in your life as adventurous—like Indiana Jones. Carefully consider the clues God gives you and just go for it. Pray right now that God will help you hear His voice each day as He prompts you to do certain things. Ask Him to help you follow through, no matter how crazy the instructions seem. The results will be phenomenal. You'll see.

Hesitation Hoedown

John 9:13–23

> *Hesitating Henry had a habit of the hobbles.*
> *He hardly ever hurried, hustled, hastened—fearing bobbles.*
> *His half-hearted, haunting hardship had him hiding in a hole.*
> *His hesitation hindered him from reaching any goal.*
>
> *He had never ever heralded or hinted of his Lord.*
> *To him it was too hard so he just hobbled—never soared.*
> *His heavenly home hidden, he had nothing else to do.*
> *But have a humdrum, humbug hopeless hunch that Jesus might shine through.*

Henry never accomplished much because he was always worried about what people might think. His fear of what others might say paralyzed him from doing much of anything.

In today's passage, the parents of the formerly blind man that Jesus healed were approached by religious authorities and questioned. The Pharisees demanded to know if their son was once blind and, if so, how he was healed. The parents hesitated to answer because they knew that anyone who openly confessed that Jesus is Lord would be cast out of the synagogue. Rather than risk the consequences, they kept their mouth shut and passed the buck along to their son.

Sometimes we Christians hesitate to make our faith known publicly. Why? We fear the consequences. Our hesitation paralyzes us into indecision, and we miss the opportunities that God provides to share Jesus. We might even pass the buck along to someone else, like the youth pastor or pastor. The name of Jesus then becomes pushed off to the side, and no one in our world has the opportunity to hear about Him. This is not how it's supposed to be. God wants every single person who you know to be very aware of your relationship with the Lord.

Do you know of anyone in your world whom you see or talk to on a regular basis who does not know about your relationship with Jesus? _____

Who are they? _____

The next time you see these people, how could you let them know in an obvious way that you are a follower of Jesus? _____

You don't have to walk around shouting, "I'm a Christian! I'm a Christian!" God just wants you to take advantage of everyday circumstances and use everyday language to turn the thoughts and hearts of others toward Jesus. Ask God right now to help you share Jesus with every single person you know. Pray for the courage to overcome any hesitation you might feel. Then, when the opportunity presents itself, don't let hesitation get the best of you.

Seeing Is Believing

John 9:23–34

> "There's no evidence for God, and I don't see the point of believing in something you can't see!" shouted Liz.
>
> Bethany struggled for the words to say. She had no photograph of God; no time machine in which to take Liz back to the Crucifixion and Resurrection; no telescope that would show her heaven. "Look, Liz. You can't see the wind, but you know it's there because you see the effects it has on the leaves in the trees. You don't look at the sun to prove to yourself that it is out today. You know the sun is out because you can see everything else. You can't see your brain, but you know you have one because you can sit here and have this conversation with me. You can't see electricity, but you use it every day when you blow-dry your hair and cook your toast. You can't see love, but you know it's there because you've told me how you feel about Robert!"
>
> "Shhhhhh!" Liz screamed in a whisper. "Someone will hear you!" Glancing around to make sure Robert was nowhere in sight, Liz said, "You've got some good points. Let me think about it."

Many people claim that they won't believe in anything until they see it. Bethany pointed out that we believe in a lot of things that we can't see. However, we can see the effects of these things in our lives.

In today's passage, a group of religious leaders questioned a formerly blind man for the second time to find out how he was healed. While the spiritual know-it-alls demanded to see some sort of proof for this miracle, the man who could now see simply told what he knew. Keep in mind that this man had never seen Jesus, because Jesus had him go wash his eyes out in a pool before he could see. All this man knew were the effects of Jesus in his life.

You cannot prove God exists, to yourself or anyone else, by seeing Him with your own eyes. He wants you to believe in Him because of the effects He has on your life. And when God gives you the opportunity to share Jesus with a friend, He doesn't expect you to prove God exists with an autographed picture of Jesus. He simply wants you to share what Jesus has done in your life. He wants you to explain how God affects you every day.

How does knowing Jesus affect you? _____

List some things that have happened to you that you believe only God could have done.

_____

Can you share these things with someone else who is not a Christian? _____

Keep your eyes open for the daily miracles of God all around you. Ask Him to allow you to experience Him in ways that you never have before. And when He does, share these experiences with others so they can see God too.

Weekly Bible Study and Prayer Review

Bible Study

Look back through some of the Scriptures you read this week. Write down the one verse or passage that God used to speak to you.

_____
_____
_____
_____

Memorize this verse or passage. You can do it if you spend just a few minutes saying it to yourself.

Now, think of at least one situation you will probably face soon in which you could use this Scripture to help you make the right decision. Write down that situation below.

_____

Quote the Scripture when you face this situation, and live by it.

Prayer Time

Take a few moments to praise God for who He is.
Now take a few moments to thank God for things He has done for you.
Now ask God to make you into the person He wants you to be.
Ask God to use you to help others become closer to God.

Below is your prayer list for the week. Keep it updated each week. If your prayer isn't answered this week, carry it over to next week's list.

Request	Date of Original Request	Date Answered
_____	___/___/___	___/___/___
_____	___/___/___	___/___/___
_____	___/___/___	___/___/___
_____	___/___/___	___/___/___
_____	___/___/___	___/___/___
_____	___/___/___	___/___/___
_____	___/___/___	___/___/___
_____	___/___/___	___/___/___
_____	___/___/___	___/___/___

Pray for the things on your list and trust God to provide.
Forgive anyone you have not yet forgiven.
Ask God to forgive you for any unconfessed sin in your life.
Ask God to keep you out of trouble with sin.
Acknowledge that God is in complete control of your life and will take care of everything.

What's with Her?

John 9:35–41

> Lori found her usual Sunday morning pew and plopped down beside her friends. The group began talking about who did what the night before, and what everyone was going to do after church tonight.
>
> Once the worship service started, Lori and her friends wrote notes to each other, whispering and giggling. This was the normal routine, and no one expected it to be any different than any other Sunday. Something was different, though. Just before the sermon started, a woman stepped up to the platform to sing a solo. Lori didn't even notice as she passed another note, but when the woman began to sing, everything changed.
>
> The music and the words to the song captured Lori's attention. She stopped writing and started listening. She leaned forward, listening intently to every word. For some reason, the lyrics gripped her heart like no song she had ever heard. The world around her began to fade as her whole mind and heart were gripped by God's undeniable presence. She closed her eyes, wiping away a tear.
>
> One friend noticed Lori's peculiar reaction and whispered to another, "What's with her?"

A more appropriate question might be *"Who's* with her?" The Lord was with Lori. The song Lori heard took away all the distractions and helped her really see Jesus, and she worshiped Him.

In today's passage, a man whom Jesus healed of blindness was thrown out of the synagogue. The man had never seen Jesus with his own eyes, but he still had faith in Him. Jesus found the man and introduced Himself as the Messiah—the Lord. The man fell down on his face in worship, lost to the world around him. The man saw no other proper response to meeting and knowing Jesus than to worship Him.

Just what is worship? Worship is seeing and experiencing God for who He really is. Often the weekly routine and the distraction of friends prevent us from really seeing God. However, when we finally open our eyes (like the blind man did) and look Jesus in the face, He reveals Himself to us like He never has before. To be able to worship, you must voluntarily remove distractions and focus on God. Forget about who's going where. Don't worry about what you're going to do later. Lock your eyes and ears on God and bask in His undeniable presence.

What distractions typically prevent you from drawing closer to God in worship? _____

What can you do to remove those distractions? _____

Describe a recent but memorable time of worship. _____

When do you plan to worship God next? _____

Jesus longs for you to see and experience Him for who He is. Ask God to help you remove any distractions that might prevent you from seeing Him clearly. Get alone, focus on the Lord, and worship Him.

The Great Escape

John 10:1–10

> A farmer was returning from the fields one day when he spotted an egg lying in his path. He had no idea what kind of egg it was, so he took it home and placed it with the other eggs in his chicken coop.
>
> Soon the egg hatched, and a tiny baby eagle crawled out. Not knowing what else to do, the eagle followed all of the other baby chicks around. The eagle grew much larger than the chickens, but it still continued to cluck, scratch the ground for worms, and flutter its wings on the ground without ever learning to fly. The eagle grew so large that its wingspan reached six feet, and yet it knew nothing other than how to be a chicken.
>
> One day as the eagle strutted around the chicken coop, it glanced upward and saw another eagle in flight. "What a magnificent bird!" the eagle said. "Oh, if I could only fly above this small, dirty place down here and see the world from new heights!"
>
> "Forget it!" a chicken clucked. "You're a chicken, and you'll never be able to fly like that."[39]

The eagle missed out on the good life because it didn't realize it had the power to fly. Jesus explained in today's passage that He is the source of the good life for the sheep—the gate in the fence. When a sheep is inside the pen, it is confined to a life of limits by the fence around it. When the shepherd opens the gate, however, he leads the sheep out of the pen and into an endless landscape of grassy hills and quiet streams—the good life.

Jesus' purpose for coming was to give us the good life. The thief, Satan, would have us believe that the good life comes through popularity, possessions, power, or pleasure. We think if we seek these things we will find happiness, but in reality it is a trap to destroy us. Jesus explains that we experience the good life by seeking Him. Just like a sheep walking through a gate to escape the pen, or an eagle stretching its wings to escape the chicken coop, you can go through Jesus to escape the limitations of an ordinary life and live the good life.

Every day you make decisions about what to do, where to go, etc. How often do you make a decision based on (1) whether or not people will notice you? _____

(2) what's in it for you (money, possessions, etc.)? _____

(3) whether or not you can be in control? _____

(4) how good it's going to feel? _____

These four motives for decision making are popularity, possessions, power, and pleasure. They are the four walls to a fence that confines you. Ask God to help you avoid making decisions based on these things, because they will limit and eventually destroy your potential. Instead, seek God's will for your life by walking with Jesus beyond these four walls and into the good life.

What Else Is There?

John 10:11–21

George made himself comfortable for the long train ride when a man a few seats in front of him fell out of his seat and into the aisle, screaming and thrashing in a wild seizure. A second man bent down onto the floor to administer aid. He held the screaming man's head, protected him from injury due to the thrashing, and talked calmly to him and the bewildered passengers. Soon, the seizure was over, and the helpful passenger placed a wet cloth on his friend's forehead.

George was astonished, but said nothing. After things calmed down, George finally slept. He was suddenly awakened again by the same man having a similar seizure. Again, the man's friend protected him and comforted him until it was over. During the course of the trip, George witnessed the same event many, many times.

When the train finally arrived at its destination, George pulled the man's friend aside and asked him what the problem was. "Well," the man replied, "this man risked his life to save mine in Vietnam. When we returned, he began having these seizures. I sold everything I had and moved in with him to take care of him. What else is there to do? I owe him my life."[40]

One man risked his life for another, and now his friend chooses to return the favor. In today's passage, Jesus revealed that He is like a shepherd who lays down His own life for the sheep. If a wolf attacks or the sheep is in any danger, a good shepherd, like Jesus, gives his life for the sheep.

Jesus gave His life for you on the cross. He continues to give His life for you by living in you and making His sole purpose to be your shepherd every day. In response, your sole purpose should be to follow the Shepherd every day no matter where He leads you. If He leads you through a tough time, don't doubt or ask why—just follow Him. If He leads you through great times, then thank Him for being the source of your fortune. If He leads you to give up a dream or habit, show Him that you prefer Him over anything else. No matter where He leads you, follow Him. Give your whole life to Him out of gratitude for what He has done for you.

If Jesus asked you to do one thing right now, what would it be? Fill in the blank. Jesus says, "I want you to _____."

What level of commitment is required for you to be able to fulfill this request? _____

How will your life change if you actually do this for Jesus? _____

What are the likely results? _____

As a good shepherd, Jesus will lead you only where He has gone before. He will make it clear to you where He wants you to go and what He wants you to do. Ask God to show you how you can change to give more of your life to Him.

Get a Grip

John 10:22–30

Carl was in church practically every time the doors were open. He paid attention to the messages most of the time and lived his life for Jesus as best he could.

His junior year, though, Carl met a girl who knocked his socks off. Against the advice of his parents, he began seeing her seriously. She didn't go to church, and before long Carl didn't either. He began sleeping with his girlfriend. She introduced him to marijuana, cocaine, and eventually heroin. Carl became so addicted to drugs that he began stealing money from his family and friends to support his habit. His girlfriend got pregnant twice, and both times Carl made her get an abortion.

One night, in a drug deal gone bad, Carl was shot in the leg. It was only a minor injury, but as he lay in bed that night he realized that he had turned his back on God. Carl feared that he had gone too far and God was so angry with him that he had no hope. In sheer despair, Carl fell on his face in his bedroom that night and said, "God, please take me back. I'm so sorry that I left You."

God smiled. "I never let you go, Carl. I never let you go."

You may not have done the same things Carl did, or you may have done things that seem much worse. Either way, there are times when you feel like you've sinned so much that God is going to abandon you.

In today's passage, Jesus explained that nothing could be further from the truth. When you become a Christian, God places you in His hand. You belong to Him, and nothing can change that—not even you and your sin. No matter how far you go, or how bad it gets, God will not let you go. In His great love and grace, He will simply wait for you to realize your sin and confess it to Him.

Does this mean you have a license to sin? Hardly. In the same passage that Jesus promises that nothing can snatch you out of God's hand, He also says that you are one of His sheep. You know Jesus' voice. You listen to Him. You follow Him. A sheep that follows Jesus but one day wanders off does not cease to be a sheep. As you follow Jesus, you may wander into sin and get into serious trouble, but you do not cease to be a Christian. God will not let you go.

Have you ever felt like you committed a sin so terrible that God was disgusted with you and let you go? _____

What did you do that was so horrible? _____

Have you confessed this sin, or sins, to God? _____

If not, do so right now.

God's grip of grace is greater than your grime. Nothing you can do will cause Him to let you go. Admit any unconfessed sin, and rest in His forgiveness. When you do, God will give you a big hand.

Get Me out of Here!

John 10:31–42

Angela knew it was going to be a rotten day the minute she woke up. "The hot water is out," her dad said matter-of-factly as she stumbled to the bathroom.

After the coldest shower of her life, Angela arrived at school. During first period, her English teacher passed out the test they had taken a week earlier. Angela almost cried when the paper plopped on her desk. She had studied so hard, only to fail miserably. On the way to third period, Angela tripped on her shoelaces and fell flat on her face in front of everyone, spraining her wrist in the process. During lunch, she found a hair in her milk.

The afternoon wasn't much better. Angela forgot about a quiz in math. She got in an argument with her best friend. She couldn't go to basketball practice because of her wrist, and she feared she might be benched for the first game in two weeks.

When Angela got home, she ran to her bedroom, closed the door, and cried. She turned on her stereo, popped in her favorite CD, closed her eyes, and just listened.

All of us have days that drive us crazy. All of us have places we go or things we do to take our minds off the bad day. Jesus was no exception.

In today's passage, we find Jesus having a rough day. He told the people around Him that He was God in the flesh, and instead of worshiping Him the people started a riot and threatened to kill Him. Jesus escaped and went to a place that would take His mind off things. He returned to the Jordan River, where His ministry first began. There He rested and recuperated.

When you have a bad day, or when circumstances begin to spin out of control, it's OK to feel like saying, "Stop the world! I want to get off." It's OK to find comfort and refuge in a special place. In following Jesus' example, that place of refuge that you go to should have spiritual significance. Jesus went to the place where His ministry first began. The place you go to or the things you do for renewal should be something that reminds you that God loves you and that His purpose for your life is still on track.

When life gets crazy, where do you go to find comfort? _____

Does this place give you temporary relief, or is it a place that draws you nearer to God?

_____

Describe something you could do or a place you could go to that would be better to renew your spirit. _____

When your world is out of control, there is only one place to go. Run to God, who is out of this world, and rest and recuperate in Him. Find a place that allows you to focus on Him and only Him. Give God your troubles. For further study, read Psalm 31:1–5.

Narrow-Minded

Luke 13:22–30

A group of people responds to the question, "What do you have to do to get into heaven?"

- Don't kill anyone or rob any banks.
- Go to church at least once a month.
- Love all people, plants, and pets.
- Fight for what is right, like environmental safety.
- God loves everyone, so we all go to heaven.
- Your good deeds have to outweigh your evil deeds.
- Say your prayers every night before you go to bed.
- Give money to the church and to those in need.
- Read your Bible every day.
- Trust in Jesus and accept Him as your Lord.

Only one of the above responses is correct. Yet the majority of non-Christians believe that there are a variety of ways to get to heaven. They think we Christians are narrow-minded for believing that Jesus is the only way to heaven.

We *are* narrow-minded. We should be. In today's passage, Jesus compared the way to heaven to a narrow door. Many people live their whole lives looking for another way into the Master's house, but those that do not enter through the narrow door of Jesus will find themselves locked out of an eternity of happiness with the Lord.

As a witness for Jesus, you can choose one of several options: (1) You can leave others looking for the narrow door by saying nothing. (2) You can try to widen the door or make new doors by telling people there are other ways to heaven besides Jesus. (3) You can stand near the narrow door and be narrow-minded enough to point to Jesus as the only true way to heaven. If you are a Christian, the first two choices are not options at all. If you choose the third option, you will be labeled as narrow-minded. That's OK, though. Jesus is the one who made these claims—not you. You are just delivering a message.

Do you know people in your world who believe there are ways to heaven other than Jesus?

_____

Who are they and what do they believe? _____

What can you do to set the record straight? _____

Follow Jesus' example by letting others know there is only one way to heaven. Pray for boldness so you won't be ashamed to make the narrow way known to people who are looking for another way. Point to Jesus, and let Him take care of the rest.

Bible Study

Look back through some of the Scriptures you read this week. Write down the one verse or passage that God used to speak to you.

_____

_____

_____

_____

Memorize this verse or passage. You can do it if you spend just
a few minutes saying it to yourself.

Now, think of at least one situation you will probably face soon in which you could use this Scripture to help you make the right decision. Write down that situation below.

_____

Quote the Scripture when you face this situation, and live by it.

Prayer Time

Take a few moments to praise God for who He is.
Now take a few moments to thank God for things He has done for you.
Now ask God to make you into the person He wants you to be.
Ask God to use you to help others become closer to God.

Below is your prayer list for the week. Keep it updated each week. If your prayer isn't answered this week, carry it over to next week's list.

Request	Date of Original Request	Date Answered
_____	__/__/__	__/__/__
_____	__/__/__	__/__/__
_____	__/__/__	__/__/__
_____	__/__/__	__/__/__
_____	__/__/__	__/__/__
_____	__/__/__	__/__/__
_____	__/__/__	__/__/__
_____	__/__/__	__/__/__
_____	__/__/__	__/__/__

Pray for the things on your list and trust God to provide.
Forgive anyone you have not yet forgiven.
Ask God to forgive you for any unconfessed sin in your life.
Ask God to keep you out of trouble with sin.
Acknowledge that God is in complete control of your life
and will take care of everything.

Go for the Gold

Luke 13:31–33

It was the summer of 1996. The U.S. Olympic women's gymnastics competition was virtually tied with Russia for first place. Kerri Strug was the last American to vault, and she had to make it count.

She took a deep breath, focused on the jump ahead, and ran toward the leather pommel horse. She sailed through the air, twisting and twirling. As she came down for her landing, something went terribly wrong. She fell down, grimacing in pain. Her ankle was dislocated, and the team was now in second place.

The pain was great, but Kerri's determination was greater. Rather than give up, Kerri returned to the starting position for her second and final jump. She took one more deep breath and sprinted down the runway on her badly injured ankle. Her vault was flawless, but the landing would determine the winner. Kerri came down on her one good foot and balanced herself on the mat. The landing was perfect.

The crowd stood to their feet and roared with applause. Kerri collapsed and was removed from the floor by stretcher. A moment later her score appeared. The U.S. Women's gymnastic team had won their first-ever gold medal.

Kerri had every reason to call it quits. Her obstacles were overwhelming. Kerri didn't see the obstacles though. She saw the goal. She saw gold.

Jesus faced His own obstacles too. King Herod had already killed Jesus' cousin, John the Baptist. Now a group of Pharisees came and told Jesus that Herod wanted to kill Him too. Jesus could have given up and left Herod's jurisdiction. He could have disbanded His disciples and gone home. He could have changed His message so it wouldn't offend Herod. Jesus didn't do any of those things. In fact, Herod's threat simply made Jesus more determined than ever to fulfill His mission.

Someone once said that an obstacle is what you see when you take your eyes off the goal. Obstacles are bound to come in your life, but they are nothing more than Satan's attempt to distract you from fulfilling your mission. Don't focus on the obstacles. Focus on Jesus—your ultimate goal. No matter what obstacles lie in your path and how difficult it may seem to go on, don't give up.

Do you have any obstacles that seem to hinder your relationship with Jesus? _____

List a few of those obstacles. _____

How have you allowed these difficulties to keep you from doing what God wants you to do?
_____

What can you do to overcome these obstacles? _____

Your obstacles are not designed to slow you down. They are designed to make you more determined than ever to become all that God wants you to be. Ask God to help you overcome the obstacles that stand in your way. Focus on Jesus, not the obstacles. Go for the gold. For further study, read Hebrews 12:1–3.

Good Grief

Matthew 23:37–39; Luke 13:34–35

Bryce and Cliff argued every day in Biology. "You're such a religious fanatic," Cliff would say to Bryce. "There is no God. Science proves it."

Bryce prayed every day that Cliff would see Jesus. One day Bryce heard about a Christian concert that would be held next month. Bryce knew that Cliff liked the style of music, so he invited Cliff to come. To his surprise, Cliff said yes.

The concert was incredible. The message of Jesus was proclaimed clearly—and loudly. There were so many people that Bryce and Cliff lost each other in the crowd. Bryce continued to pray for his friend. Near the end of the concert, the band played quietly while the lead singer preached a short message. He asked anyone who wanted to know Jesus to come to the front and talk with counselors. Out of the corner of his eye, Bryce saw Cliff standing near the front. Bryce longed for Cliff to know Jesus so much that he broke down and wept. People began to surround Bryce and ask what was wrong. Bryce said through the tears, "I want my friend to know Jesus. I want my friend to know Jesus."

Cliff did not accept the Lord that night, but Bryce continues to try and reach his friend.

In today's passage, Jesus grieved for some close to His heart—the people of Jerusalem. Jesus looked over the city and recalled how through the ages God had sent prophet after prophet to explain the depths of His love. Time after time, the people rejected His love and killed His prophets. Did that stop God? No. He longed for them to know Him so much that He would soon give His life for them.

Think about how it feels when you meet a guy or a girl who attracts you, but they don't notice you. Inside, you ache, wishing that this person would see you and like you. Multiply this feeling many times over, and you will get some idea of how Jesus felt. If you are going to be like Jesus, then you, too, will grieve for others to know God. You won't feel this grief until you love a person so much that you cannot rest until he or she knows your Lord. This kind of grief is a good grief, because it drives you to pray and witness to your friend consistently and constantly—in spite of rejection.

Do you have any friends or family members who do not know Jesus? _____

Who? _____

Have you witnessed to and prayed for them? _____

Have you given up on some of them, or does your longing for them drive you to keep trying? _____

No matter how many times the people of Jerusalem rejected God, Jesus continued to love them and long for them to know Him. Don't give up hope that your friends and family will one day believe. Turn your grief into prayer and action. Pray for them to see and accept God, and do your part to witness to them every chance you get.

Drop Everything

Luke 14:1–6

Thirteen-year-old Douglas didn't enjoy coming to church. His parents were divorced, and his mom didn't go to church. The only time he was able to spend time with a youth group was every other Sunday morning when he was visiting with his dad.

Like clockwork, Douglas sat in his Sunday school class today with the other boys his age. Since Douglas wasn't always there, and he didn't go to school with any of them, the other boys never talked to him. One day, a well-meaning class member said, "Hey, Douglas. How come you never come to any other youth events?" Douglas didn't answer. Instead, he simply walked away.

Douglas wanted so much for someone to notice him and be his friend. He was dying inside of loneliness, even though people were all around him. Finally, one Sunday as the boys walked to the church service, someone said, "Hey, Douglas. We're playing volleyball tonight in the gym after church. Why don't you come? You can be on my team."

Finally someone took the time to make Douglas feel accepted. Someone stepped outside his comfort zone and reached out to touch Douglas's life.

In today's passage, Jesus reached out and touched another neglected person. Jesus was eating at the house of a very prominent religious person and noticed a man with dropsy seated at the table. This condition caused the lower half of the man's body to swell abnormally with fluid, making him look waterlogged (which is what the word *dropsy* means). Apparently, none of the other people at the dinner noticed or cared about the man. Jesus dropped everything to take time to heal the man, even though it meant getting out of His comfort zone and experiencing rejection by those around the table.

You probably have some people in your youth group or at school who go mostly unnoticed, yet inside they long for someone to reach out and say, "Hey, I notice you. Let me help." These people, like Douglas and the man with dropsy, are often very quiet. From a distance, they may seem undesirable. For you to become friends with them may require too much effort, or it may even cause your current friends to reject you. Jesus wants you to get out of your comfort zone, drop everything, and reach out to someone new.

Name someone at your church who goes unnoticed most of the time. _____

Why do you think he or she is overlooked? _____

What can you do to reach out and befriend this person? _____

Ask God to help you get to know this person and others. Pray that you would be able to step out of your comfort zone and touch lives the way Jesus would. Drop everything, and make a difference in the life of someone else today.

Have a Seat

Luke 14:7–14

> The doors to the large gym opened, followed by the innumerable feet of screaming teenagers dashing inside toward the best seats. It was first come, first serve for the big Saturday night concert.
>
> Unbelievably, Janna managed to reach the front row first. She went straight to the very middle seat and sat down. Within five minutes the entire room was filled. Every blue, plastic portable chair was taken. All eyes focused on the stage in front. Janna surveyed her position and thought, "I've got the best seat in the house!"
>
> Suddenly, Janna heard a sound from the rear of the gym. Janna turned in her seat to see a woman standing on another platform in the back. The woman spoke into a microphone, "Good evening, everyone. I know that you will all enjoy tonight's concert. Before we begin, let me make a very important announcement. I need all of you to take your chairs and face them this way. The band will be coming out shortly on this platform. I apologize for the inconvenience."

Janna thought she had earned the best seat in the house. She discovered, to her dismay, that her efforts to be first actually caused her to be last. She now had the worst seat in the house.

In today's passage, Jesus was sitting at a banquet table. He had observed how many of the dinner guests selfishly tried to take the best seats—those near the host. Jesus pointed out that the danger of taking the best seat is that someone more important than you might show up, and you'll give up your seat in front of everyone. Instead, Jesus told them to take the worst seat, so that the host would invite them to take a better seat.

In other words, Jesus wants you to be patient and considerate of others. Don't push and shove in line in the cafeteria or the movie theater. If you drive, be courteous and let everyone else have the right of way, even if you're certain *you* have the right of way. When your brother is being selfish, let him have his way. If you notice there's only enough soda in the refrigerator for one person, offer it to someone else before you take it. When you humble yourself like this, God says that He will exalt you. If you exalt yourself in these situations, God will humble you.

When are you the most selfish? _____

Why are you selfish in this area? _____

What can you do differently to humble yourself and be less selfish in this situation?

_____

Ask God to help you be considerate of others. Pray that you would be able to conquer selfishness when it rears its ugly head. The next time the selfish side of you tells you to get your way, take a backseat and be patient. Let God be the one to offer you the best seat in the house.

Come One, Come All

Matthew 22:1–10; Luke 14:15–24

The date was set. The invitations were in the mail. Patricia was so excited about her birthday and slumber party. Everyone she talked to at school about coming seemed excited too.

When the long-awaited Friday came, Patricia was so eager that she skipped lunch to go to each of her friends and confirm that they would be at the party that night. The first person she talked to said, "I'm sorry Pat. I can't make it. My family just bought a new boat, and we're going to the lake."

Disappointed, Pat turned to another. This one said, "Oh, I forgot to tell you. Joe and I are dating now, and he asked me out tonight. We're going to the movies."

Pat couldn't believe it. She went to still another friend, who stated, "I've got a soccer game tomorrow before lunch, and I'm going to need my rest."

One by one, Patricia's friends made excuses and declined to come to the party. Patricia was at the point of tears. What was she going to do? She had a big party planned, but no one was coming.

Can you imagine how much it would hurt to have everyone you invited to a birthday party turn you down with lame excuses?

In today's passage, Jesus explained that He feels the same way. He told a parable about a man who prepared a great banquet and invited many friends. When the day of the banquet arrived, everyone made excuses. People were just too busy to come! The master was angry. He decided that since he made preparations for a party, he was going to have a party. He invited strangers and those who were poor, crippled, blind, and lame. Jesus is the master, and those who reject His invitation to heaven are the ones who refused to come to the banquet. When Jesus' invitations were rejected, He didn't give up. He invited others. He kept inviting others until His house was full.

When you share the good news of Jesus with others, you will face rejection. Many that you talk to will have excuses about why they do not want to commit their lives to Jesus. Do not be discouraged. When one person rejects Jesus, turn to another. Often those who need to hear the message the most are those you might not normally talk to. Jesus went to the poor, crippled, blind, lame, and strangers. You can take the message of Jesus to people who are hurting, because they are more likely to listen to you and less likely to make excuses.

Have you ever shared Christ with someone and been rejected? _____ What was this person's excuse? _____ Did you get discouraged? _____ _____ Can you think of any strangers or hurting people around you who need to hear about Jesus? _____ Who are they? _____ When and how will you share Jesus with them? _____

Never let the choice of others to reject Jesus discourage you. Let it make you more bold in witnessing to others. Ask God to open your eyes and show you those who need to hear His message the most.

Think About It

Luke 14:25–35

"Elle, you better slow down," Mikala urged. "You're going to get a speeding ticket, and your father will take the car away. Then we'll miss out on the senior trip next weekend."

"Would you shut your face already?" Elle countered. "I know what I'm doing. I'm following that sports car up ahead. He'll get a ticket before I will."

Elle pressed the accelerator, trying to keep up with the car in front of her. She was already doing twenty miles per hour over the limit. She glanced in the rearview mirror, and her face fell. "Oh no!" she squealed. The flashing red and blue lights made her heart leap. Elle pulled over on the shoulder and waited.

The police officer was not impressed by Elle's excuses, and he showed no mercy. He quietly wrote out the ticket, tore it from his pad, and handed it to Elle. "You ladies slow it down and have a nice day."

Elle was almost in tears. She knew her dad would take the car away from her and she would miss the senior trip next weekend. "What was I thinking?" she asked herself. "I knew this would happen."

Elle knew what would happen if she was caught speeding. She knew the cost of her mistake, but she didn't count the cost. Now she would pay more than one hundred dollars in fines and miss the trip of a lifetime.

In today's passage, Jesus explained that if you want to follow Him, you must count the cost before you begin. What is the cost of following Jesus? Everything. Your love for Jesus must be so great that it dwarfs the love you have for anything else—family, friends, possessions, money, etc. You must be willing to come to Jesus without conditions and say, "Lord, no matter what, I will follow You."

You may not realize it, but you may have placed conditions on following God. For instance, will you follow Jesus if He calls you to be single for the rest of your life? What if God wants you to go to the jungles of Africa to be a missionary? Would you follow Jesus if He asked you to die protecting a friend? What if God required you to be poor and never own your own car? Would you still follow Jesus if He allowed you to go to prison for a crime you did not commit? While these may be extreme cases, they may help you to recognize that you have placed conditions on how far you will follow Jesus.

Describe something you would be unwilling or afraid to do if God asked. _____

Why is this so difficult for you? _____

What must you do to overcome your inhibitions? _____

God may not ask you to do any of the things listed above, but He could. Be prepared to go anywhere and do anything for God. Pray that God would help you count the cost and throw away the conditions. Follow Jesus wherever He leads. Don't miss the trip of a lifetime.

Weekly Bible Study and Prayer Review

Bible Study

Look back through some of the Scriptures you read this week. Write down the one verse or passage that God used to speak to you.

_____
_____
_____
_____

Memorize this verse or passage. You can do it if you spend just
a few minutes saying it to yourself.

Now, think of at least one situation you will probably face soon in which you could use this Scripture to help you make the right decision. Write down that situation below.

_____

Quote the Scripture when you face this situation, and live by it.

Prayer Time

Take a few moments to praise God for who He is.
Now take a few moments to thank God for things He has done for you.
Now ask God to make you into the person He wants you to be.
Ask God to use you to help others become closer to God.

Below is your prayer list for the week. Keep it updated each week. If your prayer isn't answered this week, carry it over to next week's list.

Request	Date of Original Request	Date Answered
_____	__/__/__	__/__/__
_____	__/__/__	__/__/__
_____	__/__/__	__/__/__
_____	__/__/__	__/__/__
_____	__/__/__	__/__/__
_____	__/__/__	__/__/__
_____	__/__/__	__/__/__
_____	__/__/__	__/__/__
_____	__/__/__	__/__/__

Pray for the things on your list and trust God to provide.
Forgive anyone you have not yet forgiven.
Ask God to forgive you for any unconfessed sin in your life.
Ask God to keep you out of trouble with sin.
Acknowledge that God is in complete control of your life
and will take care of everything.

Animals Do the Dumbest Things

Luke 15:1–7

The sheep is by far one of the dumbest animals alive. Sheep are prone to get themselves into trouble over and over again. In every case, the trouble starts when they wander away from the shepherd.

Often a sheep will spy a stream of water and leave the flock to get a drink. As it wades into the water to drink, the water from the stream will soak the sheep's wool, making it very heavy. This pulls the sheep underwater as it fights to get out, and it drowns.

Sheep will also leave the herd to nibble on grass. As it wanders further and further away, its wool is caught in the bushes, and it can no longer move. A wolf spots the helpless sheep and devours it.

Sheep can also become cast—that is, they lay down and roll over too far and can no longer get up. This is similar to what happens to turtles that turn upside down on their shells. The sheep is totally helpless and will die unless the shepherd comes to rescue it.

In each of the three situations described above, the sheep did not intend to get into danger. It only wanted to investigate the possibilities on its own. Each time the sheep found itself in danger. Each time the only way out was for the shepherd to come to the rescue.

In today's passage, Jesus compared humans to a flock of sheep. We often unintentionally wander away from God to investigate the possibilities on our own. It doesn't take long to realize that we made a mistake and to experience the consequences of our sin. At this point, we often feel that God will zap us with a lightning bolt in His anger. Today's parable says quite the opposite. Jesus becomes more concerned with you when you sin. Why? Because you are lost and He wants to find you.

Though we are prone to unintentionally wander away from God, Jesus will always be there for us. When we feel trapped and hopeless in our sin and its harmful consequences, Jesus comes looking for us. He will not be satisfied until He has found us and can take us home on His shoulders.

Have you ever committed unintentional sins? _____

List a few things that you find yourself doing that you never intended to do. _____

What were some of the consequences of your sin? _____

Because you are human, you may find yourself caught in unintentional sin. If so, confess that sin right now, and ask God to forgive you and rescue you. He longs to come and get you, no matter how far He has to go.

Finders Keepers

Luke 15:8–10

The mall was packed, and Alyce and Krista navigated the busy crowd as they shopped. They paused for a moment to rest and get a snack from the food court, and then resumed their journey.

"Let's go in here," Alyce said. Suddenly, she stopped in her tracks. "Nobody move!" she screamed. Krista thought Alyce had lost her mind. "I lost my contact. It just popped out."

Quickly Krista dropped to the floor and began scouring the surface for any sign of Alyce's lost contact. Meanwhile, Alyce politely asked everyone around her to please avoid stepping anywhere near possible resting places. "Do you see it?" asked Alyce.

"Not yet," said Krista. "I'm looking." Krista's keen eye scanned up and down the floor. After a few moments, it seemed hopeless. Alyce finally said, "Come on, Krista. Let's just go home so I can tell my parents and get this over with."

"Wait," urged Krista, as she continued to crawl. Suddenly, a tiny reflection of light caught her eye. She reached out and carefully picked up the contact.

"You found it! You found it!" Alyce screamed, jumping up and down. She was so excited that the people walking by wondered if she was crazy.

If you wear contacts, or a retainer, or anything else of value, then you know what it feels like to lose something important. Your heart pounds, and you'll do just about anything to get it back.

Today's passage talks about a woman who lost a very valuable coin. It was worth about one full day's wages. She apparently dropped it by accident, and it rolled somewhere on the floor out of view. She knew it was nearby, but she couldn't see it. She lit a candle and scoured every nook and cranny carefully until she found it. When she did find it, she was so excited that she threw a party.

Sometimes you experience unforeseen, accidental circumstances. A relative or friend gets very sick. Your parents divorce. Your girlfriend or boyfriend doesn't care about you anymore. You fail a test that you studied for all night. Your pet is lost or dies. These and similar events tend to take our minds off of God and put them on the circumstances. Before we know it, we are far away from God. Is God angry with you? Hardly. He is doing His best to find you and bring you back to His side.

Have you experienced circumstances in your life that seemed to pull you away from God?

_____

Describe at least one event. _____

How did you feel when it happened? _____

How do you feel now? _____

Jesus cares a great deal about what you experience in moments like these. Don't let the circumstances carry you away from Him. Call out to God in prayer, and ask Him to rescue you and make you close to Him once again. He longs to do so, and when He does, He plans on having a party to celebrate.

What Are You Waiting For?

Luke 15:11–32

"Fine!" screamed Lauren as she slammed the front door. She ran down the steps on her side-walk and fumbled with her keys. All she wanted to do was leave and never come back.

Lauren fought back the tears as she drove away. "I'm going to be just fine," she assured herself. "I've got the money my parents were saving for college tuition, and I've got friends who'll let me stay with them until I can find a place of my own."

For the next eight months, Lauren stayed with various friends. She spent her money on junk food, parties, and cigarettes. She stayed out late every night and never got around to finding a job. When the money ran out, so did her welcome. Her friends didn't want her any-more, and Lauren found herself on the street with nowhere to turn. She stayed in a shelter for a couple of weeks, but soon realized that she wanted to go home.

She went to a pay phone, lifted the receiver, and thought for a long time about what she would say. She dialed the number, waited, and heard her mom pick up. "Mom!" Lauren cried.

"Lauren! Thank God you're alive! Tell me where you are, and I will come and get you—no questions asked."

No questions asked. Just the fact that Lauren called was enough for her mom. The prodigal daughter returned home.

In today's passage, Jesus told the story of the prodigal son. Like Lauren, the prodigal son committed a deliberate and well-planned rebellion against his family and against God. It was fun for awhile, but one day the money and friends were gone. The prodigal son realized how foolish he had been and longed to return home. He carefully planned what he would say to his father as he walked the long road home, but he never had a chance to say it. The father welcomed him home—no questions asked.

Deliberate and willful sin against God is the most heinous crime you can commit. You know what God wants, but you want something different. So you turn your back on God's instructions, and you walk away to live life your way. You think you'll have more fun. You think you'll be free. The truth is, if you walk away from God, you're going to hit rock bottom one day. You'll realize you were wrong, and you'll turn back to the Lord. When you do, He'll be waiting.

Are you actively involved in something that you know is contrary to God's will? _____

What are you doing? _____

Why are you doing it? _____

When are you going to give up this sin and turn back to God? _____

Ask God to help you give up any deliberate, sinful habits in your life. Pray that God would help you let them go. All it takes is your willingness to come back to God, and He will take care of the rest—no questions asked. For further study, read Psalm 19:13.

Spread It Around

Luke 16:1–17

Saturday afternoon was beautiful. It was partly cloudy, 70 degrees, and perfect for a game of football with friends. Shane and his buddies spent two hours running up and down the practice field at the high school.

When the game was over, Shane was so thirsty that he hopped into his car and went to the local convenience store for a large, thirst-quenching sports drink. He returned to the field to talk with his friends. As he was walking over to them, Rodney also returned. Rodney had gone to a convenience store too. He was carrying a large plastic bag filled with twenty-ounce drink bottles for everyone else.

Shane stopped in his tracks. Rodney was not a Christian, but he had spent his own money to get drinks for everyone, while Shane, the only Christian in the group, did not even think of how thirsty everyone else was. Shane watched the guys gulp their drinks down and thank Rodney for thinking of them. Shane was ashamed, but he vowed to be more generous in the future.

Though Rodney was not a Christian, in this case he did what Jesus would have done. He thought of others and spent his money on them. They were very appreciative.

In today's passage, Jesus told an often-misunderstood parable. Jesus pointed out that often unbelievers are wiser with money than Christians are. Jesus wants us to learn a lesson from them and use the wealth of the world to help others. Don't spend all your money on yourself. Make it obvious to the people around you that you care about them by spending your money on them. When you do, your generosity can make your friends more open to the good news of Christ.

Ask any financial planner what you should do with your money, and the answer will be, "Save it. Invest it." In other words, keep it for yourself so you can spend it on yourself later. This mentality so pervades our culture that we simply forget to be generous. Jesus wants you to change this way of thinking and use your money to point the way to God.

What is the most generous thing someone has ever done for you? _____

Why did this act impress you? _____

What is the most generous thing you have ever done for someone else? _____

How can you show your generosity this week to someone who doesn't know Jesus?

_____

Ask God to help you be generous with your money. Pray for the opportunity to give. When others question your motive, let them know that you're just doing what Jesus would do.

Going Home

Luke 16:19–31

> The boss called his best carpenter into his office. "Harrison, I want you to build this house," he boomed, sliding the blueprints across the desk. "You take complete charge of the whole thing. Find the workers. Order the materials. Oversee the labor. Everything. Here's a check for the estimated cost. Let me know when you're done."
>
> Harrison stormed out of the boss's office. He thought, I've been working here for years doing projects like this, and I've never been rewarded. I'm tired of building big houses for other people and having nothing to show for it. I'll show him. Harrison bought second-grade wood and hired less-experienced carpenters. He built the house for half as much as it would normally cost, and he secretly pocketed the difference in his own bank account. When the house was finished, it looked great, but Harrison knew that over time it would fall apart. Harrison returned to his boss and stated flatly, "The house is finished!"
>
> The boss grinned and stood. "Harrison," he thundered, "you've worked for me for years, and I've never really rewarded you. You know that house you just built? It's yours! Here are the keys."[41]

Oops. Harrison didn't realize he was building his own house. His reward was getting what he had built with his own hands.

In today's passage, Jesus explained that heaven and hell are rewards that we choose on earth. The poor man, Lazarus, went to heaven because God was Lazarus's only hope (the name *Lazarus* means "God, the Helper"). The rich man went to hell because money was his hope. Lazarus built a home in heaven. The rich man built a home out of money, which isn't found in heaven. God allowed each man's eternal destiny to be what he had built with his own hands.

Sometimes hell just doesn't seem fair. How could a loving God punish someone for eternity? God doesn't send anyone to hell. He simply allows people to live in the house they build themselves. If someone chooses to live their entire life on earth without Jesus, then God allows them to continue that way after death, and the only place in the universe without Jesus is hell. Those who choose to walk with Jesus now are allowed to do so in eternity and go to heaven. It's that simple.

What do you think hell is going to be like? _____

When people stand before God and realize that their eternal destiny is hell, what do you think their chief objection will be? _____

Do you know of anyone who is headed for this dreadful place? _____

What will you do to help them see that there is an alternative? _____

Hell is very real, but no one has to go there. After death, everyone gets to live in the house he or she built. Pray that God would make you more bold in sharing Jesus with your friends. Help them to see that living with Jesus in this life means that they can also enjoy heaven in the next life, instead of the alternative.

The Driver's Seat

Luke 17:1–4

> Scott was driving down the road with his two-year-old daughter, Savannah. Savannah was quiet. She didn't know very many words, and she didn't talk much. Scott watched her in the rearview mirror as he drove. He was contemplating what to teach his youth Sunday school class the next day when suddenly, it happened.
>
> The driver in the lane next to Scott passed him, moved over into his lane, and then slammed on the brakes. Scott swerved the car to the right and slammed on his brakes to avoid hitting the other driver. Very quietly to himself Scott muttered, "Stupid idiot."
>
> Scott eventually got over his anger and returned his thoughts to the Sunday school class. Eventually, he arrived home. As he stepped out of the car and opened the back door to retrieve his daughter, Savannah smiled at her daddy and screamed, "Stupid idiot! Stupid idiot!"
>
> "Shhhhhh!" Scott urged. "Do you want to get your daddy in trouble with Mommy?"
>
> "Stupid idiot!" Savannah replied. Scott sighed amidst the relentless words of his daughter.

Scott didn't realize that his daughter was listening. He didn't even know she could say words that big. He found out the hard way.

In today's passage, Jesus gave a strong warning to those who cause children to sin. He said that it would be better for them to have a big rock tied around their neck and be thrown into the sea than to influence a little one to commit evil. Why is Jesus so concerned about how we influence children?

You are in the driver's seat of your life. You make choices about where to go and how fast you are going to get there. You must realize, though, that there are other people riding with you in your car. The choices you make can influence your little brother or sister, a young child at church, an easily influenced friend at your school, and many others. When you make choices, Jesus wants you to stop and ask yourself, "If I do this, how is it going to affect the people around me?" Don't be guilty of leading someone else astray.

List some people around you who are easily influenced by your actions. _____

Have you ever seen any of them imitate something you have done? _____

Was it good or bad? _____

What kind of influence do you want to be to them? _____

What kind of changes do you need to make to be a better influence? _____

Be conscious of the others around you when you make choices. Pray that God would make you sensitive to their precious little eyes and ears as they watch and listen to you. Remember, you are in the driver's seat. Where are you taking them?

Weekly Bible Study and Prayer Review

Bible Study

Look back through some of the Scriptures you read this week. Write down the one verse or passage that God used to speak to you.

_____

_____

_____

_____

Memorize this verse or passage. You can do it if you spend just
a few minutes saying it to yourself.

Now, think of at least one situation you will probably face soon in which you could use this Scripture to help you make the right decision. Write down that situation below.

_____

Quote the Scripture when you face this situation, and live by it.

Prayer Time

Take a few moments to praise God for who He is.
Now take a few moments to thank God for things He has done for you.
Now ask God to make you into the person He wants you to be.
Ask God to use you to help others become closer to God.

Below is your prayer list for the week. Keep it updated each week. If your prayer isn't answered this week, carry it over to next week's list.

Request	Date of Original Request	Date Answered
_____	__/__/__	__/__/__
_____	__/__/__	__/__/__
_____	__/__/__	__/__/__
_____	__/__/__	__/__/__
_____	__/__/__	__/__/__
_____	__/__/__	__/__/__
_____	__/__/__	__/__/__
_____	__/__/__	__/__/__

Pray for the things on your list and trust God to provide.
Forgive anyone you have not yet forgiven.
Ask God to forgive you for any unconfessed sin in your life.
Ask God to keep you out of trouble with sin.
Acknowledge that God is in complete control of your life
and will take care of everything.

The Big in the Small

Luke 17:5–6

> Beth opened the door quietly as she watched and listened to her piano teacher playing a moving composition. She sat down on the bench next to him and whispered, "Can you teach me to play that?"
>
> "Why certainly, Beth. All it takes is practice. Let's begin, shall we?" Beth's enthusiasm quickly waned as she was reduced to playing major and minor scales with her left hand. After fifteen minutes of pure drudgery, she slammed on the keys in frustration. "What's wrong, Beth?" the instructor asked.
>
> "I want to play like you," Beth pouted. "All this stuff you're making me do is boring. When can I play that song you were playing?"
>
> "Beth," the instructor countered, "I am teaching you to play that song even as we speak. As soon as you learn all of the scales with both hands, then you can do this." The instructor played a simple harmony. "Then, when you learn how to do that, you will do this." He proceeded to add a part that made the song sound even better. "Finally, you will be able to do this," he said, playing the song she heard.
>
> "But," the instructor insisted, "it all starts with this." He took Beth's hand and played the same scale she had given up on earlier.

Beth had to realize that the small things she did now would help her do big things later. In today's passage, Jesus tried to explain the same thing to His disciples about faith.

The disciples said, "Lord, we want to have great faith like You!" Jesus, their instructor, said, "Start with what little faith you do have now, and work your way up." He suggested that if they had faith as small as a mustard seed, they could make a tree come out of the ground and fly into the sea. In other words, great faith doesn't come all at once. It grows with practice.

For instance, if you don't yet have the faith to witness to a room full of people, start by sharing your faith with one person at a time. If you feel your faith is too small to pray for a big miracle, then pray for a small one first. If you're afraid to become a leader in your youth group, try being a leader to one person who needs guidance. Don't fret that you can't do great things yet. Start now by putting your faith into practice and let God increase it as you go.

If you could be doing anything for God ten years from now, what would it be? _____

What steps would you have to take to get there between now and then? _____

What is the first step? _____

Can you work on that first step now? _____

Take the first step toward doing great things for Jesus with your faith. Ask God to help you overcome discouragement and focus on practicing what He has given you to do now. Let Him show you the big in the small.

Extra Credit

Luke 17:7–10

Dwight scratched his head, trying in vain to do his chemistry homework. "I can't balance equations," he said aloud. "I've spent five whole minutes trying to do this. I quit."

The next day at school—in Chemistry—Dwight received a zero on his homework. "But Mrs. Walters!" he cried. "I tried." Mrs. Walters didn't budge and told Dwight to come and see her after school if he didn't understand the problems.

That night, Dwight worked longer on his chemistry. After a bit of study and a phone call with a friend, he figured out how to balance equations. He finished every homework problem, patting himself on the back along the way.

When homework was graded in Chemistry the next day, Dwight received a perfect score. "Look there, Mrs. Walters. I did it. I think that since I did so well today, you can throw out that zero I made yesterday. Right?"

Mrs. Walters responded, "Dwight, I'm proud of you for getting all the right answers, but you simply did what I asked. That's no reason for me to change another grade."

In today's passage, Jesus explained that if and when we take care of the responsibilities (or duties) that He has given us, we shouldn't throw a big party to celebrate. An obedient servant does not get an extra reward for simply fulfilling his daily duties. His reward is knowing that he has done the right thing.

Sometimes you may feel like you deserve more credit than you actually do. You might expect an allowance from your parents for taking care of chores around the house, when in fact God wants you to do your part at home whether you get an allowance or not. When you're playing basketball and you make a great defensive play, but the referee calls a foul, you may demand that the officials see things your way. If you come in to work ten minutes early one day, you might argue with your boss that you have the right to come in ten minutes late the next day. The truth is, Jesus wants you to be humble about your responsibilities. Take care of them, but don't expect extra credit.

What responsibilities do you have at home? _____

At school? _____

At church? _____

Do you take care of these responsibilities? _____

How could you improve in each area? _____

Ask God to help you take care of every responsibility you have. Pray for humility so that you will not expect to be rewarded for doing your duty. Remember, God sees what you do and will one day reward you richly for your obedience. For further study, read 1 Peter 1:3–8.

Looking for Answers

John 11:1–16

> *I asked for strength that I might achieve;*
> *I was made weak that I might learn humbly to obey.*
> *I asked for health that I might do greater things;*
> *I was given infirmity that I might do better things.*
> *I asked for riches that I might be happy;*
> *I was given poverty that I might be wise.*
> *I asked for power that I might have the praise of men and women;*
> *I was given weakness that I might feel the need of God.*
> *I asked for all things that I might enjoy life;*
> *I was given life that I might enjoy all things.*
> *I got nothing that I asked for;*
> *But everything that I had hoped for.*
> *Almost despite myself my unspoken prayers were answered.*
> *I am among all people most richly blessed.*

These words, penned by an unknown soldier during the ravages of the Civil War, illustrate how God often answers our prayers in ways we do not expect.

In today's passage, Lazarus was sick and near the point of death. Mary and Martha got word quickly to Jesus, but He did not come. The Bible says that though Jesus loved Mary and Martha, He deliberately waited until after Lazarus had died before coming to them. Jesus did this not to hurt them but to give them the indescribable joy of seeing their brother raised from the dead.

Your prayers will sometimes seem to go unanswered. You may feel that God did not hear you, or that He does not love you. The verses you just read clearly show that neither is true. God hears your prayers, and His love for you is indescribable. Because God hears you and loves you, He often responds to your prayers with an answer that's even better than what you asked. The waiting period between your prayer and the answer can be painful, but rest assured that God will provide the best answer of all.

Are you waiting on God to answer a prayer? _____

What is your prayer? _____

How do you want God to answer this prayer? _____

Name a completely different way that God might choose to answer this prayer. _____

Trust God to answer your prayer in His way and in His timing. Ask God once more to take care of this need in your life, and wait patiently for His response. He loves you and He hears your prayer. He will richly bless you with an answer that you never expected.

Help Wanted, Part 1

John 11:17–27

> The New York City traffic was typically horrible as two men sat in the backseat of a cab. When they reached their destination, one of the men said to the cab driver, "Thanks for the lift. You drove superbly today." The driver glared at the man suspiciously. He wasn't used to compliments.
>
> In California, two women sat in a restaurant. When the waitress returned to the table after the meal was over, one of the women said, "Could I please speak to your manager?" The waitress nodded her head and went to get the manager, almost in tears for fear that she had done something wrong. When the manager arrived, the woman who had asked to see her said, "I just want you to know that my waitress was the best I've had in a long time. The food was great, and I appreciate the way you're running the place." Both the manager and the waitress were speechless.
>
> In a small Texas town, a senior in high school noticed her dad walking out the door on the way to his night shift at the post office. She knew her dad dreaded working all night, so as he was about to leave she said, "Dad, I just want to say thanks for all the hard work you do to provide for this family. Thanks for the clothes, the gas money, the food, and all the other stuff I have." Her dad had the best night at work he could remember.

Words. They are powerful. We can use them to criticize or to encourage. In a matter of seconds, we can tear people down or lift their spirits.

In today's passage, Jesus found two very dear friends in the depths of despair. Mary and Martha had been grieving over the death of their brother, Lazarus, for four days. Martha fell at Jesus' feet in despair, and Jesus chose to encourage her with His words. He shared with her the promise that she would see Lazarus alive again. He told her that He is the source of all life. Martha was encouraged by these words.

Sometimes it's hard to know exactly what to say to your friends when they are discouraged. If you follow Jesus' example, just say something positive that is true. Let them know that you care. Think about how the following words might feel to someone who is down: "I love you." "Remember the time that you and I . . ." "You really made me feel good when . . ." "I really like the way that you . . ." "Can I pray for you?" "God knows and understand what you're going through. He cares, and so do I." "Why don't you and I get out of here and go . . ."

What are the most encouraging words someone has ever spoken to you? _____

Do you have any friends who are discouraged? _____

What can you say to them to make them feel better? _____

God gave you your mouth, so use it for good. Ask God to show you what to say to your friends who need comfort. For further study, read Ephesians 4:29.

Help Wanted, Part 2

John 11:28–33

Ludwig van Beethoven composed some of the most beautiful music the world will ever know. Though completely deaf, he was able to weave together spectacular melodies and harmonies.

He was often frustrated, however, at attempts to talk with friends because of his hearing problem. Often he would retreat to himself rather than strain to be part of a normal conversation. Once, however, a close friend of Beethoven's was grieving over the death of a son. When Beethoven heard the news, he agonized over how to comfort his friend. He wanted to say the right words, but he did not know how.

Beethoven immediately went to his friend, still wondering what he could possibly say or do. When he arrived, he noticed the piano in the room where his friend sat in sadness. Without a single word, Beethoven walked over to the piano, sat down, and began to play like he had never played before. His fingers danced across the keys for some time, flooding the room with music. When he finished, he got up from the piano bench and left. Later, his friend commented to others that he had been comforted more by Beethoven's visit than anyone else's.[42]

Sometimes words just won't do the trick. People can be so discouraged that they don't want to hear talk. They just want someone to be with them without saying a word. That's exactly what Beethoven did. That's exactly what Jesus did.

In today's passage, Jesus comforted Mary in a very different way than He comforted Martha in yesterday's devotion. As He did with Martha, Jesus approached Mary gently. He made Himself available and waited for her to come to Him. When she did, He didn't say a word. The Bible says that Jesus was deeply moved in His spirit. Deep inside He felt a pain and sorrow so great that it was visible to those around Him. Jesus comforted Mary with His presence, not His words.

If you have some friends who are discouraged, sad, or depressed, go to them. You don't have to know the right words to say. Simply make yourself available to them and be there for them. If you can't think of anything to say, don't say anything at all. Give them a big hug. Listen to them tell their story and cry with them. Bring over a favorite snack and a funny movie and spend a few hours together. Take care of their chores around the house. Your actions and your presence can sometimes speak much louder than words.

Do you have any friends who seem down? _____

What can you do to encourage them that doesn't involve words? _____

When do you plan on going to them? _____

Ask God to show you the best way to offer encouragement to your friends. Then make yourself available and comfort them with your presence.

Come and See

John 11:34–38

"Ouch! That hurts," complained Tina. During cheerleading practice she had fallen and dislocated her shoulder. The doctor was gently trying to move it back into place.

The doctor placed her left arm in a sling and instructed her not to use it for at least four weeks. "Four weeks!" Tina grumbled. "I won't be able to cheerlead at homecoming."

On the way home, Tina sat in the car in silence, trying to imagine sitting in the stands at the football games. She couldn't stomach the idea one bit. Her mom tried to comfort her, but to no avail.

Later at home, Tina's father came in the door. He saw only the back of Tina's head as she sat on the couch. He asked her how her day was. She stood up and said, "Daddy, look!" She held up her arm in the sling. Dad already knew what had happened; he had talked with Mom earlier on the phone. He bent down, kissed her shoulder, and hugged her tightly.

"Why don't you suit up with the other girls at the games?" he said, brushing away her tear. "You may not be able to do the routines, but you'll probably get lots of attention from the guys with your sling."

It was as if her dad had read her mind. He kissed her right where it hurt and made things better. Tina could see in her father's eyes that he cared.

In today's passage, Jesus saw people all around Him who were grieving. Lazarus was dead, and his friends and family were hurting. Jesus asked the small crowd where Lazarus's body was, and they replied, "Come and see." They wanted Jesus to see their pain, just like Tina wanted her daddy to see her pain. Jesus knew He was about to raise Lazarus from the dead. He knew everything was going to be OK. Yet, when He saw the people He loved in pain, He hurt with them. Jesus wept.

When you hurt, either on the outside or deep inside, you want someone to notice and care. If you injure yourself, you might say to others, "Look what happened." You say that so that they will see your pain. When you hurt on the inside, you may try and tell someone how you feel so that they will understand. Jesus wants you to know that He cares for you deeply. When you hurt, He hurts. He wants you to run to Him when you suffer and say, "Look, God. Look what happened." When you do, He will cry with you and hold you. He'll kiss you where it hurts and make it better.

Do you hurt? _____ If so, what has caused this pain? _____

Who have you gone to for comfort? _____

Have you taken this ache to Jesus in prayer? _____

Jesus cares about your pain. Go to Him right now in prayer and say, "Look what happened, God. It hurts." He understands. Let Him make it better.

Weekly Bible Study and Prayer Review

Bible Study

Look back through some of the Scriptures you read this week. Write down the one verse or passage that God used to speak to you.

_____

_____

_____

_____

*Memorize this verse or passage. You can do it if you spend just
a few minutes saying it to yourself.*

Now, think of at least one situation you will probably face soon in which you could use this Scripture to help you make the right decision. Write down that situation below.

_____

Quote the Scripture when you face this situation, and live by it.

Prayer Time

*Take a few moments to praise God for who He is.
Now take a few moments to thank God for things He has done for you.
Now ask God to make you into the person He wants you to be.
Ask God to use you to help others become closer to God.*

Below is your prayer list for the week. Keep it updated each week. If your prayer isn't answered this week, carry it over to next week's list.

Request	Date of Original Request	Date Answered
_____	__/__/__	__/__/__
_____	__/__/__	__/__/__
_____	__/__/__	__/__/__
_____	__/__/__	__/__/__
_____	__/__/__	__/__/__
_____	__/__/__	__/__/__
_____	__/__/__	__/__/__
_____	__/__/__	__/__/__
_____	__/__/__	__/__/__

*Pray for the things on your list and trust God to provide.
Forgive anyone you have not yet forgiven.
Ask God to forgive you for any unconfessed sin in your life.
Ask God to keep you out of trouble with sin.
Acknowledge that God is in complete control of your life
and will take care of everything.*

Smell the Possibilities

John 11:39–45

In the late 1800s, Methodist churches from across the United States held their annual convention in Indiana. One year, the president of the college where the meeting was held gave the opening address. In his speech, he said, "I believe that we are entering a very exciting age. I believe that we will see incredible inventions, and that one day soon man will be able to fly."

Milton Wright, the presiding bishop, shot up out of his seat and declared the president's statements to be false. "Flight is reserved for the angels. We will hear no more talk of such things." Still angry about the statement, Bishop Wright returned home to his family. Over dinner one evening, he told his wife and children what the president of the college had said. "Have you ever heard of anything so ludicrous?" he asked.

Sitting at the dinner table were two of the bishop's sons—Orville and Wilbur. Perhaps they took their father's statement as a personal challenge. No one knows. But twenty-three years later the two boys, after years of hard work, flew the first airplane at Kitty Hawk, North Carolina.[43]

Bishop Wright made an assumption that limited his possibilities. Orville and Wilbur saw no end to the possibilities. In today's passage, Lazarus had been dead for four days and lay rotting in his tomb. Jesus stood at the door to the tomb and asked for the stone door to be rolled away. Martha objected, because all she expected was a bad odor. Jesus calmed her, telling her to believe, because He expected an answered prayer from His Father. Then what everyone considered impossible happened right before their eyes. Lazarus walked out of his tomb alive.

We often limit God by making assumptions about what is possible and what is impossible. For instance, which is easier for God to do—provide you with $10 or $10,000? To God, either is the same. To you, one may seem easy and the other impossible. Suppose you have a friend who is sick. Is it easier for God to heal a cold than it is for Him to heal AIDS? God can heal either. Perhaps you have committed a sin. Will God forgive an evil thought but not an evil deed? Both are sin. God forgives either if you ask. No matter what your need, nothing is impossible with God. Don't limit God by only asking for what seems possible.

If you could ask God for anything in the world that you or someone else honestly needs, what would it be? _____

If this is your biggest prayer request, what would be your smallest and most insignificant prayer request? _____

Which of these two prayer requests is easier for God to answer? _____

Your biggest prayer request and your smallest are no different to a God with whom nothing is impossible. Don't be afraid to ask God for anything. Take both of these prayer requests to God right now, and pray for them with the same amount of faith for each one. Then let God do what only God can do. For further study, read Ephesians 3:20–21.

Death Row

John 11:46–57

On February 3, 1998, Karla Faye Tucker was strapped to a table in the Walls Prison Unit in Huntsville, Texas. Her lawyers had exhausted all appeals, and Governor George W. Bush gave his approval for the execution to proceed.

Years earlier, Karla admitted she brutally killed Deborah Thornton with a pickax. Deborah was in such horrible agony during her attack that she pleaded for Karla to finish the job and kill her. She suffered in ways that perhaps human words could never describe before she died after being stabbed over two dozen times. The courts found Karla guilty of the crime and sentenced her to die.

Outside the prison on the night of her execution, four groups waited in vigil. One group demanded that Karla pay for her crimes. Another pointed to Karla's Christian conversion and pleaded for mercy. A third group shared drinks and threw a party, not caring whether or not Karla lived or died. The media hovered impatiently until the word came that Karla had indeed been executed for her crime.

Karla Faye Tucker sealed her own fate for this life on the day she murdered Deborah Thornton. However, she sealed her fate for the next life when she gave her heart to Jesus in prison.

In today's passage, Jesus sealed His own fate for this life. His recent actions had so infuriated the Pharisees that they decided Jesus must die. They claimed that His death was necessary. His death was necessary, but for reasons that they could never have comprehended at the time.

Jesus was not at the mercy of these envious, evil men. He knew He would soon die. He willingly came to earth to give His life for the sins of others. Jesus died to pay the price of a pickax murder. He would die to atone for the sins of lust, hate, greed, pride, cheating, stealing, lying, gossip, homosexuality, and a multitude of additional sins. He died for every sin that you have committed, are committing, and will ever commit. You are as guilty as Karla Faye Tucker. You deserve the death penalty for your sin. Yet God loves you so much that He chose to come to earth and take your place. He paid your death penalty. He died so you could live.

List some of the sins that Jesus paid for when He died for you. _____

How does it feel to know that you will never have to pay for these sins? _____

How does knowing Jesus died for you affect your decision to participate in sin? _____

Always remember the price that Jesus paid for you to be free from the death penalty of sin. Thank Him for giving His life for you. When you are faced with temptation, remind yourself of the cross.

I've Got Two Words for You

Luke 17:11–19

The top ten ways to say "thank you" for a birthday gift

10. Let the dog play with it in the backyard.
9. Give it to someone else for his or her birthday.
8. Have it bronzed and make it a nice boat anchor.
7. Return it to the store for something you really wanted.
6. Sell it for cash at your next garage sale.
5. Grind it up into pieces and fertilize the lawn.
4. Leave it as a tip for your waitress.
3. Put it in the offering plate at church.
2. Use it for third base at the next softball game.
1. Don't say or do anything at all. Just take it.

None of these things say "thank you." In fact, they show no gratitude whatsoever. You may not have actually tried the first nine, but you are probably guilty of number one.

Today's passage tells us about ten lepers. These men had experienced the horror of watching their flesh waste away before their eyes. They knew the depth of despair as the doctors told them there was no hope. They felt the shame of living outside of the city in small groups, shouting, "Unclean!" as others approached. Jesus saw their pain, knew their grief, sensed their despair. At their request, He healed them. Yet only one of the ten came to thank Jesus.

Why are those two simple words so difficult to say? Why are they so easy to forget? You probably forget to give thanks to people and to God every day. When is the last time you thanked your working parents for providing a house and food for you to enjoy? Can you remember the last time you told one of your teachers thanks for giving you an education? Have you recently expressed your gratitude to your pastor and youth pastor for the work they do? Do you let your waiter or waitress know how grateful you are by leaving a generous tip? Have you thanked God today for His countless blessings?

Name some people in your life who need to hear you say, "Thanks. I really appreciate you."

_____

Besides simply saying the words, how else can you express your gratitude to them? _____

How can you express your gratitude to God for the things He has done? _____

Ask God to help you be a thankful person. Pray that He will make you aware of the people in your life who deserve a little appreciation. Finally, thank God for all of the things He has done for you. He loves to hear those two little words.

Kingdom Come

Luke 17:20–21

Mrs. Sommersby taught the third grade in Vacation Bible School at her church every year for fifteen years, always being careful to make every child feel special. This class was a special challenge because one of her students had only one arm. Oliver had lost his left arm in an automobile accident. Mrs. Sommersby had gone the extra mile to make sure that Oliver felt accepted.

Today, however, Mrs. Sommersby was so excited to be finishing her class that she forgot about Oliver's missing arm. She said, "Children, put your hands together like this. Lock your fingers together like this. Watch what I do, and repeat after me. This is the church, and this is the steeple. Open the doors and see all the people."

As Mrs. Sommersby demonstrated to the children how to make a church with their hands, to her horror she suddenly remembered Oliver. She glanced toward him, and to her surprise she saw a young girl offer Oliver her left hand. Working together, the two children were able to form one church.[44]

Mrs. Sommersby learned her own lesson that day. It takes Christian people working together to make the church of Jesus Christ work.

In today's passage, someone asked Jesus what the kingdom of God will look like when it gets here. Jesus responded, perhaps with a wink, that the kingdom of God is not something that just appears or disappears. He explained that the kingdom of God was already here among them. A kingdom requires two things: a king and his subjects. If the people had taken the time to look around, they would have seen Jesus and His followers. They are the kingdom of God.

The kingdom of God is represented on earth today by the church. Your youth group; your church; the church down the road—all of these are part of the kingdom of God if they follow Jesus. Sometimes you may not feel that you have Christian brothers and sisters all around you. Don't be discouraged. Look around you. The kingdom of God surrounds you.

Are there people in your youth group whom you do not know well? _____

Are there people in your church whom you do not know very well? _____

Are there Christians at your school whom you may not be aware of? _____

What can you do to get to know all of these people better? _____

How can you work with them to make Jesus known to the world? _____

Don't ever be discouraged because you think you are alone as you follow Jesus. Don't ever be satisfied with your own little Christian clique. Get to know the Christian strangers around you. Strengthen the body of Christ by weaving your lives together. Ask God to help you meet some new Christians this week. Pray that you would be able to work together as loyal subjects in the kingdom of God.

Ready or Not

Luke 17:22–37

> Monday morning was normal. All across the world, people were busy going to work, sleeping, eating, driving, talking on the phone, and doing the things they normally do. Then it happened.
>
> Cars that suddenly had no drivers careened off the road and crashed. A husband lying next to his wife in bed saw the covers suddenly go flat where she had been lying. A boss giving a meeting to a room full of employees disappeared before their eyes. In Central Park, pets without owners sat and sniffed at the motionless pile of clothes next to them. Airplanes that suddenly lost their pilots began plummeting toward earth.
>
> The television interrupted all regularly scheduled programming for the horrific announcement: "Millions of people have suddenly vanished!" The commentators speculated that an unseen alien force had randomly kidnapped a large portion of the earth's population. Before long, one news anchor reached this startling conclusion: "It appears that everyone who vanished was a follower of Jesus Christ."

An unseen alien force did abduct these people—it was Jesus. Though this event has not occurred just yet, it will—perhaps it will be today.

In today's passage, Jesus described the day that He returns. It will be sudden, unpredictable, and lightning fast. Every true believer will be snatched away to the clouds to be with Jesus forever. Some Christians call this event the *rapture*. Whatever you call it, it will happen just like Jesus said it would. Jesus told His followers to be prepared for this day.

If you are alive when the rapture occurs, you will be snatched away suddenly from whatever it is you were doing. You could be arguing with your parents when you suddenly meet the Father. You may be holding a slice of pizza inches away from your lips when, without warning, your mouth drops open even wider at the sight of your Savior. In the twinkling of an eye, you will be snatched away to be with Jesus from wherever you are, no matter what you are doing.

This gives you an incentive to be more like Jesus each day because you want Him to find you doing His work at the moment He returns. When you know that He could return at any moment, you are more likely to serve Him and turn away from worldly things.

If Jesus had come yesterday at this time, what would He have found you doing? _____

What about three hours ago? _____

One hour ago? _____

Tomorrow at 1:23 P.M.? _____

Ask God to make you more aware of Jesus' imminent return. Pray that you would be able to focus on doing His will. Ready or not, Jesus is coming soon. When He does, what will He find you doing?

Don't Stop Now

Luke 18:1–8

Each of the people above had one common characteristic: persistence. Though they faced countless obstacles, they continued forward until they accomplished wonders.

This type of persistence is described in today's passage. Jesus told the story of a widow who wouldn't give up until she reached her goal. In Jesus' day, widows were the most helpless people in society. If a widow had no family, she had no hope of help from anyone. This particular widow turned the tables, though. She was so persistent with the judge that he finally granted her request.

When you pray, sometimes you may expect an answer immediately. However, God is not a fast-food restaurant. You don't just pull up to a drive-through window and order a couple of prayer requests and a side order of fries. Jesus says that our prayers must be persistent. If we don't get an answer the first time, or fifth time, or forty-fourth time, Jesus says to continue praying and never give up. Our persistence will pay off.

Describe something you have prayed for over a period of time without receiving an answer.

_____

Have you given up, or do you feel like giving up? _____

Do you think you could bring this request to God persistently until you receive an answer?

_____

Sometimes the answer to a prayer is no, but often you miss out on a yes because you give up too soon. Don't stop now. Take that prayer to God again, and remind Him that you are still waiting for an answer.

Weekly Bible Study and Prayer Review

Bible Study

Look back through some of the Scriptures you read this week. Write down the one verse or passage that God used to speak to you.

_____

_____

_____

Memorize this verse or passage. You can do it if you spend just a few minutes saying it to yourself.

Now, think of at least one situation you will probably face soon in which you could use this Scripture to help you make the right decision. Write down that situation below.

_____

Quote the Scripture when you face this situation, and live by it.

Prayer Time

Take a few moments to praise God for who He is.
Now take a few moments to thank God for things He has done for you.
Now ask God to make you into the person He wants you to be.
Ask God to use you to help others become closer to God.

Below is your prayer list for the week. Keep it updated each week. If your prayer isn't answered this week, carry it over to next week's list.

Request	Date of Original Request	Date Answered
_____	__/__/__	__/__/__
_____	__/__/__	__/__/__
_____	__/__/__	__/__/__
_____	__/__/__	__/__/__
_____	__/__/__	__/__/__
_____	__/__/__	__/__/__
_____	__/__/__	__/__/__
_____	__/__/__	__/__/__

Pray for the things on your list and trust God to provide.
Forgive anyone you have not yet forgiven.
Ask God to forgive you for any unconfessed sin in your life.
Ask God to keep you out of trouble with sin.
Acknowledge that God is in complete control of your life and will take care of everything.

Go Down to Get Up

Luke 18:9–14

Malcolm Witherspoon sat in his sleek, black limousine, sipping on fresh coffee. As the chauffeur drove him toward the downtown cathedral for church on this cold, wintry morning, Malcolm sifted through the morning paper. "My, my," he said, shaking his head at the headlines. "What is this world coming to?"

As the chauffeur pulled up alongside a downtown mission, Malcolm glanced out of his tinted window and saw a group of people standing around a trash barrel with a small fire inside. The group, of a different race than Malcolm, stared back at the limousine. Malcolm shook his head again and said, "Dear God, I thank You that I am not like these men. I have worked hard with the money You gave me. I am going to church, unlike these rapscallions who have nothing better to do but loiter in the streets on Sunday morning. I'll write You a large check this morning and place it in the offering. Dear Lord, get me out of here!"

As the limousine pulled away, the "rapscallions" heard the church bell in the mission. They went inside for the service, where they all knelt, prayed, and begged God for forgiveness for their sins.

Which of these men does God honor—Malcolm or the men at the mission? The answer to this question is found in today's passage. Jesus told a very similar story about two men who went to the temple to pray. The "rapscallion" went home justified, but the Pharisee did not.

Notice what is happening here. God does not think more highly of people with a lot of money or better houses, cars, and clothes than you—even if it means they will give more to the church. God does not favor those who live in a better part of town than you do. God doesn't even think more of others who have a better record of church attendance than you do.

You have no reason to feel inferior to anyone. God does not favor others over you. The world may do its best to rank you according to your grades at school, clothes you wear, the complexion of your skin, the shape of your body, and where you go on Saturday night. If you feel inadequate in these or other areas, don't let it get you down. God looks at you and loves you just the way you are.

Do you feel inferior to other people? _____

In what ways? _____

If you didn't feel inferior in these areas, how do you think it would change the way you live?

_____

You are not inferior to anyone. Go to God right now and tell Him how you feel. Pour out your insecurities, fears, and feelings of inferiority to Him. Ask for forgiveness for your sin. Then, when you get up, you can walk away confident that you are tops in God's eyes.

It Cuts Like a Knife

Matthew 19:1–12; Mark 10:1–12; Luke 16:18

"I'm sorry, Andrew. Your mother and I have decided. It's final." The words cut like a knife. Andrew went to his room and slammed the door. He couldn't believe his parents were actually going to get a divorce.

What about Mandy? Andrew thought. She's only five. She won't understand. This will kill her. And I won't even see her that much anymore! She'll be with Mom and I'll be with Dad. The more Andrew thought about it, the angrier he got. He cranked up the stereo and lay on the floor, staring at the ceiling. Is it my fault? Andrew mulled. They've been upset with me about my grades and my attitude. What if this is because of me?

Suddenly, there was a knock at the door. Andrew recognized the sound. "Come in, Mandy," he said. He tried to muster a smile.

"Mommy and Daddy said we're going to go live in different places," Mandy said quite calmly, with an innocence that Andrew wished he still had. "What does that mean?"

Andrew held his little sister and fought to find the right words to say. They never came. Inside, all he could think was, This isn't how it's supposed to be."

Divorce isn't supposed to happen. God never designed marriage to be a temporary journey in life. It's meant to last a lifetime. In today's passage, Jesus explained that when two people marry, they are joined together by God—and no one should ever try to break what God has put together.

If your parents are divorced, you know how hard it can be. Sometimes you're with Mom, sometimes Dad. You can get away with certain things with one parent, but not the other. Mom complains about Dad, and Dad insults Mom. You have good friends near one house, none at the other. You just want to stop the madness.

You can't do anything about someone else's divorce, but you can decide right now what you will do with your marriage. You can make a decision before you ever meet your future husband or wife that you will stay married for life. How can you prepare to make such a big decision? Two things. First, pray that God will bring you a godly spouse. Put Him in charge of your marriage now. Second, keep yourself sexually pure for your mate-to-be. If you are faithful now, you are more likely to be faithful then.

Are your parents divorced? _____

If so, describe how you feel about that. _____

Do you want to marry someone who you will eventually divorce? _____

What can you do now to make your marriage divorce-proof? _____

Ask God to prepare your future spouse for the time you two will meet, date, and eventually marry. Pray that God would keep you pure for your mate. Who knows? Somewhere out there your future spouse may be praying for you at this very moment.

Jesus Loves the Little Children

Matthew 19:13–15; Mark 10:13–16; Luke 18:15–17

The telephone barely rang at all before a three-year-old, quiet voice answered, "Hello."

"Hello," the salesman said. "May I speak with your mother?"

"She's busy," came the whispered reply.

"Oh, OK. May I speak with your father?" Again, the same reply. "Well, is anyone else at home?" the salesman persisted.

"The police," the child whispered.

"The police! Can I speak with them?"

"They're busy," was the only reply.

The salesman was quite curious at this point and said, "Is anyone else at home?"

"Firemen," said the boy.

"Firemen! I suppose they are busy too?" the salesman asked. When the boy affirmed his question, the salesman asked, "What are all of these people so busy doing?"

The boy replied very quietly, "Shhhhhh. They're looking for me."

Children can do and say some of the funniest things. Sometimes they make us laugh. Sometimes we get frustrated with them. Sometimes we just want them to go away.

In today's passage, Jesus showed that He has a special place in His heart for children. Parents were bringing their children to Jesus to be blessed. Though His disciples just wanted the children to go away, Jesus took extra time to hold each child and bless them all.

Children are often abandoned in today's world. Thousands of babies are aborted each day. Many more get sick and die of malnutrition and starvation. Infants and toddlers wait in orphanages and foster homes for someone to take them home to a real family. Some who have families face the horrors of emotional, sexual, or physical abuse.

What can you do to be more like Jesus to children like these? Your family may sponsor a child in another country for just a few cents a day. You might write an essay that points out the horrors of abortion on both the mother and the baby. You could treat your little brother or sister with greater care.

What children do you know who are in need? _____

What needs do they have? _____

What can you do to help meet those needs? _____

Don't be like the disciples in this story. Don't turn your back on the little ones who need your help. Ask God to show you how you can become a better minister to the children of the world.

You've Got Me All Wrong

Matthew 19:16–26; Mark 10:17–27; Luke 18:18–27

A computer expert spent her entire day helping people with computer problems over the phone. One of her conversations went something like this.

"Good morning. How may I help you?"

"Yes," the man's voice said, "I'm having trouble with the cup holder on my new computer. It's stuck open."

Bewildered, the woman probed further. "Sir, could you tell me what computer model you have. I don't recall any of our computers having cup holders."

"Oh, this one does," the man insisted. "It's the Breakneck 2000."

The woman said, "Could you describe the cup holder, please?"

"Oh, yes. When I press the button under the monitor, the cup holder slides out."

Barely able to contain herself, the woman said, "Hold, please." With that, she burst into laughter. Turning to her coworkers, the woman said, "This guy thinks his CD-ROM tray is a cup holder!"

Some people just don't get it. The rich young ruler in today's passage made several assumptions that just weren't true. First, he believed money and possessions would make him happy; but if that were true, he wouldn't have sought Jesus. Second, he thought Jesus was just a good teacher, but Jesus revealed that He was God in saying that only God is good. Third, the man assumed that in order to get to heaven, you have to do something, like keep all the commandments. Jesus revealed that the only way to heaven is to follow Him.

Lots of people have misconceptions about God—myths and assumptions that aren't based on reality. Part of your job as a Christian is to present a true and accurate picture of Jesus to others by using your words and actions to dispel common myths. How do you accomplish this? First, your actions will be the only picture of Jesus that many people see. What they see in you will determine what they believe about Jesus. Second, you can use your mouth to explain who Jesus is and what He is like. If you overhear someone say something about Jesus that isn't true, offer to explain what the Bible really says.

List at least one myth that you have heard other people discuss about God. _____

What is wrong with this assumption? _____

What are the facts that contradict this myth? _____

How can you help stop this myth from spreading? _____

God wants the people around you to see Him clearly. You have the opportunity to paint an accurate portrait of Jesus with your words and actions. Ask God to help you live a life that lets others see Jesus in you.

Reward Offered

Matthew 19:27–30; Mark 10:28–31; Luke 18:28–30

Candace asked Jesus to be the Lord of her life during her sophomore year of high school. She was in the middle of a very strong dating relationship with Will, who was not a Christian. They got along great and had awesome times together—until now.

Will didn't understand Candace anymore, and she began to realize that this relationship was pulling her away from God. She shared her faith with Will, but he wanted nothing to do with it. Candace was torn. She loved Will so much, and she couldn't imagine life without him. Yet it became very clear that Jesus could not be the center of this relationship.

Candace agonized in prayer. She called her youth pastor in tears for advice. Finally, she took the initiative and told Will they shouldn't see each other anymore. There was a big argument, and Will stormed out of the house. Candace cried for weeks with a broken heart.

Candace would not have another boyfriend in high school. It was very hard for her, but she managed. She grew in her relationship with Jesus, and shortly after graduation, she met a strong Christian man who would one day be her husband. Candace once again fell in love.

Candace gave up a lot for Jesus—a relationship that at one time was the most important thing in her life. Jesus honored that commitment, and after time, gave her another relationship that was a hundred times better.

In today's passage, Peter was concerned about what he and the other disciples had given up to follow Jesus. They had left their jobs and families and even risked their lives to be with Jesus. Peter wanted to know what the reward would be. Jesus assured His disciples that anyone who gives up anything to follow Him will receive at least a hundred times as much, both in this life and in the life to come.

Following Jesus has its price. As you grow closer and closer to the Lord, you will find that you may have to give up time, effort, money, possessions, friends, and other relationships—anything that hinders you from becoming what God has called you to be. These decisions won't be easy. They will cost you. They will hurt. They will beg you to not let go. The only comfort you have is Jesus' promise that if you give it up, He will see to it that you are rewarded many times over.

Name something you have given up to follow Jesus. _____

Have you seen any reward yet? _____ *If so, describe the reward.* _____

Is there anything in your life right now that you feel God asking you to give up for Him?

_____

What? _____

When are you going to make a decision to let this go? _____

Ask the Lord to help you let go of those things that hinder your relationship with Him. Don't hesitate, and don't be afraid. Let it go. Then wait patiently in God's arms for the promised reward. He won't let you down.

To Serve or Deserve

Matthew 20:1–16

> *I deserve to have my clothes washed by someone else.*
> *I don't deserve the lousy parents I have.*
> *I deserve to win the lottery.*
> *I don't deserve to pay taxes.*
> *I deserve a better grade on this paper.*
> *I don't deserve all this homework.*
> *I deserve to have fun all weekend long.*
> *I don't deserve all the chores I have.*
> *I deserve to have my order right at the drive-through window.*
> *That waiter doesn't deserve a tip.*
> *I deserve to know why.*
> *She doesn't deserve an apology—it was her fault.*
> *I deserve to have dessert.*

It's amazing what we think we deserve or don't deserve. We walk around with a sense of *entitlement*—a feeling that we have something coming to us.

Jesus addressed the issue of entitlement in today's passage. He told a simple story about five groups of workers who were hired to do a job. Some worked twelve hours, while others worked only one. At the end of the day, the landowner paid them all the same amount. Those who worked longer were furious because they felt that they were entitled to more—even though they agreed at the beginning of the day that their wages were fair.

If you spend your time getting upset over not getting what you deserve, you'll be miserable. Notice the word *deserve*. The prefix *de-* can often mean "the opposite of." So the word *deserve* could be translated "the opposite of serve." When you have a sense of entitlement, you expect others to serve you. When you gratefully accept whatever God gives you, you serve others. See the difference? Jesus doesn't want you to wait for others to serve you, but to take the initiative to serve others. When you do, you will be rewarded fairly according to God.

Name some things you often feel entitled to have. _____

Why do you feel you deserve these things? _____

List one or more ways you could serve others and help them get what they deserve.

_____

Let go of your sense of entitlement. Forget about what *you* deserve. Focus on others around you and what you can do to serve them. Pray that God will humble your heart and allow you to be a servant to others and not yourself.

Weekly Bible Study and Prayer Review

Bible Study

Look back through some of the Scriptures you read this week. Write down the one verse or passage that God used to speak to you.

_____

_____

_____

_____

Memorize this verse or passage. You can do it if you spend just a few minutes saying it to yourself.

Now, think of at least one situation you will probably face soon in which you could use this Scripture to help you make the right decision. Write down that situation below.

_____

Quote the Scripture when you face this situation, and live by it.

Prayer Time

Take a few moments to praise God for who He is.
Now take a few moments to thank God for things He has done for you.
Now ask God to make you into the person He wants you to be.
Ask God to use you to help others become closer to God.

Below is your prayer list for the week. Keep it updated each week. If your prayer isn't answered this week, carry it over to next week's list.

Request	Date of Original Request	Date Answered
_____	__/__/__	__/__/__
_____	__/__/__	__/__/__
_____	__/__/__	__/__/__
_____	__/__/__	__/__/__
_____	__/__/__	__/__/__
_____	__/__/__	__/__/__
_____	__/__/__	__/__/__
_____	__/__/__	__/__/__

Pray for the things on your list and trust God to provide.
Forgive anyone you have not yet forgiven.
Ask God to forgive you for any unconfessed sin in your life.
Ask God to keep you out of trouble with sin.
Acknowledge that God is in complete control of your life and will take care of everything.

That's Not What I Expected

Matthew 20:17–19; Mark 10:32–34; Luke 18:31–34

> I expected my car to run, but the battery is dead.
> I expected the light to come on, but the bulb is out.
> I expected to be killed, but the airbag saved my life.
> I expected to make a bad grade, but there was a curve.
> I expected to get a small paycheck, but my boss gave me a raise.
> I expected it to rain today, but the sun is out.
> I expected to watch my favorite show tonight, but the President is on.
> I expected it to taste bad, but the eggplant was delicious.
> I expected a cheeseburger, but they messed up my order.
> I expected to be tired, but I feel good this morning.
> I expected to watch the eclipse today, but it is too cloudy.
> I expected company, but no one came.

Every day you have expectations of how things will turn out. Often, there are exceptions to your expectations. Your plans change because your expectations are not met.

In today's passage, Jesus explained His approaching death to His disciples for the third time. All three times, the disciples were clueless. They did not understand because they had different expectations of what Jesus' purpose was. They thought the Messiah would become king and rule the world from Jerusalem. They expected things to work out according to their plan—not God's.

Even if you trust God, you probably have certain expectations of how He will do things and what your life will be like. You may expect God to answer your prayers a certain way. You might assume that God will give you the career of your choice. You probably expect to be alive one year from now. These are all normal assumptions, but they may or may not coincide with what God plans to do with you. Be careful not to expect God to work within the limits of your own understanding. He sees and does things from His point of view and according to His will—not yours. When events and circumstances interrupt your plans, don't be discouraged. You don't have to understand what God is doing. You just have to trust that He is doing it with your best interests in mind.

Name some things that you expect God to do in your life over the next ten years. _____

How would you feel if God were to do something completely different with your life—something you cannot begin to understand? _____

When unexpected circumstances alter your plans, what will you do? _____

Learn to let go of your expectations and take one day at a time. Ask God to help you trust Him to take care of you no matter what the circumstances or how you feel. Even if you don't understand, trust Him.

Digging Deeper

Matthew 20:20–28; Mark 10:35–45

The elevator door opened and a middle-aged gentleman named George, with thick salt-and-pepper hair, walked onto the second floor of Stanton's Department Store. There he noticed everyone hard at work—everyone, that is, except the floor manager.

Carter, the floor manager of this department store, was barking orders at four employees who were busy taking inventory. "We've got to be done by midnight. I want to go home to my family! Can't you move any faster?" His booming voice echoed throughout the store.

Without a word, George knelt down on the floor with the other employees and smiled. "Hi. Need a hand?" George began assisting with the inventory and helped them meet the deadline. Just before midnight, as the tired crew headed out the door, George turned to Carter and said, "If you ever need an extra hand with inventory again, let me know."

Carter replied, "And who are you?"

George grinned and said, "Stanton—George Stanton. This is my store."

Carter's view of authority was forcing others to do work. George's view of authority was to lead by example and help those under his care.

In today's passage, Jesus explained that if you want to be great in the eyes of others, you must first become a servant of all. James and his brother, John, wanted the greatest seats in heaven, but Jesus let them know that those seats are reserved for the greatest servants.

You can have a servant's heart or a selfish heart. You can help clean up after a church event, or you can just walk out while laughing with friends. You can help around the house, or you can complain about your assigned chores. You can help your little sister with her homework, or you can call her names. You can say hello to a new student at school, or you can sit with your clique. You can give some money to God through your church, or keep it all to yourself. You can be great by becoming a servant, or you can become average by expecting others to do the dirty work.

Name some areas in which you truly serve by performing needed duties. _____

Name some areas in which you are normally selfish, expecting others to serve you.

_____

What can you do to become a better servant? _____

George Washington did not join the army to order others around. He joined to serve his fellow man. Jesus did not come to the earth to be served, but to serve. Your purpose in life is not to have others serve you, but for you to serve others. Ask God to help you be a better servant. Pray that He would show you the selfish areas of your life and help you trade them in for a servant's heart. Grab your shovel and dig a little deeper.

On the Defensive

> "The Bible is too full of discrepancies," Todd pointed out. "You just can't believe a book that contradicts itself like that."
>
> "What contradictions?" challenged Amanda. "Give me an example." Amanda was just sure Todd wouldn't be able to think of one. She was wrong.
>
> "OK. Matthew, Mark, and Luke all tell the story of a blind man being healed by Jesus. Matthew says there were two men, but Mark and Luke say there was only one. Matthew and Mark say that Jesus was leaving Jericho when this happened, but Luke says that Jesus was approaching Jericho. The mere fact that these three writers contradict each other proves that the Bible is false. I rest my case."
>
> Todd sat back from the lunch table quite satisfied that he had dismantled Amanda's faith completely. Amanda said, "Todd, you've obviously done your homework. To be totally honest, I'm not very familiar with the story you mentioned. Let me go home tonight and read it, and then tomorrow I'll come back and we'll discuss it further. Fair enough?"
>
> "Fair enough," Todd shot back with a satisfied grin.

Todd was right about the apparent discrepancy. He was wrong, however, about these writers contradicting each other. In fact, upon closer investigation, the three versions of the story give more evidence that the Bible is historically accurate.

Jericho was one of the oldest cities in the world. It was so old, in fact, that many people decided to relocate the city about a mile away from the original site. Historical records indicate that some folks stayed in the old Jericho, while others moved to the new Jericho. Jesus was between old and new Jericho when the miracle happened. Matthew and Mark say Jesus was leaving Jericho, but they were referring to old Jericho. Luke says Jesus was approaching Jericho, but he was referring to new Jericho. As for how many blind men Jesus healed, there were two. Mark and Luke only mention one, but that doesn't mean there weren't others.

When unbelievers point out supposed inconsistencies in the Bible, don't let your faith be shaken. If you don't have an answer right away, don't be afraid to say you need some time to study the issue. Talk to a friend, your youth pastor, or pastor about the problem. Examine the Bible passage carefully. God wants you to study His Word and be ready to help others see the indisputable evidence that God's Word is always true and accurate.

Have you ever noticed or been told about seeming contradictions in the Bible? _____

How did you react? _____

Have you studied God's Word enough to be able to explain these supposed discrepancies?

_____

Study God's Word closely. Ask for help from others. Ask the Lord to give you wisdom and insight into what you read. Pray for the opportunity to defend your faith.

Three Strikes and You're In

Luke 19:1–9

"I have three strikes against me," Zacchaeus mumbled to himself, brushing his hair on this crisp spring morning. His thoughts plagued him as he prepared to go out of the house.

"I'm short. Look at me! People walk by and make remarks about my size. I'm sick of it. Oh, if I were just a few inches taller! I can't even see where I'm going in a crowd because everyone else is taller than I am. Maybe I should just move to some city where everyone is my size.

"And I've got this thing around my neck," Zacchaeus said, fingering the metal goblet attached to a leather strap. All the chief tax collectors wore one to signify their official right to collect taxes. *"People take one look at it and turn their eyes away in disgust or fear. They walk on the other side of the hallway. They avoid me like the plague. Don't they know it's my job to collect taxes?*

"Worst of all, there's my name. 'Zacchaeus'—which means 'pure.' What were my parents thinking? I hate that name. It sounds funny, and people say I'm impure, not pure. Why couldn't I have just had an ordinary name?" Zacchaeus sighed, set down his brush, and walked outside.

We don't know for certain that Zacchaeus felt this way about himself, but his height, job, name, and reputation were definitely strikes against him.

In today's passage, Zacchaeus heard Jesus was in town. He tried to see Him but could not because he was too short to see past the crowd. In desperation, he ran ahead of the crowd to climb a tree that would provide him with a better view when Jesus came by. He was probably hiding and didn't want to be seen by the crowd because the leaves in a sycamore-fig tree are very thick. However, when Jesus came by, He saw Zacchaeus and called him down so they could go have dinner together.

You probably feel sometimes like you have one or more strikes against you. You look in the mirror and wonder why God made you with that face. You ache over the divorce of your parents and wonder if it is your fault. You have a physical handicap that prevents you from doing things that you want to do. You have a nickname or reputation at school that you would do anything to change. As a result, you feel small and insignificant. Like Zacchaeus, you have to make an extra effort to rise above the crowd.

List three strikes you feel prevent you from being the person you really want to be.

(1) _____ (2) _____ (3) _____

How have these things hindered you? _____

What would you change about each one if you could? _____

Let God be the one to change things. Zacchaeus's height, name, and job didn't change, but his perception of himself changed when he met Jesus. He found significance in giving instead of taking. Stop hiding behind your limitations, and ask God to show you how the strikes against you can work to your advantage. You will find significance in who you are if you let God show you the way.

Hide and Go Seek

Luke 19:10

> "One, two, three, four, five, six-seven-eight-nine-ten." Jimmy popped his head up from its perch and began scouring the heavily wooded area for his five friends.
>
> Rather than run through the thicket at random hoping to find someone, Jimmy stood very still, listening carefully for movement. He allowed his eye to adjust to the light and shadows, looking for colors that didn't match the dull brown of this February afternoon.
>
> He spotted Rachel trying to stand hidden behind a tree. He heard the snap of a twig and whirled to see Ronnie squatting behind a bush. He detected Chris lying flat on the ground in a small ravine, half-covered with leaves. Jimmy heard giggling and looked up to see Erin directly overhead in a tree. He stumbled across Ryan wedged tightly between two large rocks.
>
> After the game was over, the group sat down to laugh and talk about whose hiding place was the best. After the merriment died down, Jimmy said, "I love being out here with all of you. This must be what Jesus feels like. He spends His time trying to get people to come out of their hiding places so they can spend time with Him."

Like Jimmy's friends, people who do not know Jesus spend much of their time trying to find unique hiding places where they will not be found. They want to remain where they are, but Jesus wants to find them and spend time with them.

In today's short passage, we discover Jesus' purpose on earth: *to seek and save those who are lost*. He longs to get others to emerge from their hiding places. Jimmy's friends had nothing on the creative ways that people hide from God. Some hide behind the temporary pleasure of drugs and alcohol. Others try to camouflage themselves with attempts to be popular or famous. Some hide by running away and trying to start a new life on their own. Others disguise themselves with masks, pretending to be someone they are not. Some bounce from one sexual relationship to the other, crawling through the dirt of unfaithfulness and sexually transmitted diseases.

What should your response be to those who cloak themselves in these hiding places? *Seek them. Save them.* Don't ask yourself how they got there. Don't discuss which hiding places are better or worse. Don't stand on the front porch of your church and simply shout, "Come out, come out, wherever you are!" Go find them. Spend your days and your nights diligently trying to take Jesus right to their hiding place.

Do you know others who are lost (hiding from God)? _____

What are their hiding places (sins or lifestyle choices that keep them from the Lord)?

_____

How can you expose the hiding places and introduce these people to Jesus? _____

Ask God to make you aware of the lost people around you. Pray for the wisdom to share Jesus with each of them in a unique way. Take a deep breath, count to ten, and leave the comfort of where you are to begin seeking and saving those who are lost.

You're Going to Do What?

Matthew 26:6–13; Mark 14:3–9; John 12:1–8

"What are you going to do this summer?" Gwen asked Olivia as the two bounded down the high school steps for the last time this year.

"I'm going to sleep for hours the first week," Olivia mused. "Then, I'm going to work on my tan. I'll probably go on vacation with my parents. You know, the usual. What are you going to do?"

Gwen bit her bottom lip and tried to find the right words. "I'm going to leave next Monday for a little town in Texas just north of the Mexican border. I'm going to spend the whole summer with this church, helping the English- and Spanish-speaking congregations. I'll go into Mexico several times to take food and clothes to the poor. And I'm going to spend ten days on the Yucatan Peninsula, helping a church there reach others for Jesus."

Olivia stopped dead in her tracks, looked Gwen in the eye, and asked, "You're not kidding me, are you?" Gwen shook her head in response. "No offense, Gwen, but that sounds like a waste to me. Think of all the things you could do with your summer besides work."

Gwen didn't care for the criticism, but that didn't stop her from going on her trip to Mexico. In fact, the trip changed her life forever.

In today's passage, another young woman was criticized for doing something she felt was important. Mary, the sister of Martha and Lazarus, took a very expensive jar of perfume into the room with her where a dinner party was being held for Jesus. In front of everyone else, she broke open the jar, poured the perfume on Jesus' head and feet, and wiped off the excess with her hair. The perfume was worth well over one year's wages, and several people criticized Mary for wasting it. Jesus, however, said that Mary did a great thing.

Mary had very deep feelings for Jesus, and she expressed those feelings in a unique way. She didn't care what others thought. Like Mary, you will experience criticism from others when you do something great for God. Whether you go on a summer mission trip, go to church on Wednesday night, say a blessing before lunch, stand up for the lives of unborn children, express your beliefs that God created the world, or stay sexually pure before marriage—you will face criticism from the world. Do what Mary did. Ignore the criticism and follow your heart.

Name something that you want to do for God, but you are afraid to because of the possible criticism. _____

Why do you feel that God wants you to do this? _____

How can you overcome the fear of the criticism and do what God is leading you to do?

_____

Don't let criticism stop you from doing what God has called you to do. Ask Him right now to provide you with confidence and boldness. Pray that God will show you the right time. Then make your move. God will honor you when you do.

Weekly Bible Study and Prayer Review

Bible Study

Look back through some of the Scriptures you read this week. Write down the one verse or passage that God used to speak to you.

_____

_____

_____

_____

Memorize this verse or passage. You can do it if you spend just
a few minutes saying it to yourself.

Now, think of at least one situation you will probably face soon in which you could use this Scripture to help you make the right decision. Write down that situation below.

_____

Quote the Scripture when you face this situation, and live by it.

Prayer Time

Take a few moments to praise God for who He is.
Now take a few moments to thank God for things He has done for you.
Now ask God to make you into the person He wants you to be.
Ask God to use you to help others become closer to God.

Below is your prayer list for the week. Keep it updated each week. If your prayer isn't answered this week, carry it over to next week's list.

Request	Date of Original Request	Date Answered
_____	__/__/__	__/__/__
_____	__/__/__	__/__/__
_____	__/__/__	__/__/__
_____	__/__/__	__/__/__
_____	__/__/__	__/__/__
_____	__/__/__	__/__/__
_____	__/__/__	__/__/__
_____	__/__/__	__/__/__
_____	__/__/__	__/__/__

Pray for the things on your list and trust God to provide.
Forgive anyone you have not yet forgiven.
Ask God to forgive you for any unconfessed sin in your life.
Ask God to keep you out of trouble with sin.
Acknowledge that God is in complete control of your life
and will take care of everything.

Because of You

John 12:9–11

Caleb was quiet and shy but nice to everyone. He was considered the leader of his little youth group. During church services, Caleb and a few friends sat on the back row. Caleb was quiet, but he spent his time drawing pictures, whispering jokes, and writing notes. He never disturbed anyone.

On a snow ski trip, Caleb spent most of his time with Sheena. Sheena was a brand-new Christian, and it showed. Caleb saw a light in her eyes that he could not explain. Sheena had something that he didn't, and he couldn't stop thinking about it.

Around 1:00 A.M. on the bus trip home, Caleb sat wide-awake in his seat. He began thinking about his so-called Christian life. He began to realize that he never prayed or read the Bible outside of church. He had no relationship with Jesus. As he pondered his situation, someone a few seats in front of him flipped on a reading light. Caleb leaned forward to see who else was awake at this hour. Sheena was sitting quietly in her seat with her Bible open to the book of Obadiah.

Caleb leaned back in his seat, dumbfounded. "Why would anybody read Obadiah? No one's making her do that." That night, Caleb realized he was not a Christian. Two months later, he gave his life to Jesus. He credits the living witness of his friend, Sheena, as the reason for his new life.

One girl, without even realizing it, helped a friend become a Christian. She didn't mean to. She just couldn't help it.

In today's passage, Lazarus found himself in the same position as Sheena. Because Jesus had raised him from the dead, people from all over the country came to see Lazarus. Lazarus couldn't help it, but his life convinced many people to place their faith in Jesus.

Sometimes you may look at witnessing as something you do—as a moment in time that you set aside for the purpose of sharing Jesus with someone else. Being a witness is not just something you do on certain occasions. It's who you are. You cannot help but draw others to Jesus when you follow Him. When you privately read God's Word and pray, people will notice the light in your eyes. When you live the Christian life at home, school, work, and everywhere else, people will want to know what you have that they don't. You may not mean to, and you may not be able to help it, but people around you will be face to face with Jesus.

Answer the following questions as if you were someone else—a non-Christian who has watched your life closely over the past year. How is this person most like Jesus? _____

Name one event where this person made you want to become a Christian. _____

Now, answer this question as yourself. What can you do to become a better witness in everything that you say and do? _____

Whether you realize it or not, people around you are making the decision whether or not to become a Christian because of you. Ask God to help you be a natural, daily witness for Him. Pray that your life would influence others for Jesus.

You've Got to See This

Matthew 21:1–11; Mark 11:1–11; Luke 19:28–44; John 12:12–19

"What are we going to do?" Lori asked worriedly. "We're both flat broke. We have just enough food to last until we get paid, but we have no laundry detergent. Tomorrow is Sunday, and we can't go to church because we have no clean clothes."

Lisa, her college roommate, suggested, "Let's pray about it. Maybe somehow God will provide us with money or detergent. I know it sounds crazy, but what have we got to lose?"

Lori and Lisa rolled out of their twin beds on this lazy Saturday morning and prayed that God would take care of their needs. Then they got up and took turns taking a shower and putting on comfortable (but dirty) clothes for the day.

Shortly after lunch, Lori walked out to the mailbox on their doorway. She lifted the lid, reached inside, and felt a package. As she pulled it out, she could not believe her eyes. She ran back inside and screamed, "Lisa. Lisa! Come here. You've got to see this."

Lisa came into the living room. Lori showed her the package. It was an advertisement for laundry detergent. Included was a free sample with enough soap to take care of two loads of clothes.

Before Lori and Lisa ever prayed, God knew what their needs were. He heard them before they called Him. He answered before they asked.

In today's passage, Jesus was approaching Jerusalem. He knew that today was the big day. He would fulfill prophecy by riding a donkey toward the city while others recognized Him as the Messiah and laid palm branches on the road in front of Him. One problem—He needed a donkey. Jesus didn't worry, though. He was certain that His Father would provide the donkey. He confidently instructed two of His disciples to go find the donkey and bring it back. The donkey was waiting. God put it there before anyone even thought about it.

When you have needs, you can develop one of two attitudes. You can confidently expect God to take care of you, or you can wring your hands and worry about it. The first attitude will lead you to prayer and peace. The second will bring anxiety and frustration. Which do you prefer? God knows what you need before you ask Him. He's already sending the answer before you pray. When you trust Him to provide and pray, He allows the answer to come. Don't worry, just pray and look for the answer.

What needs do you typically worry about? _____

Why do you doubt that God will provide these needs for you? _____

What will you do to turn these worries into confident prayer? _____

Practice praying for each and every need you have. Remember that God loves you and answers your prayers even before you ask them. Stop worrying and start praying. Stop thinking about what will happen if your needs aren't met, and start looking for the answer. It could be just around the corner. For further study, read Jeremiah 33:3.

Why Is It That . . . ?

Matthew 21:12–17; Mark 11:15–19; Luke 19:45–48

Why do we drive on parkways and park on driveways? If it's one goose and two geese, why isn't it one moose and two meese? If writers write, why don't hammers ham? Why is it that a slim chance and a fat chance are the same thing? Why is it that if the stars are out, you can see them, but if the lights are out, you can't see them?

Why are boxing rings square? Why isn't phonetic spelled the way it sounds? Why is the word abbreviation so long? Why are the words cough, rough, through, dough, and bough all pronounced differently? What color is a mirror? Why doesn't glue stick to the inside of its container? Why are there flotation devices under airplane seats instead of parachutes? Why do doctors and lawyers call what they do a practice? Why do they call it a TV set if you only get one?

Why is it that when cells multiply they divide? Why do baby clothes have pockets? If the black box in airplanes never gets destroyed, why don't they just build the whole plane out of the same material?

Some things just don't make sense. Why, for instance, did Jesus find people buying, selling, and cheating people in the temple when He had already cleansed it once at the beginning of His ministry (John 2:13–25)? Why did He have to do it again?

The temple was supposed to be a quiet place of prayer and worship. Instead, people had turned it into a place to make a quick buck. They didn't learn the first time, and Jesus was angry. He expressed His anger by driving everyone out of the temple so that it could once again be a place of worship.

When you get caught or punished for doing something wrong, why do you go back and do it again? It doesn't make sense. If you know something is wrong, you should choose not to do it. If you know something is right, you should choose to do it. God gets angry when you deliberately and willfully sin against Him. He's angry because He loves you. He's angry because He knows that your sin can harm and kill you. He doesn't want you to be harmed—He wants you to be all that you are meant to be. Sin prevents you from becoming all you are meant to be, and God gets angry. He uses His anger to shout a warning that you need to change the way you are living.

Describe something you did recently that you knew was wrong. _____

Did you face harmful consequences as a result of your actions? _____

Do you want to experience those consequences again? _____

You may get away with sin for awhile, but eventually God is going to shout a warning that will get your attention. When He does, use the warning as an opportunity to ask for forgiveness and turn away from your sin. And remember that His anger is not nearly as fierce as His love for you. For further study, read Hebrews 12:4–13.

Something in Common

John 12:20–22

Each of the following three things has something in common. Can you figure out what it is?

1. Mercury, Venus, Mars
2. Apple, Bar, Cane
3. Nail, Paint, Tip
4. Roller, Shoulder, Fan
5. Electric, Liver, Pipe
6. Super, Model, Wood
7. Tax, Hair, Paper
8. Circus, Wedding, Phone
9. Paint, Hair, Tooth
10. Swiss, Steak, Army

(Answers: 1. planets; 2. things associated with the word "candy"; 3. things associated with the word "finger"; 4. things with blades; 5. types of organs; 6. types of glue; 7. types of cuts; 8. things with rings; 9. types of brushes; 10. types of knives)

In today's passage, we see Andrew's third mention in the New Testament. There are only three stories about Andrew, but they all have something in common. Can you figure out what it is (John 1:41–42; 6:5–9; and 12:20–22)? In all three cases, Andrew brought someone to Jesus. In the first example, Andrew brought his brother to Jesus. In the second example, Andrew brought a boy with food to Jesus. In today's example, Andrew brought a group of foreigners to see Jesus. Andrew's lifestyle was to bring people to Jesus. He was different from his brother, Peter, who talked a lot. Andrew simply brought people directly to Jesus so they could see Him for themselves. He made it a habit.

Perhaps you are uncomfortable witnessing to someone else with your words. Don't let that stop you from sharing Jesus with someone else. Take a friend to a Christian concert. Invite someone to your weekly youth group meeting. Give a Bible to someone as a birthday gift. These ideas don't require you to be a Bible scholar or television evangelist. Simply take the time to offer others the chance to see Jesus for themselves. Make it a pattern. Make it a habit.

Name three friends who need to know Jesus. _____, _____,
and _____

What can you do this week to take each one of them to Jesus? _____

Ask God to grant you the opportunity this week to bring each of these three friends to Jesus in some way. First take them to Jesus in prayer. Then take them to Jesus using one of the ideas listed above or using a unique idea of your own.

Suffering Succotash

John 12:23–36

The year is A.D. 44. The apostles have been preaching and teaching the good news about Jesus for eleven years. Things are going well—at least they were.

James, the brother of John, has been falsely accused of a crime he did not commit. He sits in a jail cell, awaiting his fate. His cellmates expect James to be depressed and suicidal. Instead, he is enthusiastic about his impending doom. He considers it an honor to die for his Lord.

On the day of his execution, as he is being led from the jail cell to the ax of the executioner, his accuser arrives to taunt him. During the long, slow walk—in which most men cry out in terror—James's accuser ridicules and sneers at him. The accuser's purpose is to get some last-minute pleasure out of watching James suffer in anticipation of certain death.

James is so peaceful and calm by the time they reach the chopping block that the accuser is overcome with guilt and a longing to have what James has. He falls to his feet and begs to know Jesus. Moments later, both men are beheaded with the same ax.[45]

James, the first apostle to be martyred, won someone to the Lord during a time of terrible suffering. God often uses the suffering of His children to draw others to Him.

In today's passage, Jesus explained his approaching death to the crowds. He said a seed that wants to produce life must first fall to the ground and die; He declared that a person must lose his life if he wants to find it. He stated that when He is lifted up (on the cross), all people will be drawn to Him. In other words, Jesus' suffering will attract others to God. Everyone is curious about what goes through the mind of a human who experiences suffering. When they see love instead of hate, and peace instead of fright, they want to know why. They will ask questions. They will see God.

Jesus did not suffer so you would not have to. Jesus suffered to give you an example, so that you could learn to suffer in the same way He did. Jesus' suffering on the cross is a model for you to follow. God does not promise you a life free from pain. Instead, He allows you to experience pain so that others will be curious and watch your reaction. They expect you to complain and become depressed. If you learn to accept the pain without complaint and look for the good that can come out of this situation, others around you will want to know why. They will ask questions. They will see Jesus in you.

When you experience pain, whether physical or emotional, how do you react? _____

What are some examples of pain that you are experiencing right now? _____

How can you change your reaction to the suffering in a way that others can see Jesus in you? _____

Don't look at suffering as unfair. Take it as an opportunity to be a witness to those who see your suffering. Ask God to help you endure the pain. Pray that your Christlike attitude would draw others to Jesus. For further study, read 1 Peter 3:14–16.

I Don't Believe It

John 12:37–43

> There was a lull in football practice, and Sean took the opportunity to chat with his friend, Chad. Sean had been praying for and witnessing to Chad almost every day.
>
> "So, Chad," Sean said. "What is it going to take for me to convince you that you need Jesus?"
>
> Chad shot back, "Sean, look. I'm sick and tired of talking about God every chance we get. I don't believe in God. There's just no proof. I'm not going to believe in something I can't see."
>
> Sean was surprised at Chad's blunt reply, but that didn't stop him. He knew Chad wasn't being totally honest. "Chad, you're my friend. You know that. You know there is plenty in the Bible that proves that Jesus is God and that He loves you. That can't be the real reason." Sean looked Chad in the eyes through his face mask and waited for an answer.
>
> Chad stared at the ground and said, "OK, Sean. You want the real reason? Here goes. I do believe in God, but I am not about to give up my life to Him and do what He wants. I want to do things my way. So, enough talk about Jesus. I'm not going to join your little club."

Sean finally got to the heart of the matter. Chad did believe, he just didn't want to commit.

In today's passage, Jesus faced a group of Chads. He had performed count-less miracles in their presence. He had spoken words that no other teacher had ever spoken before. He had held out His hand in an open invitation to anyone who would come to Him. Yet most of the people there still refused to follow Jesus. The bottom line was, they probably did believe what they saw; but they didn't want to commit. Notice that even the few who did commit were afraid to admit it because they were afraid of what people would think.

Notice that not one of the people who rejected Jesus stated their excuses out loud, but Jesus knew the reason. Their hidden motives were exposed in the words of the Bible. When you share your faith with others and they refuse to accept Jesus, don't take it personally and don't be discouraged. God knows their heart. He knows the real reason that they do not respond to Jesus. Depend on God's Spirit to guide you as you continue witnessing to those who have rejected Jesus already.

Have you ever shared your faith with people who rejected what you said? _____

How did you feel? _____

Have you since given up, or do you continue to witness to them? _____

What can you do this week to be a witness to these same people? _____

Ask God to help you be persistent in your witness to those who reject Jesus. Pray that God would help them see their true reasons for resisting Him.

Weekly Bible Study and Prayer Review

Bible Study

Look back through some of the Scriptures you read this week. Write down the one verse or passage that God used to speak to you.

_____

_____

_____

_____

*Memorize this verse or passage. You can do it if you spend just
a few minutes saying it to yourself.*

Now, think of at least one situation you will probably face soon in which you could use this Scripture to help you make the right decision. Write down that situation below.

_____

Quote the Scripture when you face this situation, and live by it.

Prayer Time

*Take a few moments to praise God for who He is.
Now take a few moments to thank God for things He has done for you.
Now ask God to make you into the person He wants you to be.
Ask God to use you to help others become closer to God.*

Below is your prayer list for the week. Keep it updated each week. If your prayer isn't answered this week, carry it over to next week's list.

Request	Date of Original Request	Date Answered
_____	__/__/__	__/__/__
_____	__/__/__	__/__/__
_____	__/__/__	__/__/__
_____	__/__/__	__/__/__
_____	__/__/__	__/__/__
_____	__/__/__	__/__/__
_____	__/__/__	__/__/__
_____	__/__/__	__/__/__
_____	__/__/__	__/__/__

*Pray for the things on your list and trust God to provide.
Forgive anyone you have not yet forgiven.
Ask God to forgive you for any unconfessed sin in your life.
Ask God to keep you out of trouble with sin.
Acknowledge that God is in complete control of your life
and will take care of everything.*

Mirror, Mirror

John 12:44–50

Kate stumbled into the bathroom and flipped on the light. She splashed cold water on her face and dried off with a hand towel. Then she looked in the mirror. To her surprise, she didn't see what she expected. Her reflection was not imitating her! Instead, it had taken on a mind of its own. Kate's reflection stood with her hands on her hips, staring back at Kate, who was still crouched over the sink.

"I've had it with you," the reflection said. "I hate cold water. I refuse to continue this tortuous morning routine of yours. I'd rather sleep later and look sloppy."

Kate rubbed her eyes, thinking, I must be dreaming. She lifted her arms and turned around, watching the reflection to see if it followed her, but it did not. Kate finally said, "Look, this just isn't possible. You have to do what I do. You can't do your own thing."

"Oh, yeah?" her reflection shot back. "You just watch and see. I'm tired, and I'm going back to bed. You do what you want." Kate's double disappeared through the bathroom doorway, leaving Kate facing a mirror with no reflection.

You would probably check yourself into the loony bin if you and your reflection had a disagreement. Reflections aren't supposed to talk back. They are supposed to do exactly what you do.

In today's passage, Jesus explained that He is a perfect reflection of His Father in heaven. Jesus only speaks the words of His Father. His Father tells Him what to say and how to say it. If we followed Jesus' example, we would probably all stay out of trouble when it comes to what we say.

You probably have said things you regret. Curse words, gossip, back-talking, name-calling, and threats are just a few of the ways that you can misuse the mouth that God made for you. You can avoid these pitfalls by doing what Jesus did. Check with God first. Don't say anything without thinking about it first. When you are tempted to say curse words, say *bless* words. When you feel like calling someone a name, compliment her instead. If you sense you are about to talk back to your parents, hold your tongue and agree with them. These are just some of the ways you can imitate Jesus with your words.

What kinds of sins do you commit with your mouth? _____

Do you regret saying these things? _____

How can you sanitize your words and learn to say only the things that God would want you to say? _____

Ask God to help your mouth become a mirror of His. Pray that your words would be a perfect reflection of Jesus' words. For further study, read Ephesians 4:29; Colossians 4:6; and James 3:2–12.

Through the Roof

Matthew 21:18–22; Mark 11:20–26

Micah knelt down at the foot of her bed. She buried her tear-stained face in her folded arms. "God, where are You?" she sobbed.

For two long months, Micah's prayer life had been dead. When she tried to pray, it seemed her words never made it past the ceiling. She thought, God doesn't hear me. Why should I bother? So, very gradually, she stopped praying at all. Now she found herself in dire straits. Her younger brother had just run away during a family argument, and no one knew where he was.

"God, please, if You'll just hear this prayer, I'll never ask You for anything else. Bring my brother back safely. Please, God. Please." Though Micah couldn't see it, God smiled. He heard every word she spoke. He was so glad to hear her talking to Him again.

Micah finally stopped praying and joined the rest of her family in looking for her brother. Four hours later, he walked back inside the house. "I thought about running away for good, but something changed my mind," he said.

Micah's prayers didn't have to make it past the ceiling because all along Jesus was right there inside of her heart listening to every word.

In today's passage, Jesus encouraged His disciples to pray with confidence and faith. He explained that a prayer of faith can move mountains.

There are many obstacles that hinder your faith when you pray. If you feel that your prayers are not making it past the ceiling, remember that God is not some distant Spirit way out there somewhere. He lives inside of you. He hears every prayer you utter, even if you don't feel like He does. In addition, the Bible lists several faith blockers that you may need to remove before you pray. James 4:3 says that your prayers will not be answered if you are praying for something out of selfish motives. Psalm 66:18 explains that if you are holding onto a favorite sin, God will not answer you. Daniel 10:1–14 reveals that sometimes your prayer is delayed by spiritual forces of evil, so don't be alarmed if your answer doesn't come right away.

Do you ever feel as if your prayers never make it past the ceiling? _____

What makes you doubt? _____

How do you feel when you go days, weeks, or even months without talking to God?

_____

How can you learn to pray and have faith, even when you don't feel like God is listening?

_____

Remember that God hears every prayer you utter, no matter what your doubts may tell you. Ask God to help you remove anything that is hindering your faith. Then pray for each item on your prayer list, picture God answering that prayer, and believe in your heart that He will.

Don't Get Sidetracked

Matthew 21:23–27; Mark 11:27–33; Luke 20:1–8

> Every Monday morning, Parker met with a few friends in the band hall for a small Bible study before school. On this particular day, the group was about finished when someone interrupted them.
>
> "Hey, preacher boys," Benny said. "Why don't you get a life? There's no God, and you know it. If your God is real, then prove it right now!"
>
> Parker and the others looked at each other, wondering what to say. Parker could think of a hundred ideas but finally settled on one. He turned to the interloper and said, "How about this. I'll prove that my God is real if you prove something that you believe in first."
>
> "OK," Benny said. "What do you want me to prove?"
>
> Parker asked, "Do you love your father?"
>
> Benny looked confused and said, "Of course I do. What's that got to do with anything?"
>
> Parker said, "Prove it."
>
> Benny opened his mouth to reply and then stopped. He finally said, "Good point."

Parker could have started an argument that lasted all day. Instead, he gave Benny some food for thought.

In today's passage, Jesus was teaching people in the temple courts, an area without a roof where people came to listen to various teachers explain the Bible. A group of other teachers were jealous because Jesus was drawing most of the crowd. They wanted to start an argument with Jesus and embarrass Him in front of the crowds. So they asked a tough question. Jesus could have gotten sidetracked and argued with them all day, but instead He asked His own question and stumped them. Then Jesus returned to teaching the people.

You will have many opportunities to argue about your faith. Don't do it. Arguments are always a trap designed to get you sidetracked from spreading God's love. How can you show love during an argument? Instead of arguing, turn the tables on your opposition. When they ask questions, ask some of your own. If they raise their voices, lower yours. When they frown, you smile. No matter what happens, keep your cool.

Have you ever argued about your faith with someone? _____

What do you feel like you accomplish after an argument like that? _____

The next time you are tempted to argue, what do you intend to do instead? _____

Don't get sidetracked from sharing God's love with others. Never argue about your faith. Ask God to help you to stay levelheaded when you feel an argument coming on. Pray for the patience to keep your cool and the wisdom to say the right thing with a smile. For further study, read 2 Timothy 2:23–26.

Just Do It

Matthew 21:28-32

Once upon a time there were fraternal twin brothers—Ronny and Randy. They were alike in just about every way you could imagine. They had their differences, though. Randy loved chocolate, but Ronny couldn't stand it. Ronny was very athletic, whereas Randy was studious.

One day, their father came into their bedroom where they were busy playing video games. He boomed, "Boys, that yard needs mowing pronto. I need you both to get out there in the next five minutes and take care of it for me. OK?"

Both boys immediately hopped up. Randy said, "Dad, I told a friend I'd help him with his homework. He'll fail if I don't help." Before his dad could respond, Randy disappeared.

Ronny quirked, "I'll do it, Dad. No problem." Ronny went downstairs, into the garage, and dragged out the mower. He had trouble getting it to start, so he gave up and pushed it back into the garage. Moments later, Randy came walking back down the sidewalk, feeling guilty for lying to his dad. He noticed the tall grass and decided to mow after all. After some work, he started the mower. He spent the rest of the afternoon taking care of the yard.

Randy told his dad that he wouldn't do it. Ronny said he would. However, Ronny gave up and Randy actually got the job done.

In today's passage, Jesus told a very similar story. The point of both stories is this: obedience isn't complete until the job is done. Many Christians are sensitive to God's leading and have good intentions at first, but they give up when the things get tough. Youth camp is a prime example. Every summer hundreds of thousands of teenagers say, "God, I will do what You want me to do." Three weeks into the school year, however, many give up because of the hard work and persecution.

There is a long road between the time you make a commitment to God and the time you actually get the job done. If God leads you to pray for a friend until she comes to know the Lord, how long will you pray—two weeks, or two decades? When God asks you to be obedient to your parents, will you stick to it when they interrupt your plans and ask you to do chores? If you make a commitment to break a bad habit, what will you do when the temptation seizes you again?

Which of the two brothers sounds more like you—the one who talked the talk or the one who walked the walk? _____

What normally discourages you from completing a commitment that you have made to God? _____

What must you do to follow through with your commitment? _____

Search your heart for broken commitments. Ask God to forgive you where you have failed. Then make up your mind to be like the second brother. Turn your life around, and get busy doing what God has called you to do. Don't say you'll do it or think about it. Just do it.

The Cornerstone

Matthew 21:33–46; Mark 12:1–12; Luke 20:9–19

> After several hours cleaning the old garage of his new home, Carl managed to have most of the junk boxed up and ready for the trash truck. As he neared the rear of the garage something caught his eye. It was an old motorcycle. Carl studied it and could tell that it was a model from the 1950s. It was in fair shape, but it did not run. Carl wrote down the serial number and decided to call the manufacturer of the motorcycle and see if it was worth anything.
>
> Carl described his find and gave the serial number to a technician from the manufacturer. The technician asked a variety of questions, and Carl answered them all. After some time, the technician said, "Sir, please hold. The president of the company would like to speak with you."
>
> The president asked Carl to go outside to the motorcycle, lift the seat, and look underneath. Carl did so, returned to the phone, and said, "All it says is 'THE KING.'"
>
> Carl's jaw dropped to the floor when the president said, "Sir, that motorcycle belonged to Elvis Presley. I'll pay you $300,000 for it right now."[46]

Carl suddenly realized that the dilapidated old motorcycle had more value than the previous owner knew. The motorcycle that others rejected actually had belonged to Elvis Presley.

In today's passage, Jesus tried to explain to the people that He is like that motorcycle. He is like a stone that a group of construction workers decided wasn't worth anything. However, that rock eventually became the cornerstone of the entire building. Jesus is the rock that became the cornerstone of life, but some people still don't recognize His value. Instead of seeing Jesus as a rock to be used to build their life on, many see Jesus as nothing more than an annoying stone that blocks their path and causes them to stumble (1 Peter 2:4–8).

Your responsibility as a Christian is to make the rock of Jesus as big as possible. For instance, for some Christians, Jesus is a small pebble that they keep in their pocket. Occasionally, they will pull the pebble out of their pocket and try to convince others that this little rock is the meaning of life. No one will stumble over a single pebble. No one will be impressed with a tiny rock hidden away in your pocket. Don't reduce Jesus to the size of a pebble. Make Him as big and as impressive as you can. Sure, some people will stumble over what you share about Jesus, but others will see the rock as the cornerstone of their lives.

If Jesus was a rock, and His size was determined by how much you share your faith with others, how big would He be? _____

What can you do to make that rock bigger—to make Jesus more obvious to the people around you? _____

You may be the only Jesus that some people ever see. Ask God to help you make Jesus famous. Share Jesus in a big way, and let others see that He is the cornerstone of life.

Changing Clothes

Matthew 22:11–14

"Gayle, you march right back in here, young lady." Mom was obviously displeased. "What happened on your report card this time? Until you can raise these grades back up, you are grounded from the phone and TV. Do you understand?" Gayle nodded quietly, kicking the carpet as she returned to her room.

Gayle was still thinking about her report card as she drove to work. Suddenly, red and blue lights flashed in her rearview mirror. "Oh, no! I can't get a ticket now!" The police officer disagreed and handed her a yellow slip of paper.

When Gayle finally arrived at work, she was five minutes late. Her boss screamed at her for being late and made her clean the grease trap. Later, when she was helping a customer at the drive-through window, she misunderstood the order. The man driving the pickup truck began complaining. He told Gayle that she was a lazy, good-for-nothing idiot.

Gayle thought to herself, God must really hate me. I'm always messing up.

School, work, speed limits—they all have the same message: "If you blow it, you're going to get it." Sometimes we think God is the same way. We think that if we blow it, He's going to abandon us.

In today's passage, Jesus explained that nothing could be further from the truth. Notice the man at the wedding who was not wearing wedding clothes. The wedding clothes were white robes that were passed out to each guest as they arrived. The man must have refused the clothes when he entered, which was a tremendous insult to the king. The king responded by sending him away.

You cannot get to heaven in your own clothes. In other words, you cannot earn your way to heaven. No matter how good you try to be, you're going to blow it. Rather than abandon you, though, God provides you with Jesus Christ. He is the robe that covers your sin and makes you presentable for heaven. If anyone refuses Jesus Christ, he is refusing the wedding clothes the king provided and will not be allowed into heaven. Once you realize that you can't earn your way to heaven, you also learn that God still loves you when you fail Him.

Have you ever tried to earn the approval of someone else? _____

Who? _____

What did you do to win this person's favor? _____

How have you tried to earn God's approval? _____

Have you ever felt like you failed God and that He no longer loved you? _____

Don't let your failures make you think that God does not love you. Equally, don't ever feel like you have to earn God's approval in the things you do. Ask God to help you understand the depths of His unconditional love for you. Take off your old clothes (trying to win God's approval), and put on the new (Jesus). For further study, read Ephesians 2:8–9.

Weekly Bible Study and Prayer Review

Bible Study

Look back through some of the Scriptures you read this week. Write down the one verse or passage that God used to speak to you.

_____

_____

_____

_____

Memorize this verse or passage. You can do it if you spend just
a few minutes saying it to yourself.

Now, think of at least one situation you will probably face soon in which you could use this Scripture to help you make the right decision. Write down that situation below.

_____

Quote the Scripture when you face this situation, and live by it.

Prayer Time

Take a few moments to praise God for who He is.
Now take a few moments to thank God for things He has done for you.
Now ask God to make you into the person He wants you to be.
Ask God to use you to help others become closer to God.

Below is your prayer list for the week. Keep it updated each week. If your prayer isn't answered this week, carry it over to next week's list.

Request	Date of Original Request	Date Answered
_____	__/__/__	__/__/__
_____	__/__/__	__/__/__
_____	__/__/__	__/__/__
_____	__/__/__	__/__/__
_____	__/__/__	__/__/__
_____	__/__/__	__/__/__
_____	__/__/__	__/__/__
_____	__/__/__	__/__/__

Pray for the things on your list and trust God to provide.
Forgive anyone you have not yet forgiven.
Ask God to forgive you for any unconfessed sin in your life.
Ask God to keep you out of trouble with sin.
Acknowledge that God is in complete control of your life
and will take care of everything.

Good Answer

Matthew 22:15–22; Mark 12:13–17; Luke 20:20–26

"OK, if you believe in God tell me this," Hank posed. "Is your God all-powerful? Can He do anything?"

"Sure He can," Eddie countered. "God is omnipotent."

"Fine. Answer this. Is your God powerful enough to make a rock so big that He can't lift it?" Hank sat back, folded his arms across his chest, and waited for Eddie to try to get out of this one.

Eddie realized that there was no answer to this question and squirmed in his seat for the right way to respond. Then God seemed to give him the perfect reply. Eddie leaned forward and said, "Hank, you're looking for a yes or no answer. If I answer yes, then God isn't powerful enough to lift the rock. If I answer, no, then God isn't powerful enough to make such a rock. Consider this. God is powerful enough to make a rock big enough so that He can't lift it, because He is powerful enough to limit His own powers. If someone is truly all-powerful, doesn't it mean he is powerful enough to restrain his own powers?"

It was Eddie's turn to sit back and wait for an answer. Hank didn't know what to say. He didn't expect an answer like that.

In today's passage, a smug group of men were so intent on embarrassing Jesus in public that they devised an evil plan. They decided to ask Jesus publicly if Jews should pay taxes to Caesar. They knew that if Jesus answered yes, then the Jews would hate Him, because they hated paying taxes to a foreign government. If Jesus answered no, He would be arrested by the Romans for encouraging tax evasion. The men thought their plan was foolproof. They didn't count on Jesus' very wise answer.

You may sometimes find yourself between a rock and a hard place, so to speak. Someone may try to trap you by asking a question that seems to have only two wrong answers. Don't panic. Do what Jesus always did. Respond to their question with another question, or consider an answer that they don't expect. Study the Bible diligently, and be prepared to field the questions about God that may come your way.

Have you ever been stumped by a seemingly unanswerable question about your faith? __

What was the question? _____

How do you think Jesus would answer this question? _____

Don't ever panic when the tough questions come. Ask God in that moment to give you the wisdom you need to come up with a good answer. Pray now that you will be adequately prepared for those questions. For further study, read 2 Timothy 2:15.

Rule Number One

An unknown female author wrote the following ten rules for dating and marriage.

1. The girl always makes THE RULES.
2. THE RULES are subject to change without notice.
3. No guy can possibly know all THE RULES.
4. If the girl suspects the guy knows all THE RULES, she must immediately change some of them.
5. The girl is never wrong.
6. If it appears the girl is wrong, it is because of something the guy did or said wrong.
7. The girl can change her mind at any time.
8. The guy must never change his mind without the express written consent of the girl.
9. The girl has every right to be angry or upset at any time.
10. The guy must remain calm at all times, unless the girl wants him to be angry or upset.

The most important rule, at least according to this author, appears to be that the girl makes the rules.

In today's passage, Jesus shared the most important rule of all time. It's very simple: "Love the Lord your God will all your heart, soul, mind, and strength." Of all the rules that God could have given us, He chose one as the most important. "Love Me," He says.

How do you love God with all your heart, soul, mind, and strength? Your heart is the control center of your life (Proverbs 4:23). By loving God with all your heart, you always seek God's will and allow Him to be in control. Your soul is your self-consciousness of who you are. To love God with all your soul is to find your entire identity in Him. Your mind includes all of your thoughts. When you love God with your entire mind, you make every one of your thoughts obedient to Jesus (2 Corinthians 10:5). Your strength includes everything that you do in life. Loving God with all your strength means making sure that everything you do is devoted to God.

On a scale of one to ten, with ten being the best, how would you rate your love for God in each of the following areas: Heart _____ Soul _____ Mind _____ Strength _____

Name one thing in each area that you can change so that your love for God will increase: Heart _____ Soul _____

Mind _____ Strength _____

For each of these four areas, ask God how you can love Him more. Pray that He would open your eyes and help you see how you need to change. No matter where you go or what you do, always remember Rule Number One.

Rule Number Two

Matthew 22:34–40; Mark 12:28–34

> "The greatest love of all is learning to love yourself," the pop artist said in a hit song.
>
> "I'm pursuing the American dream," boasted the college graduate. "In five years I'll own my own business and be rich beyond my wildest dreams."
>
> The psychiatrist stated resolutely, "Your inner self is crying out for attention, Take some time off just for you today."
>
> "Mom and Dad," said the young man, "I've decided to buy a motorcycle and spend a few years traveling across the country to find myself."
>
> "Let's talk about you," the financial investment broker said. "Let's forget about everybody else and talk about how we can build up your retirement account."

Do you notice the common elements in all of the above statements? Everyone is concerned about him- or herself. Now, there's nothing wrong with loving yourself and doing good things for yourself. Loving ourselves comes naturally for most of us. However, we are to take the love we have for ourselves one step further.

In today's passage, Jesus gave a rule that is for real. It's the second greatest command in the Bible. Jesus said, "Love your neighbor in the exact same way that you love yourself."

If you are honest with yourself, you would probably agree that most of your days are spent thinking about yourself. You think things like, "Does she like me? I really want an 'A' in this class. I can't stand my history teacher. Why doesn't my mother leave me alone? What's for dinner? I need a car. It's not fair that my brother gets to stay out later than me. Why is this happening to me? God, will You please answer this prayer?" What would happen if you started thinking things like, "How can I help that person feel wanted? I'll write a thank-you note to my history teacher. My little brother could probably use a hug. I wonder if my parents need help making dinner." Do you see the difference? Once you learn to focus on the needs of others and not just yourself, you can learn to meet their needs in the same way you meet your own.

What percentage of the time do you spend thinking about yourself? _____

What percentage of the time do you spend thinking about how you can love the people around you? _____

What can you do this week to show your love in a visible way to all the people in your life?
_____

Ask God to help you think less about yourself and more about the people He has placed in your life. Pray that He would show you how to demonstrate your love. If you have trouble obeying Rule Number Two, see Rule Number One.

Been There, Done That

Matthew 22:41–46; Mark 12:35–37; Luke 20:41–44

1. A man stands in a dark stairway, staring at a portrait on the wall. He points to the picture and says, "Brothers and sisters have I none, but this man's father is my father's son." Who is in the picture?

2. A man and his son are on a fishing trip when lightning strikes, killing the man instantly and critically wounding his son. The boy is quickly rushed to the hospital, where it is determined that he needs immediate surgery. The hospital's top surgeon comes in, takes one look at the boy, and states, "I cannot operate on this young man. He is my son!" Who is the doctor?

3. I am the oldest man who ever lived, according to the Bible. Who am I?

The answers are (1) the man's son is in the picture, (2) the doctor is the boy's mother, and (3) Methuselah (Genesis 5:27).

In today's passage, Jesus made up His own riddle, asking the Pharisees, "Who am I?" It's a tricky question. He asked the Pharisees how the Messiah, or Christ, could be a descendant of David (human) and David's Lord (God) at the same time. The Pharisees didn't know what to say. How could the Messiah be fully God and fully human?

Though it sometimes seems like a mysterious riddle, Jesus is fully God and fully human at the same time. What does this mean for you? Think about it. God Himself, because He became human, knows how you feel when you suffer. He knows what it is like to be hurt by a friend. He understands how it feels to have your parents upset with you or to have your siblings invading your space. No matter what situation you face, Jesus has been there. Knowing that Jesus has been in your shoes gives you confidence to pray to the God who understands. You can ask for help from the one who has been there and done that.

Are you currently experiencing a temptation or trial that is difficult for you? _____

Explain. _____

Can you think of a time in Jesus' life when He faced a similar situation? _____

What did He do in that situation? _____

What should you do in your situation? _____

Always remember that God knows and understands what you are going through. He has been where you are, and He knows where to go from here. Ask God to show you how you should deal with your trials and temptations. For further study, read Hebrews 4:14–16.

I Want to Be Your Hero

Matthew 23:1–12; Mark 12:38–40; Luke 20:45–47

> "Class, I want you to write a one-page paper tonight entitled 'My Hero.' Choose someone you admire, and tell me who he is, what he has done, why you admire him, how you plan to be more like him, and so on. Any questions?"
>
> David sat in front of the computer that evening to work on his paper while listening to the news on television. He typed, "I admire Dunking Don Dunston, the basketball player. He is the most incredible person who has ever lived. He can dunk a basketball forward, backward, and upside-down. He glides through the air like an eagle. He . . ." David stopped typing when he heard Dunking Don's name on the news.
>
> "Today Dunking Don Dunston was arrested at his summer cottage for beating his wife. Sources close to the basketball star say Don has beaten his wife many times before, but this is the first time she called police. Dunston will be arraigned on Friday, and . . ."
>
> David looked back at his report and then again at the television.

Dunking Don let David down. David needed a new report. David needed a new hero.

In today's passage, Jesus warned us to be careful about whom we admire. In Jesus' day, many people looked up to the Pharisees as role models because on the outside they seemed so genuine and so important. Jesus exposed their hypocrisy, warning us not to be anything like them, because everything they did was for a show. On the inside, they were rotten. Jesus goes on to say that God is our only real hero. He is our one true Master, Father, and Teacher.

God is not a harsh Master. He is gentle and understanding. Listen to His will for your life, and be obedient to His commands, because they will bring you happiness. God is a compassionate and forgiving Father. He is the only one who will always take care of you. When you have a need, God will listen. When you have a problem, God can take care of it. When you've sinned, be honest and tell Him and He will forgive you. God is the perfect Teacher. If you're wondering what to do in a certain situation, He can point you in the right direction. If you need answers, He will give them to you. If you're looking for a hero, look to God.

Name someone that you once admired until he or she let you down. _____

How did that person disappoint you? _____

What qualities did he or she have that you wanted to imitate? _____

What qualities does Jesus have that you want to imitate? _____

Don't set yourself up for disappointment. Be careful whom you admire. Ask God to help you let Jesus be your ultimate hero. He will never disappoint you.

Motivate Yourself

Matthew 23:13–36

Two blurry-eyed district attorneys sat around a table piled high with research materials and dusty law books. They were trying to make their case against a murder suspect.

"Look," Gene said, rubbing his eyes. "We know he was at the scene of the crime. We know the gun belonged to him. We have his fingerprints on the weapon. Why do we need anything more?"

"We don't know his motive," Sarah insisted. "Why would he kill his wife and mother-in-law? It makes no sense. He seemed happily married and got along well with his mother-in-law."

Just then, a law clerk opened the door and placed a plain, brown envelope on the table. Sarah opened it and read for a few moments. "This is it!" she shouted excitedly. "Now we know his motive."

"I'm listening!" Gene said impatiently. "What is it?"

Sarah said, "Listen to this. Two weeks before the murders, our suspect talked his wife into taking out a large life insurance policy on his mother-in-law. His wife was the beneficiary. But since she died, too, the money automatically goes to her husband—our suspect. His motive was greed."

If you ever watch television or know anything about law, you know that a suspect cannot normally be convicted of a criminal offense without establishing a reason, or motive, for the crime.

In today's passage, Jesus exposed the hidden motives of the Pharisees. Jesus was so disgusted with their hypocrisy that He read their list of crimes like a prosecuting attorney. Notice that in all the things they did, their primary motive was *selfishness*. They wanted everyone to look at them and praise them. Jesus pointed out that their true motives should have been *justice, mercy,* and *faithfulness*.

God wants you to serve Him, but He wants you to serve Him for the right reasons. He wants your motives to be pure. He lists three primary motives that should be the foundation for the things you do. First, practice justice by making sure that you do everything honestly and fairly. Never lie or cheat, and fight for the rights of those who are treated unjustly. Second, practice mercy by learning to forgive those who hurt you. Finally, practice faithfulness by being consistent in your walk with the Lord. You exhibit faithfulness when you serve God even though you might not feel like it.

List some things you do out of selfish motives. _____

List some things you do out of pure motives. _____

How would your life be different if you started doing everything for the right reasons?

_____

Motivate yourself to serve God for the right reasons. Ask God to expose your selfish motives, and to instill pure motives, like justice, mercy, and love. For further study, read Micah 6:8.

Weekly Bible Study and Prayer Review

Bible Study

Look back through some of the Scriptures you read this week. Write down the one verse or passage that God used to speak to you.

_____

_____

_____

_____

Memorize this verse or passage. You can do it if you spend just a few minutes saying it to yourself.

Now, think of at least one situation you will probably face soon in which you could use this Scripture to help you make the right decision. Write down that situation below.

_____

Quote the Scripture when you face this situation, and live by it.

Prayer Time

Take a few moments to praise God for who He is.
Now take a few moments to thank God for things He has done for you.
Now ask God to make you into the person He wants you to be.
Ask God to use you to help others become closer to God.

Below is your prayer list for the week. Keep it updated each week. If your prayer isn't answered this week, carry it over to next week's list.

Request	Date of Original Request	Date Answered
_____	__/__/__	__/__/__
_____	__/__/__	__/__/__
_____	__/__/__	__/__/__
_____	__/__/__	__/__/__
_____	__/__/__	__/__/__
_____	__/__/__	__/__/__
_____	__/__/__	__/__/__
_____	__/__/__	__/__/__
_____	__/__/__	__/__/__

Pray for the things on your list and trust God to provide.
Forgive anyone you have not yet forgiven.
Ask God to forgive you for any unconfessed sin in your life.
Ask God to keep you out of trouble with sin.
Acknowledge that God is in complete control of your life and will take care of everything.

What Gives?

Mark 12:41–44; Luke 21:1–4

During his sophomore year of college, Kyle agreed to become a Big Brother in the juvenile justice system. He volunteered to spend at least two hours a week with a sixteen-year-old boy named Bryan who had been arrested for aggravated sexual assault.

Kyle would spend every Thursday afternoon and evening with Bryan. They would go to the movies, video arcades, the city park—anyplace to hang out and have some fun. One sunny Thursday afternoon as Kyle was taking Bryan back home, Bryan said, "Hey, look. I've never asked you for money before, and I don't plan on ever doing it again. My mom is $30 short of being able to pay bills this month. I was wondering if I could borrow some from you."

Kyle thought for a moment. He had exactly $30 in his wallet, but it was all he had to live on for the next five days. Before he had the chance to change his mind he said, "Sure, Bryan. Here you go." The next day, someone happened to ask Kyle to install a disk drive on his computer. Kyle intended to do it for free, but the man wouldn't hear of it. He paid Kyle exactly $30.

You may not realize it at the time, but God sees the little sacrifices you make each day. When you give until it hurts, God knows it.

In today's passage, Jesus was at the temple. He deliberately sat near the place where people gave their money in offerings to God. Many rich people came by and threw in large amounts of money, but Jesus wasn't impressed. He was stirred, however, by the sacrificial gift of an old widow who gave only a few pennies. It wasn't much, but it was all she had to live on.

When you are faced with an opportunity to give money to God, you have two choices. You can keep the money and use it for yourself, or you can let go of it and give it to God. The first choice is the most natural. You think, "I need this" or "My gift really won't make a difference." The widow could have thought either of those things, but she didn't. She gave it all. Making the same choice the widow did requires true sacrifice—giving until it hurts.

How much do you give to God each week? _____

Is this amount a sacrifice? _____

How much more would you have to give before it hurts? _____

Are you willing to make this sacrifice? _____

Your sacrifices don't go unnoticed. Jesus saw the widow, and He will see you. Ask God to help you give more to your church and to people in need. Pray that you would be able to give until it hurts.

What Is the World Coming To?

Matthew 24:1–35; Mark 13:1–31; Luke 21:5–33

Derik sat down on his couch to watch the world news. The anchor began the first of several grim stories. "Today, thirty-five people in a cult committed suicide. They believed that Jesus was coming back in a UFO and that in order to board the spacecraft they had to kill themselves.

"The Middle East is still in turmoil, as bombs in Israel went off in three separate locations. Rumors circulate that war is inevitable. The famine in Africa claimed more than one hundred lives today alone as officials scramble to find a solution. An earthquake struck southern California today, killing three and injuring hundreds more. In the Far East, a group of missionaries have been kidnapped. Family members remain hopeful that their loved ones are still alive, but little evidence exists to support this. And, in other news . . ."

Derik switched off the television and sighed. "What is this world coming to?" he muttered under his breath as he headed for his room, continuing his thoughts. "Cults, wars, famines, earthquakes, persecution—it just keeps getting worse and worse. I sure wish Jesus would come back before this world just falls completely apart."

The headlines that Derik saw on a typical day are all too familiar. What is this world coming to?

In today's passage, Jesus described modern headlines in vivid detail. He explained to His disciples what the world will be like as His Second Coming gets closer and closer. False prophets, war and rumors of war, famines, earthquakes, persecution—all of these things will increase, like the birth pains of a woman in labor. Jesus goes on to describe even more details of the final days before His return. Though for awhile it seems darker than ever, Jesus rescues His children and takes them home to be with Him in heaven forever.

Jesus does not want you to get too bogged down with the details of what will happen in the last days. He does, however, want you to do two things. First, do not be afraid when you see the world spinning out of control. The headlines will get worse, but keep in mind that God is still in complete control. He knows what He is doing. Second, remember the end of the story. No matter how bad things get, Jesus is coming back. When He does, He will rescue you from all of the headaches in this world and take you home to be with Him for eternity.

What headlines do you see in your world today that correspond with Jesus' prophecies about the last days? _____

How do you feel when you read or hear about these problems? _____

What should your attitude be as you race toward the final days of planet Earth? _____

Don't let the headlines get you down. Ask God to help you keep your head up when the world seems to spin out of control. Remember that Jesus is going to rescue you and take you home.

Our Hour

Matthew 24:36–51; Mark 13:32–37; Luke 21:34–38

"What time does Mom get home today?" Timmy asked Brianna. "We've got to get all of the chores on this list done before she gets here."

"I know," replied Brianna. "It's about noon now. Surely she won't be home before 5:00 P.M. That gives us four hours to goof off and the last hour to get everything done."

"What if she gets home before that?" Timmy insisted. "She said we should have all of these things finished before she comes home."

"Relax," Brianna suggested. "She'll be here at 5:00 P.M. I'm sure of it. You go do what you want, and I'll go do what I want. Let's meet back here at 4:00, and we'll start working on this."

With that, the two went their separate ways. Brianna went outside to play soccer with _____ computer. At four o'clock they both dropped _____ ngs on Mom's list.

_____ kids. I'm home. Did you get everything done?"

_____ ould come home, but she was wrong. _____ ores done.

_____ ry clear that no one will know the day _____ at any time. In spite of Jesus' words, _____ 1) they assume Jesus will come back a _____ und to doing what God has asked them _____ at Jesus will return and plan everything _____ s is worth the risk of being wrong.

_____ finish reading this sentence. This should _____ If you really believe that Jesus is coming _____ things. You will share Jesus with as many _____ e. You will spend a lot of time on your _____ rd regularly. You will resist temptation at _____ ossessions or money because you know that you can't take them with you. other words, you will live the way Jesus wants you to live.

How does knowing that Jesus can return at any moment change the way that you live?

_____

What would you change about your life if you knew that Jesus was coming back in one week?

Don't wait to make these changes. Make them now because Jesus could come back well before the week is over. Ask God to help you prepare yourself for Jesus' coming. Pray that you would be found faithful at the moment of His return.

Fools give full vent to their rage,
but the wise bring calm in the end.
—*Proverbs 29:11* (NIV)

14

Monday
SEPTEMBER

Check the Oil

Matthew 25:1–13

Five members of Thornton Community Church's youth group piled into Katrina's car after church Sunday night and headed for Taco Temptations. They planned to have a great time.

Their plans were interrupted by the drunk driver who broadsided their car, killing all five instantly. Katrina, Chris, Sean, Josh, and Michelle suddenly found themselves standing before God. The Lord spoke to Katrina first, "Well done, my good and faithful servant. Come and enjoy the place I have prepared for you." Katrina stepped forward and stood next to a magnificent angel, facing her four friends. The Lord spoke again to Josh and Sean, inviting them to come forward.

The Lord's eyes grew sad as he turned to Chris and Michelle, saying, "Depart from Me, the two of you, because I never knew you."

Chris and Michelle fell to their faces, saying, "But Lord, we are church members. We come to youth group all the time. We even took notes during a few sermons. We . . ."

The Lord spoke again, "You did all of those things, but you never asked Me to come inside your heart."

Billy Graham and other Christian leaders speculate that anywhere from 20 to 60 percent of church members are not Christians. They show up at church, but they do not have Jesus on the inside.

In today's passage, Jesus illustrated this tragic reality with a story about ten bridesmaids. Five of the girls took oil for their lamps, but the other five did not. The girls without oil looked just like the other girls. They wore the same clothes and were meeting in the same place. However, when the groom arrived, he found only the five with oil were ready to go home with him.

A church member who does not know Jesus looks just like a church member who does. They both meet in the same place. The only difference is that one has Jesus on the inside and one does not. How can you tell the difference? You may never know until you die or Jesus returns to take you home. Rather than sit around and try and figure out who is a Christian and who is not, you should simply check the oil for your own lamp.

How do you know that you are a Christian? _____

When did you become a Christian? _____

What was your life like before you met Jesus? _____

What was your life like after you met Jesus? _____

Check the oil in your lamp. Make sure that you are not a church member who pretends to know God on the outside but has never asked Jesus to come inside. If you know you're a Christian, praise God for the salvation He's given you. If you have doubts, talk to a Christian friend or youth pastor and get things right today.

Double or Nothing

Matthew 25:14–30; Luke 19:11–27

> "Joey, I'll pay you $10 per hour," Mr. Johnson said. "How does that sound?"
>
> Joey thought for a moment and said, "How about this instead? I'll work all day the first day for one penny." Mr. Johnson looked shocked. "Then, I'll work the second day for two cents, the third day for four cents, and so on. Just double my pay each day."
>
> Mr. Johnson thought to himself, I'm only hiring this young man for thirty days. This sounds like a great deal to me. The two shook hands and Joey began work.
>
> On the first day Joey walked home with one cent in his pocket. On the second day, his wages totaled three cents. By the fifth day he had earned a total of thirty-one cents. After he worked ten days he had $10.23. After twenty days his earnings had grown to $10,485.75. At the end of his final day of work, Joey walked away with a total of $10,737,418.23. In only thirty days, he earned more than ten million dollars.
>
> If you double something over and over, it can add up fast. It holds true for money, and it also holds true for people.

In today's passage, Jesus told a story about three men. There are two different versions of the story, so Jesus probably told the story twice. In each of the two stories, a master gave three men a sum of money and asked them to earn more with it. The first two earned much more, and the master was pleased. The third man earned nothing and was condemned. The point? God wants you to take what He has given you and earn more souls for His kingdom.

When you become a Christian, God doesn't want you to sit back and hide your faith, like the third man in the parable. He wants you to share your faith with others, like the first two men in the parable. Think about it this way. If you win two people to the Lord every six months, and those two go on to win two more every six months, then the entire world would be Christian in sixteen years. God doesn't ask for you to win the entire world all by yourself. He just asks that you try and win one or more in your lifetime.

Who would you say is most responsible for sharing Jesus with you? _____

What would your life be like if this person had not shared his or her faith? _____

Have you ever played a part in winning someone else to the Lord? _____

Who can you share your faith with this week? _____

Someone else brought you to Jesus. Now it's your turn. You can either hide your faith or share it. Ask God to help you share your faith with at least one person this week. It's double or nothing.

Least, but Not Last

Matthew 25:31–46

"Charlene, this is Jesus. I'm coming to your house today." Charlene abruptly awoke in a cold sweat.

Charlene raced through her morning routine on this beautiful summer morning. Her parents were at work, and she frantically ran through the house, trying to figure out what to do first when the phone rang.

"Hello, this is your local Salvation Army," the voice said. "We were calling to see if you had any old clothes that you could donate for the poor."

"Um, sure," Charlene said. Following the caller's instructions, she went to her closet, found some old shoes and clothes, boxed them up, and placed them on the front porch.

While she was outside, a young boy came to the door and said, "Miss, could you donate one dollar to help fight leukemia?" Charlene nodded, pulled out two one-dollar bills, and handed them to the boy. She went back inside, only to find the phone ringing again. Charlene's next-door neighbor needed a baby-sitter immediately for the rest of the day. Charlene knew she wouldn't get much pay, but she agreed.

What if Jesus comes to my house while I'm next door? she asked herself.

Jesus had already come to Charlene's house three times, in the form of the Salvation Army, a young boy, and her next-door neighbor. When Charlene offered her help to these people, she was helping Jesus.

Today's passage illustrates this point vividly. Jesus explained that how we treat others is how we treat Him. For instance, if we feed the hungry and offer water to the thirsty, then we are doing the same for Jesus. If we fail to provide clothes to those who need them, then we fail to minister to Jesus. When we care for the sick, we are caring for Jesus. When we ignore those in prison, we are ignoring Jesus.

Jesus comes to you every day in the form of a variety of people with different needs. He may come in the form of your parents, who are overloaded with household chores and need your help. He might slip up behind you in the form of your little brother or sister, wanting some attention and love. He could come in the form of that person who really gets on your nerves, needing some help with homework; or your math teacher, who needs a "thank you." When Jesus comes disguised as someone in need, will you help or pretend you didn't notice?

What needs have you deliberately ignored this week? _____

What needs have you met? _____

What can you do to improve the way you respond to the people in need around you?

_____

Don't turn Jesus away when He comes in the form of someone who needs your help. Ask God to show you how to minister to others around you. Pray that you would make ministering to the least of Jesus' brothers and sisters your first priority.

Weekly Bible Study and Prayer Review

Bible Study

Look back through some of the Scriptures you read this week. Write down the one verse or passage that God used to speak to you.

_____

_____

_____

_____

*Memorize this verse or passage. You can do it if you spend just
a few minutes saying it to yourself.*

Now, think of at least one situation you will probably face soon in which you could use this Scripture to help you make the right decision. Write down that situation below.

_____

Quote the Scripture when you face this situation, and live by it.

Prayer Time

*Take a few moments to praise God for who He is.
Now take a few moments to thank God for things He has done for you.
Now ask God to make you into the person He wants you to be.
Ask God to use you to help others become closer to God.*

Below is your prayer list for the week. Keep it updated each week. If your prayer isn't answered this week, carry it over to next week's list.

Request	Date of Original Request	Date Answered
_____	__/__/__	__/__/__
_____	__/__/__	__/__/__
_____	__/__/__	__/__/__
_____	__/__/__	__/__/__
_____	__/__/__	__/__/__
_____	__/__/__	__/__/__
_____	__/__/__	__/__/__
_____	__/__/__	__/__/__
_____	__/__/__	__/__/__

*Pray for the things on your list and trust God to provide.
Forgive anyone you have not yet forgiven.
Ask God to forgive you for any unconfessed sin in your life.
Ask God to keep you out of trouble with sin.
Acknowledge that God is in complete control of your life
and will take care of everything.*

Losing Your Religion

Matthew 26:1–5; Mark 14:1–2; Luke 22:1–2

Every year a group of so-called religious leaders holds an annual conference. Their stated purpose is to determine the truth about Jesus: who He was, what He said, and what He means to us today.

These religious leaders have concluded that all of the eyewitness testimony of Jesus' apostles are not trustworthy. They say that the virgin birth never happened. They say that Judas Iscariot was not as guilty as he has been made out to be. They say that Jesus' hometown of Nazareth did not even exist when He was growing up. They say that He married an unknown woman. They say that when He fasted forty days and forty nights in the desert He hallucinated. They say Jesus did die on a cross, but that He never rose from the dead.

They say He was not a savior, not the Lord, not the way to heaven. They say He was nothing more than a revolutionary, another ancient prophet, the founder of a religion.

The annual Jesus Seminar claims that its purposes are noble, but in reality they seek to destroy Jesus by denying the truth about Him that has been preserved for us in God's Word.

Some modern religious leaders are no different than the religious leaders in Jesus' day. Their purpose is to stop His message by destroying who He is.

In today's passage, the religious leaders of Jesus' day held a meeting to decide what to do about Jesus. They did not like His message. They did not believe the things that He said. They decided that the only way to stop Jesus was to devise a cunning plot to arrest and kill Him. Which religious leader are you more likely to believe in—someone who says, "Let's commit murder" or someone who says, "God loves you, and you can go to heaven if you follow Me"? The motives of the so-called religious leaders prove that they were not religious at all.

Christianity is not a religion. *Religion* can be defined as "a human attempt to find and reach God." Christianity can be defined as "God's attempt to find and reach humans." Do you see the difference? All of the religions of the world are nothing more than rules and regulations set up by humans in a futile attempt to try to work their way to God. Christianity is the exact opposite of those religions. Jesus says that you cannot work your way to God. The only way to know God is to know Jesus, who is God. So beware of religions. Their only purpose is to destroy the message of Jesus. You don't need religion. You need Jesus.

What kinds of religious beliefs do you see around you? _____

How do these religious beliefs contradict what Jesus says? _____

How can you continue to share the good news of Jesus in spite of all of the other beliefs out there? _____

Ask God to help you discern the difference between religion and following Jesus. Pray for the wisdom and patience to keep sharing Jesus with others, even when popular religion tries to destroy your message.

Even Trade

Matthew 26:14–16; Mark 14:10–11; Luke 22:3–6

The final item up for bid at the auction was an old cedar chest. It was ornately carved, and it dated back to the Civil War. The auctioneer asserted that the locked chest had never been opened and no one knew what was inside.

Justin got goose bumps just thinking about what mysteries lay just out of reach in the old chest. He checked his wallet and whispered to Susan, "That thing could be a gold mine. Let's bid." Susan objected, saying that she would rather save their money for something certain, but Justin persisted.

The bidding war began, and within ten minutes Justin's offer of $100 won him the chest. He loaded it into his pickup truck, and he and Susan drove home. Quickly, he unloaded the chest and pried open the old lock. The trunk was packed tight with one-hundred-dollar bills.

"We're rich!" Justin cried. "Look at all this money! I told you, Susan. Our trade paid off."

Susan hated to disappoint Justin. She said, "Justin. That's all Confederate money. It's just paper. It was worth something in the South during the Civil War, but today it's worthless."

Justin gave up $100 for nothing. His trade was not even. He lost on the deal. In today's passage, we discover that one of the disciples made an uneven trade.

Judas Iscariot made the worst trade of all time. He decided that he would rather have money than have Jesus. He auctioned Jesus off to the highest bidder, and in return received thirty pieces of silver. Satan deceived Judas into giving up Jesus for a worthless handful of coins.

Satan is a masterful auctioneer, who wants you to trade Jesus for sin, but it's always an uneven trade. Don't ever think you will come out ahead if you choose sin over Jesus. You may think lying to your parents about where you go Saturday night will give you a night of fun, but when they find out they will no longer trust you. You might believe that a few moments of lustful passion are worth the pleasure, but in the end your future spouse will lose a part of you meant only for him or her. You may suppose that cheating on your math test is an easy ticket to a good grade, but in the long run you will lose out on a good education. Sin isn't worth it, no matter how good Satan makes it look.

Have you ever traded in your principles and your faith in God for the pleasures of a momentary sin? _____ *Describe a recent example.* _____

What consequences did you suffer, or what consequences do you think you will suffer?

_____

How can you avoid falling into the same sinful trap again? _____

Sin feels good, but only for a fleeting instant. Ask God to help you avoid trading your faith in Him for the momentary pleasures of sin. Pray for the strength to overcome the temptation of sinful habits. Don't make an uneven trade. Hang on to Jesus. You'll never get a better offer. For further study, read Hebrews 11:25.

The Inside Track

Matthew 26:17–19; Mark 14:12–16; Luke 22:7–13

Every Saturday morning, sixteen-year-old Collin rode in the church van to a little country church to play basketball. The blonde, blue-eyed new Christian loved to play basketball.

Every time they traveled to the church where the games took place, they passed a maximum-security prison, where the average age of the inmates was nineteen years old—all violent offenders. Each week, as the van passed the prison, Collin seemed inexplicably drawn to it. He began to think, How do the guys in there go to church? Who teaches them about Jesus? Over a series of weeks, Collin began to sense God calling him to go inside and share the good news with the prisoners. But how was God going to get him inside?

A few weeks later, Collin began dating Kim, whose father was a pastor in another city. Collin told Kim about his desire to reach the prisoners for Jesus. Kim introduced Collin to a man who went to that very same prison every Wednesday night to share Jesus. "Collin," the man said, "it just so happens that we need someone else to come with us and lead a Bible study each Wednesday night. Would you be willing?"

God told Collin to share Jesus with the inmates before He showed him how he would get inside. Because Collin was willing, God showed him the way.

In today's passage, Jesus asked Peter and John to go and make preparations for the Passover meal, an annual feast that required much preparation. Peter and John said, "We'll do it, but where and how?" Jesus told them to go into the city, look for a man carrying a water jar (in that day normally women carried the water jars), and everything would be taken care of. Jesus just wanted them to be willing to follow His instructions, even if they weren't exactly sure where they were headed. He had already made the necessary arrangements in advance.

The same holds true when God calls you to serve Him in a particular way. He is not necessarily going to give you a list of instructions that tells you exactly what to do and when to do it. More likely, He will give you a gentle nudge in the direction you should go, saying, "Don't worry. Everything will be taken care of. I've already made the necessary arrangements." So if you sense that God is calling you to do something, don't worry if you don't know all of the details yet. Just be ready, willing, and able. God has already gone ahead of you to make the necessary arrangements. Just do what He asks, and you will get the inside track as you go.

What do you sense God calling you to do? _____

What questions would you like to have answered before you start? _____

Are you willing to start heading in that direction, even if God doesn't give you all the answers at first? _____

God will never send you somewhere that He has not already been. He will always make the necessary arrangements for you in advance. Ask God to help you follow His leading, even if you're not sure where you'll end up.

Sole Desire

John 13:1–20

Mother Teresa was one of the most revered Christians who ever lived. The world mourned for her on the day she died. She gave her life ministering to the poor and sick in Calcutta, India. It was a tremendously tiresome and dirty job, but it was her ministry, and she made a tremendous difference.

Before she died, there was a young man who greatly admired Mother Teresa and the work that she did. He wrote her a letter and asked her how he could become as great as she was. He placed the letter in the mail and prayed, "Dear God, please allow Mother Teresa to have the time to answer my letter. I really want to be like her."

Every day, the young man checked his mailbox, but it was empty. After many days passed, he became discouraged. He began to feel that he would never receive an answer. One day, however, a wrinkled envelope arrived with a return address from Calcutta, India. Trembling with excitement, the young man opened the letter. Mother Teresa wrote only four words, but they changed his life forever. The letter read, "Find your own Calcutta."

Find your own Calcutta. In other words, find a specific ministry in your world where you can make a difference. When you find it, give it your all. Make it your sole desire.

In today's passage, Jesus illustrated true ministry. He assumed the role of a common house slave and began washing each disciple's feet. In Jesus' day, this was a detestable job. Everyone wore sandals and walked in dust all day long. By dinnertime, a person's feet were tremendously dirty. Jesus didn't see the dirt or the sweat, though. He was thinking about His disciples and what He could do to help them be a stronger team after He was gone. He told the disciples to imitate Him by washing the feet of others whenever they had the chance.

If you are to imitate Jesus, what does it mean to wash someone else's feet? Does it mean that you should take off someone else's shoes and start scrubbing? Not necessarily. It means that you are to humble yourself and be willing to do the things that no one else is willing to do. It means finding your own Calcutta. Don't think about how dirty the job is. Think about how you can help the team (your church and youth group). Grab a vacuum after the next youth event and start cleaning. Be extra nice to the person no one else likes. Offer to mow or pull weeds around your church for free. Come early to your next Bible study and ask if you can help set up.

What are some of the jobs in your church or youth group that no one wants to do? ____

When is the last time you helped with one of the grubby tasks? _____

What job could you do on a regular basis for the sake of the team? _____

Ask God to show you your Calcutta. Pray that He would show you what your ministry is. Don't walk away from the dirty jobs. Follow Jesus' example and get busy scrubbing.

Face to Face

Matthew 26:20–25; Mark 14:17–21; Luke 22:21–23; John 13:21–30

Tracy couldn't believe her ears. From just around the corner in the school hallway, she heard one of her friends talking. Her words cut like a knife. Tracy's friend was telling lies about her.

Tracy reversed her direction and walked the long way to her next class. She was in a daze. Why would her friend lie about her? What had she done to deserve this? How would she convince people that the rumors were not true? During geometry class, Tracy couldn't concentrate. Her sadness slowly turned to resentment and anger. She began to plot revenge.

As she walked back to her locker in silence, her friend spotted her and said, "Hey, Tracy. Are you ready to face Mr. Driver in English next period?" Tracy looked her friend in the eye, grasping for something to say. Instead of responding with anger or revenge, Tracy just leaned against her locker. She looked her friend in the eye and said, "I heard what you said about me. You know it's not true. You really hurt me. If you're going to keep saying those things, go ahead. Just don't pretend to be my friend anymore."[47]

Nothing hurts more than the betrayal of a friend. When you face a situation like this, you can choose to get revenge, or you can face your betrayer with gentleness and honesty.

In today's passage, Jesus shared with His disciples that He was aware that one of them would betray Him. Each of them reacted by asking, "It's not me, is it?" Judas had already agreed to betray Jesus, but he feigned his innocence by saying, "Surely it isn't me." Jesus could have exploded in anger. He could have called on an angel to kill Judas right there on the spot. Instead, Jesus responded with gentle words. He looked Judas in the eye and told him if he was going to betray Him, then to get it over with.

When someone you care about hurts you, it hurts. You can't avoid pain, and you can't choose not to be hurt. You can, however, choose your response to the person. You can get angry and stew about it, but you'll only feel worse. You can get even by hurting your friend as much or more as you were hurt. Or you can do what Jesus did and gently bring the problem out in the open. Tell your friend how you feel. Let him or her know you are hurt. Then leave the choice to your friend to make amends or walk away.

Have you recently been hurt by a friend? _____ How? _____

Did you tell your friend how you felt, or did you try to get even? _____

If things are not fully resolved between the two of you, what can you do to make things right? _____

Ask God to help you get past the pain, and talk things out with those who hurt you. Pray that He would help you let go of your anger and thoughts of revenge. Work things out openly and honestly, face to face.

Dinner Is Served

Matthew 26:26–30; Mark 14:22–26; Luke 22:14–20

> A weary desert traveler stopped to rest. He sat down, leaned against a boulder, and opened his canteen. He drank deeply as he thought about the long road ahead.
>
> After a moment's rest, he set out again, traveling westward. Before long he reached a wide ridge at the top of a large mountain. He looked down into the valley and gasped. There, stretched out below, were hundreds of thousands of people. In the center of their camp was a large, ceremonial tent. The people were camped around the tent on four sides. Their arrangement formed an elongated cross that faced him. He said to himself, "Perhaps these people are friendly and they will provide me with food for my journey."
>
> The man soon arrived in the camp and was greeted cordially by the people. Their leader, Moses, asked the stranger to join them at dusk for an annual feast called the Passover. There the man was treated to a meal of fresh lamb, unleavened bread, bitter herbs, and wine.

The people of Israel celebrated the Passover long before Jesus came to earth. In Numbers 2, if you do the math, you will find that the arrangement of their camp formed the shape of a cross.

In today's passage, Jesus celebrated His last supper with the disciples. It was the night before Jesus would die on a cross. It was also the evening of the annual Passover meal—a time when the Israelites slaughtered and sacrificed a perfect lamb, remembering the day that the Lord delivered them from their slavery in Egypt. On this night, Jesus instituted a new Passover meal. The bread symbolized Jesus' body, broken on the cross. The wine symbolized His blood, spilled on the cross. Jesus asked His disciples to celebrate this meal to remember what He did on the cross.

The cross is the center of the gospel story. It is foreshadowed in the Old Testament in the Israelite camp around the Tabernacle. The New Testament shows us that the cross is the very reason Jesus came to earth. Today, churches celebrate the Last Supper, or Communion, to remember what Jesus did on the cross. You are to pick up and carry your own cross and follow Jesus daily (Luke 9:23). The answer to the question "What would Jesus do?" is found only in the cross. Jesus gives you the perfect example of loving God and loving others. If you really want to know how to be more like Jesus, look to the cross.

In what ways are you most like Jesus? _____

In what ways are you least like Jesus? _____

What needs to change in your life today for you to become more like Jesus? _____

Remember the cross. Share the message of the cross with others. Take up your own cross and follow Jesus. Ask God to help you abandon the things of this world that keep you from being more like Jesus. Pray that the cross will always be the center of your attention. For further study, read 1 Corinthians 1:18, 2:2; Galatians 6:14; and Philippians 2:5–8.

Weekly Bible Study and Prayer Review

Bible Study

Look back through some of the Scriptures you read this week. Write down the one verse or passage that God used to speak to you.

_____
_____
_____
_____

Memorize this verse or passage. You can do it if you spend just
a few minutes saying it to yourself.

Now, think of at least one situation you will probably face soon in which you could use this Scripture to help you make the right decision. Write down that situation below.

_____

Quote the Scripture when you face this situation, and live by it.

Prayer Time

Take a few moments to praise God for who He is.
Now take a few moments to thank God for things He has done for you.
Now ask God to make you into the person He wants you to be.
Ask God to use you to help others become closer to God.

Below is your prayer list for the week. Keep it updated each week. If your prayer isn't answered this week, carry it over to next week's list.

Request	Date of Original Request	Date Answered
_____	__/__/__	__/__/__
_____	__/__/__	__/__/__
_____	__/__/__	__/__/__
_____	__/__/__	__/__/__
_____	__/__/__	__/__/__
_____	__/__/__	__/__/__
_____	__/__/__	__/__/__
_____	__/__/__	__/__/__
_____	__/__/__	__/__/__

Pray for the things on your list and trust God to provide.
Forgive anyone you have not yet forgiven.
Ask God to forgive you for any unconfessed sin in your life.
Ask God to keep you out of trouble with sin.
Acknowledge that God is in complete control of your life
and will take care of everything.

Table for One

Luke 22:24–30

Serving God is like being a waiter in a restaurant. Jesus comes in, asks for a table for one, and sits down. You have been assigned to His table.

In today's passage, Jesus' disciples got into an argument about who was going to be the greatest. They'd already had this discussion once before, but they still didn't get it. Jesus explained to His friends that the greatest person is the one who serves the best. He pointed to His own life as an example, saying, "Don't you remember how I served you?" Their model for becoming great was to imitate Jesus' life as a servant.

You want to be great at something, right? You strive to make the highest grade, run the fastest mile, eat the most pieces of pizza, make first chair in band, or be the most popular at school. You say the right words and do the right things, hoping you will one day rise above the rest and be noticed. If you really want to be great, Jesus says to become the greatest servant of all. Stop trying to impress people and start helping them. Jesus was the greatest person who ever lived because He served. If you want to be great, learn to serve the way Jesus did.

What are the things you strive to be great at? _____

Why do you want to be great in these areas? _____

Would you say that you are a great servant? _____ *Why or why not?* _____

How can you become a better servant? _____

Never forget that your purpose on earth is to serve Jesus. You can become greater than you ever dreamed if you dare to devote your life to serving the Lord. Ask God to show you how you can become a better servant. Pretend that you are a waiter in a restaurant and Jesus is your only customer. Ask Him, "What can I do for You today?"

A Devil of a Time

Your eyes slowly begin to adjust to the magnificent light all around you. You see angels encircling a throne, where God Almighty reigns in glorious splendor. You see the silhouettes of people everywhere, prostrate before their King, singing praises.

Suddenly, an eerie feeling crawls up and down your spine. You look, and a dark, hooded figure approaches the throne. Instinctively, you know it is the Evil One. "Why is he here?" you ask yourself. "This is heaven. He doesn't belong here."

Satan steps in front of the throne. It appears that he is having a conversation with the Lord. You strain to hear the voices. The discussion appears to be about someone on earth. Satan is asking the Lord for permission to test this young person. Satan makes a wager with the Lord that this person will be overcome during the trial and give up on God. The Lord smiles and says, "I have confidence in My child. Test as you wish. We will see who wins this victory." As Satan turns away with an evil grin, he wrings his hands together, saying your name over and over. He's going to test you!

This story is not so farfetched. It already happened once in the book of Job (Job 1–2). It happened again to Peter.

In today's passage, Jesus explained to His disciples that they would all abandon Him that night. He explained to Peter that Satan had asked to test him. Jesus hinted that for a time Peter would be overcome by this test, but then later he would turn back. He indicated that when Peter did turn back, he would strengthen the other disciples. Peter would become strong through his trial, even though at first he would be weak and deny the Lord three times.

On occasion, Satan will stand before God in heaven and beg to have a crack at making you crack. It may not seem fair, but sometimes God will give Satan permission to test you. During this time of testing, you may feel that God has abandoned you. The suffering you experience may seem unfair. Satan's purpose for this time of testing is to get you to turn away from God. God's purpose for this time of testing is to strengthen your faith in Him. He knows that you may stumble and fall in weakness during your test, but He also has confidence that you will turn back to Him and be stronger. Then you will be able to strengthen others when they go through trials.

How has Satan tried to make you turn away from God? _____

How have you denied or failed Jesus during your trial? _____

How has your faith been strengthened because of what you endured? _____

Don't lose heart during the test. Your suffering won't last forever. Ask God to help you endure the testing that comes. Pray for strength to overcome your weaknesses. Have faith in God. He has faith that you will overcome your trial and be strong again. For further study, read what Peter wrote after his trial in 1 Peter 1:6–7.

It's a Big, Big House

John 14:1–3

In the early nineteenth century, a small ship carried passengers from England to the United States. The ride went smoothly until late one night an unexpected storm hit.

The winds and waves became so violent that most feared that the ship would sink and that they all would die. One woman, however, chose to remain calm. She pulled out her small, well-worn Bible and began reading stories to all who would listen. Many gathered around the woman of faith and received peace from the things she read.

After what seemed like days, the storm ceased, and the ship continued on its journey. The captain of the ship, interested to know the source of the woman's quiet strength, pulled her aside. He said, "Why were you able to remain so calm when everyone else feared the ship would sink?"

The woman replied, "I have two daughters. One has died and lives in heaven. The other lives in New York. I knew that when this trip was over I would see one of them—and it didn't really matter to me which one."

This woman knew that if she didn't live through the storm, heaven was waiting. She had peace in the midst of panic because she knew where her true home was.

Jesus took the time to talk to His disciples about what heaven would be like. He described heaven as a big house, owned and managed by His Father and filled with many rooms. Jesus said that He was going to heaven to prepare your room and make it just right. Then, at just the right time, He is going to come back and take us all home to live in heaven with Him.

Why did Jesus take the time on the evening before His crucifixion to give us a glimpse into heaven? He considered it important enough to share with us and encourage us. Jesus doesn't want us to get too comfortable down here on earth. Instead, we should keep reminding ourselves that this life we live is only temporary. Can you even begin to imagine what it will be like to live forever with Jesus, walking on streets of gold in a city where there are no tears, disease, or death? The more you time you spend thinking about heaven, the more likely you are to spend your time doing things that will matter.

What do you hope you can do in heaven? _____

What do you want to see in heaven? _____

If you could design heaven yourself, what kinds of things would you include? _____

_____

Is there anyone you know whom you could invite to come to heaven with you? _____

Spend a few minutes with your eyes closed, dreaming about the day that you arrive in heaven and see Jesus face to face for the first time. Ask God to show you how to make your life count for eternity.

I Just Want Three Things

John 14:4–7

An atheist and a Christian sat together at lunch. They ate together once a week, and the discussion frequently turned to God.

"So," the Christian asked, finishing his dessert, "since you are an atheist, tell me this. What do you want out of life? After all, since you don't believe in God, you think this is the only life you have. What do you want to do and experience before you die?"

"That's a good question!" his friend responded. "Let me see. I just want three things. First, I want to have a plan. I've got a list of goals I want to accomplish, and they provide me direction and focus. Second, I want to be able to distinguish what is true and what is false, so that I live by what is true. Finally, I want to experience a good life. Since I only have so many years on this planet, I want to live life to the fullest. I want to make memories, have fun, and laugh a lot. These three things are precisely why I am not a Christian."

The Christian smiled and said, "The three things you described are direction, truth, and life. I want these too. In fact, I have them. They are precisely why I'm a Christian. Jesus once said, 'I am the way, the truth, and the life.' I have found these three things through Jesus."[48]

Today's passage contains the very verse that the Christian quoted to his atheist friend. Jesus said, "I am the way, the truth, and the life." These three things are what everyone wants out of life. Everyone wants direction—a purpose and a plan to follow. Everybody has a natural desire to know the truth, whether it's about the way things work (science), the innocence or guilt of a person on trial (law), or the question of God's existence (religion/philosophy). Everyone hopes to have a memorable life filled with wonderful relationships and experiences. Jesus is the source of all of these things. Only through Him will you have them all.

Sometimes people think that to become a Christian you must live a boring life, carry a big fat Bible everywhere, and never have any fun. Nothing could be further from the truth. When you follow Jesus, you will find everything you need for a full and meaningful life. You will find the way—your purpose on this planet and how to fulfill it. You will know the truth—knowing the difference between what is real and what is not. You will experience the life—memorable experiences and relationships with God and people.

How would you describe your purpose in life? _____

How do you normally distinguish what is true from what is false? _____

What do you hope to accomplish and experience in your life before you die? _____

Will you try and obtain these things on your own, or will you allow Jesus to provide them for you? _____

Ask God to show you your purpose. Pray that you will be able to tell the difference between what is true and what is not. Ask the Lord for a meaningful life. Never forget that He is the one and only source of these three things.

Look a Little Closer

John 14:8–14

"Do you see it?" Jessica asked impatiently.

"No!" Greg cried in frustration. "All I see are a bunch of random dots. There's nothing else there."

Jessica tried to help once more. "You have to look past the picture—look through it. Try and focus your eyes as if you were looking way behind the picture."

Greg rolled his eyes and took a deep breath. "OK, I'll try again." Greg tried Jessica's suggestions but it still wasn't working. "It's no use. I just can't see it and I never will."

"But you've just got to," insisted Jessica. She thought for a moment and then said, "Here's one more idea." Jessica walked about ten feet behind the picture, which was sitting on an easel in the store, and said, "Now look just above the picture and focus on my face. Got it? OK, now without changing the focus of your eyes, slowly point your eyes back at the picture."

Greg followed Jessica's instructions to the letter. He focused on Jessica's face and then lowered his eyes toward the picture. "I see it!" he cheered. "I see it!" It's three-dimensional and it just pops right out at you. Wow! I had no idea what I was missing!"

When Greg learned to take his eyes off the picture and focus on Jessica, he saw the three-dimensional image he had been missing. Before, all he saw was a two-dimensional mess.

In today's passage, Philip is having trouble seeing God. His eyes have not yet been able to see what Jesus has been trying to show him all along. Jesus explains, "Philip, take your eyes off everything else and look at me. When you look at me, you will see God because the Father is in me. Everything I say and everything I do is a perfect reflection of Him and His work." Hopefully, Philip was able to refocus and take his walk with Jesus into a new dimension.

Sometimes the ordinariness of life and the problems we face can blur our vision. We can't see God and we feel weak and powerless in our Christian walk. What do you do when this happens to you? It's time to refocus. It's time to look past the two-dimensional life you are living here on earth and focus on the face of Jesus, who is behind the scenes, quietly working things out in His own way, in another dimension. When you focus on Jesus and then point your eyes back at your life, you will see God working in you.

Name some areas of life where you long to see God working in you. _____

Name some areas of your life where you already know God is working. _____

God longs for you to know that He lives in you and works in you, in spite of the circumstances that you see and feel around you. Take your eyes off of what's happening down here on earth and refocus on Jesus. Pray that He will help you to see Him in your life and in your world. For further study, read Colossians 3:2.

What's Gotten into You?

John 14:25–31

> "Logan, what's gotten into you?" his mother asked as he walked past her with his head in the clouds. "You never wear nice clothes like that to school. Your hair is combed, and you smell nice. What's going on?"
>
> Logan said, "Nothing, Mom. I just thought I would look nice, you know?" Logan grabbed his books and headed for the bus stop. When he arrived, he could see Shelley coming down the road from her house. His heart skipped a beat.
>
> "Good morning, Shelley," he said sweetly. "Can I carry your books for you?"
>
> "Sure, Logan." Shelley replied. "You look nice today."
>
> "Thanks," Logan said. "So do you. Hey, listen. I was thinking. My big brother has two tickets to a concert next Thursday night. Would you like to go?"
>
> Shelley said, "I thought you played basketball on Thursday nights. You never miss basketball."
>
> Logan said, "I'd miss it for you."

Yuck. Logan used to be a normal guy. Now he's in love with Shelley, and he's doing things differently. What's gotten into him? *Love.*

In today's passage, Jesus said that if you love Him, you will act differently. You will be obedient to His commands. He doesn't say, "If you obey My commands, it proves that you love Me." Instead, Jesus says, "If you love Me, you will (automatically) keep My commands." There's a big difference between these two statements. The first says that obedience proves love. The second says that obedience is a by-product of love. If you love Jesus, obedience will come naturally.

Your relationship with Jesus should be based on one thing: *love,* not obligation. If you love Jesus, you will naturally do the things that He commands. You will sacrifice your time to be with Him every day. You will ask His advice. You will not hesitate to give money, time, and effort to others. You will keep your thought life pure. You will honor your parents and be honest with them. You will be patient with your little brother. You will be nice to your teachers. You will do many other things simply because you love Jesus and want to please Him.

Which of God's commands do you obey because you love Him? _____

Which commands do you obey out of obligation? _____

Which commands do you disobey? _____

Your answers to the second two questions will help you see where your love for Jesus needs to improve. Ask God to help you love Jesus more. Pray that you would serve Him and obey Him out of love and not obligation. Before long, your life will be very different. People will ask, "What's gotten into you?" For further study, read 1 Corinthians 13.

Weekly Bible Study and Prayer Review

Bible Study

Look back through some of the Scriptures you read this week. Write down the one verse or passage that God used to speak to you.

_____

_____

_____

_____

Memorize this verse or passage. You can do it if you spend just
a few minutes saying it to yourself.

Now, think of at least one situation you will probably face soon in which you could use this Scripture to help you make the right decision. Write down that situation below.

_____

Quote the Scripture when you face this situation, and live by it.

Prayer Time

Take a few moments to praise God for who He is.
Now take a few moments to thank God for things He has done for you.
Now ask God to make you into the person He wants you to be.
Ask God to use you to help others become closer to God.

Below is your prayer list for the week. Keep it updated each week. If your prayer isn't answered this week, carry it over to next week's list.

Request	Date of Original Request	Date Answered
_____	__/__/__	__/__/__
_____	__/__/__	__/__/__
_____	__/__/__	__/__/__
_____	__/__/__	__/__/__
_____	__/__/__	__/__/__
_____	__/__/__	__/__/__
_____	__/__/__	__/__/__
_____	__/__/__	__/__/__

Pray for the things on your list and trust God to provide.
Forgive anyone you have not yet forgiven.
Ask God to forgive you for any unconfessed sin in your life.
Ask God to keep you out of trouble with sin.
Acknowledge that God is in complete control of your life
and will take care of everything.

Don't Lose Your Head

John 14:15–31

Patricia placed her sack of groceries in the backseat. She sat down, put on her seat belt, and placed the key in the ignition. That's when it happened.

BOOOOOM! The explosion in Patricia's ears came simultaneously with the jolt to the back of her head. I've been shot! Patricia thought, panicking. She reached up to feel the place where she had been hit and all she felt was thick goo. My head has been blown wide open! she told herself, and then she immediately passed out.

Sometime later, she awoke, still in her same position in the car. No one had noticed her plight. She reached again for the back of her head and felt the wet, sticky substance. My brains are falling out. I've got to hold them in until someone comes to help. Patricia sat, petrified with fear that the slightest movement would kill her instantly. Finally, an employee of the grocery store noticed that Patricia had not moved for some time. He looked through the window and noticed that a can of biscuits from her grocery sack had exploded. The dough was all over the back of her head.[49]

Patricia thought she was losing her mind, but in reality nothing was wrong. Instead of being at peace, she went to pieces.

In today's passage, Jesus told His disciples that the Holy Spirit would give them peace. Jesus said, "Don't let your hearts be troubled, and don't be afraid because I am giving you real peace—not the kind of peace the world offers, but true and lasting peace." He does this by allowing His Spirit, the Holy Spirit, to live inside the heart of every Christian. When worry and fear strikes the rest of the world, the true believer can still experience peace because God is present. God is in control. God cares.

You probably get uptight and lose your head over a variety of things. During these times, it is easy to allow your feelings to take control. You feel like God is not aware of your problems. You feel as if your prayers fall on deaf ears. You feel that perhaps God does not care about your plight. You feel like you will never experience peace. Don't let your feelings determine how you react. Your feelings can betray you. Patricia felt like her brains were falling out, but she was totally wrong. You can't depend on your feelings. Instead, you must depend on the Holy Spirit who lives inside you. Let Him be the source of your peace.

When do you feel like God doesn't care? _____

How often do you feel like your prayers go unanswered? _____

How do you typically act when you feel this way? _____

How can you learn to depend more on the Holy Spirit instead of your feelings? _____

Don't lose your head over your circumstances. Don't let your feelings take control. Ask God, who is right there inside you, to help you depend less on your feelings and more on His Spirit. Pray that you will experience His peace.

Houston, We Have a Problem

John 15:1–8

James Lovell and his crew on Apollo 13 had just finished a TV broadcast when something went wrong. The astronauts were performing a routine stirring of an oxygen tank, when suddenly, BANG!

"Houston, we have a problem," Lovell said nervously into his microphone. They were 250,000 miles from home, all alone, and losing oxygen fast. Ninety minutes after the explosion, one oxygen tank was completely empty, and the second was in danger of doing the same. Without oxygen, the men would not be able to breathe, and they would die. Without oxygen, the ship would lose power and simply float in space until the end of time. Without oxygen, they could do nothing.

Mission Control feverishly hashed out a contingency plan with the astronauts to save their lives. Hundreds of obstacles stood in their way, but they all worked together to make sure that the precious oxygen would last long enough to get the men home. When they finally attempted a very questionable reentry procedure, the ship lost communications with the ground for four full minutes as the world waited in anticipation. Suddenly, the landing capsule appeared, floating gently into the ocean. When the doors opened, three men breathed lungs full of fresh oxygen—something they previously had taken for granted.

Oxygen is something we take for granted every day, and yet without it we can do nothing. In today's passage, Jesus explains that without Him, we can do nothing. He is as valuable to us as the air we breathe.

Do you hold your breath when you go to school? Of course not. You have to breathe. But do you take Jesus to school with you? Do you study like Jesus would; treat your teachers like Jesus would; tell your friends about Jesus? You don't hold your breath whenever you're at home, so why would you leave Jesus out of your family life? Do you honor your father and mother; treat your siblings with patience; take care of your chores on time? You don't stop breathing when you enter your room, but do you take Jesus with you to your private places? Do you take every thought captive and make it obedient to Jesus? When no one else is looking, do you still do what Jesus would do?

No matter what you think, say, and do—you are breathing oxygen. No matter what you think, say, and do—Jesus should be the reason for it. Honor Him; serve Him; share Him. This is the meaning and purpose of life.

List some areas of your life where Jesus is in control. _____

List some areas of your life where Jesus is not in control. _____

What can you do to allow Jesus to have control of these areas? _____

Don't leave Jesus out of anything. Let Him have and be a part of every facet of your life. Ask God to help you yield control to Jesus in the areas you listed above. You'll breathe easier when you make living for Jesus a moment-by-moment habit.

To Die For

John 15:9–17

A young teenage girl was diagnosed with a rare blood disease. The doctors gave her only one hope of surviving until her sixteenth birthday. She needed a blood transfusion from a donor with a perfect match. After an intensive search of blood donor databases, it became apparent that the only viable donor for the girl was her six-year-old brother, David.

The parents sat down with David and said, "Son, your sister is very sick. The only way she will get better is if we take some blood out of your body and put it into hers. Would you be willing to do that?" David was very quiet and asked his parents if he could take a walk to think about it. The boy walked outside and paced up and down the sidewalk while his parents watched through the front window. Finally, he came back inside and said, "I'll do it. I'll do it because I love my sister."

The next day, doctors connected David and his sister to a machine. David and his sister lay down side by side as the life-giving blood began to flow. Dad sat next to David, and Mom sat next to his sister. After about five minutes, the little boy turned to his father and said, "Dad, when do I die?"[50]

David thought giving blood to his sister meant he would die, and yet he was still willing to help his sister. This little boy illustrated the greatest love of all. He was willing to give his life. He was willing to die so that someone else could live.

In today's passage, Jesus challenged us with a new command to have the same love for each other as this little boy had for his sister. Jesus did not command us to do something that He was not willing to do Himself. The very next day He would willingly allow Himself to be beaten and crucified for us so that we could live. He asks us to follow His example and love our Christian brothers and sisters so much that we would be willing to die for them.

Love is not a feeling. Love is an unselfish act or acts that you *do* for someone else with no thought of what will happen to you or what reward you might receive. Love is helping your parents when you aren't asked. Love is spending your own money to provide food and clothing for a hungry child in another country. Love is holding your tongue when someone else hurts you. Love is offering to give up your Saturday afternoon plans to baby-sit your little sister. Love is giving every moment of your life to sharing Jesus with others. Love is losing your life, if necessary, so that others can live.

Who around you needs to be shown this kind of love? _____

What specific things can you do to illustrate your love? _____

Ask God to help you love every single person around you. Pray for the opportunity to express that love in unselfish acts that help others see Jesus. People will be drawn to Jesus when you live out this kind of love. It's to die for.

What People Think

John 15:18–16:4

Many years ago in ancient China, the story goes that a father and son were walking down the road with their donkey. As they traveled, a person going the other way said, "How silly! You have a strong donkey who could be ridden, and yet the two of you walk."

After the man's comments, the father and son climbed on the donkey and began riding him. Before long, they came upon another traveler who said, "How cruel! No donkey that size should ever bear the weight of two grown men."

The son then hopped off the donkey and allowed his father to ride while he walked beside him. They met yet another traveler with another opinion. "How selfish!" he bellowed. "What father would force his son to walk while he rides a donkey?"

The father and son sighed and switched places. As they rounded a bend, an approaching traveler cried, "How rude! How could a son force his old father to walk while he rides?"

The son hopped down, and they both realized they only had one choice left. Together, the two men bent down and struggled with all their might. They continued down the road, carrying the donkey.

This father and son learned the hard way that they couldn't please everyone. By responding to every criticism, they spent most of their trip under a donkey.

In today's passage, Jesus warns us that we will face immense criticism from others. If people criticized, hated, and finally killed Jesus, then we can expect similar treatment. Jesus explained that when this form of persecution comes, we are not to respond to the criticism by changing our message. Instead, we are to become even bolder through the Holy Spirit and spread the good news of Jesus even more.

Criticism and persecution will strike you in many forms. If you have family members who are not Christians, they may belittle you for believing in God or attending church. Perhaps you have experienced the biting words of a fellow student at school who ridiculed your faith. Maybe someone poked fun at you for carrying your Bible or praying at lunch. You might even know what it feels like to have someone hate you for the message you proclaim. Don't change your message, and don't lose heart. Jesus knows how you feel. He's been there. His Spirit will help you continue to share the good news about Him.

Have you ever changed your behavior because of someone else's criticism? _____

Have you ever backed away from sharing Jesus because of what someone else might say or do? _____

How would your life be different if you always did what was right regardless of persecution? _____

Ask God to help you get the donkey of criticism off your back. Pray that you will follow Jesus, and not the faultfinding of others. Make a conscious choice to follow the Spirit's leading no matter where it may take you or what others may think.

It's an Inside Job

John 16:5–15

Karla was apprehensive, but she felt strongly that the Lord was in this moment. As part of an assignment for her youth group, she had to go to someone's home and share Jesus. She drew a deep breath and prepared to ring the doorbell.

When the door opened, Karla couldn't believe her eyes. Inside, a birthday party was in full swing, and there were at least ten adults and as many children in the house. Karla started to apologize and walk away, but she was invited inside.

She sat down on the couch with the woman of the house, who asked her why she had come. Trembling, Karla looked to her left and her right. "Everyone else seems to be busy. I guess I can do this with one person. Here goes." Karla opened her mouth and began to explain the story of Jesus—how He died on the cross to provide forgiveness for sin. As she spoke, she did not see the seven other adults slowly walk up to the couch behind her, listening to every word.

When Karla finished, she said, "Would you like to ask Jesus into your life?" To her surprise, eight people said, "Yes."

If you had asked Karla to share her faith with eight adults, she would have never done it. The Holy Spirit, however, wanted those people to hear the gospel. The Spirit planned that birthday party and Karla's timely visit.

In today's passage, Jesus explained to His disciples that the Holy Spirit has two primary roles in situations where a believer witnesses to an unbeliever. First, the Holy Spirit is the one who convicts the unbeliever of sin. Second, the Holy Spirit gives you an understanding of the truth so that you will know how to witness to each unbeliever specifically. In other words, the Holy Spirit does all the work. You simply have to be available for Him to use you.

You don't have to fear sharing Jesus with someone else for two reasons. First, you are not responsible for the other person's response. The Holy Spirit is the one who will convict the person and urge him or her to accept Jesus. The Holy Spirit has likely been working on this person long before you came along and will continue to work on this person long after you share your faith. Second, you do not need to worry about what to say. If you pray and read God's Word, He will make sure that the Spirit provides you with the words to say.

Do you fear sharing your faith with others? _____

Why? _____

What role does the Holy Spirit have in alleviating your fears? _____

How can you become more sensitive to the Holy Spirit's guidance in witnessing situations?
_____

Don't let fear shut your mouth. Ask God to make you bold in witnessing to others around you. Let His Spirit do the leading. You just provide the mouth, and let Him do the rest of the work.

Blood Bath

John 16:16–33

Dr. Felix Ruh agonized over the loss of his granddaughter. In the days before microscopes and a belief in germs, no one knew what caused it. Ruh, however, believed a certain type of germ had caused it, and he was determined to isolate the cause of his granddaughter's death.

Working with Louis Pasteur, Ruh grew a large culture of black diphtheria germs. He took the germs and deliberately infected twenty horses. Within a short time, nineteen of those horses died from the disease. The twentieth horse became deathly ill and everyone feared that it, too, would die. The horse held on for a few more days while the two men waited and watched to see what would happen.

Surprisingly, the horse's fever began to drop, and within twenty-four hours it was back on its feet and taking water and food. When Dr. Ruh realized that the horse had survived the infection, he killed it. He siphoned every last drop of blood from the horse into a container, which he and Pasteur took to a hospital in Paris. There, they injected the blood of the horse into three hundred babies who had contracted diphtheria and were expected to die. They waited, and to everyone's amazement, all but three of the babies recovered from the disease and went home to be with their families.[52]

Why did the horse blood cure the babies? The horse had overcome the diphtheria, and his immune system had developed a defense against the disease. Dr. Ruh transferred blood to the babies so that they, too, could overcome the disease.

Jesus ends today's passage with the statement, "In this world you will face many troubles, but be encouraged, because I have overcome the world." When you become a Christian, you receive the blood of Jesus, who overcame the world.

Jesus' blood overcomes the deadly consequences of sin and cures you by giving you forgiveness. The reason you have the right to go to God and ask Him to forgive you is because of the blood that Jesus freely gave away on the cross. His blood cleanses you of sin once and for all. You don't ever have to ask for forgiveness of the same sin twice. When you have sinned, and the guilt begins to overcome your conscience, simply go to Jesus and kneel at the foot of the cross. Admit that you have sinned, and you will be forgiven.

Do you carry any guilty feelings for something you have done? _____

Of what are you guilty? _____

Would you like to be free of these feelings of guilt? _____

Have you specifically admitted this sin to God? _____

If you have not already, confess your sin to God. Be specific—let Him know what you did and that you know it was wrong. Once you have done so, God will completely cleanse you of your sin and take away the guilt. For further study, read Hebrews 10:19–23.

Weekly Bible Study and Prayer Review

Bible Study

Look back through some of the Scriptures you read this week. Write down the one verse or passage that God used to speak to you.

_____

_____

_____

_____

*Memorize this verse or passage. You can do it if you spend just
a few minutes saying it to yourself.*

Now, think of at least one situation you will probably face soon in which you could use this Scripture to help you make the right decision. Write down that situation below.

_____

Quote the Scripture when you face this situation, and live by it.

Prayer Time

Take a few moments to praise God for who He is.
Now take a few moments to thank God for things He has done for you.
Now ask God to make you into the person He wants you to be.
Ask God to use you to help others become closer to God.

Below is your prayer list for the week. Keep it updated each week. If your prayer isn't answered this week, carry it over to next week's list.

Request	Date of Original Request	Date Answered
_____	___/___/___	___/___/___
_____	___/___/___	___/___/___
_____	___/___/___	___/___/___
_____	___/___/___	___/___/___
_____	___/___/___	___/___/___
_____	___/___/___	___/___/___
_____	___/___/___	___/___/___
_____	___/___/___	___/___/___
_____	___/___/___	___/___/___

Pray for the things on your list and trust God to provide.
Forgive anyone you have not yet forgiven.
Ask God to forgive you for any unconfessed sin in your life.
Ask God to keep you out of trouble with sin.
*Acknowledge that God is in complete control of your life
and will take care of everything.*

The Center of Attention

John 17:1–5

When a group of children were asked to say something to God, here is what they wrote.

- Are You really invisible or is that just a trick?
- I think about You sometimes even when I'm not praying.
- I bet it is very hard for You to love all of everybody in the whole world. There are only four people in our family and I can never do it.
- We read that Thomas Edison made light. But in Sunday school they said You did it. So I bet he stole Your idea.
- I do not think anybody could be a better God. Well, I just want You to know but I am not just saying that because You are God.
- I didn't think orange went with purple until I saw the sunset You made Tuesday. That was cool.
- I don't ever feel alone since I found out about You.

Kids ask and say some of the funniest things. These kids had a writing assignment that made God the center of attention. God has an assignment for you that will make Him the center of attention too.

In today's passage, Jesus prayed to His Father in a garden on the night before His death. He made a particular comment that really sticks out. He said that eternal life is to know God the Father and His Son, Jesus. He also used the word *glory* or *glorify* several times. Do you know what that means? To glorify something is to make it the center of attention.

Your purpose in life is to glorify God. In other words, no matter where you go or what you do, you should make God the center of attention. God wants you to do this so that people who don't know Him will have the chance to meet Him personally. How do you make God the center of attention in all that you do? You can pray at meals and acknowledge that God has provided your food. You might start a conversation with someone by saying, "God is so cool. Today He . . ." You could tell your friends about an answered prayer. You can wear a T-shirt or bracelet with a Christian theme or message.

How can you make Jesus the center of attention at home? _____

At school? _____ *At work?* _____

At a party? _____ *While you drive?* _____

Ask God to help you glorify Him in all that you do wherever you are. Make Him the center of attention so that those around you will have a chance to meet Him. For further study, read Proverbs 3:6 and 1 Corinthians 10:31.

Pure for Sure

John 17:6–19

A young boy on the farm with his grandfather noticed an old, wooden box leaning against the big, red barn. He picked it up, noticing that the bottom of the box was full of tiny square holes, most of which were plugged with dirt. "Grandpa, what's this?" he asked curiously. His grandfather explained that it was a sieve once used to strain the water in the creek for gold.

With a twinkle in his eye, the grandfather challenged the boy to take the dirty old sieve down to the creek, lower the sieve in the water, and bring it back. The boy accepted the dare and ran to the creek. Of course, by the time he returned, the water was completely gone. The grandfather invited the boy to try it again. This time he ran even faster, but still he was unable to collect one drop of water. After the third try, the boy said, "Grandpa, it's just not possible."

The old man smiled and replied, "Look at the sieve. It used to be full of dirt. Now it is clean because you ran the water through it so many times."

The point of Grandpa's challenge was not to see how much water the boy could collect, but to clean the sieve. The sieve was purified, or *sanctified*.

In today's passage, Jesus prayed that His disciples would be sanctified. He added that it could only happen through the Word of God, or the Bible. Think of the followers of Jesus as the sieve, often becoming dirty with sin. The Bible is like pure water. When we submerge ourselves in the Bible and allow its cleansing effects to go through us, we will become clean. We may not remember everything we read, just like the sieve did not hold any water, but we will be sanctified.

You may sometimes feel that reading the Bible is a waste of time. Like the boy running back and forth to the creek, you wonder if you should just give up. Remember, the reason you spend time in God's Word is not so you can memorize everything you read or be zapped by some amazing experience, but to cleanse you through and through on the inside. Every word you read is alive and works its way deep into the crevices of your heart where sin still tries to hold on. It loosens the dirt of your evil thoughts and ways and challenges you to be more like Jesus.

Do you ever feel like reading the Bible is a waste of time? _____ *Why?* _____

What do you think your life would be like if you never spent time in God's Word?

_____

How do you think your life would change if you spent more time in God's Word?

_____

You may not see it at first, but every moment you spend with God in His Word is invaluable. Ask God to give you a greater desire to read the Bible. Pray for the wisdom to see how God's Word is working in your life to sanctify you. Don't give up. You're becoming pure for sure.

All for One

John 17:20–26

> They were ready. Their eyes were focused on the 100 yards before them and the finish line at the end. They poised themselves and listened for the sound of the gun.
>
> All nine contestants wanted to win. All nine had an equal chance. Each of them wanted to be able to go home and say, "I won a gold medal at the Special Olympics." The time had come. The moment was now.
>
> The gun sounded, and they bolted off the starting line. One young boy, however, stumbled on his first step and tumbled to the ground head over heels on the track. Knowing that all hope of winning was gone, he began to cry. The others heading down the track heard the boy's cry. They hesitated, and then they stopped. They turned around and saw the boy sitting on the track in tears. Then not one but all the contestants walked back to the boy. A girl with Down syndrome leaned over and kissed him. Others picked the boy up. Together, all nine linked arms and walked across the finish line as one.
>
> The crowd stood on its feet and cheered wildly. For ten solid minutes, the nine winners received a standing ovation.[53]

These Special Olympic contestants valued unity over competition. They sacrificed their individual goals for the good of the group.

Jesus wants the same kind of unity in your youth group and your church. In today's passage, Jesus actually said a prayer for you—for *you*. Since this is the only place in the Bible where Jesus said a prayer for believers who are not yet born, it must be extremely important. What was the focus of Jesus' prayer? Unity. Jesus prayed that all Christians, including you, would be one. No competition. No division. Just one big happy family.

Jesus' one prayer for the future Church is that all are one. This says a lot about you and your youth group—you and your church. God wants you to be unified with every other Christian brother and sister you know. Unity is not easy, either. It takes work. You've got to forgive others in your church who have hurt you. You must learn to help encourage someone else when she is down. When you see division between two youth group members, you need to do all you can to make peace. When you hear gossip, you've got to stamp it out at the source. You need to be on your knees, like Jesus, praying for unity in your church.

Is your youth group or church living in perfect unity? _____

List some problem areas that are causing disunity. _____

What can you do to help bring about more unity? _____

Pray that God would bring unity to your youth group and church. Be an answer to Jesus' prayer by doing your part to unify those around you. Sacrifice your individual goals and interests for the good of the group.

Yours or Mine?

Matthew 26:36–46; Mark 14:32–42; Luke 22:39–46

"If you're going to make the team," the coach insisted, "Here's what it's going to take. You've got to run the mile in under six minutes. You must be able to do seventy-five push-ups and fifty sit-ups. You'll have to sprint forty yards in less than six seconds. You have to bench at least 150 pounds. Any questions?"

The guys trying out for the boys' track team looked at each other in silence. They knew it was going to be tough. They knew that some of them wouldn't make it. Roland decided right then and there that he was going to make the team no matter what it took.

For the next three weeks, Roland did push-ups and sit-ups every morning. He ran two miles before breakfast and three miles after dinner. He went to the weight room after school every day. One evening after dinner as he headed outside to run, Roland's older sister asked, "Why do you like running and exercising so much?"

Roland responded, "Right now, I don't want to run. I'd rather be watching TV. I don't want to do push-ups, sit-ups, or weight training either. But I want to make the track team, so I'll do what I don't want to get what I want."

In today's passage, Jesus didn't want to suffer and die on the cross, but He did want to do His Father's will. After praying earnestly on three separate occasions, Jesus accepted His Father's will. He chose to do what He didn't want in order to get what He really wanted—the satisfaction that He had successfully completed what His Father had asked Him to do. Jesus illustrated the most important prayer of all time, "Father, I don't want what I want. I want what You want."

Your spirit is willing to be obedient to God, but your flesh is weak. What is the solution? Prayer. Jesus said to pray so that you will not fall into temptation. When you pray, your spirit becomes strong. Your will conforms to God's will. When you don't pray, the earthly desires of your body become strong. Your will conflicts with God's will. You choose whether your spirit or your body wins the fight. You hold the answer in your folded (or unfolded) hands.

Do you ever avoid doing things you know you should because you don't feel like it?

_____

What things do you avoid doing? _____

Why don't you feel like doing them? _____

How can prayer help you do the things you know you should? _____

Spend some time in prayer strengthening your spirit. Let God conform your will to His. Pray about those things you know you should be doing. Keep praying until you can say, "Not my will, but Yours be done."

Kiss of Death

Matthew 26:47–50; Mark 14:43–45; Luke 22:47–48; John 18:1–3

Once upon a time a turtle lay sleeping peacefully on the shore of slow-moving river. He opened his eyes groggily just in time to see a large scorpion make its way toward him.

The turtle sprang to life and was about to jump into the river when the scorpion spoke. "Please, Mr. Turtle. Won't you give me a ride across the river? I can't swim, but I need to reach the other side."

The turtle replied, "Why would I risk my life for you? You will just sting me, and I will die."

The scorpion shook his head and said, "No, Mr. Turtle, I would not. Besides, if I stung you what good would that do me? You would drown, and we would both die."

The turtle thought for a moment about the scorpion's logic and eventually changed his mind. "OK, scorpion. Hop on. Let's go."

The two were halfway across when, without warning, the scorpion stung the turtle. Just before the turtle slipped under the water, he said, "Why did you sting me? Now we both will die."

The scorpion shrugged and said, "I couldn't help it. I'm a scorpion."[54]

The scorpion did what came naturally, even though it cost him his life. He could have lived a long and happy life if only he had temporarily resisted his natural inclinations.

In today's passage, a scorpion named Judas Iscariot led an army of soldiers to the garden where Jesus often went to pray. Pretending to greet Jesus, he gave Him the traditional kiss on the cheek, which normally symbolized friendship and allegiance. Instead, Judas offered a kiss of death, betraying the trust of a friend for his own selfish reasons. That same night, Judas hung himself. Judas could have experienced eternal life if he had resisted his natural inclinations and become a true follower of Jesus.

Inside of your body are two natures: the old you that wants to do evil for your own selfish reasons, and the new you that has been transformed by Jesus. These two natures are in constant battle for control of your will. You choose which one you will follow. When you give in to your natural inclinations, you may experience temporary pleasure, but you are being deceived by a kiss of death. When you submit to God's Spirit inside you, you experience a lasting and pleasing life.

Have you ever done something because you thought it would feel good, only to feel the sting of sin after you were done? _____ Explain. _____

What has this experience taught you? _____

Don't be deceived by the kiss of death—the temporary pleasures of sin. Ask God to help you resist the temptation to give in to sin. Pray for the wisdom to be able to tell the difference between the good and evil that battle for control within you. For further study, read Romans 8:5–17.

Lend Me Your Ear

Matthew 26:51–56; Mark 14:46–52; Luke 22:49–53; John 18:4–11

Something happened tonight that I will never forget. I was just doing my job, serving the high priest, when my life changed forever.

I stood next to the high priest when we went to arrest Jesus of Nazareth. When we arrived, Jesus almost looked as if He were expecting us. As we were explaining why we were there, one of His disciples pulled out a small sword and lunged for the high priest. My boss ducked behind me, and before I knew what happened, the sword struck me full force. I fell to my knees in agony, holding my head and staring at the ground where my ear lay in the dirt. Jesus said something, but I couldn't hear what. Then, He reached down and touched the right side of my head. I felt this tingly sensation, and then the pain vanished instantly. Suddenly, I could hear again. He had healed me completely.

For the rest of the weekend, all I could think about was what Jesus had done for me. I came to arrest Him and get Him killed, and He knew it. Yet He took the time to reach out and touch me where it hurt. Why would He do that? Why would He care about me?

Jesus touched Malchus. He loved him and cared for him, even though Malchus did not believe in Jesus. That night probably changed Malchus's life forever.

In today's passage, you read the four accounts of what happened that night. Why do you think Jesus showed such compassion for Malchus? Malchus did not believe in Jesus. In fact, Malchus was there to help arrest Jesus and get Him crucified. Yet, when Jesus saw that Malchus was in need, He reached out and met that need. He touched Malchus where it hurt. He made things better. He loved Malchus and cared for Him just like he was one of His own disciples.

When you see someone in need—even if the person is not a Christian—God wants you to reach out and touch that person's life. Don't discriminate between Christians and non-Christians when it comes to showing compassion. Treat everyone the same. Your kindness will be obvious to those who don't believe in Jesus, and they will wonder why you are so generous. They will want to know the source of the love in your heart. This will give you a perfect opportunity to tell them about Jesus.

Do you try and meet the needs of others around you? _____

How are you meeting the needs of your Christian brothers and sisters? _____

How are you meeting the needs of those who do not believe in Jesus? _____

Practice loving and caring for non-Christians in the same way that Jesus cared for Malchus. Ask God to help you see and meet the needs of those who do not believe in Him. Your compassion just may get their attention long enough for you to say, "Lend me your ear, and I'll tell you about Jesus."

Weekly Bible Study and Prayer Review

Bible Study

Look back through some of the Scriptures you read this week. Write down the one verse or passage that God used to speak to you.

_____

_____

_____

_____

Memorize this verse or passage. You can do it if you spend just
a few minutes saying it to yourself.

Now, think of at least one situation you will probably face soon in which you could use this Scripture to help you make the right decision. Write down that situation below.

_____

Quote the Scripture when you face this situation, and live by it.

Prayer Time

Take a few moments to praise God for who He is.
Now take a few moments to thank God for things He has done for you.
Now ask God to make you into the person He wants you to be.
Ask God to use you to help others become closer to God.

Below is your prayer list for the week. Keep it updated each week. If your prayer isn't answered this week, carry it over to next week's list.

Request	Date of Original Request	Date Answered
_____	__/__/__	__/__/__
_____	__/__/__	__/__/__
_____	__/__/__	__/__/__
_____	__/__/__	__/__/__
_____	__/__/__	__/__/__
_____	__/__/__	__/__/__
_____	__/__/__	__/__/__
_____	__/__/__	__/__/__
_____	__/__/__	__/__/__

Pray for the things on your list and trust God to provide.
Forgive anyone you have not yet forgiven.
Ask God to forgive you for any unconfessed sin in your life.
Ask God to keep you out of trouble with sin.
Acknowledge that God is in complete control of your life
and will take care of everything.

The Truth Hurts

John 18:12–24

The story of George Washington and the cherry tree is false. It was a story invented by a parson named Mason Locke Weems to illustrate the first President's character. However, there is a true story about George Washington that is similar.

Washington's mother owned a colt. She loved the animal dearly, but it was a wild and unruly thing. One day, George decided he wanted to ride the colt. He cornered the colt with some of his brothers and bridled it. George jumped onto the horse, and the battle was on. The colt bucked and jumped, once even standing straight up on its hind legs in an attempt to throw off young George. The horse fought valiantly, but George managed to maintain his position.

Suddenly, the horse dropped to the ground in sheer exhaustion and collapsed. A moment later the colt was dead. George's antics had killed one of his mother's favorite animals. As George and his brothers walked back into the house, his mother said, "How is my colt doing?"

Without a moment's hesitation, George replied, "He is dead, Mother, and I am the one who killed him."[55]

George's mother was very upset that George killed her colt, but she told her son that she was honored that he told the truth, even though it hurt.

In today's passage, Jesus told the truth when it hurt—literally. Annas, one of the high priests, was questioning Jesus about His teachings and His disciples. Jesus, knowing Annas's true motives, said, "Annas, you know what I'm all about. I have taught openly since the beginning. Why are you asking Me these questions?" Even though Jesus just spoke the truth, a man reached over and slapped Him hard in the face. Jesus asked, "Why did you hit Me when I told the truth?"

Sometimes telling the truth can hurt. If you do something that you know your parents will be angry about, you are tempted to lie and place the blame on someone else. You may find yourself afraid to share your faith with someone, even though you know it is true, because you fear being rejected or laughed at. When your community or government supports something that is wrong, you figure it is easier to keep your mouth shut than to stand up for what is right. Face it, the truth hurts.

Describe a time when you told a lie to cover up for a mistake you made. _____

Describe a time when you failed to witness to someone or stand up for the truth because you feared the pain of rejection. _____

Why do you lie or keep quiet when you know you should tell the truth? _____

Ask God to help you become a man or woman of truth. Don't ever be afraid to tell the truth, even when you know it is going to hurt. You may get a slap in the face like Jesus did, but truth is always going to win in the end.

Major Mistake

Matthew 26:57–68; Mark 14:53–65; Luke 22:66–71

A prominent surgeon lay peacefully sleeping at his home in the middle of the night when the phone rang. Startled from his slumber, he answered the phone. A small child had been in a terrible accident, and the surgeon was the only one who could help. He quickly got ready and headed for the hospital.

The surgeon slowed for a traffic light at an intersection in a rough neighborhood. Without warning, the car door opened and a man pulled the surgeon out of the car. The surgeon pleaded with him, trying in vain to explain the urgency of the situation. The man would not listen and drove off in the doctor's car. The surgeon frantically tried to find a taxi or a phone.

One hour later, when the doctor finally managed to arrive by taxi, he rushed inside. A nurse told the doctor that he was too late. The little boy had died only minutes earlier. The nurse told the doctor that the father was in the chapel, weeping and asking, "Why didn't the doctor come?"

The surgeon walked down to the chapel to comfort the man and explain to him why he had not arrived sooner. As the doctor opened the door to the chapel, he saw a man sitting on the front row with tears in his eyes. It was the man who had stolen his car.

The father wanted desperately to be with his son, but in his hurry to get there, he threw away his one chance for his only son to live.

In today's passage, Jesus stood trial before a group of men who hated Him. They wanted Him dead. They held a mock trial and asked Him plainly if He was the long-awaited Messiah. Jesus looked them in the eye and said, "Yes, I am. And one day you will see Me coming on the clouds of heaven with My Father." The men, who were supposed to be religious, went into a frenzy. They condemned Jesus to death. What they did not realize was that they had just thrown away their only chance of finding true life.

You may not reject Jesus the way these men did, but you may be rejecting Him in other ways. For instance, do you obey your parents like Jesus did, or do you dishonor them by disobeying them? Are you honest and truthful with your schoolwork, or do you cheat a little to make things easier? Do you always tell the truth, or do you lie to cover your tracks? Do you follow God's leading, or do you go your own way?

List some habitual sins that you have trouble overcoming. _____

How have you tried to conquer these habits? _____

What is it going to take for you to give up this sinful behavior? _____

Sin is a choice, even when it involves a habit. If you choose to continue the sin instead of letting it go, you are rejecting Jesus' will for your life. Ask God to show you what areas of your life need changing. Pray that you would be innocent of rejecting Jesus. Make a habit of breaking bad habits.

Seize the Day

Matthew 26:69–75; Mark 14:66–72; Luke 22:54–62; John 18:25–27

The professor of a philosophy class at a major university was a devout atheist. Every year, after a long semester of lectures on the nonexistence of God, the professor would end his last class this way. He would hold up a piece of chalk, face his class of three hundred students, and say, "If anyone in here still believes in God, stand up!" No one ever dared to stand, including some timid Christians in the group. The professor would say, "If God were real, he could stop this piece of chalk from breaking when it hit the floor." With that, he would drop the chalk, and it would fall to the ground and shatter.

For twenty years, no one ever challenged the professor. One year, however, the professor stood up on the last day of class and said, "If anyone still believes in God, stand up!" One lone, bold Christian student stood up. The professor was dumbfounded. He said, "You fool! If God were real, he could keep this piece of chalk from breaking when it hits the floor." With that, he let go of the chalk. The piece of chalk bounced off his cuff, rolled down his pants leg onto his shoe, and gently landed unbroken on the floor. The professor, trembling from the experience, made a hasty exit from his classroom.

The Christian student seized the opportunity. Walking to the front of the class, he shared his faith in Jesus Christ with three hundred students.[56]

Why did it take so long for a Christian student to stand up for Jesus? How many Christians denied Jesus by remaining seated during the professor's challenge?

In today's passage, Peter denied Jesus. Three times someone clearly challenged Peter and his relationship to the Lord. Three times Peter denied that he even knew Jesus. After the third time, a rooster crowed, and Jesus looked Peter in the eye without saying a word. Peter, realizing what he had done, ran away and wept.

You can deny Jesus one of two ways. Like Peter, you can deny Jesus openly with your words when someone asks you if you are a Christian. Or, like the students at the university, you can deny Jesus by your silence when given the opportunity to share your faith. Both forms of denial are equally wrong. When people deny Jesus, they normally do it out of fear. They are afraid of what people will think, say, or do. You must realize, however, that God provides opportunities for you to stand up for Jesus for two reasons: (1) so you can grow stronger in your faith as you overcome fear, and (2) so others will realize that Jesus is alive and well today.

Describe a time when you denied Jesus with your words. _____

Describe a time when you denied Jesus with your silence. _____

How did you feel after you became aware that you denied your Lord? _____

What can you do in the future to stand up for Jesus? _____

Ask God to make you bold. Pray that you would recognize opportunities to stand up for Jesus. Seize the day and let Jesus become the center of attention.

Admit One

Matthew 27:1–10

> When I kept my mouth shut,
> My insides turned to mush.
> I felt sick all day long.
> Every day and night
> Your hand pressed hard against me.
> I had no strength at all.
> It felt like I was suffocating in the summer heat.
> Finally, I admitted my sin to you.
> I stopped hiding it.
> I said, "I will tell God what I have done."
> Then you forgave me
> And all the guilt went away.

This is a paraphrase of King David's words in Psalm 32:3–6. David's words illustrate how your life can waste away when you refuse to confess your sin to God.

In today's passage, Judas Iscariot realized he had sinned. However, he did not go to Jesus. He tried to clear his guilt by returning the money he was paid. When the priests refused to take the money back, Judas threw the money in the temple and walked away. He sauntered away in his remorse, but he never asked Jesus for forgiveness. Instead, he was so eaten with guilt that he committed suicide.

When you commit a sin, you experience feelings of guilt. Guilt is your body's way of telling you that you were wrong and you need to make things right. Guilt can come from God or from Satan. Guilt that comes from Satan tells you that God does not love you and will not forgive you. This form of guilt can lead to depression and even suicide. Godly guilt tells you that God loves you and will forgive you if you can simply confess your sin to God. Judas gave in to the wrong kind of guilt, and it killed him. Don't let that happen to you. Take your sin to God right now and allow Him to forgive you.

What sins do you feel guilt over? _____

Would you say the source of your guilt is God or Satan? _____

What can you do to get rid of these guilty feelings? _____

Don't be like Judas. Don't let ungodly guilt depress you and drive you away from God. You will never be free from those feelings until you admit your sin to God. Your ticket to freedom is just around the corner. Admit your sins to God, one by one, and He will forgive you and take the guilt away.

Bragging Rights

Matthew 27:11–14; Mark 15:1–5; Luke 23:1–5; John 18:28–38

"Mrs. Thomas said my English paper was the best one of all," Nancy bragged. "She said I chose a hard subject and handled it very well."

The others at the cafeteria table rolled their eyes, thinking, Here we go again. Miss Nancy is going to tell us why she is better than everybody else.

Nancy continued. "Who is everyone going to the prom with?" Before anyone could answer, she said, "I'm going with Doug. He asked me last Friday. He said he wouldn't consider taking anyone else but me. His father drives a limousine so we're going in style."

Nancy barely took a breath between bites. "My father says he is going to get me a red Corvette when I turn seventeen. It's going to have T-tops and tinted windows. He also said that if I ever get pulled over by a policeman, that I should just tell him who my father is and he'll let me off the hook. My father knows everyone. One time he . . ."

No one else ever had a chance to say a word. Nancy was so busy telling half-truths, trying to get everyone to like her, that she failed to see that her bragging made people dislike her.

In today's passage, Jesus had the perfect opportunity to brag. He stood in a trial that would determine whether He lived or died. Pilate asked Him, "Are you the King of the Jews?" Jesus simply said, "Yes." Jesus said relatively nothing after that. Pilate was amazed at how quiet Jesus was. Jesus could have said, "Yes, I'm a king. I'm the King of kings. I'm the Lord of lords. You should fall down on your face right this minute and worship Me because I made you. My Father could kill you right now if I asked Him to." Jesus didn't say any of these things. His words were few.

You often will be tempted to brag—to make yourself look better in someone else's eyes by talking about how great you are. Don't spend time talking about yourself. Don't think you have to defend yourself or make yourself look good by flapping your jaws. If someone says something untrue about you, don't waste a lot of breath trying to prove yourself. If you do well in school or in an extracurricular activity, don't flaunt it. Use your words to build up the image of God or someone else, not your own.

Do you ever brag? _____ How? _____

Do you think you are helping or hurting your image when you talk about yourself? ____

_____

The next time you are tempted to brag, what can you do differently? _____

Bite your tongue the next time you feel the need to boast. Ask God to help you to keep your words about yourself at a minimum. When you do talk, use your words to make God and others look good. Give away your bragging rights, and let God be the one to brag on you on the day you stand before Him.

Expect the Unexpected

Luke 23:6–12

Sully became a Christian when he was fourteen years old. His life changed completely. He began to see the world in a new light. For two years, he was happier than he had ever been before.

When he was sixteen, though, things changed. His parents started arguing a lot, and they were threatening divorce. Sully began to pray. He prayed hard. He prayed persistently, believing that God was going to make things right in his family.

Instead of getting better, though, things got worse. Sully's parents separated. Sully's older sister was so despondent over the family crisis that she turned to drugs. Sully never saw his father anymore. Sully's mother became a different person, always depressed and in her bedroom with the door closed. Sully changed too. He stopped praying. He stopped reading his Bible. He stopped going to church.

Before long, Sully drifted far away from Jesus. Inside he blamed God for what happened. He was no longer happy. He was bitter and disappointed with God.

Sully expected God to do things a certain way. When God didn't live up to Sully's expectations, his attitude changed. He sent Jesus away.

In today's passage, someone else was disappointed with Jesus. Pilate sent Jesus to King Herod, who was greatly pleased to see Him. Herod had wanted to meet Jesus for a long time. Herod expected Jesus to perform a miracle. He expected Jesus to answer his questions. Jesus did neither. Jesus was silent. Herod's attitude changed. He became disappointed with what he saw in Jesus, so he sent Him away.

Sometimes God does not live up to your expectations. You expect Him to answer a certain prayer, but He doesn't (at least not yet). You expect Him to protect your home, but your house burns down and you lose everything. You expect Him to help you with your grades, but you fail another test. You expect Him to keep your family together, but they get divorced anyway. You become disappointed with God. Don't be like Herod and turn Jesus away. Keep believing. Keep trusting. Wait on God to show you how everything is going to work out for the best. God loves you and cares about you. Don't let the trials of life turn you away from God.

Are you ever disappointed with God? _____ Explain. _____

How do you turn Jesus away when He does not live up to your expectations? _____

How can you continue to trust in God, even when you are disappointed in Him?

_____

Herod missed out by turning Jesus away. He missed the opportunity to really get to know Him and discover that Jesus loved him and would take care of him. Ask God—the same God you are sometimes disappointed in—to help you trust Him even when He does not do what you expect. Let go of your expectations, and learn to expect the unexpected from God.

Weekly Bible Study and Prayer Review

Bible Study

Look back through some of the Scriptures you read this week. Write down the one verse or passage that God used to speak to you.

_____

_____

_____

_____

Memorize this verse or passage. You can do it if you spend just a few minutes saying it to yourself.

Now, think of at least one situation you will probably face soon in which you could use this Scripture to help you make the right decision. Write down that situation below.

_____

Quote the Scripture when you face this situation, and live by it.

Prayer Time

Take a few moments to praise God for who He is.
Now take a few moments to thank God for things He has done for you.
Now ask God to make you into the person He wants you to be.
Ask God to use you to help others become closer to God.

Below is your prayer list for the week. Keep it updated each week. If your prayer isn't answered this week, carry it over to next week's list.

Request	Date of Original Request	Date Answered
_____	__/__/__	__/__/__
_____	__/__/__	__/__/__
_____	__/__/__	__/__/__
_____	__/__/__	__/__/__
_____	__/__/__	__/__/__
_____	__/__/__	__/__/__
_____	__/__/__	__/__/__
_____	__/__/__	__/__/__
_____	__/__/__	__/__/__

Pray for the things on your list and trust God to provide.
Forgive anyone you have not yet forgiven.
Ask God to forgive you for any unconfessed sin in your life.
Ask God to keep you out of trouble with sin.
Acknowledge that God is in complete control of your life and will take care of everything.

Don't Wash Your Hands

Matthew 27:15–26; Mark 15:6–15; Luke 23:13–25; John 18:39–19:16

Tanya, Sylvia, Holly, and Bethany were all watching a scary movie at Tanya's house, curled up under a blanket on the couch with all of the lights turned off. Every time something unexpected happened, they all screamed in unison—then laughed. They were having so much fun.

A scary scene ended, and the TV screen zoomed in on the faces of young children in another country who were starving to death. They lived in one-room straw houses and played in streets lined with raw sewage. Their chance of surviving to adulthood was very slim. According to the commercial spokesperson, if someone would be willing to donate $20 per month it would save the life of one of these children.

Sylvia sat up and said, "Hey, there are four of us here. Let's each put in $5 a month and send it to one of these children." Sylvia's suggestion was quickly shot down with a barrage of excuses from the other three including, "The kids probably never see your money," "I can't afford $5 each month," "How can $20 feed one child for an entire month?" Sylvia sighed. The commercial ended. The scary movie started again, and the starving children were forgotten.

Sylvia had a great idea. She and her friends could have helped save a child's life. But after all their excuses and doubts, they washed their hands of the whole idea.

In today's passage, Pilate washed his hands of another idea. He held the power to release Jesus so that He would not be crucified. He tried several times to convince the crowd that Jesus did not deserve to die. However, Pilate gave in to the shouts of the crowd. Pilate was worried about what his boss, Caesar, would think if he let a man claiming to be the "King of the Jews" go free. So, rather than take responsibility for his actions, Pilate washed his hands of the whole deal and turned Jesus over to be crucified.

When you see someone else in need, but all you do is change the TV channel or otherwise ignore what you see, you are washing your hands of Jesus. Jesus helped everyone He saw. He never turned anyone away who asked for His help. How can you turn away when you see someone in need? Maybe you can't sponsor a child in another country all by yourself, but perhaps you can get a few friends and do it together. When you see piles of trash along the road or in a local park near where you live, you can ignore what you see or get your youth group together to volunteer a Saturday to clean it up.

What needs do you see in your world? _____

How have you ignored doing your part to meet these needs? _____

What can you do to make a difference? _____

Ask God to show you what you can do to help others in their time of need. When He answers that prayer, don't wash your hands before you become involved. Wash your hands afterward because you got them dirty doing all you could do.

The Doormat

Matthew 27:27–31; Mark 15:16–20

> Jonathan grabbed the basketball as Adam locked the doors. The two headed for the basketball court, joining their teammates as the game of the century was about to begin.
>
> As the game started, it became apparent that the other team was playing dirty—throwing elbows, pushing, and tripping. The referees weren't calling many fouls, and Jonathan and Adam were getting more and more frustrated. As Adam went in for a layup, someone slammed into him and knocked him down. Adam couldn't take any more. He jumped up, turned to the perpetrator, and screamed, "Come on, big shot! Let's see what you've got."
>
> Those watching the game began to yell, and Adam was ready for a fight. The referee stopped the clash before it started and called a technical foul on Adam. Adam began screaming at the referee who then threw him out of the game. Jonathan, in the meanwhile, continued to play. He was also pushed, shoved, and abused, but he never said a word. He just kept playing and scoring points for his team.

Adam had a right to be upset. The other team was wrong. The referee was wrong. However, Adam did not respond the way Jesus would. Jonathan did.

In today's passage, Jesus had a right to be upset. A group of Roman soldiers was taking advantage of their spare time by abusing Jesus. They had already beaten Him. Now they twisted together a crown of thorns and rammed it down on Jesus' head. They put a purple robe on Him and mockingly referred to Him as their king. They spit in His face. They pulled the hair out of His beard (Isaiah 50:6). They took a wooden staff and hit Him in the head over and over. They added insult to injury with their words. How did Jesus react? He took it. He said nothing. He let them have their way with Him.

When violence strikes, the world says, "Hey, don't let them walk all over you. Defend yourself." Jesus, by His example, says, "Let them walk all over you. Trust in God to provide your defense." When someone insults you or calls you names, respond by saying something nice or saying nothing at all. If you're playing sports and the opposing team is playing dirty, ignore it and keep playing. When someone tries to pick a fight with you, offer a smile or just walk away.

Describe an incident where someone harmed you, whether verbally or physically. _____
_____*How did you react?* _____
How can you prepare yourself to be more like Jesus the next time violence strikes?

_____

Ask God to help you let others see Jesus in you by responding to violence with kindness. Pray for the inner strength to endure whatever someone may throw your way. Be a doormat. People who wipe their feet on a doormat will always find themselves at a doorway. While they are walking over you, God will open the door and allow them to see Jesus. For further study, read 1 Peter 2:21–23.

The Eyes Have It

Matthew 27:32–34; Mark 15:21–23; Luke 23:26–32; John 19:17

Tammy and her family braced for the oncoming storm. They boarded up all the windows, bought extra food and water, and prepared for the worst. In just a short while, the hurricane would strike.

Tammy lay in her bed listening to the sounds of the storm. The rain fell in pulsating sheets. Tree branches began to snap and break under the tremendous strain caused by high winds. The tempest raged on into the night for what seemed like hours. Suddenly, around midnight, the storm ceased. The rain stopped. The winds grew quiet.

Tammy hopped out of bed, put on her robe, and went into the living room. Her mother and father were standing at the front door, looking outside.

"Is the storm over?" Tammy asked.

"No," her father said. "The eye of the hurricane is passing right over us. We've still got more wind and rains coming, but for now it's quiet and peaceful. We get to have a short little break before it starts all over again."

God designed hurricanes to have an eye—a place of peace and quiet in the middle of the storm. God provides something similar for the storms in your life.

In today's passage, Jesus was being led out to die. He was so tired and weary from all that He had been through so far that He collapsed under the weight of His cross. He couldn't go any further. He couldn't take it anymore. Jesus needed help. The guards found a man named Simon and forced him to carry Jesus' cross. Simon didn't know it, but God had chosen him to be the eye of the storm for Jesus. He gave Jesus a much-needed break.

There are times when you want to collapse under the weight of life's pressures and problems. You find that you just can't go on. Do you know what? It's OK to feel like that. When you reach your boiling point, God has carefully prepared a peaceful eye in the middle of your storms to give you temporary relief from what you are going through. Sometimes the eye comes in the form of a friend who helps carry part of your load. Perhaps it arrives at just the right time in a favorite song or Bible verse. It could come in the shape of blue skies and a day full of sunshine.

What hardships are you encountering right now? _____

What kind of relief do you want from your burdens? _____

Describe something God has done for you recently that served as an eye in your storm.

_____

Ask God to give you rest from the struggles you face. Pray for someone or something to come along soon and make your load a little lighter. You never know where or how God is going to speak to you in the storm. Keep your eyes open.

Double Cross

Matthew 27:35–44; Mark 15:24–32; Luke 23:33; John 19:18–24

> Shane cried the day his dog died at the old age of fourteen. After a tearful good-bye, Shane's father buried the dog in the backyard. A few days later, Shane was thinking about all the good times he'd had with Fluffy. Shane walked outside and sat near the grave of his beloved pet. He missed Fluffy so much. Shane thought to himself, I have to see Fluffy just one more time. He began digging. He scraped away the dirt until Fluffy's curly white hair became visible. He continued his exhumation until Fluffy's entire body was exposed.
>
> Shane thought, Maybe I should take Fluffy for one more walk. He went to the garage, found the leash, and attached it to Fluffy's collar. Shane pulled his old dog out of the grave and began walking around the neighborhood with Fluffy in tow. He soon became very tired of pulling all of that dead weight, so he returned Fluffy to the grave and covered him back up with dirt.
>
> Now and then, you may find Shane heading into the backyard with a leash and a shovel.

You can breathe a sigh of relief—this is *not* a true story. Surely no one would dig up something dead and take it for a walk—unless you are talking about sin.

In today's passage, Jesus was crucified. The Roman soldiers stripped Him of His clothes and forced Him to lie down on the back they had just beaten. Standing on Jesus' hands, they pounded six-inch long nails through His left hand, and then His right. They drove one long nail right through both feet. The soldiers then lifted the cross until it was fully upright, sliding it into a deep hole with a sudden jolt. Jesus endured this pain and gave up His life for two reasons: (1) to pay the full price for your sin, and (2) to show you how you must crucify sin.

Jesus paid the price for your sin. He crucified it on the cross. Sometimes, though, you act like Shane. You go digging up the sin that Jesus paid for so you can play with it just one more time. How do you stop this terrible habit of playing with what is dead? You do what Jesus did. You allow yourself to be crucified—meaning that you voluntarily give up your right to commit a particular sin. You endure the pain of temptation. You stay on your cross, even when you want to come down and participate in the things you know you must not do.

Do you continue to participate in certain sins even though Jesus paid the price for them on the cross? _____ List the sins of which you are most guilty. _____

Why do you continue to play with these dead things? _____

What kind of pain must you endure on your cross to be crucified and die to these sins?

_____

Ask God to help you put your sinful habits to death. Allow yourself to be crucified with Christ. Though it may be very painful to endure the temptation as you suffer on your cross, remember this: if you die with Jesus, you will also live with Him. For further study, read Romans 6:6–12 and Galatians 2:20, 5:24.

Let It Go

Luke 23:34–38

Just after Thanksgiving, Gerald lined the front lawn of his new country home with Christmas lights. He drove short wooden stakes into the ground and strung the lights along the sidewalk and street about six inches high. When night fell, the lights twinkled softly but brilliantly.

One evening, however, the lights did not come on when Gerald flipped the switch. After careful examination, he discovered that someone had deliberately cut the wires in several places. Muttering to himself, Gerald patched up the breaks until the lights worked again. Sometime that night, however, the unknown culprit struck again. Gerald was furious. Who would do such a thing? Once again he repaired the lights. Once again, sometime during the night the wires were cut.

In sheer desperation, Gerald vowed to catch the perpetrator. Gerald rigged up a video surveillance system and left it running all night. Sure enough, the next morning Gerald discovered that the wires were cut. He fast-forwarded through last night's video. About 2:00 A.M., several rabbits emerged from the nearby woodlands and chewed through the wires.

Would it make sense for Gerald to punish the rabbits for their behavior? Of course not. The rabbits had no idea that what they were doing was wrong.

In today's passage, Jesus hung on the cross in silence, contemplating His situation. Pilate had callously sentenced Him to die while claiming no responsibility for the deed. The religious leaders had spread false rumors about Jesus and held a mock trial that resulted in this cruel punishment. The Roman guards had just driven long metal spikes through Jesus' hands and feet. The people around Jesus made fun of Him, daring Him to come down from the cross. Jesus took one look at all of these people and said His first words from the cross, "Father, forgive them. They have no idea what they are doing."

Jesus chose to forgive everyone for the part they played in causing His pain. He didn't pardon the simple sins and refuse to forgive the greater sins. He forgave them all. You, too, must learn to forgive all sin. Sometimes you subconsciously make a list of sins that are worth forgiving. You may pardon your little brother for breaking your pencil, but will you forgive him for breaking your video game? Perhaps you would excuse someone for accidentally running over your pet cat, but would you forgive a drunk driver who killed your best friend?

List sins that you consider easy to forgive. _____

Now make a list of sins that seem unforgivable. _____

Whom in your life have you still not forgiven for something they did? _____

When will you choose to forgive them? _____

Don't carry bitterness and resentment in your heart. Forgive those around you for the part they have played in causing your pain. Ask God to show you any unforgiveness that may still be in your heart. When He does, pray for the strength to let it go.

Hi, Mom

John 19:25–27

Doug and his friends walked into the house, exhausted from their afternoon of skateboarding. They went immediately to the refrigerator, practically emptying it of its contents.

They all sat on the couch, watching Saturday afternoon sports, when the phone rang. One of the guys tossed the cordless phone over to Doug. He answered, "Hello."

"Doug, is that you?" his mom asked. "Listen, I'm in a jam. I have a flat tire, and I'm on the side of the freeway about ten miles from you. Is Dad home yet?"

"No, Mom," Doug responded. "Dad left a message on the coffee table saying he wouldn't be home for a few more hours. The guys and I are about to go see a movie."

"Doug, listen. I need your help. Could you bring the pickup out here and help me change this tire? The groceries are going to spoil."

Doug looked at his chums and thought about the movie he was dying to see. He asked himself what Jesus would do and told his mom, "I'm on my way. I should be there in about fifteen minutes."

Doug faced a tough decision. He could do what he had planned to do and go to the movies with his friends or miss out by changing a flat tire for his mother. He decided to think of Mom.

In today's passage, we find Jesus on the cross. He suffered from blinding pain, and yet when He looked down at the crowd around Him, He saw His mother. She was in need. Who would take care of her when Jesus was dead? Rather than think of Himself, Jesus thought of His mother's needs. He handed the care of His mother over to the apostle John. Jesus had every right to think only of Himself, but He still took care of His mother.

Your parents will sometimes, or perhaps often, require assistance that goes above and beyond your daily chores. They shouldn't have to ask for your help. You can do like Jesus did and take the initiative to help your parents when they are in need. Help them bring in the groceries and put them away. Take out the trash when you notice it overflowing. Do the dishes even if it isn't your turn. Clean your room before they have a chance to make you do it. Surprise whoever is mowing the yard with a tall glass of lemonade. Do whatever it takes to let your parents know that you care about them.

What do your daily chores include? _____

What are some needs that your parents have outside of your list? _____

How can you help meet those needs? _____

Jesus honored His mother and met her needs until the day He died. God wants you to do the same for your parents. Ask God to show you how you can be more like Jesus with your parents. Look for opportunities to help them. Take the initiative and be there for them whenever they have a need.

Weekly Bible Study and Prayer Review

Bible Study

Look back through some of the Scriptures you read this week. Write down the one verse or passage that God used to speak to you.

_____

_____

_____

_____

Memorize this verse or passage. You can do it if you spend just
a few minutes saying it to yourself.

Now, think of at least one situation you will probably face soon in which you could use this Scripture to help you make the right decision. Write down that situation below.

_____

Quote the Scripture when you face this situation, and live by it.

Prayer Time

Take a few moments to praise God for who He is.
Now take a few moments to thank God for things He has done for you.
Now ask God to make you into the person He wants you to be.
Ask God to use you to help others become closer to God.

Below is your prayer list for the week. Keep it updated each week. If your prayer isn't answered this week, carry it over to next week's list.

Request	Date of Original Request	Date Answered
_____	__/__/__	__/__/__
_____	__/__/__	__/__/__
_____	__/__/__	__/__/__
_____	__/__/__	__/__/__
_____	__/__/__	__/__/__
_____	__/__/__	__/__/__
_____	__/__/__	__/__/__
_____	__/__/__	__/__/__

Pray for the things on your list and trust God to provide.
Forgive anyone you have not yet forgiven.
Ask God to forgive you for any unconfessed sin in your life.
Ask God to keep you out of trouble with sin.
Acknowledge that God is in complete control of your life
and will take care of everything.

Paradise Found

Luke 23:39–43

Alexis was about to go crazy. Though it was her senior year in high school, nothing seemed to go right. Her family argued any time they found themselves in the same room together. She had no boyfriend. She had no idea what she wanted to do with her life after she graduated. The pressures were intense. Alexis thought that when she became a Christian last year that life would become easier. Instead, it seemed to get harder.

Every day after school, Alexis would take Matt home. Matt was not a Christian. One day, Matt began to tell Alexis about the problems in his life. Alexis did not want to hear about someone else's problems. She had enough of her own. However, she listened. Before long, she forgot about herself and began to feel compassion for Matt and his situation.

Alexis began to share with Matt how she met Jesus and how He had changed her life. She couldn't believe her own words, but before long she told Matt how to become a Christian. When she dropped him off at his house, she said, "Think about what I said." Matt did think about it. That night in his room he gave his life to Jesus.

Alexis was going through some difficulties, but she didn't let that stop her from sharing Jesus with someone else. She took her eyes off herself and gave, even when she felt like there was nothing to give.

Jesus did the same thing in today's passage. While hanging on the cross in unbelievable agony, a common thief asked Jesus to remember him. Jesus could have said, "Excuse me! Can't you see that I'm dying here? I gave everything, and I have nothing left to give." Jesus did no such thing. He looked the thief in the eyes and said, "Sure, I will remember you. In fact, this very day you and I will be in Paradise together."

Sometimes when things get rough you might stop and have a pity party. You start thinking about how lousy your life is, and you forget that God's mission is still the same. He cares about what you are going through, but He also cares about what everyone else is going through. In the middle of your darkest moment, God may send someone your way who needs to hear the good news about Jesus. Will you be ready and willing to share God's love with someone else when that time comes?

Are you currently experiencing troubles that make you focus on yourself instead of others?

_____

Instead of thinking of those, think about the people God has placed in your life. Who around you needs to know the Lord? _____

What can you do to share Jesus with these people? _____

Being a Christian does not mean that you are immune to pain and suffering. You can, however, still be a minister to others in spite of your troubles. Ask God to help you see past your pain to the opportunities around you to witness to others.

I Told You So

John 19:28–29

The Bible has more than three hundred Old Testament prophecies of the Messiah's life, all of which Jesus fulfilled. Examples include the following: Jesus would be born of a virgin (Isaiah 7:14). He would be born in Bethlehem (Micah 5:2). He would ride into Jerusalem on a donkey (Zechariah 9:9). The person who betrayed Jesus would be a close friend who ate with Him (Psalm 41:9). Jesus' betrayer would trade Him for thirty pieces of silver (Zechariah 11:12). Jesus would remain silent when He was condemned to death (Isaiah 53:7). Both His hands and feet would be pierced (Psalm 22:16). He would be crucified alongside thieves (Isaiah 53:12). Someone would cast lots for His clothes (Psalm 22:18). None of His bones would be broken (Psalm 34:20). He would experience thirst while hanging on the cross (Psalm 22:15).

George Heron, a French mathematician, calculated the odds that Jesus could have fulfilled just forty-eight Old Testament prophecies concerning the Messiah. He said the odds are 1 in 10,157. These odds are so astronomically high that for one man to fulfill them all indicates that he must have been who he claimed to be.

In today's passage, Jesus fulfilled the final Old Testament prophecy concerning His life. He experienced thirst from the cross. Imagine going home after the crucifixion and opening your Bible to Psalm 22 for your daily devotion. You would be amazed to see a very detailed description of the day's events. You would be so startled that perhaps you would believe that Jesus is who He claimed to be. That is the purpose of Old Testament prophecy about Jesus—it proves He is the one and only Messiah.

The Old Testament is full of valuable lessons. The Book of Genesis tells the story of Creation and stories of the founding mothers and fathers of the faith. Exodus through Deuteronomy gives us the story of Moses and the law. Joshua through Esther contain historical stories of great men and women of God. Job through Song of Solomon include lessons and sayings on wisdom. The rest of the books in the Old Testament, Isaiah through Malachi, tell the stories of the lives and messages of great prophets.

What Old Testament book have you read the most? _____

What book have you read the least? _____

What is your favorite verse or story in the Old Testament? _____

Do you regularly study the Old Testament during your quiet times? _____

If you have not already, start a daily Bible reading plan that includes readings from the Old Testament. You could start at the beginning and just read a chapter or story each day along with your other readings. Ask God to speak to you through the Old Testament. You will be amazed at how often you see Jesus in its pages.

A Prescription for Pain

Matthew 27:45–49; Mark 15:33–36

Kendra's face fell. The doctor's words seemed to echo down a distant corridor. "He couldn't be talking to me," she thought, trembling as she looked first at her mother and then at her father. The expressions on their faces brought her back to reality.

"Leukemia can be treated in a variety of ways," the doctor continued. Kendra didn't hear another word. Her head was spinning. She saw her entire life flash before her eyes. Her parents held her tightly, but even they couldn't console her.

For the next few months, nothing could comfort Kendra. She couldn't eat or sleep. Every day was a nightmare. She turned away from her parents, her friends, and from God. Six weeks after her diagnosis, she picked up her Bible for the first time. She asked God to speak to her, and she opened it to Psalm 102. The words seemed to be written just for her. In tears, she read the words over and over again. She realized that God had not abandoned her. She fell on her face in prayer and begged God to allow her to experience His presence and comfort once again.

Kendra found a prescription for her pain in the Psalms. The words met her right where she hurt.

In today's passage, Jesus was experiencing excruciating pain. Not only was His physical body in torment, but His mind and emotions encountered pain as well. In sheer agony, Jesus cried out, "My God, My God—why have You forsaken Me?" To some, this may sound like Jesus wondered where His Father was. In reality, Jesus was comforting Himself with the words of Psalm 22. This psalm, like many others, begins with a cry of desperation. It ends, however, with a song of victory and trust in God.

One of the reasons God gave you the Psalms in the Bible is to teach you how to talk to God when you are in pain. Many people run away from God when they are in pain. God wants you to run *toward* Him. The Psalms help you do that by teaching you how to pray, even when it hurts. When you read through the Psalms, you will learn things like (1) you are not alone in your pain, (2) it is OK to complain of your suffering to the Lord, (3) God understands and cares about how you feel, and (4) there is assurance that one day soon your suffering will end.

Do you ever experience suffering, whether physical, mental, or emotional? _____

Do you run toward God or away from Him when you hurt? _____

Do you ever wonder if God cares about how you feel? _____

Do you ever doubt that you will ever escape your misery? _____

God wants you to run toward Him when you are suffering. Use the Psalms as your guide. Read one per day and share your difficulties and your victories with your Father in heaven. Ask God to help you learn to practice His presence during your pain through the Psalms. Within those pages, you will find a successful prescription for pain.

It Is Finished

John 19:30

> "He was born in an obscure village, the child of a peasant woman. He grew up in still another village, where he worked in a carpenter's shop until he was thirty, then for three years he was a preacher.
>
> "He never wrote a book. He never had an office. He never had a family or owned a house. He didn't go to college. He never visited a big city. He never traveled more than two hundred miles from the place where he was born. He did none of the things usually associated with greatness. He had no credentials but himself. He was only thirty-three when the tide of public opinion turned against him. His friends ran away. He was turned over to his enemies and went though a mockery of a trial. He was nailed to a cross between two thieves. While he was dying, his executioners gambled for his clothing, the only property he had on earth. When he was dead, he was laid in a borrowed grave through the pity of a friend.
>
> "Twenty centuries have come and gone, and today he remains the central figure of the human race and the leader of mankind's progress. All the armies that ever marched, all of the navies that ever sailed, all the parliaments that ever sat, all the kings that have ever reigned, put together, have not affected the life of man on this planet so much as that one solitary life."

The author of the above illustration is unknown, but the words summarize the story of the most well-known life of all. When Jesus said, "It is finished," His life—and yours—was complete.

Jesus accomplished everything that He came to earth to do. He lived a sinless life. He touched the lives of thousands of people. He healed the sick, raised the dead, cast out demons, taught the people, trained a band of disciples, and offered eternal life to anyone who would acknowledge Him. His life was complete.

You may feel sometimes as if your life is going nowhere. You sit down and think about all the negatives. "I've never done this. I can't do that. I'm no good at this, and no one cares that I did that." You start to feel as if your life will never amount to anything. Remember, though, that Jesus didn't do any of the normal things that make a person great. He simply focused on His mission in life and carried it out to completion. You can't say "It is finished" until you know what *it* is.

What would you say is your mission in life? _____

Name some things that distract you from your mission. _____

How do you overcome these distractions to stay focused on your mission? _____

How do you plan to fulfill your mission between now and the end of your life? _____

Ask God to show you what your mission in life is. Pray for the strength to stay focused. Pray for the ability to overcome any distractions and obstacles that stand in your way. Though you will make mistakes along the way, live your life in such a way that when you face death, you will be able to state with confidence, "It is finished."

What a Rip

Luke 23:44–46

Felicia stood at her locker in disbelief. She couldn't remember the combination! Her five-page English paper was due in her next class, but it was in the locker. "OK, calm yourself down, Felicia," she mumbled to herself, "You've had this locker for three months. You can remember."

When the tardy bell was only thirty seconds away, Felicia gave up and ran to English. She sat down just as the bell rang. As the rest of the class handed in their papers, she tried in vain to explain her predicament to her English teacher. Mrs. Ogilvie was skeptical but knew Felicia to be a good student. "Go to the office and see if they have your combination on file."

Felicia went to the office, but of course her combination was not on file. "This is the story of my life," Felicia grumbled. "How am I ever going to get in there?"

The vice-principal said, "Felicia, if you want, we have some steel cutters that can break the lock. You'll have to pay $10 for a new lock, but at least you'll be able to get to your English paper."

Felicia agreed. The custodian took the steel cutters and broke open Felicia's locker.

Now Felicia could get to her English paper. Now she could start over with a new combination. And this time she would write it down!

In today's passage, something else was broken open. Jesus cried His final words from the cross and died. When He did, the curtain in the temple was ripped in half, from top to bottom. What did that mean? The curtain separated the rest of the temple from the Most Holy Place—the place where God dwelled on earth. No one was ever allowed into the Most Holy Place, except the high priest—and he could only enter once a year. When Jesus died and the curtain was torn in two, He allowed everyone to start over with a new combination for reaching God.

Sometimes people think that when you step into a church building, you must act differently. You've probably heard someone say, "Don't do that—this is a church!" When Jesus ripped open the curtain, however, He showed that the Most Holy Place is now *inside* you, so you should be holy wherever you go. You shouldn't pretend to be more holy when you walk into a church building. You should always be on your best behavior, imitating Jesus in all you do no matter where you are.

When are you usually on your best behavior? _____

When do you usually act your worst? _____

What makes you act differently from one situation or place to the other? _____

If God is always with you, how should you act in every situation? _____

Ask God to help you do what Jesus would do in any and every situation you face. He lives inside of you and goes with you wherever you go. Make everything you do holy—set apart for the purpose of honoring Jesus.

Two Sides to Every Story

Matthew 27:57–61; Mark 15:42–47; Luke 23:50–56; John 19:38–42

> Teardrops stained the notebook paper and smudged the ink as Darla penned her last words. She wrote, "I just can't take it anymore. Mom and Dad, forgive me. It's not your fault. I just can't deal with the pain I'm feeling inside. No one understands, and it's never going to go away. This is the only thing I can do to find rest."
>
> Darla wrote many other words, but they seemed so empty. *I can't even write a suicide note,* she thought. She sealed the envelope and placed it on her dresser. She caught a glimpse of herself in the mirror and wept even more. She slowly fell to the floor, holding the bottle of sleeping pills in one hand and a glass of water in the other. She leaned against her bed, cocked her head back, and opened her mouth. She emptied the contents of the bottle and dropped it in her lap. She raised the glass to her lips, and . . .

Stop. No more. This scene is too painful to even imagine. Suicide is not Darla's way out. She may feel as if she has no other choice, but she does.

In today's passage, Jesus was dead. His lifeless body hung limply as the sun began to set. The love in His eyes was gone. The healing in His hands had been replaced with jagged wounds. Two men, Joseph and Nicodemus, came for the body of Jesus. They saw only death. They wrapped Jesus in cloth and laid Him in a tomb. They rolled a huge stone against the door, assuming that this was the end of the story. They didn't see any other way to deal with what had happened.

You know the rest of the story. Jesus rose again. For awhile, though, death seemed like it was the only answer. Joseph and Nicodemus had no hope that Jesus would rise, or they wouldn't have buried Him as they did.

Someday, perhaps even now, you may experience so many problems that you feel death is the only answer. You don't see any other way to escape the pain, so you begin to imagine or even plan suicide. Stop. No more. The thought is too painful to even imagine. There are two sides to every story. Suicide is one side. The other side is life. Jesus could have stayed in His tomb, but He rose again. He overcame the pain He suffered on the cross and saw life again. You can rise again too.

Have you ever considered suicide? _____ *If so, why?* _____

If not, do you know someone else who has thought about, attempted, or committed suicide?

_____

Is suicide really the answer to anything? _____

What can you do, either for yourself or someone else, to prevent suicide? _____

If you are considering suicide, tell someone *now.* Let them help you. Tell God. Let Him help you. If you are not considering suicide, look around. Someone close to you may be because of the troubles they face. Ask God to help you choose life and overcome the pain that may cause you or someone you know to consider suicide.

Weekly Bible Study and Prayer Review

Bible Study

Look back through some of the Scriptures you read this week. Write down the one verse or passage that God used to speak to you.

_____

_____

_____

_____

Memorize this verse or passage. You can do it if you spend just
a few minutes saying it to yourself.

Now, think of at least one situation you will probably face soon in which you could use this Scripture to help you make the right decision. Write down that situation below.

_____

Quote the Scripture when you face this situation, and live by it.

Prayer Time

Take a few moments to praise God for who He is.
Now take a few moments to thank God for things He has done for you.
Now ask God to make you into the person He wants you to be.
Ask God to use you to help others become closer to God.

Below is your prayer list for the week. Keep it updated each week. If your prayer isn't answered this week, carry it over to next week's list.

Request	Date of Original Request	Date Answered
_____	__/__/__	__/__/__
_____	__/__/__	__/__/__
_____	__/__/__	__/__/__
_____	__/__/__	__/__/__
_____	__/__/__	__/__/__
_____	__/__/__	__/__/__
_____	__/__/__	__/__/__
_____	__/__/__	__/__/__

Pray for the things on your list and trust God to provide.
Forgive anyone you have not yet forgiven.
Ask God to forgive you for any unconfessed sin in your life.
Ask God to keep you out of trouble with sin.
Acknowledge that God is in complete control of your life
and will take care of everything.

No Way Out

Matthew 27:62–66

Kendall thought for a brief moment that he was in big trouble. Sometimes you find yourself in a situation in which there seems to be no way out.

In today's passage, Jesus was dead. His body lay in a tomb on the day after the crucifixion, and everything looked hopeless. Armed guards stood near the entrance of the tomb where a large rock prevented anyone from going in and anyone from coming out. For extra protection the guards placed an official government seal across the rock—warning that anyone tampering with the stone would be prosecuted to the fullest extent of the law. It seemed as if there was no way out for Jesus.

You may sometimes feel that you are in a jam that will never end. Your face breaks out with acne, and it seems to be getting worse each day. Your grades are falling even though you are doing your best. The memory of an abusive situation haunts you, giving you nightmares and irrational fears. You never seem to have enough money to buy basic necessities. What should you do in these seemingly hopeless situations? Wait. Be still. Be patient. Though it is dark on the inside and well guarded on the outside, God will rescue you in His time. Let Him be the one to move whatever stone blocks your way.

Do you ever feel like you are in a bad situation with no way out? _____

What is the stone that blocks your way to freedom? _____

What have you tried so far to remove the stone? _____

There is a way out. Stop trying to pry your way out, and start praying your way out. Let go of your solutions to the problem, and let God show you His. Be still before God and ask Him to help you through this dark time. Pray that you would have the patience to wait on God to rescue you in His timing.

Just Keep Looking

Matthew 28:1–8; Mark 16:1–8; Luke 24:1–12; John 20:1–9

Hanna checked her backpack one last time and then set out. She looked up one last time, shielding her eyes from the sun. She fixed her eyes on her destination: Elephant Rock, a large stone formation jutting through the trees at the top of the mountain in front of her. Taking a deep breath, she began her ascent.

Two hours later, Hanna stopped to rest. She leaned against a tree, taking a sip from the water in her canteen. She rubbed her aching knees, wondering to herself if this was such a good idea. I haven't seen Elephant Rock since I started because the mountain blocks my view, she thought. It's taking longer than I expected, and I could be headed in the wrong direction. What am I going to do when I get up there, anyway? Maybe I should just head back..

Hanna shook herself as if to awaken from a dream. "Stop it," she chided herself. "So what if you can't see where you're going. Just go with what you know, and you'll get there." Three hours later, Hanna did get there. She stood atop Elephant Rock and shouted, "I made it!"

Hanna had a lot of questions along the way and no solid answers. Rather than turn back, though, she continued with what she knew and finished her course.

In today's passage, Jesus rose from the dead. Before everyone knew that Jesus was alive, however, notice how many people had unanswered questions. Two women headed for the tomb had no idea who would roll the stone away for them. Later, they told Peter and John that Jesus was alive. The two disciples ran to the tomb, even though they had no idea what they would find. They arrived to find Jesus' empty grave clothes. Peter walked away, wondering what happened. John, however, believed that Jesus was alive—in spite of all his questions. These four people had many unanswered questions, but they still went looking for Jesus.

As you strive to follow God, you will probably have many questions along the way. Sometimes you won't be able to see Jesus as clearly as you would like. What should you do? Should you give up and turn away from God or keep looking for Jesus even when you can't see Him? Keep going when you're not sure what to do. Keep praying when it doesn't seem like God's listening. Keep reading your Bible when you don't seem to get anything out of it. Keep witnessing to your friends even though they don't seem interested. Keep looking for Jesus.

What doubts or questions sometimes keep you from following God as closely as you should?

_____

Where do you think God might be at work in your life when you experience these uncertainties? _____

Even though you don't know everything, take what you do know and keep following Jesus. Ask God to help you overcome your fears, doubts, and questions. Pray for the power to keep going. Keep looking for Jesus. He may seem far away, but it won't be long before you see Him again.

Something Special

Mark 16:9–11; John 20:10–18

After the crucifixion of Jesus, the angels of heaven gathered for a very important meeting. Their task was to determine who Jesus should appear to first after His resurrection.

Some suggested John since he seemed to be the most faithful disciple. Others nominated Mary, the mother of Jesus, because she had been with Jesus the longest. One angel said, "I think the first person Jesus should appear to is Pilate, so that coward will be scared senseless."

After a brief moment of laughter, the angels continued their discussion. One group voted that Jesus should appear to all of the disciples at once. Some felt Peter should be first since he would one day be the leader of the apostles. Still others thought that the Jews who had Jesus arrested should see Him first so they would finally admit He was the Messiah.

Finally, one small angel raised his hand and said, "What about Mary Magdalene?"

"Mary Magdalene!" the others teased. "Why should Jesus appear to her first?"

"Why not?" the angel posed. "Doesn't our Lord consider everyone to be special?"

The angels probably didn't actually decide who would be first. Jesus had already decided that it would be Mary Magdalene, a woman from whom He had once cast out seven demons.

If you search the entire Bible to find out about Mary Magdalene, you won't find much. All we know is that she followed Jesus from the beginning of His ministry after He cast seven demons out of her (Luke 8:1–3). There was nothing else special about her. Jesus, however, made her someone special. He honored her faithfulness to Him by making her the first person in history to see Jesus after His resurrection.

You may sometimes feel you are almost a nobody. You tell yourself there is nothing special about you. You convince yourself you are too insignificant to be of any worth to God or anyone else. Jesus, however, makes you someone special. With Him in your life, He transforms you from a nobody into a somebody. While other people may see nothing special about you, Jesus sees a unique person like no other. Mary Magdalene is the only person mentioned in the Bible to have seven demons cast out of her. You are the only person in history who can fulfill the call that God has placed on your life.

Do you ever feel like you are nothing special? _____

Why? _____

Name one thing that is unique about you—something that no one else can claim. _____

How might God use this unique quality for His purpose? _____

You are unique. You are special. Stop letting the voices of Satan and the world convince you otherwise. Ask God to help you see how special and unique you really are. Pray for an understanding of God's call on your life—it's something special.

Tell It Like It Is

Matthew 28:8–10

On the third night of youth camp, something happened. When it was time for the camp pastor to speak, he didn't. He said everyone should keep singing and worshiping God. So they did. That's when it happened.

Near the back of the auditorium, one youth group experienced God like they never had before. Ryan realized that he had been playing the church game for too long. He fell on his face and wept, begging God to forgive him. Three brothers—Cory, Jason, and Tim—kneeled in a circle with their arms locked and prayed for a very long time. Many others simply embraced each other with tears in their eyes, asking for forgiveness and sharing prayer requests. A youth group was reborn.

After the service, the group walked in silence to a place called "The Rock." It was a small, stone seating area just big enough for everyone to gather and share their experiences. Everyone agreed that they had all seen God move in a powerful way. Their greatest desire was to go home and tell everyone else in the youth group and church what happened.

Some experiences are meant to be shared. This youth group shared theirs, and those who missed camp sensed that something truly amazing happened that week.

In today's passage, something truly amazing happened to a small group of women. They had already heard the angels' message that Jesus was alive, and they were on their way to tell the disciples when it happened. Suddenly, Jesus appeared. They saw and experienced God like never before. They fell on their faces and worshiped Jesus. They wanted to stay there forever, but Jesus told them to get up and go share their experience with the other disciples.

You may be alone or in a group, but you will occasionally see God as you have never seen Him before. You read a special verse in the Bible that speaks right to your heart. You see an answer to prayer right in front of your eyes. You hear a song on a new CD that touches your spirit to the core. You feel God's unconditional forgiveness when you finally confess a hidden sin. God wants you to share these and similar experiences with others so that they will know He is still working in the hearts and lives of His children.

Describe your most intimate experience with God. _____

Whom have you told about this encounter? _____

How did they react? _____

Ask God for a fresh encounter with Him. Share your intimate moments with God with your church family, youth group, and Christian friends. Don't keep these experiences to yourself. Let others know what God is doing in your life.

True or False

Matthew 28:11–15

Casey said to his friends, "I've got a story. One day I stopped for gas near my house. After filling up my car, I went inside to grab a candy bar and soda. This lady inside started following me. I tried to get away from her, but she cornered me near the ice cream. She said, 'Young man, you look just like my son. He died last August in a car accident. His name was Tommy. Can I call you Tommy?' I didn't say a word. I just ducked into the bathroom to get away from her."

"I waited until she was gone, then went to check out. The clerk added up my total and said, 'Your mother said you would pay for her stuff too.' That lady was trying to make me pay for her stuff! I told the clerk that the woman was not my mother. I ran outside to get in my car while the clerk caught up with the woman in the parking lot. She got away from the clerk, ran over to me, fell on the ground, and started begging me to help her. She called me Tommy, and started pulling on my leg—just like I'm pulling your leg right now."

Casey's story was false, but it kept everyone interested for a while. Casey's story was for fun, but in some cases, lies can get out of hand.

In today's passage, we find one of the greatest cover-ups of all time. Sixteen Roman guards who kept watch over Jesus' tomb returned to the chief priests who killed Jesus to tell them the truth about what happened Sunday morning. Afterwards, the chief priests paid the guards to change their story. The guards began to circulate the false story that the disciples had stolen the body while the guards slept. Many people chose to believe this version of the story instead of the truth.

False stories about Jesus still circulate today. Jehovah's Witnesses say Jesus is not God but only a created being like an angel. Mormonism teaches that you can become a god equal to Jesus. Islam (whose followers are called Muslims) says that Jesus was merely a prophet, and that Allah is the true God. Buddhism teaches that there are many gods, and Jesus is only one. These false religions have many followers, some of whom you'll meet. When you do, remember three things. First, do not be swayed by false teachings. Second, make sure you know the truth about Jesus by studying the Bible and getting the facts straight. Finally, never argue about who's right and who's wrong. Simply state the truth and leave it at that.

Name a false religion or a false view of God that some people around you believe. _____

Why is their version of the story false? _____

Do they point to the Bible as their source of truth, or some other writing? _____

If you know someone who believes in a false religion or false view of Jesus, pray for them by name right now. Then, whenever you have the opportunity, share the true story of Jesus with them. Love them. Be gentle with them. Love them. And be very careful that you are able to determine what is true and what is false. For further study, read 2 Timothy 2:23–26.

Now I Get It

Mark 16:12–13; Luke 24:13–35

Jennifer carefully opened the envelope she found on her front porch. Inside was a simple, two-line poem that read, "Just as the man with hair of snow, so is the coin that's lost its glow." Inside was a picture of an old man, and an old silver dime. Jennifer wondered what this meant.

The next night another envelope appeared. The message in this one said, "Just as the sun on a cloudless day, so is the coin that shines today." Inside was a picture of the sun, along with a brand new dime.

On the third night, another message: "Just as the time that quickly soars, so are the things that are not yours." Inside the envelope was a picture of a clock, along with a pair of her sister's earrings.

Jennifer could hardly contain herself when the fourth night yielded yet another mysterious poem. This one read, "Just as the sky at noonday clear, so is the object you see here." Inside was a beautiful blue swatch of cloth.

Jennifer pondered the four gifts, wondering what they could mean. She knew her boyfriend was sending them, but what was he trying to say? Suddenly, it hit her. "Something old, something new, something borrowed, something blue!" she squealed to herself. "He wants to marry me!"

Jennifer didn't understand the messages at first; but once she put them all together, they made perfect sense.

In today's passage, two men walked home from Jerusalem on a quiet Sunday morning, discouraged by recent events. They witnessed Jesus' death, and it just didn't make sense. Quietly and unexpectedly, Jesus slipped up behind them and joined their conversation. He used Scripture to put all of God's messages together, explaining why He had to die. When Jesus broke bread, it hit them. It all made sense.

Your life is a series of events that God uses to speak to you, but sometimes you miss what God is saying. You may forget about God altogether when things are going well. During the tough times, you might wonder why God seems to be so far away. Sometimes, you may feel like your life doesn't make sense. When you feel that way, you may not be aware of it at first, but Jesus will quietly slip up behind you and whisper words of encouragement to you from His Word. He will pull the events of your life together and show you they all make perfect sense.

Do you ever feel like your life doesn't make sense? _____

Why? _____

If you consider all of the events and experiences of your entire life, what do you think God might be trying to say to you? _____

Don't be discouraged by who you are or the things that you experience. God is in complete control of your life, even when you can't see it for yourself. Ask God to help you see His hand in all that happens. Pray that you would be able to recognize Jesus as He walks with you along the way.

Weekly Bible Study and Prayer Review

Bible Study

Look back through some of the Scriptures you read this week. Write down the one verse or passage that God used to speak to you.

_____

_____

_____

_____

Memorize this verse or passage. You can do it if you spend just
a few minutes saying it to yourself.

Now, think of at least one situation you will probably face soon in which you could use this Scripture to help you make the right decision. Write down that situation below.

_____

Quote the Scripture when you face this situation, and live by it.

Prayer Time

Take a few moments to praise God for who He is.
Now take a few moments to thank God for things He has done for you.
Now ask God to make you into the person He wants you to be.
Ask God to use you to help others become closer to God.

Below is your prayer list for the week. Keep it updated each week. If your prayer isn't answered this week, carry it over to next week's list.

Request	Date of Original Request	Date Answered
_____	__/__/__	__/__/__
_____	__/__/__	__/__/__
_____	__/__/__	__/__/__
_____	__/__/__	__/__/__
_____	__/__/__	__/__/__
_____	__/__/__	__/__/__
_____	__/__/__	__/__/__
_____	__/__/__	__/__/__
_____	__/__/__	__/__/__

Pray for the things on your list and trust God to provide.
Forgive anyone you have not yet forgiven.
Ask God to forgive you for any unconfessed sin in your life.
Ask God to keep you out of trouble with sin.
Acknowledge that God is in complete control of your life
and will take care of everything.

Phobiafest

Luke 24:36–43; John 20:19–23

Do you have any of the following phobias?

Claustrophobia: fear of enclosed places
Hydrophobia: fear of water
Acrophobia: fear of heights
Odynophobia: fear of pain
Ochlophobia: fear of crowds
Mysophobia: fear of germs
Opthalmophobia: fear of being stared at
Taphophobia: fear of being buried alive
Blennophobia: fear of slime

Agoraphobia: fear of open places
Xenophobia: fear of strangers
Pathophobia: fear of disease
Nyctophobia: fear of the dark
Ergophobia: fear of work
Pyrophobia: fear of fire
Peniaphobia: fear of being poor
Eisoptrophobia: fear of mirrors
Panophobia: fear of just about everything

Fear is a natural human response to an unwanted circumstance. Sometimes, though, phobias can paralyze us, leaving us helpless in the hands of fear.

In today's passage, Jesus' disciples were paralyzed with fear. Jesus' body was missing. A few women had told them that Jesus was alive. Jews spread the rumor that the disciples had stolen the body. The disciples locked the doors and hid, fearing that someone would come and arrest them or even kill them. Suddenly, at the height of their phobia, Jesus appeared. His first word to them was, "Peace." Jesus knew they were frightened of just about everything, including the sight of Him, so He said to them, "Peace to you." He didn't want them to be afraid. He wanted them to be at peace.

Your fears may sometimes keep you from becoming all God intends you to be. For instance, you may fear speaking in public, but God intends for you to become a preacher or traveling evangelist. Perhaps you fear hospitals, but God wants you to hold the hand of a sick or dying friend and comfort her. Maybe you have peniaphobia, but God wants you live among and minister to the poor. God has great plans for your life, and they don't include being paralyzed by fear. He wants you to let go of your fears and trust in Him.

What are some things that you're afraid of? _____

How do you normally act when you are afraid? _____

What goes through your mind? _____

How can you experience God's peace during the height of your fears? _____

Don't lock yourself out of allowing God to shape you according to His will. Ask God to remove any phobias that prevent you from becoming more like Jesus. Spend time in His presence and allow Him to melt away your fears. For further study, read Psalm 32:7 and Psalm 56:3.

No Way

Mark 16:14; John 20:24–31

"I don't believe it," Chandler said, shaking his head. "No way. You guys are pulling my leg."

"We are not!" Crystal insisted. "I'm telling you that while you were in the bathroom, the President of the United States came in here and got a cheeseburger."

Chandler stared at all the faces, searching for the punchline, but he could find none. The story wasn't farfetched. After all, Chandler and his youth group were on a mission trip in Washington D.C., and the White House was only three blocks away. Still, he wasn't convinced.

"I don't care what the rest of you say," Chandler said, shaking his head. "I'm not going to let you make a fool out of me. I won't believe the President was in here until I see him myself."

Just then, the doors to the restaurant swung open and a dozen or so men in dark suits and sunglasses appeared, forming an impenetrable barrier. In walked the President of the United States. He said to the cashier, "Can I get an order of fries and a hot apple pie?"

Everyone in the youth group looked at Chandler and said, "Now do you believe us?"

Chandler didn't believe until he saw the President with his own eyes. Sometimes it's easier to wait until we can see things with our own eyes before we take a risk and believe what we hear.

In today's passage, doubting Thomas refused to believe that the rest of the disciples had seen Jesus alive. He stated emphatically, "No way. I won't believe it until I see the nail marks in His hands and feel them with my fingers." One week later, Thomas did see Jesus with his own eyes. He saw the nail marks. He felt the scars. He believed because he saw. Jesus said what Thomas did was good, but those who believe before they see do even better.

As you walk with Jesus, God will ask you to believe things that you can't see. God tells you that things are going to work out for the best, but all you see right now is a painful trial (Romans 8:28). When you pray for something that you need, God wants you to believe that you will receive the answer before you do (Matthew 21:22). God has a great plan for your life, but at the moment you just can't see it happening (Jeremiah 29:11–13). You can choose to believe His promises before you see them, or remain skeptical and be like doubting Thomas.

Name a promise in the Bible that you sometimes find hard to believe. _____

Why is this promise so difficult to accept? _____

How would your life be different if you chose to believe this promise wholeheartedly?

_____

God never breaks a promise. Everything He has said in His Word is true. Everything that He has spoken to you is true. Ask God to help you overcome your doubt and accept His Word completely. Pray for the faith to believe what you cannot see. For further study, read Hebrews 11.

Who Gets the Credit?

John 21:1–14

Palindromes are coincidences of the English language. They just happen to work the way they do. No one is responsible for them—they just happen.

In today's passage, Jesus' disciples had spent the entire night fishing with no luck. At dawn they headed for shore. A stranger suggested that they try casting their net on the other side of the boat. They did, and they caught 153 large fish. They could have labeled the experience a coincidence. They could have assumed they just had dumb luck. They could have given themselves credit for being expert fishermen. John, however, saw beyond all that. He saw that Jesus was responsible.

Sometimes we don't recognize God in the so-called coincidences of life. We chalk them up to chance or give credit to ourselves. You get a great paying summer job, and you give credit to your friend who put in the good word for you. You make a good grade on a difficult test, and you pat yourself on the back. You find a ten-dollar bill lying on the ground and figure you're having good luck today. How often do you remember to give credit to God for the good things that happen in your life?

Name some good things that have happened to you recently. _____

Did you take time to acknowledge and thank God for each of these? _____

If you did not, who or what else got the credit? _____

All good things come from God. Take time right now to thank the Lord for the good things He has done for you. Ask God to help you recognize Jesus at work in your life during the positive experiences you have in the future. Remember to give credit where credit is due. For further study, read James 1:17.

I've Fallen, and I Can Get Up

John 21:15–25

Hungary's only gold medal in the 1948 Olympics came from a pistol-wielding sharpshooter who almost never made it to the Games.

In the 1930's the young man was the European pistol champion of the decade. But in 1938, he lost his right arm in a terrible accident. The man was right-handed, and his loss prevented him from continuing to perfect his skills. In great despair, he retreated to himself and would talk to no one. He spent days in seclusion, thinking about what had happened. One day, he jumped up, grabbed his pistol, and headed out the door. His wife, seeing her husband leave in such a hurry, wondered what he was doing. Suddenly, she heard a shot. Fearing her husband had committed suicide, she froze. Then another shot rang out, and another. She ran outside.

To her amazement, she saw her husband holding the pistol in his left hand and firing at the target where he once practiced for the Olympics. He resolved that day to be as good with his left hand as he was with his right. Ten years later, he competed in the 1948 Olympics and won the gold medal. And in 1952, he won the gold again.[57]

He could have given up. He could have sat in his chair and wasted away. Instead, he got up and became better than he was before.

In today's passage, Jesus had a long talk with Peter. If you remember, just before Jesus died, Peter denied even knowing Jesus on three separate occasions. Peter was so overcome with grief over his sin against God that he wept bitterly. Peter was still down about his failure, and Jesus knew it. Rather than lecture him, Jesus had a better idea. Three times Jesus asked Peter if he loved Him. Three times Peter responded, "Yes, Lord. I love You." Peter's three failures were replaced with his three confessions of love for Jesus. Jesus restored him and even predicted that Peter would one day be so faithful that he would die for his Savior.

Many times in your life you will fail or experience problems that seem to stop you dead in your tracks. You may get discouraged and turn away from God or give up on your dreams. When you fall, God doesn't want you to stay there. He's there to help you. When you sin, He is there to forgive you. When bad things happen, He is there to comfort and strengthen you so that you can go on. When an obstacle blocks the path to your goals, He is there to show you the way around it. You will fall many times, but God is always there to help you up.

What discourages you the most? _____

How have you let these circumstances keep you from becoming all that God intends you to be? _____

If anything good could come out of this situation, what do you think it would be? _____

Don't be discouraged by circumstances. When you fall down, let God show you the way back up. Ask God to help you see the positives. Pray that you would be able to overcome your despair and rise to become all that God wants you to be.

Get Going

Matthew 28:18–20; Mark 16:15–18

> Dear Children,
>
> I am going away for a short while. During the time that I am gone, here are your instructions. Go into every part of the world and make disciples of every nation. Baptize them in the name of the Father, Son, and Holy Spirit. Teach them to imitate everything that I have taught you. Remember, I will be with you no matter where you go.
>
> Jesus
>
> Dear Jesus,
>
> After carefully considering Your proposal, we have decided to take an alternate approach. We feel that we can reach more people with Your message by asking them to come to us. We can save time, money, and effort if we sit on the inside and wait for those on the outside to come in. Thanks anyway for Your very valuable input.
>
> The Children

Sadly, this make-believe correspondence reads true in many churches. We have lost the desire to go, and instead we sit inside of our comfortable buildings, hoping that the lost find the front door.

In today's passage, Jesus gave His disciples what has come to be known as the Great Commission. Today, lots of people are talking about it. Many churches are discussing it. Some organizations frame the words and hang them on the wall. However, many Christians today have forgotten that Jesus said go, not sit. Our purpose is not merely to sit in church pews on Sunday mornings, but to go into every part of the world the rest of the week and make disciples.

Making disciples involves much more than simply sharing the good news. When someone responds to the message and accepts Jesus, you still have lots of work to do. After you lead others to Jesus, encourage them to make that decision public in a local church by being baptized. Then, do your part to teach them the basic principles of the faith. Spend time with them on a regular basis, answering their questions and helping them to make a habit of reading God's Word, praying, attending church, growing in their faith, and completing the circle by learning to witness.

Have you ever led someone to Jesus? _____

Describe what happened and how you felt. _____

Did you do your part in making sure this person continued to grow as a Christian by learning more about Jesus? _____

How can you play your part this week in following Jesus' command to make disciples?

_____

Don't be a Sunday morning Christian who merely sits in a pew one day a week. Get out of your seat, onto your feet, and into the street. Ask God to help you do your part in fulfilling the Great Commission. When you are done praying, get going.

A Better Understanding

Luke 24:44–49

> "I just don't understand what I'm reading sometimes," Laura said. "Why should I read the Bible at all if it doesn't make any sense?"
>
> Barry thought for a few moments and replied, "Just suppose that God sometimes doesn't want you to understand what you are reading until after you read it."
>
> "What?" interrupted Laura. "What would be the purpose of that?"
>
> Barry continued, "One time I grabbed my Bible and headed out the door on a sunny afternoon to find a nice quiet place to get alone with God. I finally settled on this little park about five miles from my house. I got out of my Jeep, walked over to the edge of a trickling brook, and sat down on the green grass. I sat there for a good while, just enjoying the view. Then I opened my Bible to read. I read Psalm 23. I've read or heard that psalm at least one thousand times in my life. However, I never really understood it. But when I read it lying in the green grass next to the quiet waters, I had a whole new perspective. God really opened my eyes and helped me see how He is my Shepherd."

Barry began to understand the Bible better when he actually experienced what he read. God used the circumstances in conjunction with His Word to speak to Barry.

In today's passage, Jesus was talking with His disciples after the Resurrection. Jesus had spoken God's Word to these men for three years, and yet they still did not understand. However, when they saw the resurrected Jesus, God opened their eyes, and they began to understand. Jesus made sense of the words He had spoken. He made sense of the Old Testament. He tied everything together, and, finally, they understood.

Do not get worried or become discouraged when you read the Bible and you don't understand everything. God may choose to help you understand what you read at a later time, using events and circumstances that will bring the Scriptures to life. So, if you don't understand what you read right away, take a look around you. Expect God to teach you what you read through something that you experience that day, that week, or sometime in the future.

Have you ever read a verse or passage in the Bible that you didn't understand? _____

How do you typically react when that happens? _____

How do you think God might use the circumstances in your life to explain His Word to you this week? _____

When you don't understand what you read in the Bible, ask God to explain it to you. Pray for wisdom and understanding. Then, let God open your eyes as you begin to look around for the answer. You never know what God is going to do.

Weekly Bible Study and Prayer Review

Bible Study

Look back through some of the Scriptures you read this week. Write down the one verse or passage that God used to speak to you.

_____

_____

_____

Memorize this verse or passage. You can do it if you spend just a few minutes saying it to yourself.

Now, think of at least one situation you will probably face soon in which you could use this Scripture to help you make the right decision. Write down that situation below.

_____

Quote the Scripture when you face this situation, and live by it.

Prayer Time

Take a few moments to praise God for who He is.
Now take a few moments to thank God for things He has done for you.
Now ask God to make you into the person He wants you to be.
Ask God to use you to help others become closer to God.

Below is your prayer list for the week. Keep it updated each week. If your prayer isn't answered this week, carry it over to next week's list.

Request	Date of Original Request	Date Answered
_____	__/__/__	__/__/__
_____	__/__/__	__/__/__
_____	__/__/__	__/__/__
_____	__/__/__	__/__/__
_____	__/__/__	__/__/__
_____	__/__/__	__/__/__
_____	__/__/__	__/__/__
_____	__/__/__	__/__/__
_____	__/__/__	__/__/__

Pray for the things on your list and trust God to provide.
Forgive anyone you have not yet forgiven.
Ask God to forgive you for any unconfessed sin in your life.
Ask God to keep you out of trouble with sin.
Acknowledge that God is in complete control of your life and will take care of everything.

Beyond Belief

> After Jesus had spoken a few final words of blessing, He ascended and disappeared behind a cloud. The disciples stared into the sky in wonder, waiting to see what would happen next. Their first inclination was to stay there forever. They didn't want to leave that spot, almost fearing that if they took their eyes off the clouds, Jesus would disappear from their minds as well as their view. Suddenly, two angels stood among them. They said, "Men of Galilee, what are you looking at? Stop staring into the sky. Jesus will return one day in the exact same way that He left." Then, as quickly as they had come, the angels vanished.
>
> In the silence that followed, the disciples were silent, lost in the thoughts of the things that Jesus had said and done over the past three years. They were in awe. Finally John turned to Peter and asked the question that everyone else was thinking. "What do we do now?"
>
> Peter thought for a moment, and said, "Well, what would Jesus do?"

Thankfully, the disciples did not stay on that mountain. They returned to Jerusalem excitedly and expectantly. From there, they changed the world by doing what Jesus did.

How did the disciples change the world? Notice what they did. (1) They worshiped Jesus. Though they could no longer see Him, they praised Him. (2) They were filled with excitement and joy, knowing that Jesus would one day come again. (3) They obeyed Jesus by returning to Jerusalem just as He asked. (4) They waited for the promised Holy Spirit. They didn't try to do things in their own power. (5) They stayed close to each other. They were all unified, having the same purpose. (6) They prayed. They spent lots of time on their knees. (7) They spread the good news boldly all over the world to everyone they met.

How can you do what Jesus would do? How can you change your world? Follow the example of those who followed Jesus. Worship God, by yourself and as part of a youth group and church family. Live your faith with excitement, reminding yourself every day that Jesus could return at any moment. Be obedient to God's Word. Don't just read it. Live it. Depend on the power of the Holy Spirit for everything that you do. Spend lots of time with your youth group and your church, making friends and learning from others. Pray every chance you get. Finally, share the story of Jesus with every single person that you meet.

Of the seven things the disciples did, which one do you do the best? _____

Which one do you need to work on the most? _____

Suppose you gave Jesus total control of yourself for a period of twenty-four hours. During that time, you decided not to do anything without asking yourself, "What would Jesus do?" How would your life, your world, change? _____

Ask God to help you commit yourself totally to Him each day. Pray that your life will change the world. Go beyond the words you have read about Jesus. Go beyond belief in Jesus. Live like Jesus. Imitate Him. Go and do what Jesus would do.

Endnotes

1. Jim Burns and Greg McKinnon, *Illustrations, Stories, and Quotes* (Ventura, Calif.: Gospel Light, 1997), 173–74.
2. Wayne Rice, *More Hot Illustrations for Youth Talks* (Grand Rapids: Zondervan Publishing House, 1995), 55.
3. Jack Canfield and Mark Victor Hansen, *Chicken Soup for the Soul* (Deerfield Beach, Fla.: Health Communications Inc., 1994), 236–37.
4. http://www2.gospelcom.net/rbc/ds/q0206/point4.html
5. Sergei Kourdakov, *The Persecutor* (Old Tappan, N.J.: Fleming H. Revell, 1973).
6. *Pulpit Helps* (January, 1991), 14.
7. Alice Gray, comp., *More Stories from the Heart* (Sisters, Oreg.: Multnomah Publishers, 1997), 126–27.
8. Rice, *More Hot Illustrations,* 84.
9. http://www.cyberantiquemall.com/featuredarticles/sotheby.html
10. *See You at the Pole,* promotional video, (Ft. Worth, Tex.: Student Discipleship Ministries).
11. Chuck Colson, *The Body* (Dallas: Word Publishing, 1992), 51–61.
12. Rice, *More Hot Illustrations,* 127–28.
13. Wayne Rice, *Hot Illustrations for Youth Talks* (El Cajon, Calif.: Youth Specialties, 1994), 81–82.
14. Rice, *More Hot Illustrations,* 140.
15. Gray, *More Stories from the Heart,* 55–59.
16. Rice, *Hot Illustrations,* 50–51.
17. Ibid., 58–60
18. Billy Beacham, et al., *Everyone, Everywhere* (Ft. Worth, Tex.: Student Discipleship Ministries, 1990), 51–52.
19. Rice, *More Hot Illustrations,* 169–70.
20. Ibid., 155.
21. Ibid.,
22. Ibid., 19–20.
23. Ibid., 31–32.
24. Ibid, 120.
25. Rice, *Hot Illustrations,* 161–62.
26. Canfield and Hansen, *Chicken Soup for the Soul,* 65–66.
27. Burns and McKinnon, *Illustrations, Stories, and Quotes,* 103.
28. Charles R. Swindoll, *Simple Faith* (Dallas: Word Publishing, 1991), 95–96.
29. Rice, *More Hot Illustrations,* 109.
30. Burns and McKinnon, *Illustrations, Stories, and Quotes,* 115–16.
31. Ibid., 35–36.
32. Ibid., 131.

33. Ibid., 197.

34. Ibid., 47.

35. Rice, *More Hot Illustrations,* 58–60.

36. Rice, *Hot Illustrations,* 68–69.

37. Burns and McKinnon, *Illustrations, Stories, and Quotes,* 31.

38. Ibid., 147.

39. Ibid., 67.

40. Ibid., 149.

41. Ibid., 123–24.

42. Gray, *More Stories from the Heart,* 25.

43. Burns and McKinnon, *Illustrations, Stories, and Quotes,* 45.

44. Ibid., 171.

45. John Foxe, *Foxe's Christian Martyrs of the World* (Chicago: Moody Press), 27.

46. Gray, *More Stories from the Heart,* 228–31.

47. Burns and McKinnon, *Illustrations, Stories, and Quotes,* 159.

48. Gray, *More Stories from the Heart,* 269.

49. Burns and McKinnon, *Illustrations, Stories, and Quotes,* 41.

50. Ibid., 13.

51. Rice, *More Hot Illustrations,* 72.

52. Rice, *Hot Illustrations,* 42–43.

53. Joy Evans, quoted in "It Sometimes Takes 'Special People' to Lead the Way," *The Brand* (Hardin-Simmons University), 14 February, 1997.

54. http://www.harvest.org/tools/ffl/man2.html.

55. Ed Sanders, http://www.edsanders.com/histool.html.

56. http://www.faderballistics.com/sean/relig.html.

57. David Wallechinsky, *The Complete Book of the Olympics* (Boston: Little, Brown & Co., 1992), 444.

Scripture Index

Topical Index

Topical Index

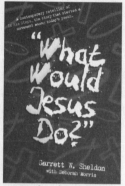
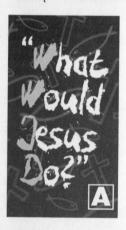